THE
TREASURED
WRITINGS
OF
KAHLIL
GIBRAN

THE TREASURED WRITINGS OF KAHLIL GIBRAN

CASTLE

The content of The Treasured Writings of Kahlil Gibran is composed of works originally published in:

A Treasury of Kahlil Gibran, translated by Anthony Rizcallah Ferris and edited by Martin L. Wolf, copyright 1951 by The Citadel Press, a division of Lyle Stuart Inc., and copyright 1947 and 1949 by Philosophical Library, Inc.

A Second Treasury of Kahlil Gibran, translated by Anthony R. Ferris, copyright © 1962 by The Citadel Press, a division of Lyle Stuart Inc. and copyright © 1957, 1958, 1959 and 1960 by Anthony R. Ferris.

A Third Treasury of Kahlil Gibran, edited by Andrew Dib Sherfan, copyright © 1975, 1973, 1966, 1965 by Philosophical Library, Inc.

The Treasured Writings of Kahlil Gibran
is published by
CASTLE BOOKS
A division of Book Sales, Inc.
114 Northfield Avenue, Edison, NJ 08837

ISBN 0-89009-389-X

Manufactured in the United States of America.

Table of Contents

A SELF-PORTRAIT   *643*

MIRRORS OF THE SOUL   *723*

THE WISDOM OF KAHLIL GIBRAN

THE CREATION

T HE GOD separated a spirit from Himself and fashioned it into beauty. He showered upon her all the blessings of gracefulness and kindness. He gave her the cup of happiness and said, "Drink not from this cup unless you forget the past and the future, for happiness is naught but the moment." And He also gave her a cup of sorrow and said, "Drink from this cup and you will understand the meaning of the fleeting instants of the joy of life, for sorrow ever abounds."

And the God bestowed upon her a love that would desert her forever upon her first sigh of earthly satisfaction, and a sweetness that would vanish with her first awareness of flattery.

And He gave her wisdom from heaven to lead her to the all-righteous path, and placed in the depth of her heart an eye that sees the unseen, and created in her an affection and goodness toward all things. He dressed her with raiment of hopes spun by the angels of heaven from the sinews of the rainbow. And He cloaked her in the shadow of confusion, which is the dawn of life and light.

Then the God took consuming fire from the furnace of anger, and searing wind from the desert of ignorance, and sharp-cutting sands from the shore of selfishness, and coarse earth from under the feet of ages, and combined them all and fashioned Man. He gave to Man a blind power that rages and drives him into a madness which extinguishes only before gratification of desire, and placed life in him which is the spectre of death.

And the God laughed and cried. He felt an overwhelming love and pity for Man, and sheltered him beneath His guidance.

HAVE MERCY ON ME,
MY SOUL!

WHY ARE you weeping, my Soul?
Knowest thou my weakness?
Thy tears strike sharp and injure,
For I know not my wrong.
Until when shalt thou cry?
I have naught but human words
To interpret your dreams,
Your desires, and your instructions.

Look upon me, my Soul; I have
Consumed my full life heeding
Your teachings. Think of how
I suffer! I have exhausted my
Life following you.

My heart was glorying upon the
Throne, but is now yoked in slavery;
My patience was a companion, but
Now contends against me;
My youth was my hope, but
Now reprimands my neglect.

5

Why, my Soul, are you all-demanding?
I have denied myself pleasure
And deserted the joy of life
Following the course which you
Impelled me to pursue.
Be just to me, or call Death
To unshackle me,
For justice is your glory.

Have mercy on me, my Soul.
You have laden me with Love until
I cannot carry my burden. You and
Love are inseparable might; Substance
And I are inseparable weakness.
Will e'er the struggle cease
Between the strong and the weak?

Have mercy on me, my Soul.
You have shown me Fortune beyond
My grasp. You and Fortune abide on
The mountain top; Misery and I are
Abandoned together in the pit of
The valley. Will e'er the mountain
And the valley unite?

Have mercy on me, my Soul.
You have shown me Beauty, but then
Concealed her. You and Beauty live
In the light; Ignorance and I are
Bound together in the dark. Will
E'er the light invade darkness?

Your delight comes with the Ending,
And you revel now in anticipation;
But this body suffers with life
While in life.
This, my Soul, is perplexing.

You are hastening toward Eternity,
But this body goes slowly toward
Perishment. You do not wait for him,
And he cannot go quickly.
This, my Soul, is sadness.

You ascend high, through heaven's
Attraction, but this body falls by
Earth's gravity. You do not console
Him, and he does not appreciate you.
This, my Soul, is misery.

You are rich in wisdom, but this
Body is poor in understanding.
You do not compromise
And he does not obey.
This, my Soul, is extreme suffering.

In the silence of the night you visit
The Beloved and enjoy the sweetness of
His presence. This body ever remains
The bitter victim of hope and separation.
This, my Soul, is agonizing torture.
Have mercy on me, my Soul!

TWO INFANTS

A PRINCE stood on the balcony of his palace addressing a great multitude summoned for the occasion and said, "Let me offer you and this whole fortunate country my congratulations upon the birth of a new prince who will carry the name of my noble family, and of whom you will be justly proud. He is the new bearer of a great and illustrious ancestry, and upon him depends the brilliant future of this realm. Sing and be merry!" The voices of the throngs, full of joy and thankfulness, flooded the sky with exhilarating song, welcoming the new tyrant who would affix the yoke of oppression to their necks by ruling the weak with bitter authority, and exploiting their bodies and killing their souls. For that destiny, the people were singing and drinking ecstatically to the health of the new Emir.

Another child entered life and that kingdom at the same time. While the crowds were glorifying the strong and belittling themselves by singing praise to a potential despot, and while the angels of heaven

were weeping over the people's weakness and servitude, a sick woman was thinking. She lived in an old, deserted hovel and, lying in her hard bed beside her newly-born infant wrapped with ragged swaddles, was starving to death. She was a penurious and miserable young wife neglected by humanity; her husband had fallen into the trap of death set by the prince's oppression, leaving a solitary woman to whom God had sent, that night, a tiny companion to prevent her from working and sustaining life.

As the mass dispersed and silence was restored to the vicinity, the wretched woman placed the infant on her lap and looked into his face and wept as if she were to baptize him with tears. And with a hunger-weakened voice she spoke to the child saying, "Why have you left the spiritual world and come to share with me the bitterness of earthly life? Why have you deserted the angels and the spacious firmament and come to this miserable land of humans, filled with agony, oppression, and heartlessness? I have nothing to give you except tears; will you be nourished on tears instead of milk? I have no silk clothes to put on you; will my naked, shivering arms give you warmth? The little animals graze in the pasture and return safely to their shed; and the small birds pick the seeds and sleep placidly between the branches. But you, my beloved, have naught save a loving but destitute mother."

Then she took the infant to her withered breast and clasped her arms around him as if wanting to

join the two bodies in one, as before. She lifted her burning eyes slowly toward heaven and cried, "God! Have mercy on my unfortunate countrymen!"

At that moment the clouds floated from the face of the moon, whose beams penetrated the transom of that poor home and fell upon two corpses.

THE LIFE OF LOVE

SPRING

Come, my beloved; let us walk amidst the knolls,
For the snow is water, and Life is alive from its
Slumber and is roaming the hills and valleys.
Let us follow the footprints of Spring into the
Distant fields, and mount the hilltops to draw
Inspiration high above the cool green plains.

Dawn of Spring has unfolded her winter-kept gar-
  ment
And placed it on the peach and citrus trees; and
They appear as brides in the ceremonial custom of
The Night of Kedre.

The sprigs of grapevine embrace each other like
Sweethearts, and the brooks burst out in dance
Between the rocks, repeating the song of joy;
And the flowers bud suddenly from the heart of
Nature, like foam from the rich heart of the sea.

Come, my beloved; let us drink the last of Winter's
Tears from the cupped lilies, and soothe our spirits

11

With the shower of notes from the birds, and wander
In exhilaration through the intoxicating breeze.

Let us sit by that rock, where violets hide; let us
Pursue their exchange of the sweetness of kisses.

SUMMER

Let us go into the fields, my beloved, for the
Time of harvest approaches, and the sun's eyes
Are ripening the grain.
Let us tend the fruit of the earth, as the
Spirit nourishes the grains of Joy from the
Seeds of Love, sowed deep in our hearts.
Let us fill our bins with the products of
Nature, as life fills so abundantly the
Domain of our hearts with her endless bounty.
Let us make the flowers our bed, and the
Sky our blanket, and rest our heads together
Upon pillows of soft hay.
Let us relax after the day's toil, and listen
To the provoking murmur of the brook.

AUTUMN

Let us go and gather the grapes of the vineyard
For the winepress, and keep the wine in old
Vases, as the spirit keeps Knowledge of the
Ages in eternal vessels.

Let us return to our dwelling, for the wind has
Caused the yellow leaves to fall and shroud the
Withering flowers that whisper elegy to Summer.

Come home, my eternal sweetheart, for the birds
Have made pilgrimage to warmth and left the chilled
Prairies suffering pangs of solitude. The jasmine
And myrtle have no more tears.

Let us retreat, for the tired brook has
Ceased its song; and the bubblesome springs
Are drained of their copious weeping; and
The cautious old hills have stored away
Their colourful garments.

Come, my beloved; Nature is justly weary
And is bidding her enthusiasm farewell
With quiet and contented melody.

WINTER

Come close to me, oh companion of my full life;
Come close to me and let not Winter's touch
Enter between us. Sit by me before the hearth,
For fire is the only fruit of Winter.

Speak to me of the glory of your heart, for
That is greater than the shrieking elements
Beyond our door.
Bind the door and seal the transoms, for the
Angry countenance of the heaven depresses my
Spirit, and the face of our snow-laden fields
Makes my soul cry.

Feed the lamp with oil and let it not dim, and
Place it by you, so I can read with tears what
Your life with me has written upon your face.

Bring Autumn's wine. Let us drink and sing the
Song of remembrance to Spring's carefree sowing,
And Summer's watchful tending, and Autumn's
Reward in harvest.

Come close to me, oh beloved of my soul; the
Fire is cooling and fleeing under the ashes.
Embrace me, for I fear loneliness; the lamp is
Dim, and the wine which we pressed is closing
Our eyes. Let us look upon each other before
They are shut.
Find me with your arms and embrace me; let
Slumber then embrace our souls as one.
Kiss me, my beloved, for Winter has stolen
All but our moving lips.

You are close by me, My Forever.
How deep and wide will be the ocean of Slumber;
And how recent was the dawn!

THE HOUSE OF FORTUNE

MY WEARIED heart bade me farewell and left for the House of Fortune. As he reached that holy city which the soul had blessed and worshipped, he commenced wondering, for he could not find what he had always imagined would be there. The city was empty of power, money, and authority.

And my heart spoke to the daughter of Love saying, "Oh Love, where can I find Contentment? I heard that she had come here to join you."

And the daughter of Love responded, "Contentment has already gone to preach her gospel in the city, where greed and corruption are paramount; we are not in need of her."

Fortune craves not Contentment, for it is an earthly hope, and its desires are embraced by union with objects, while Contentment is naught but heartfelt.

The eternal soul is never contented; it ever seeks exaltation. Then my heart looked upon Life of Beauty and said, "Thou art all knowledge; en-

lighten me as to the mystery of Woman." And he answered, "Oh human heart, woman is your own reflection, and whatever you are, she is; wherever you live, she lives; she is like religion if not interpreted by the ignorant, and like a moon, if not veiled with clouds, and like a breeze, if not poisoned with impurities."

And my heart walked toward Knowledge, the daughter of Love and Beauty, and said, "Bestow upon me wisdom, that I might share it with the people." And she responded, "Say not wisdom, but rather fortune, for real fortune comes not from outside, but begins in the Holy of Holies of life. Share of thyself with the people."

SONG OF THE WAVE

THE STRONG SHORE is my beloved
And I am his sweetheart.
We are at last united by love, and
Then the moon draws me from him.
I go to him in haste and depart
Reluctantly, with many
Little farewells.

I steal swiftly from behind the
Blue horizon to cast the silver of
My foam upon the gold of his sand, and
We blend in melted brilliance.

I quench his thirst and submerge his
Heart; he softens my voice and subdues
My temper.
At dawn I recite the rules of love upon
His ears, and he embraces me longingly.

At eventide I sing to him the song of
Hope, and then print smooth kisses upon
His face; I am swift and fearful, but he
Is quiet, patient, and thoughtful. His
Broad bosom soothes my restlessness.

17

As the tide comes we caress each other,
When it withdraws, I drop to his feet in
Prayer.

Many times have I danced around mermaids
As they rose from the depths and rested
Upon my crest to watch the stars;
Many times have I heard lovers complain
Of their smallness, and I helped them to sigh.

Many times have I teased the great rocks
And fondled them with a smile, but never
Have I received laughter from them;
Many times have I lifted drowning souls
And carried them tenderly to my beloved
Shore. He gives them strength as he
Takes mine.

Many times have I stolen gems from the
Depths and presented them to my beloved
Shore. He takes in silence, but still
I give for he welcomes me ever.

In the heaviness of night, when all
Creatures seek the ghost of Slumber, I
Sit up, singing at one time and sighing
At another. I am awake always.

Alas! Sleeplessness has weakened me!
But I am a lover, and the truth of love
Is strong.
I may weary, but I shall never die.

A POET'S DEATH IS HIS LIFE

The dark wings of night enfolded the city upon which Nature had spread a pure and white garment of snow; and men deserted the streets for their houses in search of warmth, while the north wind probed in contemplation of laying waste the gardens. There in the suburb stood an old hut heavily laden with snow and on the verge of falling. In a dark recess of that hovel was a poor bed in which a dying youth was lying, staring at the dim light of his oil lamp, made to flicker by the entering winds. He was a man in the spring of life who foresaw fully that the peaceful hour of freeing himself from the clutches of life was fast nearing. He was awaiting Death's visit gratefully, and upon his pale face appeared the dawn of hope; and on his lips a sorrowful smile; and in his eyes forgiveness.

He was a poet perishing from hunger in the city of living rich. He was placed in the earthly world to enliven the heart of man with his beautiful and profound sayings. He was a noble soul, sent by the Goddess of Understanding to soothe and make gen-

tle the human spirit. But alas! He gladly bade the cold earth farewell without receiving a smile from its strange occupants.

He was breathing his last and had no one at his bedside save the oil lamp, his only companion, and some parchments upon which he had inscribed his heart's feeling. As he salvaged the remnants of his withering strength he lifted his hands heavenward; he moved his eyes hopelessly, as if wanting to penetrate the ceiling in order to see the stars from behind the veil of clouds.

And he said, "Come, oh beautiful Death; my soul is longing for you. Come close to me and unfasten the irons of life, for I am weary of dragging them. Come, oh sweet Death, and deliver me from my neighbours who looked upon me as a stranger because I interpret to them the language of the angels. Hurry, oh peaceful Death, and carry me from these multitudes who left me in the dark corner of oblivion because I do not bleed the weak as they do. Come, oh gentle Death, and enfold me under your white wings, for my fellowmen are not in want of me. Embrace me, oh Death, full of love and mercy; let your lips touch my lips which never tasted a mother's kiss, nor touched a sister's cheeks, nor caressed a sweetheart's fingertips. Come and take me, my beloved Death."

Then, at the bedside of the dying poet appeared an angel who possessed a supernatural and divine beauty, holding in her hand a wreath of lilies. She

embraced him and closed his eyes so he could see no more, except with the eye of his spirit. She impressed a deep and long and gently withdrawn kiss that left an eternal smile of fulfillment upon his lips. Then the hovel became empty and nothing was left save parchments and papers which the poet had strewn about with bitter futility.

Hundreds of years later, when the people of the city arose from the diseased slumber of ignorance and saw the dawn of knowledge, they erected a monument in the most beautiful garden of the city and celebrated a feast every year in honour of that poet, whose writings had freed them. Oh, how cruel is man's ignorance!

PEACE

THE TEMPEST calmed after
bending the branches of the trees and leaning heavily
upon the grain in the field. The stars appeared as
broken remnants of the lightning, but now silence
prevailed over all, as if Nature's war had never been
fought.

At that hour a young woman entered her chamber and knelt by her bed sobbing bitterly. Her heart
flamed with agony but she could finally open her
lips and say, "Oh Lord, bring him home safely to
me. I have exhausted my tears and can offer no more,
oh Lord, full of love and mercy. My patience is
drained and calamity is seeking possession of my
heart. Save him, oh Lord, from the iron paws of
War; deliver him from such unmerciful Death, for
he is weak, governed by the strong. Oh Lord, save
my beloved, who is Thine own son, from the foe,
who is thy foe. Keep him from the forced pathway
to Death's door; let him see me, or come and take
me to him."

Quietly a young man entered. His head was wrapped in bandage soaked with escaping life.

He approached her with a greeting of tears and laughter, then took her hand and placed against it his flaming lips. And with a voice which bespoke past sorrow, and joy of union, and uncertainty of her reaction, he said, "Fear me not, for I am the object of your plea. Be glad, for Peace has carried me back safely to you, and humanity has restored what greed essayed to take from us. Be not sad, but smile, my beloved. Do not express bewilderment, for Love has power that dispels Death; charm that conquers the enemy. I am your one. Think me not a spectre emerging from the House of Death to visit your Home of Beauty.

"Do not be frightened, for I am now Truth, spared from swords and fire to reveal to the people the triumph of Love over War. I am Word uttering introduction to the play of happiness and peace."

Then the young man became speechless and his tears spoke the language of the heart; and the angels of Joy hovered about that dwelling, and the two hearts restored the singleness which had been taken from them.

At dawn the two stood in the middle of the field, contemplating the beauty of Nature injured by the tempest. After a deep and comforting silence, the soldier looked to the east and said to his sweetheart, "Look at the Darkness, giving birth to the Sun."

THE CRIMINAL

A YOUNG man of strong body, weakened by hunger, sat on the walker's portion of the street stretching his hand toward all who passed, begging and repeating the sad song of his defeat in life, while suffering from hunger and from humiliation.

When night came, his lips and tongue were parched, while his hand was still as empty as his stomach.

He gathered himself and went out from the city, where he sat under a tree and wept bitterly. Then he lifted his puzzled eyes to heaven while hunger was eating his inside, and he said, "Oh Lord, I went to the rich man and asked for employment, but he turned away because of my shabbiness; I knocked at the school door, but was forbidden solace because I was empty-handed; I sought any occupation that would give me bread, but all to no avail. In desperation I asked alms, but Thy worshippers saw me and said, "He is strong and lazy, and he should not beg."

"Oh Lord, it is Thy will that my mother gave

24

birth unto me, and now the earth offers me back to You before the Ending."

His expression then changed. He arose and his eyes now glittered in determination. He fashioned a thick and heavy stick from the branch of the tree, and pointed it toward the city, shouting, "I asked for bread with all the strength of my voice, and was refused. Now I shall obtain it by the strength of my muscles! I asked for bread in the name of mercy and love, but humanity did not heed. I shall take it now in the name of evil!"

The passing years rendered the youth a robber, killer, and destroyer of souls; he crushed all who opposed him; he amassed fabulous wealth with which he won himself over to those in power. He was admired by colleagues, envied by other thieves, and feared by the multitudes.

His riches and false position prevailed upon the Emir to appoint him deputy in that city—the sad process pursued by unwise governors. Thefts were then legalized; oppression was supported by authority; crushing of the weak became commonplace; the throngs curried and praised.

Thus does the first touch of humanity's selfishness make criminals of the humble, and make killers of the sons of peace; thus does the early greed of humanity grow and strike back at humanity a thousandfold!

THE PLAYGROUND OF LIFE

ONE HOUR devoted to the pursuit of Beauty
And Love is worth a full century of glory
Given by the frightened weak to the strong.

From that hour comes man's Truth; and
During that century Truth sleeps between
The restless arms of disturbing dreams.

In that hour the soul sees for herself
The Natural Law, and for that century she
Imprisons herself behind the law of man;
And she is shackled with irons of oppression.

That hour was the inspiration of the Songs
Of Solomon, and that century was the blind
Power which destroyed the temple of Baalbek.

That hour was the birth of the Sermon on the
Mount, and that century wrecked the castles of
Palmyra and the tower of Babylon.

That hour was the Hegira of Mohammed, and that
Century forgot Allah, Golgotha, and Sinai.

One hour devoted to mourning and lamenting the
Stolen equality of the weak is nobler than a
Century filled with greed and usurpation.

It is at that hour when the heart is
Purified by flaming sorrow, and
Illuminated by the torch of Love.
And in the century, desires for Truth
Are buried in the bosom of the earth.
That hour is the root which must flourish.
That hour is the hour of contemplation,
The hour of meditation, the hour of
Prayer, and the hour of a new era of good.

And that century is a life of Nero spent
On self-investment taken solely from
Earthly substance.

This is life.
Portrayed on the stage for ages;
Recorded earthily for centuries;
Lived in strangeness for years;
Sung as a hymn for days;
Exalted for but an hour, but the
Hour is treasured by Eternity as a jewel.

SONG OF FORTUNE

Man and I are sweethearts
He craves me and I long for him,
But alas! Between us has appeared
A rival who brings us misery.
She is cruel and demanding,
Possessing empty lure.
Her name is Substance.
She follows wherever we go
And watches like a sentinel, bringing
Restlessness to my lover.

I ask for my beloved in the forest,
Under the trees, by the lakes.
I cannot find him, for Substance
Has spirited him to the clamourous
City and placed him on the throne
Of quaking, metal riches.

I call for him with the voice of
Knowledge and the song of Wisdom.
He does not hearken, for Substance
Has enticed him into the dungeon
Of selfishness, where avarice dwells.

I seek him in the field of Contentment,
But I am alone, for my rival has
Imprisoned him in the cave of gluttony
And greed, and locked him there
With painful chains of gold.

I call to him at dawn, when Nature smiles,
But he does not hear, for excess has
Laden his drugged eyes with sick slumber.

I beguile him at eventide, when Silence rules
And the flowers sleep. But he responds not,
For his fear over what the morrow will
Bring, shadows his thoughts.

He yearns to love me;
He asks for me in his own acts. But he
Will find me not except in God's acts.
He seeks me in the edifices of his glory
Which he has built upon the bones of others;
He whispers to me from among
His heaps of gold and silver;
But he will find me only by coming to
The house of Simplicity which God has built
At the brink of the stream of affection.

He desires to kiss me before his coffers,
But his lips will never touch mine except
In the richness of the pure breeze.

He asks me to share with him his
Fabulous wealth, but I will not forsake God's
Fortune; I will not cast off my cloak of beauty.

He seeks deceit for medium; I seek only
The medium of his heart.
He bruises his heart in his narrow cell;
I would enrich his heart with my love.

My beloved has learned how to shriek and
Cry for my enemy, Substance; I would
Teach him how to shed tears of affection
And mercy from the eyes of his soul
For all things,
And utter sighs of contentment through
Those tears.

Man is my sweetheart;
I want to belong to him.

THE CITY OF THE DEAD

Yesterday I drew myself
from the noisome throngs and proceeded into the
field until I reached a knoll upon which Nature had
spread her comely garments. Now I could breathe.

I looked back, and the city appeared with its magnificent mosques and stately residences veiled by the
smoke of the shops.

I commenced analyzing man's mission, but could
conclude only that most of his life was identified
with struggle and hardship. Then I tried not to
ponder over what the sons of Adam had done, and
centered my eyes on the field which is the throne
of God's glory. In one secluded corner of the field
I observed a burying ground surrounded by poplar
trees.

There, between the city of the dead and the city
of the living, I meditated. I thought of the eternal
silence in the first and the endless sorrow in the
second.

In the city of the living I found hope and despair;
love and hatred, joy and sorrow, wealth and poverty,
faith and infidelity.

In the city of the dead there is buried earth in earth that Nature converts, in the night's silence, into vegetation, and then into animal, and then into man. As my mind wandered in this fashion, I saw a procession moving slowly and reverently, accompanied by pieces of music that filled the sky with sad melody. It was an elaborate funeral. The dead was followed by the living who wept and lamented his going. As the cortege reached the place of interment the priests commenced praying and burning incense, and the musicians blowing and plucking their instruments, mourning the departed. Then the leaders came forward one after the other and recited their eulogies with fine choice of words.

At last the multitude departed, leaving the dead resting in a most spacious and beautiful vault, expertly designed in stone and iron, and surrounded by the most expensively-entwined wreaths of flowers.

The farewell-bidders returned to the city and I remained, watching them from a distance and speaking softly to myself while the sun was descending to the horizon and Nature was making her many preparations for slumber.

Then I saw two men labouring under the weight of a wooden casket, and behind them a shabby-appearing woman carrying an infant on her arms. Following last was a dog who, with heartbreaking eyes, stared first at the woman and then at the casket.

It was a poor funeral. This guest of Death left to cold society a miserable wife and an infant to share

her sorrows, and a faithful dog whose heart knew of his companion's departure.

As they reached the burial place they deposited the casket into a ditch away from the tended shrubs and marble stones, and retreated after a few simple words to God. The dog made one last turn to look at his friend's grave as the small group disappeared behind the trees.

I looked at the city of the living and said to myself, "That place belongs to the few." Then I looked upon the trim city of the dead and said, "That place, too, belongs to the few. Oh Lord, where is the haven of all people?"

As I said this, I looked toward the clouds, mingled with the sun's longest and most beautiful golden rays. And I heard a voice within me saying, "Over there!"

SONG OF THE RAIN

I AM dotted silver threads dropped from heaven
By the gods. Nature then takes me, to adorn
Her fields and valleys.

I am beautiful pearls, plucked from the
Crown of Ishtar by the daughter of Dawn
To embellish the gardens.

When I cry the hills laugh;
When I humble myself the flowers rejoice;
When I bow, all things are elated.

The field and the cloud are lovers
And between them I am a messenger of mercy.
I quench the thirst of the one;
I cure the ailment of the other.

The voice of thunder declares my arrival;
The rainbow announces my departure.
I am like earthly life, which begins at
The feet of the mad elements and ends
Under the upraised wings of death.

I emerge from the heart of the sea and
Soar with the breeze. When I see a field in
Need, I descend and embrace the flowers and
The trees in a million little ways.

I touch gently at the windows with my
Soft fingers, and my announcement is a
Welcome song. All can hear, but only
The sensitive can understand.

The heat in the air gives birth to me,
But in turn I kill it,
As woman overcomes man with
The strength she takes from him.

1 am the sigh of the sea;
The laughter of the field;
The tears of heaven.

So with love—
Sighs from the deep sea of affection;
Laughter from the colourful field of the spirit;
Tears from the endless heaven of memories.

THE WIDOW AND HER SON

Night fell over North Lebanon and snow was covering the villages surrounded by the Kadeesha Valley, giving the fields and prairies the appearance of a great sheet of parchment upon which the furious Nature was recording her many deeds. Men came home from the streets while silence engulfed the night.

In a lone house near those villages lived a woman who sat by her fireside spinning wool, and at her side was her only child, staring now at the fire and then at his mother.

A terrible roar of thunder shook the house and the little boy took fright. He threw his arms about his mother, seeking protection from Nature in her affection. She took him to her bosom and kissed him; then she sat him on her lap and said, "Do not fear, my son, for Nature is but comparing her great power to man's weakness. There is a Supreme Being beyond the falling snow and the heavy clouds and the blowing wind, and He knows the needs of the earth,

for He made it; and He looks upon the weak with merciful eyes.

"Be brave, my boy. Nature smiles in Spring and laughs in Summer and yawns in Autumn, but now she is weeping; and with her tears she waters life, hidden under the earth.

"Sleep, my dear child; your father is viewing us from Eternity. The snow and thunder bring us closer to him at this time.

"Sleep, my beloved, for this white blanket which makes us cold, keeps the seeds warm, and these war-like things will produce beautiful flowers when Nisan comes.

"Thus, my child, man cannot reap love until after sad and revealing separation, and bitter patience, and desperate hardship. Sleep, my little boy; sweet dreams will find your soul who is unafraid of the terrible darkness of night and the biting frost."

The little boy looked upon his mother with sleep-laden eyes and said, "Mother, my eyes are heavy, but I cannot go to sleep without saying my prayer."

The woman looked at his angelic face, her vision blurred by misted eyes, and said, "Repeat with me, my boy—'God, have mercy on the poor and protect them from the winter; warm their thin-clad bodies with Thy merciful hands; look upon the orphans who are sleeping in wretched houses, suffering from hunger and cold. Hear, oh Lord, the call of widows who are helpless and shivering with fear for their young. Open, oh Lord, the hearts of all humans,

that they may see the misery of the weak. Have mercy upon the sufferers who knock on doors, and lead the wayfarers into warm places. Watch, oh Lord, over the little birds and protect the trees and fields from the anger of the storm; for Thou art merciful and full of love.' "

As Slumber captured the boy's spirit, his mother placed him in the bed and kissed his eyes with quivering lips. Then she went back and sat by the hearth, spinning the wool to make him raiment.

THE POET

He is link between this and the coming world. He is
A pure spring from which all thirsty souls may drink.

He is a tree watered by the River of Beauty, bearing
Fruit which the hungry heart craves;
He is a nightingale, soothing the depressed
Spirit with his beautiful melodies;
He is a white cloud appearing over the horizon,
Ascending and growing until it fills the face of the
sky,
Then it falls on the flowers in the Field of Life,
Opening their petals to admit the light.

He is an angel, sent by the goddess to
Preach the Deity's gospel;
He is a brilliant lamp, unconquered by darkness
And inextinguishable by the wind. It is filled with
Oil by Ishtar of Love, and lighted by Apollon of
Music.

He is a solitary figure, robed in simplicity and
Kindness; He sits upon the lap of Nature to draw his
Inspiration, and stays up in the silence of the night,
Awaiting the descending of the spirit.

He is a sower who sows the seeds of his heart in the
Prairies of affection, and humanity reaps the
Harvest for her nourishment.

This is the poet—whom the people ignore in this
 life,
And who is recognized only after he bids the earthly
World farewell and returns to his arbor in heaven.

This is the poet—who asks naught of
Humanity but a smile.
This is the poet—whose spirit ascends and
Fills the firmament with beautiful sayings;
Yet the people deny themselves his radiance.

Until when shall the people remain asleep?
Until when shall they continue to glorify those
Who attained greatness by moments of advantage?
How long shall they ignore those who enable
Them to see the beauty of their spirit,
Symbol of peace and love?
Until when shall human beings honor the dead
And forget the living, who spend their lives
Encircled in misery, and who consume themselves
Like burning candles to illuminate the way
For the ignorant and lead them into the path of
 light?

Poet, you are the life of this life, and you have
Triumphed over the ages despite their severity.

Poet, you will one day rule the hearts, and
Therefore, your kingdom has no ending.

Poet, examine your crown of thorns; you will
Find concealed in it a budding wreath of laurel.

SONG OF THE SOUL

IN THE DEPTH of my soul there is
A wordless song—a song that lives
In the seed of my heart.
It refuses to melt with ink on
Parchment; it engulfs my affection
In a transparent cloak and flows,
But not upon my lips.

How can I sigh it? I fear it may
Mingle with earthly ether;
To whom shall I sing it? It dwells
In the house of my soul, in fear of
Harsh ears.

When I look into my inner eyes
I see the shadow of its shadow;
When I touch my fingertips
I feel its vibrations.

The deeds of my hands heed its
Presence as a lake must reflect
The glittering stars; my tears

Reveal it, as bright drops of dew
Reveal the secret of a withering rose.

It is a song composed by contemplation,
And published by silence,
And shunned by clamour,
And folded by truth,
And repeated by dreams,
And understood by love,
And hidden by awakening,
And sung by the soul.

It is the song of love;
What Cain or Esau could sing it?

It is more fragrant than jasmine;
What voice could enslave it?

It is heartbound, as a virgin's secret;
What string could quiver it?

Who dares unite the roar of the sea
And the singing of the nightingale?
Who dares compare the shrieking tempest
To the sigh of an infant?
Who dares speak aloud the words
Intended for the heart to speak?
What human dares sing in voice
The song of God?

LAUGHTER AND TEARS

As the Sun withdrew his rays from the garden, and the moon threw cushioned beams upon the flowers, I sat under the trees pondering upon the phenomena of the atmosphere, looking through the branches at the strewn stars which glittered like chips of silver upon a blue carpet; and I could hear from a distance the agitated murmur of the rivulet singing its way briskly into the valley.

When the birds took shelter among the boughs, and the flowers folded their petals, and tremendous silence descended, I heard a rustle of feet through the grass. I took heed and saw a young couple approaching my arbor. They sat under a tree where I could see them without being seen.

After he looked about in every direction, I heard the young man saying, "Sit by me, my beloved, and listen to my heart; smile, for your happiness is a symbol of our future; be merry, for the sparkling days rejoice with us.

"My soul is warning me of the doubt in your heart, for doubt in love is a sin.

"Soon you will be the owner of this vast land,

lighted by this beautiful moon; soon you will be the mistress of my palace, and all the servants and maids will obey your commands.

"Smile, my beloved, like the gold smiles from my father's coffers.

"My heart refuses to deny you its secret. Twelve months of comfort and travel await us; for a year we will spend my father's gold at the blue lakes of Switzerland, and viewing the edifices of Italy and Egypt, and resting under the Holy Cedars of Lebanon; you will meet the princesses who will envy you for your jewels and clothes.

"All these things I will do for you; will you be satisfied?"

In a little while I saw them walking and stepping on flowers as the rich step upon the hearts of the poor. As they disappeared from my sight, I commenced to make comparison between love and money, and to analyze their position in my heart.

Money! The source of insincere love; the spring of false light and fortune; the well of poisoned water; the desperation of old age!

I was still wandering in the vast desert of contemplation when a forlorn and spectre-like couple passed by me and sat on the grass; a young man and a young woman who had left their farming shacks in the nearby fields for this cool and solitary place.

After a few moments of complete silence, I heard the following words uttered with sighs from weather-bitten lips, "Shed not tears, my beloved; love that

opens our eyes and enslaves our hearts can give us the blessings of patience. Be consoled in our delay, for we have taken an oath and entered Love's shrine; for our love will ever grow in adversity; for it is in Love's name that we are suffering the obstacles of poverty and the sharpness of misery and the emptiness of separation. I shall attack these hardships until I triumph and place in your hands a strength that will help over all things to complete the journey of life.

"Love—which is God—will consider our sighs and tears as incense burned at His altar and He will reward us with fortitude. Good-bye, my beloved; I must leave before the heartening moon vanishes."

A pure voice, combined of the consuming flame of love, and the hopeless bitterness of longing and the resolved sweetness of patience, said, "Good-bye, my beloved."

They separated, and the elegy to their union was smothered by the wails of my crying heart.

I looked upon slumbering Nature, and with deep reflection discovered the reality of a vast and infinite thing—something no power could demand, influence acquire, nor riches purchase. Nor could it be effaced by the tears of time or deadened by sorrow; a thing which cannot be discovered by the blue lakes of Switzerland or the beautiful edifices of Italy.

It is something that gathers strength with patience, grows despite obstacles, warms in winter, flourishes in spring, casts a breeze in summer, and bears fruit in autumn—I found Love.

SONG OF THE FLOWER

I AM A KIND WORD uttered and repeated
By the voice of Nature;
I am a star fallen from the
Blue tent upon the green carpet.
I am the daughter of the elements
With whom Winter conceived;
To whom Spring gave birth; I was
Reared in the lap of Summer and I
Slept in the bed of Autumn.

At dawn I unite with the breeze
To announce the coming of light;
At eventide I join the birds
In bidding the light farewell.

The plains are decorated with
My beautiful colours, and the air
Is scented with my fragrance.

As I embrace Slumber the eyes of
Night watch over me, and as I
Awaken I stare at the sun, which is
The only eye of the day.

47

I drink dew for wine, and hearken to
The voices of the birds, and dance
To the rhythmic swaying of the grass.

I am the lover's gift; I am the wedding wreath;
I am the memory of a moment of happiness;
I am the last gift of the living to the dead;
I am a part of joy and a part of sorrow.

But I look up high to see only the light,
And never look down to see my shadow.
This is wisdom which man must learn.

VISION

There in the middle of the field, by the side of a crystalline stream, I saw a bird-cage whose rods and hinges were fashioned by an expert's hands. In one corner lay a dead bird, and in another were two basins—one empty of water and the other of seeds. I stood there reverently, as if the lifeless bird and the murmur of the water were worthy of deep silence and respect—something worthy of examination and meditation by the heart and conscience.

As I engrossed myself in view and thought, I found that the poor creature had died of thirst beside a stream of water, and of hunger in the midst of a rich field, cradle of life; like a rich man locked inside his iron safe, perishing from hunger amid heaps of gold.

Before my eyes I saw the cage turned suddenly into a human skeleton, and the dead bird into a man's heart which was bleeding from a deep wound that looked like the lips of a sorrowing woman. A voice came from that wound saying, "I am the

human heart, prisoner of substance and victim of earthly laws.

"In God's field of Beauty, at the edge of the stream of life, I was imprisoned in the cage of laws made by man.

"In the center of beautiful Creation I died neglected because I was kept from enjoying the freedom of God's bounty.

"Everything of beauty that awakens my love and desire is a disgrace, according to man's conceptions; everything of goodness that I crave is but naught, according to his judgment.

"I am the lost human heart, imprisoned in the foul dungeon of man's dictates, tied with chains of earthly authority, dead and forgotten by laughing humanity whose tongue is tied and whose eyes are empty of visible tears."

All these words I heard, and I saw them emerging with a stream of ever-thinning blood from that wounded heart.

More was said, but my misted eyes and crying soul prevented further sight or hearing.

SONG OF LOVE

I AM the lover's eyes, and the spirit's
Wine, and the heart's nourishment.
I am a rose. My heart opens at dawn and
The virgin kisses me and places me
Upon her breast.

I am the house of true fortune, and the
Origin of pleasure, and the beginning
Of peace and tranquility. I am the gentle
Smile upon the lips of beauty. When youth
Overtakes me he forgets his toil, and his
Whole life becomes reality of sweet dreams.

I am the poet's elation,
And the artist's revelation,
And the musician's inspiration.

I am a sacred shrine in the heart of a
Child, adored by a merciful mother.

I appear to a heart's cry; I shun a demand;
My fullness pursues the heart's desire;
It shuns the empty claim of the voice.

I appeared to Adam through Eve
And exile was his lot;
Yet I revealed myself to Solomon, and
He drew wisdom from my presence.

I smiled at Helena and she destroyed Tarwada;
Yet I crowned Cleopatra and peace dominated
The Valley of the Nile.

I am like the ages—building today
And destroying tomorrow;
I am like a god, who creates and ruins;
I am sweeter than a violet's sigh;
I am more violent than a raging tempest.

Gifts alone do not entice me;
Parting does not discourage me;
Poverty does not chase me;
Jealousy does not prove my awareness;
Madness does not evidence my presence.

Oh seekers, I am Truth, beseeching Truth;
And your Truth in seeking and receiving
And protecting me shall determine my
Behaviour.

TWO WISHES

I N THE silence of the night
Death descended from God toward the earth. He
hovered above a city and pierced the dwellings with
his eyes. He saw the spirits floating on wings of
dreams, and the people who were surrendered to
the mercy of Slumber.

When the moon fell below the horizon and the
city became black, Death walked silently among the
houses—careful to touch nothing—until he reached
a palace. He entered through the bolted gates undisturbed, and stood by the rich man's bed; and
as Death touched his forehead, the sleeper's eyes
opened, showing great fright.

When he saw the spectre, he summoned a voice
mingled with fear and anger, and said, "Go away,
oh horrible dream; leave me, you dreadful ghost.
Who are you? How did you enter this place? What
do you want? Leave this place at once, for I am the
lord of the house and will call my slaves and guards,
and order them to kill you!"

Then Death spoke, softly but with smouldering thunder, "I am Death. Stand and bow!"

The man responded, "What do you want? Why have you come here when I have not yet finished my affairs? What seek you from strength such as mine? Go to the weak man, and take him away!

"I loathe the sight of your bloody paws and hollow face, and my eyes take sick at your horrible ribbed wings and cadaverous body."

After a quiet moment of fearful realization he added, "No, no, oh merciful Death! Mind not my talk, for fear reveals what the heart forbids.

"Take a bushelful of my gold, or a handful of my slaves' souls, but leave me. I have accounts with Life requiring settling; I have due from the people much gold; my ships have not reached the harbour; my wheat has not been harvested. Take anything you demand, but spare my life. Death, I own harems of supernatural beauty; your choice is my gift to you. Give heed, Death—I have but one child, and I love him dearly for he is my only joy in this life. I offer supreme sacrifice—take him, but spare me!"

Death murmured, "You are not rich, but pitifully poor." Then Death took the hand of that earthly slave, removed his reality, and gave to the angels the heavy task of correction.

And Death walked slowly amidst the dwellings of the poor until he reached the most miserable he could find. He entered and approached a bed upon which a youth slept fitfully. Death touched his eyes;

the lad sprang up as he saw Death standing by, and, with a voice full of love and hope he said, "Here I am, my beautiful Death. Accept my soul, for you are the hope of my dreams. Be their accomplishment! Embrace me, oh beloved Death! You are merciful; do not leave me. You are God's messenger; deliver me to Him. You are the right hand of Truth and the heart of Kindness; do not neglect me.

"I have begged for you many times, but you did not come; I have sought you, but you avoided me; I called out to you, but you listened not. You hear me now—embrace my soul, beloved Death!"

Death placed his softened hand upon the trembling lips, removed all reality, and enfolded it beneath his wings for secure conduct. And returning to the sky, Death looked back and whispered his warning:

> "Only those return to Eternity
> Who on earth seek out Eternity."

SONG OF MAN

I WAS HERE from the moment of the
Beginning, and here I am still. And
I shall remain here until the end
Of the world, for there is no
Ending to my grief-stricken being.

I roamed the infinite sky, and
Soared in the ideal world, and
Floated through the firmament. But
Here I am, prisoner of measurement.

I heard the teachings of Confucius;
I listened to Brahma's wisdom;
I sat by Buddha under the Tree of Knowledge.
Yet here am I, existing with ignorance
And heresy.

I was on Sinai when Jehovah approached Moses;
I saw the Nazarene's miracles at the Jordan;
I was in Medina when Mohammed visited.
Yet here I am, prisoner of bewilderment.

56

Then I witnessed the might of Babylon;
I learned of the glory of Egypt;
I viewed the warring greatness of Rome.
Yet my earlier teachings showed the
Weakness and sorrow of those achievements.

I conversed with the magicians of Ain Dour;
I debated with the priests of Assyria;
I gleaned depth from the prophets of Palestine.
Yet, I am still seeking the truth.

I gathered wisdom from quiet India;
I probed the antiquity of Arabia;
I heard all that can be heard.
Yet, my heart is deaf and blind.

I suffered at the hands of despotic rulers;
I suffered slavery under insane invaders;
I suffered hunger imposed by tyranny;
Yet, I still possess some inner power
With which I struggle to greet each day.

My mind is filled, but my heart is empty;
My body is old, but my heart is an infant.
Perhaps in youth my heart will grow, but I
Pray to grow old and reach the moment of
My return to God. Only then will my heart fill!

I was here from the moment of the
Beginning, and here I am still. And
I shall remain here until the end
Of the world, for there is no
Ending to my grief-stricken being.

YESTERDAY AND TODAY

THE GOLD-HOARDER WALKED in his palace park and with him walked his troubles. And over his head hovered worries as a vulture hovers over a carcass, until he reached a beautiful lake surrounded by magnificent marble statuary.

He sat there pondering the water which poured from the mouths of the statues like thoughts flowing freely from a lover's imagination, and contemplating heavily his palace which stood upon a knoll like a birth-mark upon the cheek of a maiden. His fancy revealed to him the pages of his life's drama which he read with falling tears that veiled his eyes and prevented him from viewing man's feeble additions to Nature.

He looked back with piercing regret to the images of his early life, woven into pattern by the gods, until he could no longer control his anguish. He said aloud, "Yesterday I was grazing my sheep in the green valley, enjoying my existence, sounding my flute, and holding my head high. Today I am a prisoner of greed. Gold leads into gold, then into restlessness, and finally into crushing misery.

"Yesterday I was like a singing bird, soaring freely here and there in the fields. Today I am a slave to fickle wealth, society's rules, the city's customs, and purchased friends, pleasing the people by conforming to the strange and narrow laws of man. I was born to be free and enjoy the bounty of life, but I find myself like a beast of burden so heavily laden with gold that his back is breaking.

"Where are the spacious plains, the singing brooks, the pure breeze, the closeness of Nature? Where is my deity? I have lost all! Naught remains save loneliness that saddens me, gold that ridicules me, slaves who curse to my back, and a palace that I have erected as a tomb for my happiness, and in whose greatness I have lost my heart.

"Yesterday I roamed the prairies and the hills together with the Bedouin's daughter; Virtue was our companion, Love our delight, and the moon our guardian. Today I am among women with shallow beauty who sell themselves for gold and diamonds.

"Yesterday I was carefree, sharing with the shepherds all the joy of life; eating, playing, working, singing, and dancing together to the music of the heart's truth. Today I find myself among the people like a frightened lamb among the wolves. As I walk in the roads, they gaze at me with hateful eyes and point at me with scorn and jealousy, and as I steal through the park I see frowning faces all about me.

"Yesterday I was rich in happiness and today I am poor in gold.

"Yesterday I was a happy shepherd looking upon my herd as a merciful king looks with pleasure upon his contented subjects. Today I am a slave standing before my wealth, my wealth which robbed me of the beauty of life I once knew.

"Forgive me, my Judge! I did not know that riches would put my life in fragments and lead me into the dungeons of harshness and stupidity. What I thought was glory is naught but an eternal inferno."

He gathered himself wearily and walked slowly toward the palace, sighing and repeating, "Is this what people call wealth? Is this the god I am serving and worshipping? Is this what I seek of the earth? Why can I not trade it for one particle of contentment? Who would sell me one beautiful thought for a ton of gold? Who would give me one moment of love for a handful of gems? Who would grant me an eye that can see others' hearts, and take all my coffers in barter?"

As he reached the palace gates he turned and looked toward the city as Jeremiah gazed toward Jerusalem. He raised his arms in woeful lament and shouted, "Oh people of the noisome city, who are living in darkness, hastening toward misery, preaching falsehood, and speaking with stupidity . . . until when shall you remain ignorant? Until when shall you abide in the filth of life and continue to desert its gardens? Why wear you tattered robes of narrowness while the silk raiment of Nature's beauty is fashioned for you? The lamp of wisdom is dimming;

it is time to furnish it with oil. The house of true fortune is being destroyed; it is time to rebuild it and guard it. The thieves of ignorance have stolen the treasure of your peace; it is time to retake it!"

At that moment a poor man stood before him and stretched forth his hand for alms. As he looked at the beggar, his lips parted, his eyes brightened with a softness, and his face radiated kindness. It was as if the yesterday he had lamented by the lake had come to greet him. He embraced the pauper with affection and filled his hand with gold, and with a voice sincere with the sweetness of love he said, "Come back tomorrow and bring with you your fellow sufferers. All your possessions will be restored."

He entered his palace saying, "Everything in life is good; even gold, for it teaches a lesson. Money is like a stringed instrument; he who does not know how to use it properly will hear only discordant music. Money is like love; it kills slowly and painfully the one who withholds it, and it enlivens the other who turns it upon his fellow men."

BEFORE THE THRONE
OF BEAUTY

O<small>NE HEAVY</small> day I ran
away from the grim face of society and the dizzying
clamour of the city and directed my weary steps to
the spacious valley. I pursued the beckoning course
of the rivulet and the musical sounds of the birds
until I reached a lonely spot where the flowing
branches of the trees prevented the sun from touching the earth.

I stood there, and it was entertaining to my soul—
my thirsty soul who had seen naught but the mirage
of life instead of its sweetness.

I was engrossed deeply in thought and my spirits
were sailing the firmament when a Houri, wearing a
sprig of grapevine that covered part of her naked
body, and a wreath of poppies about her golden
hair, suddenly appeared to me. As she realized my
astonishment, she greeted me saying, "Fear me not;
I am the Nymph of the Jungle."

"How can beauty like yours be committed to live
in this place? Please tell me who you are and whence

you come?" I asked. She sat gracefully on the green grass and responded, "I am the symbol of Nature! I am the Ever-Virgin your forefathers worshipped, and to my honour they erected shrines and temples at Baalbek and Djabeil." And I dared say, "But those temples and shrines were laid waste and the bones of my adoring ancestors became a part of the earth; nothing was left to commemorate their goddess save a pitiful few and forgotten pages in the book of history."

She replied, "Some goddesses live in the lives of their worshippers and die in their death, while some live an eternal and infinite life. My life is sustained by the world of Beauty which you will see wherever you rest your eyes, and this Beauty is Nature itself; it is the beginning of the shepherd's joy among the hills, and a villager's happiness in the fields, and the pleasure of the awe-filled tribes between the mountains and the plains. This Beauty promotes the wise into the throne of Truth."

Then I said, "Beauty is a terrible power!" And she retorted, "Human beings fear all things, even yourselves. You fear heaven, the source of spiritual peace; you fear Nature, the haven of rest and tranquility; you fear the God of goodness and accuse him of anger, while he is full of love and mercy."

After a deep silence, mingled with sweet dreams, I asked, "Speak to me of that Beauty which the people interpret and define, each one according to

his own conception; I have seen her honoured and worshipped in different ways and manners."

She answered, "Beauty is that which attracts your soul, and that which loves to give and not to receive. When you meet Beauty, you feel that the hands deep within your inner self are stretched forth to bring her into the domain of your heart. It is a magnificence combined of sorrow and joy; it is the Unseen which you see, and the Vague which you understand, and the Mute which you hear—it is the Holy of Holies that begins in yourself and ends vastly beyond your earthly imagination."

Then the Nymph of the Jungle approached me and laid her scented hand upon my eyes. And as she withdrew, I found me alone in the valley. When I returned to the city, whose turbulence no longer vexed me, I repeated her words:

"Beauty is that which attracts your soul,
And that which loves to give and not to receive."

LEAVE ME, MY BLAMER

Leave me, my blamer,
For the sake of the love
Which unites your soul with
That of your beloved one;
For the sake of that which
Joins spirit with mother's
Affection, and ties your
Heart with filial love. Go,
And leave me to my own
Weeping heart.

Let me sail in the ocean of
My dreams; wait until Tomorrow
Comes, for Tomorrow is free to
Do with me as he wishes. Your
Flaying is naught but shadow
That walks with the spirit to
The tomb of abashment, and shows
Her the cold, solid earth.

I have a little heart within me
And I like to bring him out of

His prison and carry him on the
Palm of my hand to examine him
In depth and extract his secret.
Aim not your arrows at him, lest
He take fright and vanish ere he
Pours the secret's blood as a
Sacrifice at the altar of his
Own faith, given him by Deity
When He fashioned him of Love and Beauty.

The sun is rising and the nightingale
Is singing, and the myrtle is
Breathing its fragrance into space.
I want to free myself from the
Quilted slumber of wrong. Do not
Detain me, my blamer!

Cavil me not by mention of the
Lions of the forest or the
Snakes of the valley, for
My soul knows no fear of earth and
Accepts no warning of evil before
Evil comes.

Advise me not, my blamer, for
Calamities have opened my heart and
Tears have cleansed my eyes, and
Errors have taught me the language
Of the hearts.

Talk not of banishment, for Conscience
Is my judge and he will justify me

And protect me if I am innocent, and
Will deny me of life if I am a criminal.

Love's procession is moving;
Beauty is waving her banner;
Youth is sounding the trumpet of joy;
Disturb not my contrition, my blamer.
Let me walk, for the path is rich
With roses and mint, and the air
Is scented with cleanliness.

Relate not the tales of wealth and
Greatness, for my soul is rich
With bounty and great with God's glory.

Speak not of peoples and laws and
Kingdoms, for the whole earth is
My birthplace and all humans are
My brothers.

Go from me, for you are taking away
Life-giving repentance and bringing
Needless words.

A LOVER'S CALL

WHERE are you, my beloved? Are you in that little
Paradise, watering the flowers who look upon you
As infants look upon the breast of their mothers?

Or are you in your chamber where the shrine of
Virtue has been placed in your honour, and upon
Which you offer my heart and soul as sacrifice?

Or amongst the books, seeking human knowledge,
While you are replete with heavenly wisdom?

Oh companion of my soul, where are you? Are you
Praying in the temple? Or calling Nature in the
Field, haven of your dreams?

Are you in the huts of the poor, consoling the
Broken-hearted with the sweetness of your soul, and
Filling their hands with your bounty?

You are God's spirit everywhere;
You are stronger than the ages.

Do you have memory of the day we met, when the
 halo of
Your spirit surrounded us, and the Angels of Love
Floated about, singing the praise of the soul's deeds?

Do you recollect our sitting in the shade of the
Branches, sheltering ourselves from Humanity, as
 the ribs
Protect the divine secret of the heart from injury?

Remember you the trails and forest we walked, with
 hands
Joined, and our heads leaning against each other,
 as if
We were hiding ourselves within ourselves?

Recall you the hour I bade you farewell,
And the Miriamite kiss you placed on my lips?
That kiss taught me that joining of lips in Love
Reveals heavenly secrets which the tongue cannot
 utter!

That kiss was introduction to a great sigh,
Like the Almighty's breath that turned earth into
 man.

That sigh led my way into the spiritual world,
Announcing the glory of my soul; and there
It shall perpetuate until again we meet.

I remember when you kissed me and kissed me,
With tears coursing your cheeks, and you said,

"Earthly bodies must often separate for earthly purpose,
And must live apart impelled by worldly intent.

"But the spirit remains joined safely in the hands of
Love, until death arrives and takes joined souls to
God.

"Go, my beloved; Love has chosen you her delegate;
Obey her, for she is Beauty who offers to her fol-
lower
The cup of the sweetness of life.
As for my own empty arms, your love shall remain
my
Comforting groom; your memory, my Eternal wed-
ding."

Where are you now, my other self? Are you awake in
The silence of the night? Let the clean breeze convey
To you my heart's every beat and affection.

Are you fondling my face in your memory? That
image
Is no longer my own, for Sorrow has dropped his
Shadow on my happy countenance of the past.

Sobs have withered my eyes which reflected your
beauty
And dried my lips which you sweetened with kisses.

Where are you, my beloved? Do you hear my weeping
From beyond the ocean? Do you understand my
  need?
Do you know the greatness of my patience?

Is there any spirit in the air capable of conveying
To you the breath of this dying youth? Is there any
Secret communication between angels that will carry
  to
You my complaint?

Where are you, my beautiful star? The obscurity of
  life
Has cast me upon its bosom; sorrow has conquered
  me.
Sail your smile into the air; it will reach and enliven
  me!
Breathe your fragrance into the air; it will sustain
  me!

Where are you, my beloved?
Oh, how great is Love!
And how little am I!

THE BEAUTY OF DEATH

Dedicated to M. E. H.

PART ONE—THE CALLING

Let me sleep, for my soul is intoxicated with
    love, and
Let me rest, for my spirit has had its bounty of days
    and nights;
Light the candles and burn the incense around my
    bed, and
Scatter leaves of jasmine and roses over my body;
Embalm my hair with frankincense and sprinkle my
    feet with perfume,
And read what the hand of Death has written on
    my forehead.

Let me rest in the arms of Slumber, for my open
    eyes are tired;
Let the silver-stringed lyre quiver and soothe my
    spirit;
Weave from the harp and lute a veil around my
    withering heart.

Sing of the past as you behold the dawn of hope in
my eyes, for
Its magic meaning is a soft bed upon which my
heart rests.

Dry your tears, my friends, and raise your heads as
the flowers
Raise their crowns to greet the dawn.
Look at the bride of Death standing like a column
of light
Between my bed and the infinite;
Hold your breath and listen with me to the beckon-
ing rustle of
Her white wings.

Come close and bid me farewell; touch my eyes
with smiling lips.
Let the children grasp my hands with soft and rosy
fingers;
Let the aged place their veined hands upon my head
and bless me;
Let the virgins come close and see the shadow of
God in my eyes,
And hear the echo of His will racing with my breath.

PART TWO—THE ASCENDING

I have passed a mountain peak and my soul is soaring in the
Firmament of complete and unbound freedom;
I am far, far away, my companions, and the clouds
are

Hiding the hills from my eyes.
The valleys are becoming flooded with an ocean of
    silence, and the
Hands of oblivion are engulfing the roads and the
    houses;
The prairies and fields are disappearing behind a
    white spectre
That looks like the spring cloud, yellow as the
    candlelight
And red as the twilight.

The songs of the waves and the hymns of the streams
Are scattered, and the voices of the throngs reduced
    to silence;
And I can hear naught but the music of Eternity
In exact harmony with the spirit's desires.
I am cloaked in full whiteness;
I am in comfort; I am in peace.

PART THREE—THE REMAINS

Unwrap me from this white linen shroud and clothe
    me
With leaves of jasmine and lilies;
Take my body from the ivory casket and let it rest
Upon pillows of orange blossoms.
Lament me not, but sing songs of youth and joy;
Shed not tears upon me, but sing of harvest and the
    winepress;
Utter no sigh of agony, but draw upon my face with
    your

Finger the symbol of Love and Joy.
Disturb not the air's tranquility with chanting and
   requiems,
But let your hearts sing with me the song of Eternal
   Life;
Mourn me not with apparel of black,
But dress in colour and rejoice with me;
Talk not of my departure with sighs in your hearts;
   close
Your eyes and you will see me with you forever-
   more.

Place me upon clusters of leaves and
Carry me upon your friendly shoulders and
Walk slowly to the deserted forest.
Take me not to the crowded burying ground lest
   my slumber
Be disrupted by the rattling of bones and skulls.
Carry me to the cypress woods and dig my grave
   where violets
And poppies grow not in the other's shadow;
Let my grave be deep so that the flood will not
Carry my bones to the open valley;
Let my grave be wide, so that the twilight shadows
Will come and sit by me.

Take from me all earthly raiment and place me
   deep in my
Mother Earth; and place me with care upon my
   mother's breast.

Cover me with soft earth, and let each handful be
   mixed
With seeds of jasmine, lilies, and myrtle; and when
   they
Grow above me and thrive on my body's element
   they will
Breathe the fragrance of my heart into space;
And reveal even to the sun the secret of my peace;
And sail with the breeze and comfort the wayfarer.

Leave me then, friends—leave me and depart on
   mute feet,
As the silence walks in the deserted valley;
Leave me to God and disperse yourselves slowly, as
   the almond
And apple blossoms disperse under the vibration of
   Nisan's breeze.

Go back to the joy of your dwellings and you will
   find there
That which Death cannot remove from you and me.
Leave this place, for what you see here is far away
   in meaning
From the earthly world. Leave me.

THE PALACE AND THE HUT

PART ONE

As NIGHT fell and the
light glittered in the great house, the servants stood
at the massive door awaiting the coming of the guests;
and upon their velvet garments shone golden but-
tons.

The magnificent carriages drew into the palace
park and the nobles entered, dressed in gorgeous raiment and decorated with jewels. The instruments
filled the air with pleasant melodies while the dignitaries danced to the soothing music.

At midnight the finest and most palatable foods
were served on a beautiful table embellished with
all kinds of the rarest flowers. The feasters dined
and drank abundantly, until the sequence of the
wine began to play its part. At dawn the throng dispersed boisterously, after spending a long night of
intoxication and gluttony which hurried their worn
bodies into their deep beds with unnatural sleep.

PART TWO

At eventide, a man attired in the dress of heavy work
stood before the door of his small house and knocked

at the door. As it opened, he entered and greeted the occupants in a cheerful manner, and then sat between his children who were playing at the fireplace. In a short time, his wife had the meal prepared and they sat at a wooden table consuming their food. After eating they gathered around the oil lamp and talked of the day's events. When early night had lapsed, all stood silently and surrendered themselves to the King of Slumber with a song of praise and a prayer of gratitude upon their lips.

A POET'S VOICE

PART ONE

THE POWER of charity sows deep in my heart, and I reap and gather the wheat in bundles and give them to the hungry.

My soul gives life to the grapevine and I press its bunches and give the juice to the thirsty.

Heaven fills my lamp with oil and I place it at my window to direct the stranger through the dark.

I do all these things because I live in them; and if destiny should tie my hands and prevent me from so doing, then death would be my only desire. For I am a poet, and if I cannot give, I shall refuse to receive.

Humanity rages like a tempest, but I sigh in silence for I know the storm must pass away while a sigh goes to God.

Human kinds cling to earthly things, but I seek ever to embrace the torch of love so it will purify me by its fire and sear inhumanity from my heart.

Substantial things deaden a man without suffering; love awakens him with enlivening pains.

Humans are divided into different clans and tribes, and belong to countries and towns. But I find myself a stranger to all communities and belong to no settlement. The universe is my country and the human family is my tribe.

Men are weak, and it is sad that they divide amongst themselves. The world is narrow and it is unwise to cleave it into kingdoms, empires, and provinces.

Human kinds unite themselves only to destroy the temples of soul, and they join hands to build edifices for earthly bodies. I stand alone listening to the voice of hope in my deep self saying, "As love enlivens a man's heart with pain, so ignorance teaches him the way to knowledge." Pain and ignorance lead to great joy and knowledge because the Supreme Being has created nothing vain under the sun.

PART TWO

I have a yearning for my beautiful country, and I love its people because of their misery. But if my people rose, stimulated by plunder and motivated by what they call "patriotic spirit" to murder, and invaded my neighbour's country, then upon the committing of any human atrocity I would hate my people and my country.

I sing the praise of my birthplace and long to see the home of my childhood; but if the people in that home refused to shelter and feed the needy way-

farer, I would convert my praise into anger and my longing into forgetfulness. My inner voice would say, "The house that does not comfort the needy is worthy of naught but destruction."

I love my native village with some of my love for my country; and I love my country with part of my love for the earth, all of which is my country; and I love the earth with all of myself because it is the haven of humanity, the manifest spirit of God.

Humanity is the spirit of the Supreme Being on earth, and that humanity is standing amidst ruins, hiding its nakedness behind tattered rags, shedding tears upon hollow cheeks, and calling for its children with pitiful voice. But the children are busy singing their clan's anthem; they are busy sharpening the swords and cannot hear the cry of their mothers.

Humanity appeals to its people but they listen not. Were one to listen, and console a mother by wiping her tears, others would say, "He is weak, affected by sentiment."

Humanity is the spirit of the Supreme Being on earth, and that Supreme Being preaches love and good-will. But the people ridicule such teachings. The Nazarene Jesus listened, and crucifixion was his lot; Socrates heard the voice and followed it, and he too fell victim in body. The followers of The Nazarene and Socrates are the followers of Deity, and since people will not kill them, they deride them, saying, "Ridicule is more bitter than killing."

Jerusalem could not kill The Nazarene, nor

Athens Socrates; they are living yet and shall live eternally. Ridicule cannot triumph over the followers of Deity. They live and grow forever.

PART THREE

Thou art my brother because you are a human, and we both are sons of one Holy Spirit; we are equal and made of the same earth.

You are here as my companion along the path of life, and my aid in understanding the meaning of hidden Truth. You are a human, and, that fact sufficing, I love you as a brother. You may speak of me as you choose, for Tomorrow shall take you away and will use your talk as evidence for his judgment, and you shall receive justice.

You may deprive me of whatever I possess, for my greed instigated the amassing of wealth and you are entitled to my lot if it will satisfy you.

You may do unto me whatever you wish, but you shall not be able to touch my Truth.

You may shed my blood and burn my body, but you cannot kill or hurt my spirit.

You may tie my hands with chains and my feet with shackles, and put me in the dark prison, but you shall not enslave my thinking, for it is free, like the breeze in the spacious sky.

You are my brother and I love you. I love you worshipping in your church, kneeling in your temple, and praying in your mosque. You and I and all are children of one religion, for the varied paths of

religion are but the fingers of the loving hand of the Supreme Being, extended to all, offering completeness of spirit to all, anxious to receive all.

I love you for your Truth, derived from your knowledge; that Truth which I cannot see because of my ignorance. But I respect it as a divine thing, for it is the deed of the spirit. Your Truth shall meet my Truth in the coming world and blend together like the fragrance of flowers and become one whole and eternal Truth, perpetuating and living in the eternity of Love and Beauty.

I love you because you are weak before the strong oppressor, and poor before the greedy rich. For these reasons I shed tears and comfort you; and from behind my tears I see you embraced in the arms of Justice, smiling and forgiving your persecutors. You are my brother and I love you.

PART FOUR

You are my brother, but why are you quarreling with me? Why do you invade my country and try to subjugate me for the sake of pleasing those who are seeking glory and authority?

Why do you leave your wife and children and follow Death to the distant land for the sake of those who buy glory with your blood, and high honour with your mother's tears?

Is it an honour for a man to kill his brother man? If you deem it an honour, let it be an act of worship,

and erect a temple to Cain who slew his brother Abel.

Is self-preservation the first law of Nature? Why, then, does Greed urge you to self-sacrifice in order only to achieve his aim in hurting your brothers? Beware, my brother, of the leader who says, "Love of existence obliges us to deprive the people of their rights!" I say unto you but this: protecting others' rights is the noblest and most beautiful human act; if my existence requires that I kill others, then death is more honourable to me, and if I cannot find someone to kill me for the protection of my honour, I will not hesitate to take my life by my own hands for the sake of Eternity before Eternity comes.

Selfishness, my brother, is the cause of blind superiority, and superiority creates clanship, and clanship creates authority which leads to discord and subjugation.

The soul believes in the power of knowledge and justice over dark ignorance; it denies the authority that supplies the swords to defend and strengthen ignorance and oppression—that authority which destroyed Babylon and shook the foundation of Jerusalem and left Rome in ruins. It is that which made people call criminals great men; made writers respect their names; made historians relate the stories of their inhumanity in manner of praise.

The only authority I obey is the knowledge of guarding and acquiescing in the Natural Law of Justice.

What justice does authority display when it kills the killer? When it imprisons the robber? When it descends on a neighbouring country and slays its people? What does justice think of the authority under which a killer punishes the one who kills, and a thief sentences the one who steals?

You are my brother, and I love you; and Love is justice with its full intensity and dignity. If justice did not support my love for you, regardless of your tribe and community, I would be a deceiver concealing the ugliness of selfishness behind the outer garment of pure love.

CONCLUSION

My soul is my friend who consoles me in misery and distress of life. He who does not befriend his soul is an enemy of humanity, and he who does not find human guidance within himself will perish desperately. Life emerges from within, and derives not from environs.

I came to say a word and I shall say it now. But if death prevents its uttering, it will be said by Tomorrow, for Tomorrow never leaves a secret in the book of Eternity.

I came to live in the glory of Love and the light of Beauty, which are the reflections of God. I am here living, and the people are unable to exile me from the domain of life for they know I will live in death. If they pluck my eyes I will hearken to the murmurs of Love and the songs of Beauty.

If they close my ears I will enjoy the touch of the ,breeze mixed with the incense of Love and the fragrance of Beauty.

If they place me in vacuum, I will live together with my soul, the child of Love and Beauty.

I came here to be for all and with all, and what I do today in my solitude will be echoed by Tomorrow to the people.

What I say now with one heart will be said to-morrow by many hearts.

THE BRIDE'S BED*

THE BRIDE and bridegroom, preceded by candle carriers and followed by priests and friends, left the temple accompanied by young men and women who walked by their sides singing and filling the firmament with beautiful and happy melodies.

As the procession reached the bridegroom's residence, the newly wed couple took high seats in the spacious room, and the celebrants seated themselves upon the silken cushions and velvet divans until the place became crowded with multitudes of well wishers. The servants set the tables, and the feasters commenced drinking to the health of the bride and bridegroom, while the musicians were soothing the spirits with their stringed instruments. One could hear the ringing and rattling of the drinking cups in unison with the sound of tambourines. The maidens began to dance gracefully and twist their

* This incident occurred in North Lebanon in the latter part of the nineteenth century and it was conveyed to me by a person who was related to one of the principals in this story, and who attended the function described. (*Kahlil Gibran.*)

flexible bodies to the melodies of the music, while the onlookers watched cheerfully and drank more and more wine.

In a few hours the scene was converted from a gay and pleasant wedding celebration into a coarse and profane orgy of drunkenness. Here is a young man pouring out all of his heart's sentiment and revealing his momentary, questionable love to an attractive maiden. And there is another youth endeavouring to converse with a woman, and having difficulty in bringing to his wine-drugged tongue the beautiful expressions he sought. Now and then you hear an elderly man urging the musicians to repeat a certain song that reminded him of his youthful days. In this group a woman is flirting with a man who, in turn, is looking passionately at her rival. In that corner, a grey-haired woman is watching the maidens smilingly, trying to select a wife for her only son. By the window stands a married woman who affords herself this opportunity to make plans with her lover while her husband is occupied with wine. It seemed that all were reaping the fruits of the present and forgetting the past and the future.

All this was taking place while the beautiful bride watched them with sorrowful eyes. She felt like a miserable prisoner behind the iron bars of a prison, and frequently she glanced across the room toward a young man who was sitting alone and quietly, like a wounded bird left behind by the flock. His arms were folded across his bosom as if he were try-

ing to keep his heart from bursting. He was gazing at something invisible in the sky of the room and seemed to be completely lost in a world of darkness.

Midnight came, and the exultation of the throng mounted higher until it assumed the aspects of unleashed madness, for the minds were free and the tongues were uncontrolled.

The bridegroom, who was an elderly man, already drunk, left the bride to herself and circulated amidst the guests, drinking with the feasters and adding fuel to the flames of his intoxication.

Responding to the bride's signal, a maiden came and sat close by her side, whereupon the bride turned around and looked in every direction before she whispered with a trembling voice, "I beg you, my companion, and appeal to you in the name of our friendship and everything that is dear to you in this world, to go now and tell Saleem to join me in the garden under the willow tree. Please, Susan, beg him for me and ask him to grant my request; remind him of our past and tell him that I will die if I do not see him. Tell him that I must confess my sins to him and ask him to forgive me; tell him that I want to pour out all my heart's secrets before him. Hurry, and do not fear."

Susan dispatched the bride's message with sincerity; Saleem looked at her as a thirsty man looks at a brook far off and he quietly said, "I will wait for her in the garden under the willow tree." He left the house, and a few minutes passed before the bride

followed him, stealing her way between the drunken revelers. As she reached the garden, she looked to the rear like a gazelle who is fleeing a wolf, and sped toward the willow tree where the youth awaited her. When she found herself by his side, she threw her arms about him and said tearfully, "My beloved, listen to me; I am sorry for having been hasty and thoughtless. I repented until my heart is crushed with sorrow; I love you and do not love any other; I shall continue to love you to the end of my life. They lied to me and told me that you loved another and Najeebee deceived me when she told me that you had fallen in love with her, and did so in order to induce me to accept her cousin as my bridegroom, as the family had long planned. I am married now but you are the only one I love and you are my bridegroom. Now that the veil has been removed from my eyes and truth is near, I came here to follow you to the end of life, and I will never go back to the man whom falsehood and narrow custom have selected for me as a husband. Let us hurry, my beloved, and leave this place under the protection of night. Let us go to the seacoast and embark upon a ship that will take us to a distant land where we will live together unmolested. Let us start now so when dawn comes we will be safe from the grip of the enemy; I have enough jewelry to take care of us for the rest of our lives . . . Why do you not talk, Saleem? Why do you not look at me? Why do you not kiss me? Are you listening to the wailing of my

soul and the crying of my heart? Speak, and let us make haste to leave this place! The minutes we are losing are more precious than diamonds, and dearer than the crowns of the kings."

Her voice was more soothing than Life's whispering, and more anguished than the moaning call of Death, and softer than the rustling of wings, and deeper than the message of the waves . . . it was a voice that vibrated with hope and despair, with pleasure and pain, with happiness and misery, with need for life and desire for death. The youth was listening, but within him Love and Honour fought each other . . . Honour that confronts the spirit, and Love that God places in the human heart . . . After a long silence, the youth raised his head and turned his eyes away from the bride who was quivering with anxiety and he quietly protested, "Return to your destiny, for it is now too late. Sobriety has effaced what intoxication had painted. Go back before the guests see you here and say that you betrayed your husband on the wedding night just as you betrayed me during my absence." When she heard these words, she trembled like a withering flower before a tempest and she said painfully, "I shall never go back to that house which I have left forever. I feel now like a prisoner who leaves his exile . . . do not cast me from you, saying that I betrayed you. The hands that joined your heart and mine are stronger than the Emir's and the priest's hands which committed my body to my revolting

bridegroom. There is no power that can take you from me . . . not even Death can separate our souls, for as Heaven has willed it, only Heaven can alter it."

Feigning disinterest and trying to free himself from the grip of her arms around him, Saleem retorted, "Depart from me! I love another with an intensity that causes me to forget you exist in this world. Najeebee was right when she told you that I loved her. Go back to your husband and be a faithful wife to him as the law commands."

The bride desperately protested, "No, no! I do not believe you, Saleem! I know that you love me, and I can read it in your eyes; I sense your love when I am close to you; I shall never leave you for my husband's home as long as my heart beats; I came here to follow you to the end of the world. Lead the way, Saleem, or shed my blood and take my life now." With a voice no stronger than before, Saleem returned, "Leave me, or I will shout and gather the people in this garden and disgrace you before God and man and let my beloved Najeebee laugh at you and be proud of her triumph."

As Saleem was endeavouring to unclasp her arms, she turned from a hopeful, kind, and pleading woman into a furious lioness who had lost her cubs, and she cried out saying, "No one shall ever triumph over me and take my love from me!" Having uttered these words, she drew a dagger from beneath her wedding gown, and swift as lightning, she

sheathed it in the youth's heart. He fell upon the ground like a tender branch broken by the storms and she bent over him, holding the blood-stained dagger in her hand. He opened his eyes and his lips vibrated when he faltered, "Come now, my beloved; come, Lyla, and do not leave me. Life is weaker than Death, and Death is weaker than Love. Listen to the cruel laughter of the feasters inside the house, and hear the tinkling and breaking of the drinking cups, my beloved. Lyla, you have rescued me from Life's suffering. Let me kiss the hand that broke the chains and let me free. Kiss me and forgive me, for I have not been truthful.

"Place your blood-cleansed hands upon my withering heart, and when my soul ascends into the spacious sky, place the dagger in my right hand and say that I took my own life." He choked for breath and whispered, "I love you, Lyla, and never loved another. Self-sacrifice is nobler than fleeing with you. Kiss me, oh beloved sweetheart of my soul. Kiss me, oh Lyla . . ." And he placed his hand upon his wounded heart and breathed his last. The bride looked toward the house and cried in piercing agony, "Emerge from your stupor, for here is the wedding! The bride and the bridegroom are awaiting you! Come and see our soft bed! Wake up, you madmen and drunkards; hurry to this place so we can reveal to you the truth of Love, Death and Life!" Her hysterical voice rang through every corner of the house, echoing into the guests' ears. As if

in a trance, they were drawn to the door and they walked out, looking in every direction. As they approached the scene of tragic beauty, and saw the bride weeping over Saleem, they retreated in fright and none dared come close by. It seemed that the stream of blood from the youth's heart, and the dagger in the bride's hand, had fascinated them and frozen the blood in their bodies. The bride looked at him and moaned bitterly, "Come, you cowards! Fear not the spectre of Death whose greatness will refuse to approach your littleness, and dread not this dagger, for it is a divine instrument which declines to touch your filthy bodies and empty hearts. Look at this handsome youth . . . he is my beloved, and I killed him because I loved him . . . he is my bridegroom and I am his bride. We sought a bed worthy of our love in this world which you have made so small with your ignorance and traditions. But we chose this bed. Where is that wicked woman who slandered my beloved and said that he loved her? Where is the one who believed she triumphed over me? Where is Najeebee, that hell-viper who deceived me? Where is the woman who gathered you here to celebrate my beloved's departure and not the wedding of the man she had chosen for me? My words are vague to you, for the abyss cannot understand the song of the stars. You shall tell your children that I killed my beloved on the wedding night. My name shall be upon your dirty lips uttered with blasphemy, but your grandchildren shall

bless me, for Tomorrow shall be for the freedom of truth and the spirit. And you, my ignorant husband, who bought my body but not my love, and who owns me but will never possess me, you are the symbol of this miserable nation, seeking light in darkness, and awaiting the coming of water from the rock; you symbolize a country ruled by blindness and stupidity; you represent a false humanity which cuts throats and arms in order to reach for a necklace or bracelet. I forgive you now, for the happy, departing soul forgives the sins of all the people."

Then the bride lifted her dagger toward the sky, and like a thirsty person who brings the edge of a drinking glass to his lips, she brought it down and planted it in her bosom. She fell by the side of her beloved like a lily whose flower was cut off by a sharp scythe. The women gazed upon the horrible scene and cried frightfully; some of them fell into a swoon, and the uproar of the men filled the sky. As they shamefully and reverently approached the victims, the dying bride looked at them, and with blood streaming from her stricken body, she said, "Stay away from us and separate not our bodies, for if you commit such a sin, the spirit that hovers over your heads will grasp you and take your lives. Let this hungry earth swallow our bodies and hide us in its bosom. Let it protect us as it protects the seeds from the snow until Spring comes, and restores pure life and awakening."

She came close to her beloved, placed her lips

upon his cold lips, and uttered her last words, "Look, my forever . . . look at our friends. How the jealous are gathering about our bed! Hear the grating of their teeth and the crushing of their fingers! You have waited for me a long time, Saleem, and here I am, for I have broken the chains and shackles. Let us go toward the sun, for we have been waiting too long in this confining, dark world. All objects are disappearing from my sight and I can see naught but you, my beloved. These are my lips, my greatest earthly possession . . . accept my last human breath. Come, Saleem, let us leave now. Love has lifted his wings and ascended into the great light." She dropped her head upon his bosom and her unseeing eyes were still open and gazing upon him.

Silence prevailed, as if the dignity of death had stolen the people's strength and prevented them from moving. Whereupon the priest who had performed the wedding ceremony came forth and pointed with his forefinger at the death-bound couple shouting, "Cursed are the hands that touch these blood-spattered carcasses that are soaked with sin. And cursed are the eyes that shed tears of sorrow upon these two evil souls. Let the corpse of the son of Sodom and that of the daughter of Gomorrah remain lying in this diseased spot until the beasts devour their flesh and the wind scatters their bones. Go back to your homes and flee from the pollution of these sinners! Disperse now, before the flames of hell sting you, and he who remains here shall be

cursed and excommunicated from the Church and shall never again enter the temple and join the Christians in offering prayers to God!"

Susan, who acted as the last messenger between the bride and her beloved, walked forth bravely and stood before the priest. She looked at him with tearful eyes and said, "I shall remain here, you merciless heretic, and I shall guard them until dawn comes. I shall dig a grave for them under these hanging branches and bury them in the garden of their last earthly kiss. Leave this place immediately, for the swine detest the aromatic scent of incense, and the thieves fear the lord of the house and dread the coming of the brilliant sunrise. Hurry to your obscured beds, for the hymns of the angels will not enter your ears, blocked with the hardened cement of cruel and stupid rules."

The throng departed slowly with the stern-faced priest, and Susan remained watching over Lyla and Saleem as a loving mother guards her children in the silence of the night. And when the multitude was gone, she dropped down and wept with the crying angels.

BETWEEN
NIGHT & MORN

THE TEMPEST

PART ONE

USIF EL FAKHRI was thirty
years of age when he withdrew himself from society
and departed to live in an isolated hermitage in the
vicinity of Kedeesha Valley in North Lebanon. The
people of the nearby villages heard various tales
concerning Yusif; some related that his was a wealthy
and noble family, and that he loved a woman who
betrayed him and caused him to lead a solitary life,
while others said that he was a poet who deserted the
clamourous city and retired to that place in order to
record his thoughts and compose his inspiration;
and many were sure that he was a mystic who was
contented with the spiritual world, although most
people insisted that he was a madman.

As for myself, I could not draw any conclusion
regarding the man, for I knew that there must be a
deep secret within his heart whose revelation I would
not trust to mere speculation. I had long hoped for
the opportunity to meet this strange man. I had endeavoured in devious ways to win his friendship in

order to study his reality and learn his story by inquiring as to his purpose in life, but my efforts were in vain. When I met him for the first time, he was walking by the forest of the Holy Cedars of Lebanon, and I greeted him with the finest choice of words, but he returned my greeting by merely shaking his head and striding off.

On another occasion I found him standing in the midst of a small vineyard by a monastery, and again I approached and greeted him, saying, "It is said by the villagers that this monastery was built by a Syriac group in the Fourteenth Century; do you know anything of its history?" He replied coldly, "I do not know who built this monastery, nor do I care to know." And he turned his back to me and added, "Why do you not ask your grandparents, who are older than I, and who know more of the history of these valleys than I do?" Realizing at once my utter failure, I left him.

Thus did two years pass, and the bizarre life of this strange man preyed on my mind and disturbed my dreams.

PART TWO

One day in Autumn, as I was roaming the hills and knolls adjacent to the hermitage of Yusif El Fakhri, I was suddenly caught in a strong wind and torrent rain, and the tempest cast me here and there like a boat whose rudder has been broken and whose masts have been torn by a gale in a rough sea. I

directed my steps with difficulty toward Yusif's place, saying to myself, "This is an opportunity I have long sought, and the tempest will be my excuse for entering, while my wet clothes will serve as good reason for lingering."

I was in a miserable plight when I reached the hermitage, and as I knocked on the door, the man whom I had been longing to see opened it. He was holding in one hand a dying bird whose head had been injured and whose wings had been broken. I greeted him saying, "I beg your forgiveness for this annoying intrusion. The raging tempest trapped me while I was afar from home." He frowned, saying, "There are many caves in this wilderness in which you might have taken refuge." However, he did not close the door, and the beat of my heart quickened in anticipation, for the realization of my great wish was close at hand. He commenced to touch the bird's head gently and with the utmost care and interest, exhibiting a quality important to my heart. I was surprised over the two opponent characteristics I found in that man—mercy and cruelty at the same time. We became aware of the strained silence. He resented my presence, I desired to remain.

It seemed as if he felt my thought, for he looked up and said, "The tempest is clean, and declines to eat soured meat. Why do you seek to escape from it?" And with a touch of humour, I responded, "The tempest may not desire salted or soured things, but she is inclined to chill and tender all things, and

undoubtedly she would enjoy consuming me if she grasped me again." His expression was severe when he retorted, "The tempest would have bestowed upon you a great honour, of which you are not worthy, if she had swallowed you." I agreed, "Yes, Sir, I fled the tempest so I might not be awarded an honour which I do not merit." He turned his face from me in an effort to choke his smile, and then motioned toward a wooden bench by the fireplace and invited me to rest and dry my raiment. I could scarcely control my elation.

I thanked him and sat down while he seated himself opposite, on a bench carved of rock. He commenced to dip his finger tips into an earthenware jar containing a kind of oil, applying it softly to the bird's head and wings. Without looking up he said, "The strong winds have caused this bird to fall upon the rocks between Life and Death." I replied, rendering comparison, "And the strong winds have sent me, adrift, to your door, in time to prevent having my head injured and my wings broken."

He looked at me seriously and said, "It is my wish that man would show the bird's instinct, and it is my wish that the tempest would break the people's wings. For man inclines toward fear and cowardice, and as he feels the awakening of the tempest he crawls into the crevices and the caves of the earth and hides himself."

My purpose was to extract the story of his self-imposed exile, and I provoked, "Yes, the birds possess

an honour and courage that man does not possess.
. . . Man lives in the shadow of laws and customs
which he made and fashioned for himself, but the
birds live according to the same free Eternal Law
which causes the earth to pursue its mighty path
about the sun." His eyes and face brightened, as if
he had found in me an understanding disciple, and
he exclaimed, "Well done! If you place belief in
your own words you should leave civilization and its
corrupt laws and traditions, and live like the birds
in a place empty of all things except the magnificent
law of heaven and earth.

"Believing is a fine thing, but placing those beliefs into execution is a test of strength. Many are
those who talk like the roar of the sea, but their
lives are shallow and stagnant, like the rotting
marshes. Many are those who lift their heads above
the mountain tops, but their spirits remain dormant
in the obscurity of the caverns." He rose trembling
from his seat and placed the bird upon a folded
cloth by the window.

He placed a bundle of dry sticks upon the fire,
saying, "Remove your sandals and warm your feet,
for dampness is dangerous to man's health. Dry well
your garments, and be comfortable."

Yusif's continued hospitality kept my hopes high.
I approached near to the fire, and the steam sifted
from my wet robe. While he stood at the door gazing
at the grey skies, my mind searched and scurried for
the opening wedge into his background. I asked,

innocently, "Has it been long since you came to this place?"

Without looking at me, he answered quietly, "I came to this place when the earth was without form, and void; and darkness was upon the face of the deep. And the Spirit of God moved upon the face of the waters."

I was aghast at these words! Struggling to gather my shocked and scattered wits, I said to myself, "How fantastic this man is! And how difficult is the path that leads to his reality! But I shall attack cautiously and slowly and patiently, until his reticence turns into communication, and his strangeness into understanding."

PART THREE

Night was spreading her black garment upon those valleys, and the tempest was shrieking dizzily and the rain becoming stronger. I began to fancy that the Biblical flood was coming again, to abolish life and wash man's filth from God's earth.

It seemed that the revolution of elements had created in Yusif's heart a tranquility which often comes as a reaction to temperament and converts aloneness into conviviality. He ignited two candles, and then placed before me a jar of wine and a large tray containing bread, cheese, olives, honey, and some dry fruits. Then he sat near me, and after apologizing for the small quantity—but not for the simplicity—of the food, asked me to join him.

We partook of the repast in understanding silence, listening to the wailing of the wind and the crying of the rain, and at the same time I was contemplating his face and trying to dig out his secrets, meditating the possible motive underlying his unusual existence. Having finished, he took a copper kettle from the fire and poured pure, aromatic coffee into two cups; then he opened a small box and offered me a cigarette, addressing me as "Brother." I took one while drinking my coffee, not believing what my eyes were seeing. He looked at me smilingly, and after he had inhaled deeply of his cigarette and sipped some coffee, he said, "Undoubtedly you are thinking upon the existence here of wine and tobacco and coffee, and you may also be wondering over my food and comforts. Your curiosity is justified in all respects, for you are one of the many who believe that in being away from the people, one is absent from life, and must abstain from all its enjoyment." Quickly I agreed, "Yes, it is related by the wise men that he who deserts the world for the purpose of worshipping God alone will leave behind all the enjoyment and plenty of life, contenting himself with the simple products of God alone, and existing on plants and water."

After a pause, heavy with thought, he mused, "I could have worshipped God while living among His creatures, for worship does not require solitude. I did not leave the people in order to see God, for I had always seen Him at the home of my father and

mother. I deserted the people because their natures were in conflict with mine, and their dreams did not agree with my dreams. . . . I left man because I found that the wheel of my soul was turning one way and grinding harshly against the wheels of other souls which were turning in the opposite direction. I left civilization because I found it to be an old and corrupt tree, strong and terrible, whose roots are locked into the obscurity of the earth and whose branches are reaching beyond the cloud; but its blossoms are of greed and evil and crime, and its fruit is of woe and misery and fear. Crusaders have undertaken to blend good into it and change its nature, but they could not succeed. They died disappointed, persecuted and torn."

Yusif leaned toward the side of the fireplace as if awaiting the impression of his words upon my heart. I thought it best to remain a listener, and he continued, "No, I did not seek solitude to pray and lead a hermit's life . . . for prayer, which is the song of the heart, will reach the ears of God even when mingled with the shout and cry of thousands of voices. To live the life of a recluse is to torture the body and soul and deaden the inclinations, a kind of existence which is repugnant to me, for God has erected the bodies as temples for the spirits, and it is our mission to deserve and maintain the trust reposed in us by God.

"No, my brother, I did not seek solitude for religious purposes, but solely to avoid the people and

their laws, their teachings and their traditions, their ideas and their clamour and their wailing.

"I sought solitude in order to keep from seeing the faces of men who sell themselves and buy with the same price that which is lower than they are, spiritually and materially.

"I sought solitude in order that I might not encounter the women who walk proudly, with one thousands smiles upon their lips, while in the depths of their thousands of hearts there is but one purpose.

"I sought solitude in order to conceal myself from those self-satisfied individuals who see the spectre of knowledge in their dreams and believe that they have attained their goal.

"I fled from society to avoid those who see but the phantom of truth in their awakening, and shout to the world that they have acquired completely the essence of truth.

"I deserted the world and sought solitude because I became tired of rendering courtesy to those multitudes who believe that humility is a sort of weakness, and mercy a kind of cowardice, and snobbery a form of strength.

"I sought solitude because my soul wearied of association with those who believe sincerely that the sun and moon and stars do not rise save from their coffers, and do not set except in their gardens.

"I ran from the office-seekers who shatter the earthly fate of the people while throwing into their

eyes the golden dust and filling their ears with sounds of meaningless talk.

"I departed from the ministers who do not live according to their sermons, and who demand of the people that which they do not solicit of themselves.

"I sought solitude because I never obtained kindness from a human unless I paid the full price with my heart.

"I sought solitude because I loathe that great and terrible institution which the people call civilization—that symmetrical monstrosity erected upon the perpetual misery of human kinds.

"I sought solitude for in it there is a full life for the spirit and for the heart and for the body. I found the endless prairies where the light of the sun rests, and where the flowers breathe their fragrance into space, and where the streams sing their way to the sea. I discovered the mountains where I found the fresh awakening of Spring, and the colourful longing of Summer, and the rich songs of Autumn, and the beautiful mystery of Winter. I came to this far corner of God's domain for I hungered to learn the secrets of the Universe, and approach close to the throne of God."

Yusif breathed deeply, as if he had been relieved of a heavy burden. His eyes shone with strange and magical rays, and upon his radiant face appeared the signs of pride, will, and contentment.

A few minutes passed, and I was gazing placidly

at him, and pondering the unveiling of what had been hidden from me; then I addressed him, saying, "You are undoubtedly correct in most of the things you have said, but through your diagnosis of the social ailment, you prove at the same time that you are a good doctor. I believe that the sick society is in dire need of such a physician, who should cure it or kill it. This distressed world begs your attention. Is it just or merciful to withdraw yourself from the ailing patient and deny him your benefit?"

He stared at me thoughtfully, and then said with futility, "Since the beginning of the world, the doctors have been trying to save the people from their disorders; some used knives, while others used potions, but pestilence spread hopelessly. It is my wish that the patient would content himself with remaining in his filthy bed, meditating his long-continued sores; but instead, he stretches his hands from under the robe and clutches at the neck of each who comes to visit him, choking him to death. What irony it is! The evil patient kills the doctor, and then closes his eyes and says within himself, 'He was a great physician.' No, Brother, no one on earth can benefit humanity. The sower, however wise and expert he may be, cannot cause the field to sprout in Winter."

And I argued, "The people's Winter will pass away, and then comes the beautiful Spring, and the flowers must surely bloom in the fields, and the brooks will again leap in the valleys."

He frowned, and said bitterly, "Alas! Has God

divided man's life—which is the whole creation—
into seasons like those of the year? Will any tribe
of human beings, living now in God's truth and
spirit, desire to re-appear on the face of this earth?
Will ever the time come when man settles and abides
at the right arm of Life, rejoicing with the brilliant
light of day and the peaceful silence of night? Can
that dream become reality? Can it materialize after
the earth has been covered with human flesh and
drenched with man's blood?"

And Yusif stood and raised his hand toward the
sky, as if pointing at a different world, and he continued, "This is naught but a vain dream for the
world, but I am finding its accomplishment for
myself, and what I am discovering here occupies
every space in my heart and in the valleys and in
the mountains." He now raised his intense voice,
"What I really know to be true is the crying of my
inner self. I am here living, and in the depths of my
existence there is a thirst and hunger, and I find
joy in partaking of the bread and wine of Life from
the vases which I make and fashion by my own hands.
For this reason I abandoned the boards of the people
and came to this place, and I shall remain here until
the Ending!"

He continued walking back and forth across the
room in agitation while I was pondering his sayings
and meditating the description of society's gaping
wounds. I ventured again a tactful criticism. "I hold
the utmost regard for your opinion and intentions,

and I envy and respect your solitude and aloneness, but I know that this miserable nation has sustained a great loss in your expatriation, for she is in need of an understanding healer to help her through her difficulties and awaken her spirit."

He shook his head slowly and said, "This nation is like all the nations. And the people are made of the same element and do not vary except in their exterior appearance, which is of no consequence. The misery of our Oriental nations is the misery of the world, and what you call civilization in the West is naught but another spectre of the many phantoms of tragic deception.

"Hypocrisy will always remain, even if her finger tips are coloured and polished; and Deceit will never change even if her touch becomes soft and delicate; and Falsehood will never turn into Truth even if you dress her with silken robes and place her in the palace; and Greed will not become Contentment; nor will Crime become Virtue. And Eternal Slavery to teachings, to customs, and to history will remain Slavery even if she paints her face and disguises her voice. Slavery will remain Slavery in all her horrible form, even if she calls herself Liberty.

"No, my brother, the West is not higher than the East, nor is the West lower than the East, and the difference that stands between the two is not greater than the difference between the tiger and the lion. There is a just and perfect law that I have found behind the exterior of society, which equalizes mis-

ery, prosperity, and ignorance; it does not prefer one nation to another, nor does it oppress one tribe in order to enrich another."

I exclaimed, "Then civilization is vanity, and all in it is vanity!" He quickly responded, "Yes, civilization is vanity and all in it is vanity. . . . Inventions and discoveries are but amusement and comfort for the body when it is tired and weary. The conquest of distance and the victory over the seas are but false fruit which do not satisfy the soul, nor nourish the heart, neither lift the spirit, for they are afar from nature. And those structures and theories which man calls knowledge and art are naught except shackles and golden chains which man drags, and he rejoices with their glittering reflections and ringing sounds. They are strong cages whose bars man commenced fabricating ages ago, unaware that he was building from the inside, and that he would soon become his own prisoner to eternity. Yes, vain are the deeds of man, and vain are his purposes, and all is vanity upon the earth." He paused, then slowly added, "And among all vanities of life, there is only one thing that the spirit loves and craves. One thing dazzling and alone."

"What is it?" I inquired with quivering voice. He looked at me for a long minute and then closed his eyes. He placed his hands on his chest, while his face brightened, and with a serene and sincere voice he said, "It is an awakening in the spirit; it is an awakening in the inner depths of the heart; it is an

overwhelming and magnificent power that descends suddenly upon man's conscience and opens his eyes, whereupon he sees Life amid a dizzying shower of brilliant music, surrounded by a circle of great light, with man standing as a pillar of beauty between the earth and the firmament. It is a flame that suddenly rages within the spirit and sears and purifies the heart, ascending above the earth and hovering in the spacious sky. It is a kindness that envelops the individual's heart whereby he would bewilder and disapprove all who opposed it, and revolt against those who refuse to understand its great meaning. It is a secret hand which removed the veil from my eyes while I was a member of society amidst my family, my friends and my countrymen.

"Many times I wondered, and spoke to myself, saying, 'What is this Universe, and why am I different from those people who are looking at me, and how do I know them, and where did I meet them, and why am I living among them? Am I a stranger among them, or is it they who are strange to this earth, built by Life who entrusted me with the keys?' "

He suddenly became silent, as if remembering something he had seen long before, refusing to reveal it. Then he stretched his arms forward and whispered, "That is what happened to me four years ago, when I left the world and came to this void place to live in the awakeness of life and enjoy kind thoughts and beautiful silence."

115

He walked toward the door, looking at the depths of the darkness as if preparing to address the tempest. But he spoke in a vibrating voice, saying, "It is an awakening within the spirit; he who knows it, is unable to reveal it by words; and he who knows it not, will never think upon the compelling and beautiful mystery of existence."

PART FOUR

An hour had passed and Yusif El Fakhri was striding about the room, stopping at random and gazing at the tremendous grey skies. I remained silent, reflecting upon the strange unison of joy and sorrow in his solitary life.

Later in the night he approached me and stared long into my face, as if wanting to commit to memory the picture of the man to whom he had disclosed the piercing secrets of his life. My mind was heavy with turmoil, my eyes with mist. He said quietly, "I am going now to walk through the night with the tempest, to feel the closeness of Nature's expression; it is a practise that I enjoy greatly in Autumn and Winter. Here is the wine, and there is the tobacco; please accept my home as your own for the night."

He wrapped himself in a black robe and added smilingly, "I beg you to fasten the door against the intruding humans when you leave in the morning, for I plan to spend the day in the forest of the Holy Cedars." Then he walked toward the door, carrying a long walking staff and he concluded, "If the tem-

pest surprises you again while you are in this vicinity, do not hesitate to take refuge in this hermitage. . . . I hope you will teach yourself to love, and not to fear, the tempest. . . . Good night, my brother."

He opened the door and walked out with his head high, into the dark. I stood at the door to see which course he had taken, but he had disappeared from view. For a few minutes I heard the fall of his feet upon the broken stones of the valley.

PART FIVE

Morning came, after a night of deep thought, and the tempest had passed away, while the sky was clear and the mountains and the plains were reveling in the sun's warm rays. On my way back to the city I felt that spiritual awakening of which Yusif El Fakhri had spoken, and it was raging throughout every fibre of my being. I felt that my shivering must be visible. And when I calmed, all about me was beauty and perfection.

As soon as I reached the noisome people and heard their voices and saw their deeds, I stopped and said within myself, "Yes, the spiritual awakening is the most essential thing in man's life, and it is the sole purpose of being. Is not civilization, in all its tragic forms, a supreme motive for spiritual awakening? Then how can we deny existing matter, while its very existence is unwavering proof of its conformability into the intended fitness? The present civilization may possess a vanishing purpose, but the

eternal law has offered to that purpose a ladder whose steps can lead to a free substance."

I never saw Yusif El Fakhri again, for through my endeavours to attend the ills of civilization, Life had expelled me from North Lebanon in late Autumn of that same year, and I was required to live in exile in a distant country whose tempests are domestic. And leading a hermit's life in that country is a sort of glorious madness, for its society, too, is ailing.

SLAVERY

THE PEOPLE are the slaves
of Life, and it is slavery which fills their days with
misery and distress, and floods their nights with tears
and anguish.

Seven thousand years have passed since the day
of my first birth, and since that day I have been
witnessing the slaves of Life, dragging their heavy
shackles.

I have roamed the East and West of the earth and
wandered in the Light and in the Shadow of Life.
I have seen the processions of civilization moving
from light into darkness, and each was dragged down
to hell by humiliated souls bent under the yoke of
slavery. The strong is fettered and subdued, and the
faithful is on his knees worshipping before the idols.
I have followed man from Babylon to Cairo, and
from Ain Dour to Baghdad, and observed the marks
of his chains upon the sand. I heard the sad echoes
of the fickle ages repeated by the eternal prairies and
valleys.

I visited the temples and altars and entered the

palaces, and sat before the thrones. And I saw the apprentice slaving for the artisan, and the artisan slaving for the employer, and the employer slaving for the soldier, and the soldier slaving for the governor, and the governor slaving for the king, and the king slaving for the priest, and the priest slaving for the idol. . . . And the idol is naught but earth fashioned by Satan and erected upon a knoll of skulls.

I entered the mansions of the rich and visited the huts of the poor. I found the infant nursing the milk of slavery from his mother's bosom, and the children learning submission with the alphabet.

The maidens wear garments of restriction and passivity, and the wives retire with tears upon beds of obedience and legal compliance.

I accompanied the ages from the banks of the Kange to the shores of Euphrates; from the mouth of the Nile to the plains of Assyria; from the arenas of Athens to the churches of Rome; from the slums of Constantinople to the palaces of Alexandria. . . . Yet I saw slavery moving over all, in a glorious and majestic procession of ignorance. I saw the people sacrificing the youths and maidens at the feet of the idol, calling her the God; pouring wine and perfume upon her feet, and calling her the Queen; burning incense before her image, and calling her the Prophet; kneeling and worshipping before her, and calling her the Law; fighting and dying for her, and calling her Patriotism; submitting to her will,

and calling her the Shadow of God on earth; destroying and demolishing homes and institutions for her sake, and calling her Fraternity; struggling and stealing and working for her, and calling her Fortune and Happiness; killing for her, and calling her Equality.

She possesses various names, but one reality. She has many appearances, but is made of one element. In truth, she is an everlasting ailment bequeathed by each generation unto its successor.

I found the blind slavery, which ties the people's present with their parents' past, and urges them to yield to their traditions and customs, placing ancient spirits in the new bodies.

I found the mute slavery, which binds the life of a man to a wife whom he abhors, and places the woman's body in the bed of a hated husband, deadening both lives spiritually.

I found the deaf slavery, which stifles the soul and the heart, rendering man but an empty echo of a voice, and a pitiful shadow of a body.

I found the lame slavery, which places man's neck under the domination of the tyrant and submits strong bodies and weak minds to the sons of Greed for use as instruments to their power.

I found the ugly slavery, which descends with the infants' spirits from the spacious firmament into the home of Misery, where Need lives by Ignorance, and Humiliation resides beside Despair. And the

children grow as miserables, and live as criminals, and die as despised and rejected non-existents.

I found the subtle slavery, which entitles things with other than their names—calling slyness an intelligence, and emptiness a knowledge, and weakness a tenderness, and cowardice a strong refusal.

I found the twisted slavery, which causes the tongues of the weak to move with fear, and speak outside of their feelings, and they feign to be meditating their plight, but they become as empty sacks, which even a child can fold or hang.

I found the bent slavery, which prevails upon one nation to comply with the laws and rules of another nation, and the bending is greater with each day.

I found the perpetual slavery, which crowns the sons of monarchs as kings, and offers no regard to merit.

I found the black slavery, which brands with shame and disgrace forever the innocent sons of the criminals.

Contemplating slavery, it is found to possess the vicious powers of continuation and contagion.

When I grew tired of following the dissolute ages, and wearied of beholding the processions of stoned people, I walked lonely in the Valley of the Shadow of Life, where the past attempts to conceal itself in guilt, and the soul of the future folds and rests itself too long. There, at the edge of Blood and Tears

River, which crawled like a poisonous viper and twisted like a criminal's dreams, I listened to the frightened whisper of the ghosts of slaves, and gazed at nothingness.

When midnight came and the spirits emerged from hidden places, I saw a cadaverous, dying spectre fall to her knees, gazing at the moon. I approached her, asking, "What is your name?"

"My name is Liberty," replied this ghastly shadow of a corpse.

And I inquired, "Where are your children?"

And Liberty, tearful and weak, gasped, "One died crucified, another died mad, and the third one is not yet born."

She limped away and spoke further, but the mist in my eyes and cries of my heart prevented sight or hearing.

SATAN

THE PEOPLE looked upon Father Samaan as their guide in the field of spiritual and theological matters, for he was an authority and a source of deep information on venial and mortal sins, well versed in the secrets of Paradise, Hell, and Purgatory.

Father Samaan's mission in North Lebanon was to travel from one village to another, preaching and curing the people from the spiritual disease of sin, and saving them from the horrible trap of Satan. The Reverend Father waged constant war with Satan. The fellahin honoured and respected this clergyman, and were always anxious to buy his advice or prayers with pieces of gold and silver; and at every harvest they would present him with the finest fruits of their fields.

One evening in Autumn, as Father Samaan walked his way toward a solitary village, crossing those valleys and hills, he heard a painful cry emerging from a ditch at the side of the road. He stopped and looked in the direction of the voice, and saw an unclothed

THE TREASURED WRITINGS OF KAHLIL GIBRAN

man lying on the ground. Streams of blood oozed
from deep wounds in his head and chest. He was
moaning pitifully for aid, saying, "Save me, help me.
Have mercy on me, I am dying." Father Samaan
looked with perplexity at the sufferer, and said
within himself, "This man must be a thief. . . . He
probably tried to rob the wayfarers and failed. Some
one has wounded him, and I fear that should he die
I may be accused of having taken his life."

Having thus pondered the situation, he resumed
his journey, whereupon the dying man stopped him,
calling out, "Do not leave me! I am dying!" Then
the Father meditated again, and his face became pale
as he realized he was refusing to help. His lips quivered, but he spoke to himself, saying, "He must
surely be one of the madmen wandering in the wilderness. The sight of his wounds brings fear into
my heart; what shall I do? Surely a spiritual doctor
is not capable of treating flesh-wounded bodies."
Father Samaan walked ahead a few paces when the
near-corpse uttered a painful plaint that melted the
heart of the rock and he gasped, "Come close to me!
Come, for we have been friends a long time. . . .
You are Father Samaan, the Good Shepherd, and I
am not a thief nor a madman. . . . Come close, and
do not let me die in this deserted place. Come, and
I will tell you who I am."

Father Samaan came close to the man, knelt, and
stared at him; but he saw a strange face with con-
trasting features; he saw intelligence with slyness,

ugliness with beauty, and wickedness with softness. He withdrew to his feet sharply, and exclaimed, "Who are you?"

With a fainting voice, the dying man said, "Fear me not, Father, for we have been strong friends for long. Help me to stand, and take me to the nearby streamlet and cleanse my wounds with your linens." And the Father inquired, "Tell me who you are, for I do not know you, nor even remember having seen you."

And the man replied with an agonizing voice, "You know my identity! You have seen me one thousand times and you speak of me each day. . . . I am dearer to you than your own life." And the Father reprimanded, "You are a lying imposter! A dying man should tell the truth. . . . I have never seen your evil face in my entire life. Tell me who you are, or I will suffer you to die, soaked in your own escaping life." And the wounded man moved slowly and looked into the clergyman's eyes, and upon his lips appeared a mystic smile; and in a quiet, deep and smooth voice he said, "I am Satan."

Upon hearing the fearful word, Father Samaan uttered a terrible cry that shook the far corners of the valley; then he stared, and realized that the dying man's body, with its grotesque distortions, coincided with the likeness of Satan in a religious picture hanging on the wall of the village church. He trembled and cried out, saying, "God has shown me your hellish image and justly caused me to hate you;

cursed be you forevermore! The mangled lamb must be destroyed by the shepherd lest he will infect the other lambs!"

Satan answered, "Be not in haste, Father, and lose not this fleeting time in empty talk. . . . Come and close my wounds quickly, before Life departs from my body." And the clergyman retorted, "The hands which offer a daily sacrifice to God shall not touch a body made of the secretion of Hell. . . . You must die accursed by the tongues of the Ages, and the lips of Humanity, for you are the enemy of Humanity, and it is your avowed purpose to destroy all virtue."

Satan moved in anguish, raising himself upon one elbow, and responded, "You know not what you are saying, nor understand the crime you are committing upon yourself. Give heed, for I will relate my story. Today I walked alone in this solitary valley. When I reached this place, a group of angels descended to attack, and struck me severely; had it not been for one of them, who carried a blazing sword with two sharp edges, I would have driven them off, but I had no power against the brilliant sword." And Satan ceased talking for a moment, as he pressed a shaking hand upon a deep wound in his side. Then he continued, "The armed angel—I believe he was Michael —was an expert gladiator. Had I not thrown myself to the friendly ground and feigned to have been slain, he would have torn me into brutal death."

With voice of triumph, and casting his eyes heav-

enward, the Father offered, "Blessed be Michael's name, who has saved Humanity from this vicious enemy."

And Satan protested, "My disdain for Humanity is not greater than your hatred for yourself. . . . You are blessing Michael who never has come to your rescue. . . . You are cursing me in the hour of my defeat, even though I was, and still am, the source of your tranquility and happiness. . . . You deny me your blessing, and extend not your kindness, but you live and prosper in the shadow of my being. . . . You have adopted for my existence an excuse and weapon for your career, and you employ my name in justification for your deeds. Has not my past caused you to be in need of my present and future? Have you reached your goal in amassing the required wealth? Have you found it impossible to extract more gold and silver from your followers, using my kingdom as a threat?

"Do you not realize that you will starve to death if I were to die? What would you do tomorrow if you allowed me to die today? What vocation would you pursue if my name disappeared? For decades you have been roaming these villages and warning the people against falling into my hands. They have bought your advice with their poor denars and with the products of their land. What would they buy from you tomorrow, if they discovered that their wicked enemy no longer existed? Your occupation would die with me, for the people would be safe

from sin. As a clergyman, do you not realize that Satan's existence alone has created his enemy, the church? That ancient conflict is the secret hand which removes the gold and silver from the faithful's pocket and deposits it forever into the pouch of the preacher and missionary. How can you permit me to die here, when you know it will surely cause you to lose your prestige, your church, your home, and your livelihood?"

Satan became silent for a moment and his humility was now converted into a confident independence, and he continued, "Father, you are proud, but ignorant. I will disclose to you the history of belief, and in it you will find the truth which joins both of our beings, and ties my existence with your very conscience.

"In the first hour of the beginning of time, man stood before the face of the sun and stretched forth his arms and cried for the first time, saying, 'Behind the sky there is a great and loving and benevolent God.' Then man turned his back to the great circle of light and saw his shadow upon the earth, and he hailed, 'In the depths of the earth there is a dark devil who loves wickedness.'

"And the man walked toward his cave, whispering to himself, 'I am between two compelling forces, one in whom I must take refuge, and the other against whom I must struggle.' And the ages marched in procession while man existed between two powers, one

that he blessed because it exalted him, and one that he cursed because it frightened him. But he never perceived the meaning of a blessing or of a curse; he was between the two, like a tree between Summer, when it blooms, and Winter, when it shivers.

"When man saw the dawn of civilization, which is human understanding, the family as a unit came into being. Then came the tribes, whereupon labour was divided according to ability and inclination; one clan cultivated the land, another built shelters, others wove raiment or hunted food. Subsequently divination made its appearance upon the earth, and this was the first career adopted by man which possessed no essential urge or necessity."

Satan ceased talking for a moment. Then he laughed and his mirth shook the empty valley, but his laughter reminded him of his wounds, and he placed his hand on his side, suffering with pain. He steadied himself and continued, "Divination appeared and grew on earth in strange fashion.

"There was a man in the first tribe called La Wiss. I know not the origin of his name. He was an intelligent creature, but extremely indolent and he detested work in the cultivation of land, construction of shelters, grazing of cattle or any pursuit requiring body movement or exertion. And since food, during that era, could not be obtained except by arduous toil, La Wiss slept many nights with an empty stomach.

"One Summer night, as the members of that clan

were gathered around the hut of their Chief, talking of the outcome of their day and waiting for their slumber time, a man suddenly leaped to his feet, pointed toward the moon, and cried out, saying, 'Look at the Night God! His face is dark, and his beauty has vanished, and he has turned into a black stone hanging in the dome of the sky!' The multitude gazed at the moon, shouted in awe, and shook with fear, as if the hands of darkness had clutched their hearts, for they saw the Night God slowly turning into a dark ball which changed the bright countenance of the earth and caused the hills and valleys before their eyes to disappear behind a black veil.

"At that moment, La Wiss, who had seen an eclipse before, and understood its simple cause, stepped forward to make much of this opportunity. He stood in the midst of the throng, lifted his hands to the sky, and in a strong voice he addressed them, saying, 'Kneel and pray, for the Evil God of Obscurity is locked in struggle with the Illuminating Night God; if the Evil God conquers him, we will all perish, but if the Night God triumphs over him, we will remain alive. . . . Pray now and worship. . . . Cover your faces with earth. . . . Close your eyes, and lift not your heads toward the sky, for he who witnesses the two gods wrestling will lose his sight and mind, and will remain blind and insane all his life! Bend your heads low, and with all your hearts

urge the Night God against his enemy, who is our mortal enemy!'

"Thus did La Wiss continue talking, using many cryptic words of his own fabrication which they had never heard. After this crafty deception, as the moon returned to its previous glory, La Wiss raised his voice louder than before and said impressively, 'Rise now, and look at the Night God who has triumphed over his evil enemy. He is resuming his journey among the stars. Let it be known that through your prayers you have helped him to overcome the Devil of Darkness. He is well pleased now, and brighter than ever.'

"The multitude rose and gazed at the moon that was shining in full beam. Their fear became tranquility, and their confusion was now joy. They commenced dancing and singing and striking with their thick sticks upon sheets of iron, filling the valleys with their clamour and shouting.

"That night, the Chief of the tribe called La Wiss and spoke to him, saying, 'You have done something that no man has ever done. . . . You have demonstrated knowledge of a hidden secret that no other among us understands. Reflecting the will of my people, you are to be the highest ranking member, after me, in the tribe. I am the strongest man, and you are the wisest and most learned person. . . . You are the medium between our people and the gods, whose desires and deeds you are to interpret, and

you will teach us those things necessary to gain their blessings and love.'

"And La Wiss slyly assured, 'Everything the Human God reveals to me in my divine dreams will be conveyed to you in awakeness, and you may be confident that I will act directly between you and him.' The chief was assured, and gave La Wiss two horses, seven calves, seventy sheep and seventy lambs; and he spoke to him, saying, 'The men of the tribe shall build for you a strong house, and we will give you at the end of each harvest season a part of the crop of the land, so you may live as an honourable and respected Master.'

"La Wiss rose and started to leave, but the Chief stopped him, saying, 'Who and what is the one whom you call the Human God? Who is this daring God who wrestles with the glorious Night God? We have never pondered him before.' La Wiss rubbed his forehead and answered him, saying, 'My Honourable Master, in the olden time, before the creation of man, all the Gods were living peacefully together in an upper world behind the vastness of the stars. The God of Gods was their father, and knew what they did not know, and did what they were unable to do. He kept for himself the divine secrets that existed beyond the eternal laws. During the seventh epoch of the twelfth age, the spirit of Bahtaar, who hated the great God, revolted and stood before his father, and said, 'Why do you keep for yourself the power of great authority upon all creatures, hiding

away from us the secrets and laws of the Universe? Are we not your children who believe in you and share with you the great understanding and the perpetual being?'

"The God of Gods became enraged and said, 'I shall preserve for myself the primary power and the great authority and the essential secrets, for I am the beginning and the end.'

"And Bahtaar answered him saying, 'Unless you share with me your might and power, I and my children and my children's children will revolt against you!' At that moment, the God of Gods stood upon his throne in the deep heavens, and drew forth a sword, and grasped the Sun as a shield; and with a voice that shook all corners of eternity he shouted out, saying, 'Descend, you evil rebel, to the dismal lower world where darkness and misery exist! There you shall remain in exile, wandering until the Sun turns into ashes and the stars into dispersed particles!' In that hour, Bahtaar descended from the upper world into the lower world, where all the evil spirits dwelt. Thereupon, he swore by the secret of Life that he would fight his father and brothers by trapping every soul who loved them.'

"As the Chief listened, his forehead wrinkled and his face turned pale. He ventured, 'Then the name of the Evil God is Bahtaar?' and La Wiss responded, 'His name was Bahtaar when he was in upper world, but when he entered into the lower world, he adopted successively the names Baalzaboul, Satanail,

Balial, Zamiel, Ahriman, Mara, Abdon, Devil, and finally Satan, which is the most famous.'

"The Chief repeated the word 'Satan' many times with a quivering voice that sounded like the rustling of the dry branches at the passing of the wind; then he asked, 'Why does Satan hate man as much as he hates the gods?'

"And La Wiss responded quickly, 'He hates man because man is a descendant of Satan's brothers and sisters.' The Chief exclaimed, 'Then Satan is the cousin of man!' In a voice mingled with confusion and annoyance, he retorted, 'Yes, Master, but he is their great enemy who fills their days with misery and their nights with horrible dreams. He is the power who directs the tempest toward their hovels, and brings famine upon their plantation, and disease upon them and their animals. He is an evil and powerful god; he is wicked, and he rejoices when we are in sorrow, and he mourns when we are joyous. We must, through my knowledge, examine him thoroughly, in order to avoid his evil; we must study his character, so we will not step upon his trap-laden path.'

"The Chief leaned his head upon his thick stick and whispered, saying, 'I have learned now the inner secret of that strange power who directs the tempest toward our homes and brings the pestilence upon us and our cattle. The people shall learn all that I have comprehended now, and La Wiss will be blessed, honoured and glorified for revealing to them the

mystery of their powerful enemy, and directing them away from the road of evil.'

"And La Wiss left the Chief of the tribe and went to his retiring place, happy over his ingenuity, and intoxicated with the wine of his pleasure and fancy. For the first time, the Chief and all the tribe, except La Wiss, spent the night slumbering in beds surrounded by horrible ghosts, fearful spectres, and disturbing dreams."

Satan ceased talking for a moment, while Father Samaan stared at him as one bewildered, and upon the Father's lips appeared the sickly laughter of Death. Then Satan continued, "Thus divination came to this earth, and thus was my existence the cause for its appearance. La Wiss was the first who adopted my cruelty as a vocation. After the death of La Wiss, this occupation circulated through his children and prospered until it became a perfect and divine profession, pursued by those whose minds are ripe with knowledge, and whose souls are noble, and whose hearts are pure, and whose fancy is vast.

"In Babylon, the people bowed seven times in worshipping before a priest who fought me with his chantings. . . . In Nineveh, they looked upon a man, who claimed to have known my inner secrets, as a golden link between God and man. . . . In Tibet, they called the person who wrestled with me The Son of the Sun and Moon. . . . In Byblus, Ephesus and Antioch, they offered their children's

lives in sacrifice to my opponents. . . . In Jerusalem and Rome, they placed their lives in the hands of those who claimed they hated me and fought me with all their might.

"In every city under the sun my name was the axis of the educational circle of religion, arts, and philosophy. Had it not been for me, no temples would have been built, no towers or palaces would have been erected. I am the courage that creates resolution in man. . . . I am the source that provokes originality of thought. . . . I am the hand that moves man's hands. . . . I am Satan everlasting. I am Satan whom the people fight in order to keep themselves alive. If they cease struggling against me, slothfulness will deaden their minds and hearts and souls, in accordance with the weird penalties of their tremendous myth.

"I am the enraged and mute tempest who agitates the minds of man and the hearts of women. And in fear of me, they will travel to places of worship to condemn me, or to places of vice to make me happy by surrendering to my will. The monk who prays in the silence of the night to keep me away from his bed is like the prostitute who invites me to her chamber. I am Satan everlasting and eternal.

"I am the builder of convents and monasteries upon the foundation of fear. I build wine shops and wicked houses upon the foundations of lust and self-gratification. If I cease to exist, fear and enjoyment will be abolished from the world, and through their

disappearance, desires and hopes will cease to exist in the human heart. Life will become empty and cold, like a harp with broken strings. I am Satan everlasting.

"I am the inspiration for Falsehood, Slander, Treachery, Deceit and Mockery, and if these elements were to be removed from this world, human society would become like a deserted field in which naught would thrive but thorns of virtue. I am Satan everlasting.

"I am the father and mother of sin, and if sin were to vanish, the fighters of sin would vanish with it, along with their families and structures.

"I am the heart of all evil. Would you wish for human motion to stop through cessation of my heartbeats? Would you accept the result after destroying the cause? I am the cause! Would you allow me to die in this deserted wilderness? Do you desire to sever the bond that exists between you and me? Answer me, clergyman!"

And Satan stretched his arms and bent his head forward and gasped deeply; his face turned to grey and he resembled one of those Egyptian statues laid waste by the Ages at the side of the Nile. Then he fixed his glittering eyes upon Father Samaan's face, and said, in a faltering voice, "I am tired and weak. I did wrong by using my waning strength to speak on things you already knew. Now you may do as you please. . . . You may carry me to your home and treat my wounds, or leave me in this place to die."

Father Samaan quivered and rubbed his hands nervously, and with apology in his voice he said, "I know now what I had not known an hour ago. Forgive my ignorance. I know that your existence in this world creates temptation, and temptation is a measurement by which God adjudges the value of human souls. It is a scale which Almighty God uses to weigh the spirits. I am certain that if you die, temptation will die, and with its passing, death will destroy the ideal power which elevates and alerts man.

"You must live, for if you die and the people know it, their fear of hell will vanish and they will cease worshipping, for naught would be sin. You must live, for in your life is the salvation of humanity from vice and sin.

"As to myself, I shall sacrifice my hatred for you on the altar of my love for man."

Satan uttered a laugh that rocked the ground, and he said, "What an intelligent person you are, Father! And what wonderful knowledge you possess in theological facts! You have found, through the power of your knowledge, a purpose for my existence which I had never understood, and now we realize our need for each other.

"Come close to me, my brother; darkness is submerging the plains, and half of my blood has escaped upon the sand of this valley, and naught remains of me but the remnants of a broken body which Death shall soon buy unless you render aid." Father Samaan

rolled the sleeves of his robe and approached, and lifted Satan to his back and walked toward his home.

In the midst of those valleys, engulfed with silence and embellished with the veil of darkness, Father Samaan walked toward the village with his back bent under his heavy burden. His black raiment and long beard were spattered with blood streaming from above him, but he struggled forward, his lips moving in fervent prayer for the life of the dying Satan.

THE MERMAIDS

IN THE depths of the sea, surrounding the nearby islands where the sun rises, there is a profoundness. And there, where the pearl exists in abundance, lay a corpse of a youth encircled by sea maidens of long golden hair; they stared upon him with their deep blue eyes, conversing among themselves with musical voices. And the conversation, heard by the depths and conveyed to the shore by the waves, was brought to me by the frolicsome breeze.

One of them said, "This is a human who entered into our world yesterday, while our sea was raging."

And the second one said, "The sea was not raging. Man, who claims that he is a descendant of the Gods, was making iron war, and his blood is being shed until the colour of the water is now crimson; this human is a victim of war."

The third one ventured, "I do not know what war is, but I do know that man, after having subdued the land, became aggressive and resolved to subdue the sea. He devised a strange object which carried

him upon the seas, whereupon our severe Neptune became enraged over his greed. In order to please Neptune, man commenced offering gifts and sacrifices, and the still body before us is the most recent gift of man to our great and terrible Neptune."

The fourth one asserted, "How great is Neptune, and how cruel is his heart! If I were the Sultan of the sea I would refuse to accept such payment. . . . Come now, and let us examine this ransom. Perhaps we may enlighten ourselves as to the human clan."

The mermaids approached the youth, probed the pockets, and found a message close to his heart; one of them read it aloud to the others:

"My Beloved:

"Midnight has again come, and I have no consolation except my pouring tears, and naught to comfort me save my hope in your return to me from between the bloody paws of war. I cannot forget your words when you took departure: 'Every man has a trust of tears which must be returned some day.'

"I know not what to say, My Beloved, but my soul will pour itself into parchment . . . my soul that suffers through separation, but is consoled by Love that renders pain a joy, and sorrow a happiness. When Love unified our hearts, and we looked to the day when our two hearts would be joined by the mighty breath of God, War shouted her horri-

ble call and you followed her, prompted by your duty to the leaders.

"What is this duty that separates the lovers, and causes the women to become widows, and the children to become orphans? What is this patriotism which provokes wars and destroys kingdoms through trifles? And what cause can be more than trifling when compared to but one life? What is this duty which invites poor villagers, who are looked upon as nothing by the strong and by the sons of the inherited nobility, to die for the glory of their oppressors? If duty destroys peace among nations, and patriotism disturbs the tranquility of man's life, then let us say, 'Peace be with duty and patriotism.'

"No, no, My Beloved! Heed not my words! Be courageous and faithful to your country.... Hearken not unto the talk of a damsel, blinded by Love, and lost through farewell and aloneness. . . . If Love will not restore you to me in this life, then Love will surely join us in the coming life.

Your Forever"

The mermaids replaced the note under the youth's raiment and swam silently and sorrowfully away. As they gathered together at a distance from the body of the dead soldier, one of them said, "The human heart is more severe than the cruel heart of Neptune."

WE AND YOU

WE ARE the sons of Sorrow, and you are the
Sons of Joy. We are the sons of Sorrow,
And Sorrow is the shadow of a God who
Lives not in the domain of evil hearts.

We are sorrowful spirits, and Sorrow is
Too great to exist in small hearts.
When you laugh, we cry and lament; and he
Who is seared and cleansed once with his
Own tears will remain pure forevermore.

You understand us not, but we offer our
Sympathy to you. You are racing with the
Current of the River of Life, and you
Do not look upon us; but we are sitting by
The coast, watching you and hearing your
Strange voices.

You do not comprehend our cry, for the
Clamour of the days is crowding your ears,
Blocked with the hard substance of your
Years of indifference to truth; but we hear
Your songs, for the whispering of the night

Has opened our inner hearts. We see you
Standing under the pointing finger of light,
But you cannot see us, for we are tarrying
In the enlightening darkness.

We are the sons of Sorrow; we are the poets
And the prophets and the musicians. We weave
Raiment for the goddess from the threads of
Our hearts, and we fill the hands of the
Angels with the seeds of our inner selves.

You are the sons of the pursuit of earthly
Gaiety. You place your hearts in the hands
Of Emptiness, for the hand's touch to
Emptiness is smooth and inviting.

You reside in the house of Ignorance, for
In his house there is no mirror in which to
View your souls.

We sigh, and from our sighs arise the
Whispering of flowers and the rustling of
Leaves and the murmur of rivulets.

When you ridicule us your taunts mingle
With the crushing of the skulls and the
Rattling of shackles and the wailing of the
Abyss. When we cry, our tears fall into the
Heart of Life, as dew drops fall from the
Eyes of Night into the heart of Dawn; and
When you laugh, your mocking laughter pours
Down like the viper's venom into a wound.

We cry, and sympathize with the miserable
Wanderer and distressed widow; but you rejoice
And smile at the sight of resplendent gold.

We cry, for we listen to the moaning of the
Poor and the grieving of the oppressed weak;
But you laugh, for you hear naught but the
Happy sound of the wine goblets.

We cry, for our spirits are at the moment
Separated from God; but you laugh, for your
Bodies cling with unconcern to the earth.

We are the sons of Sorrow, and you are the
Sons of Joy. . . . Let us measure the outcome of
Our sorrow against the deeds of your joy
Before the face of the Sun. . . .

You have built the Pyramids upon the hearts
Of slaves, but the Pyramids stand now upon
The sand, commemorating to the Ages our
Immortality and your evanescence.

You have built Babylon upon the bones of the
Weak, and erected the palaces of Nineveh upon
The graves of the miserable. Babylon is now but
The footprint of the camel upon the moving sand
Of the desert, and its history is repeated
To the nations who bless us and curse you.

We have carved Ishtar from solid marble,
And made it to quiver in its solidity and
Speak through its muteness.

We have composed and played the soothing
Song of Nahawand upon the strings, and caused
The Beloved's spirit to come hovering in the
Firmament near to us; we have praised the
Supreme Being with words and deeds; the words
Became as the words of God, and the deeds
Became overwhelming love of the angels.

You are following Amusement, whose sharp claws
Have torn thousands of martyrs in the arenas
Of Rome and Antioch. . . . But we are following
Silence, whose careful fingers have woven the
Iliad and the Book of Job and the Lamentations
Of Jeremiah.

You lie down with Lust, whose tempest has
Swept one thousand processions of the soul of
Woman away and into the pit of shame and
Horror. . . . But we embrace Solitude, in whose
Shadow the beauties of Hamlet and Dante arose.

You curry for the favor of Greed, and the sharp
Swords of Greed have shed one thousand rivers
Of blood. . . . But we seek company with Truth,
And the hands of Truth have brought down
Knowledge from the Great Heart of the Circle
Of Light.

We are the sons of Sorrow, and you are the
Sons of Joy; and between our sorrow and your
Joy there is a rough and narrow path which

Your spirited horses cannot travel, and upon
Which your magnificent carriages cannot pass.

We pity your smallness as you hate our
Greatness; and between our pity and your
Hatred, Time halts bewildered. We come to
You as friends, but you attack us as enemies;
And between our friendship and your enmity,
There is a deep ravine flowing with tears
And blood.

We build palaces for you, and you dig graves
For us; and between the beauty of the palace
And the obscurity of the grave, Humanity
Walks as a sentry with iron weapons.

We spread your path with roses, and you cover
Our beds with thorns; and between the roses
And the thorns, Truth slumbers fitfully.

Since the beginning of the world you have
Fought against our gentle power with your
Coarse weakness; and when you triumph over
Us for an hour, you croak and clamour merrily
Like the frogs of the water. And when we
Conquer you and subdue you for an Age, we
Remain as silent giants.

You crucified Jesus and stood below Him,
Blaspheming and mocking at Him; but at last
He came down and overcame the generations,

And walked among you as a hero, filling the
Universe with His glory and His beauty.

You poisoned Socrates and stoned Paul and
Destroyed Ali Talib and assassinated
Madhat Pasha, and yet those immortals are
With us forever before the face of Eternity.

But you live in the memory of man like
Corpses upon the face of the earth; and you
Cannot find a friend who will bury you in
The obscurity of non-existence and oblivion,
Which you sought on earth.

We are the sons of Sorrow, and sorrow is a
Rich cloud, showering the multitudes with
Knowledge and Truth. You are the sons of
Joy, and as high as your joy may reach,
By the Law of God it must be destroyed
Before the winds of heaven and dispersed
Into nothingness, for it is naught but a
Thin and wavering pillar of smoke.

THE LONELY POET

I AM A STRANGER in this world, and there is a severe solitude and painful lonesomeness in my exile. I am alone, but in my aloneness I contemplate an unknown and enchanting country, and this meditation fills my dreams with spectres of a great and distant land which my eyes have never seen.

I am a stranger among my people and I have no friends. When I see a person I say within myself, "Who is he, and in what manner do I know him, and why is he here, and what law has joined me with him?"

I am a stranger to myself, and when I hear my tongue speak, my ears wonder over my voice; I see my inner self smiling, crying, braving, and fearing; and my existence wonders over my substance while my soul interrogates my heart; but I remain unknown, engulfed by tremendous silence.

My thoughts are strangers to my body, and as I stand before the mirror, I see something in my face which my soul does not see, and I find in my eyes what my inner self does not find.

When I walk vacant-eyed through the streets of the clamourous city, the children follow me, shouting, "Here is a blind man! Let us give him a walking cane to feel his way." When I run from them, I meet with a group of maidens, and they grasp the edges of my garment, saying, "He is deaf like the rock; let us fill his ears with the music of love." And when I flee from them, a throng of aged people point at me with trembling fingers and say, "He is a madman who lost his mind in the world of genii and ghouls."

I am a stranger in this world; I roamed the Universe from end to end, but could not find a place to rest my head; nor did I know any human I confronted, neither an individual who would hearken to my mind.

When I open my sleepless eyes at dawn, I find myself imprisoned in a dark cave from whose ceiling hang the insects and upon whose floor crawl the vipers.

When I go out to meet the light, the shadow of my body follows me, but the shadow of my spirit precedes me and leads the way to an unknown place seeking things beyond my understanding, and grasping objects that are meaningless to me.

At eventide I return and lie upon my bed, made of soft feathers and lined with thorns, and I contemplate and feel the troublesome and happy desires, and sense the painful and joyous hopes.

At midnight the ghosts of the past ages and the

spirits of the forgotten civilization enter through the crevices of the cave to visit me . . . I stare at them and they gaze upon me; I talk to them and they answer me smilingly. Then I endeavour to clutch them, but they sift through my fingers and vanish like the mist which rests on the lake.

I am a stranger in this world, and there is no one in the Universe who understands the language I speak. Patterns of bizarre remembrance form suddenly in my mind, and my eyes bring forth queer images and sad ghosts. I walk in the deserted prairies, watching the streamlets running fast, up and up from the depths of the valley to the top of the mountain; I watch the naked trees blooming and bearing fruit, and shedding their leaves in one instant, and then I see the branches fall and turn into speckled snakes. I see the birds hovering above, singing and wailing; then they stop and open their wings and turn into undraped maidens with long hair, looking at me from behind kohled and infatuated eyes, and smiling at me with full lips soaked with honey, stretching their scented hands toward me. Then they ascend and disappear from my sight like phantoms, leaving in the firmament the resounding echo of their taunts and mocking laughter.

I am a stranger in this world . . . I am a poet who composes what life proses, and who proses what life composes.

For this reason I am a stranger, and I shall remain

a stranger until the white and friendly wings of Death carry me home into my beautiful country. There, where light and peace and understanding abide, I will await the other strangers who will be rescued by the friendly trap of time from this narrow, dark world.

ASHES OF THE AGES AND ETERNAL FIRE

PART ONE

Spring of the Year 116 B.C.

Night had fallen and silence prevailed while life slumbered in the City of the Sun,* and the lamps were extinguished in the scattered houses about the majestic temples amidst the olive and laurel trees. The moon poured its silver rays upon the white marble columns that stood like giants in the silence of the night, guarding the god's temples and looking with perplexity toward the towers of Lebanon that sat bristling upon the foreheads of the distant hills.

At that hour, while souls succumbed to the allure of slumber, Nathan, the son of the High Priest, entered Ishtar's temple, bearing a torch in trembling

---

* Baalbek, or the City of Baal, called by the ancients "The City of the Sun," was built in honor of the Sun God Heliopolis, and historians assert that Baalbek was the most beautiful city in the Middle East. Its ruins, which we observe at present time, indicate that the architecture was largly influenced by the Romans during the occupation of Syria. (*Editor's note.*)

hands. He lighted the lamps and censers until the aromatic scent of myrrh and frankincense reached to the farthest corners; then he knelt before the altar, studded with inlays of ivory and gold, raised his hands toward Ishtar, and with a painful and choking voice he cried out, saying, "Have mercy upon me, O great Ishtar, goddess of Love and Beauty. Be merciful, and remove the hands of Death from my beloved, whom my soul has chosen by thy will. . . . The potions of the physicians and the wizards do not restore her life, neither the enchantments of the priests and the sorcerers. Naught is left to be done except thy holy will. Thou art my guide and my aid. Have mercy on me and grant my prayers! * Gaze upon my crushed heart and aching soul! Spare my beloved's life so that we may rejoice with the secrets of thy love, and glory in the beauty of youth that reveals the mystery of thy strength and wisdom. From the depths of my heart I cry unto thee, O exalted Ishtar, and from behind the darkness of the night I beg thy mercy; hear me, O Ishtar! I am thy good servant Nathan, the son of the High Priest Hiram, and I devote all of my deeds and words to thy greatness at thy altar.

"I love a maiden amongst all maidens and made

* Ishtar was the great goddess of the Phoenicians. They worshipped her in the cities of Tyre, Sidon, Sûr, Djabeil and Baalbek, and described her as the Burner of the Torch of Life, and Guardian of Youth. Greece adored her after Phoenicia, calling her the goddess of Love and Beauty. The Romans called her Venus. (*Editor's note.*)

her my companion, but the genii brides envied her and blew into her body a strange affliction and sent unto her the messenger of Death who is standing by her bed like a hungry spectre, spreading his black ribbed wings over her, stretching forth his sharp claws in readiness to prey upon her. I come here now beseeching you to have mercy upon me and spare that flower who has not yet rejoiced with the summer of Life.

"Save her from the grasp of Death so we may sing joyfully thy praise and burn incense in thine honour and offer sacrifices at thy altar, filling thy vases with perfumed oil and spreading roses and violets upon the portico of thy place of worship, burning frankincense before thy shrine. Save her, O Ishtar, goddess of miracles, and let Love overcome Death in this struggle of Joy against Sorrow." *

Nathan then became silent. His eyes were flooded with tears and his heart was uttering sorrowful sighs; then he continued, "Alas, my dreams are shattered, O Ishtar divine, and my heart is melted within; enliven me with thy mercy and spare my beloved."

At that moment one of his slaves entered the temple, hastened to Nathan, and whispered to him, "She has opened her eyes, Master, and looked about

* During the Era of Ignorance, the Arabs believed that if a genie loved a human youth, she would prevent him from marrying, and if he did wed, she would bewitch the bride and cause her to die. This mythological superstition persists today in some small villages in Lebanon. (*Editor's note.*)

her bed, but could not find you; then she called for you, and I used all speed to advise you."

Nathan departed hurriedly and the slave followed him.

When he reached his palace, he entered the chamber of the ailing maiden, leaned over her bed, held her frail hand, and printed several kisses upon her lips as if striving to breathe into her body a new life from his own life. She moved her head on the silk cushions and opened her eyes. And upon her lips appeared the phantom of a smile which was the faint residue of life in her wasted body . . . the echo of the calling of a heart which is racing toward a halt; and with a voice that bespoke the weakening cries of a hungry infant on the breast of a withered mother, she said, "The goddess has called me, Oh Life of my Soul, and Death has come to sever me from you; but fear not, for the will of the goddess is sacred, and the demands of Death are just. I am departing now, and I hear the rustle of the whiteness descending, but the cups of Love and Youth are still full in our hands, and the flowered paths of beautiful Life are extended before us. I am embarking, My Beloved, upon an ark of the spirit, and I shall come back to this world, for great Ishtar will bring back to life those souls of loving humans who departed to Eternity before they enjoyed the sweetness of Love and the happiness of Youth.

"We shall meet again, Oh Nathan, and drink together the dew of the dawn from the cupped petals

of the lilies, and rejoice with the birds of the fields over the colours of the rainbow. Until then, My Forever, farewell." *

Her voice lowered and her lips trembled like a lone flower before the gusts of dawn. Nathan embraced her with pouring tears, and as he pressed his lips upon her lips, he found them cold as the stone of the field. He uttered a terrible cry and commenced tearing his raiment; he threw himself upon her dead body while his shivering soul was sailing fitfully between the mountain of Life and the precipice of Death.

In the silence of the night, the slumbering souls were awakened. Women and children were frightened as they heard mighty rumbling and painful wailing and bitter lamentation coming from the corners of the palace of the High Priest of Ishtar.

When the tired morn arrived, the people asked about Nathan to offer their sympathy, but were told that he had disappeared. And after a fortnight, the chief of a caravan arriving from the East related that he had seen Nathan in the distant wilderness, wandering with a flock of gazelles.

The ages passed, crushing with their invisible feet the feeble acts of the civilizations, and the goddess of Love and Beauty had left the country. A strange

* Many Asiatics pursue this belief with conviction, having derived it from their holy writings. Mohammed said, "You were dead and He brought you back to life, and He will deaden you again and

and fickle goddess took her place. She destroyed the magnificent temples of the City of the Sun and demolished its beautiful palaces. The blooming orchards and fertile prairies were laid waste and nothing was left in that spot save ruins commemorating to the aching souls the ghosts of Yesterday, repeating to the sorrowful spirits only the echo of the hymns of glory.

But the severe ages that crushed the deeds of man could not destroy his dreams; nor could they weaken his love, for dreams and affections are ever-living with the Eternal Spirit. They may disappear for a time, pursuing the sun when the night comes, and the stars when morning appears, but like the lights of heaven, they must surely return.

PART TWO

Spring of the Year 1890 A.D.

The day was over, Nature was making her many preparations for slumber, and the sun withdrew its golden rays from the plains of Baalbek. Ali El Hosseini * brought his herd back to the shed in the

then will enliven you, whereupon you shall go back to Him." Buddha said, "Yesterday we existed in this life, and now we came, and we will continue to go back until we become perfect like the God." (*Editor's note.*)
* The Hosseinese are groups comprising an Arabian tribe, at present living in tents pitched in the plains surrounding the ruins of Baalbek. (*Editor's note.*)

midst of the ruins of the temples. He sat there near the ancient columns which symbolized the bones of countless soldiers left behind in the field of battle. The sheep folded around him, charmed with the music of his flute.

Midnight came, and heaven sowed the seeds of the following day in the deep furrows of the darkness. Ali's eyes became tired of the phantoms of awakeness, and his mind was wearied by the procession of ghosts marching in horrible silence amidst the demolished walls. He leaned upon his arm, and sleep captured his senses with the extreme end of its plaited veil, like a delicate cloud touching the face of a calm lake. He forgot his actual self and encountered his invisible self, rich with dreams and ideals higher than the laws and teachings of man. The circle of vision broadened before his eyes, and Life's hidden secrets gradually became apparent to him. His soul abandoned the rapid parade of time rushing toward nothingness; it stood alone before symmetrical thoughts and crystal ideas. For the first time in his life, Ali was aware of the causes for the spiritual famine that had accompanied his youth. . . . The famine which levels away the pit between the sweetness and the bitterness of Life. . . . That thirst which unites into contentment the sighs of Affection and the silence of Satisfaction. . . . That longing which cannot be vanquished by the glory of the world nor twisted by the passing of the ages. Ali felt the surge of a strange affection and a kind tenderness

within himself which was Memory, enlivening itself like incense placed upon white firebrands. . . . It was a magic love whose soft fingers had touched Ali's heart as a musician's delicate fingers touch quivering strings. It was a new power emanating from nothingness and growing forcefully, embracing his real self and filling his spirit with ardent love, at once painful and sweet.

Ali looked toward the ruins and his heavy eyes became alert as he fancied the glory of those devastated shrines that stood as mighty, impregnable, and eternal temples long before. His eyes became motionless and the breathing of his heart quickened. And like a blind man whose sight has suddenly been restored, he commenced to see, think and meditate. . . . He recollected the lamps and the silver censers that surrounded the image of an adored and revered goddess. . . . He remembered the priests offering sacrifices before an altar built of ivory and gold. . . . He envisioned the dancing maidens, and the tambourine players, and the singers who chanted the praise of the goddess of Love and Beauty; he saw all this before him, and felt the impression of their obscurity in the choking depths of his heart.

But memory alone brings naught save echoes of voices heard in the depths of the long ago. What, then, is the bizarre relationship between these powerful, weaving memories and the past actual life of a simple youth who was born in a tent and who

spent the spring of his life grazing sheep in the valleys?

Ali gathered himself and walked amidst the ruins, and the gnawing memories suddenly tore the veil of oblivion from his thoughts. As he reached the great and cavernous entrance to the temple, he halted as if a magnetic power gripped him and fastened his feet. As he looked downward, he found a smashed statue on the ground. He broke from the grasp of the Unseen and at once his soul's tears unleashed and poured like blood issuing from a deep wound; his heart roared in ebb and flow like the welling waves of the sea. He sighed bitterly and cried painfully, for he felt a stabbing aloneness and a destructive remoteness standing as an abyss between his heart and the heart from whom he was torn before he entered upon this life. He felt that his soul's element was but a flame from the burning torch which God had separated from Himself before the passing of the Ages. He perceived the feathery touch of delicate wings rustling about his flaming heart, and a great love possessing him. . . . A love whose power separates the mind from the world of quantity and measurement. . . . A love that talks when the tongue of Life is muted. . . . A love that stands as a blue beacon to point out the path, guiding with no visible light. That love or that God who descended in that quiet hour upon Ali's heart had seared into his being a bitter and sweet affection, like thorns growing by the side of the flourishing flowers.

But who is this Love and whence did he come? What does he desire of a shepherd kneeling in the midst of those ruins? Is it a seed sown without awareness in the domain of the heart by a Bedouin maiden? Or a beam appeared from behind the dark cloud to illuminate life? Is it a dream that crept close in the silence of the night to ridicule him? Or is it Truth that existed since the Beginning, and shall continue to exist until the Ending?

Ali closed his tearful eyes and stretched forth his arms like a beggar, and exclaimed, "Who are you, standing close to my heart but away from my sight, yet acting as a great wall between me and my real self, binding my today with my forgotten past? Are you the phantom of a spectre from Eternity to show me the vanity of Life and the weakness of mankind? Or the spirit of a genie appeared from the earth's crevices to enslave me and render me an object of mockery amongst the youths of my tribe? Who are you and what is this strange power which at one time deadens and enlivens my heart? Who am I and what is this strange self whom I call "Myself?" Has the Water of Life which I drank made of me an angel, seeing and hearing the mysterious secrets of the Universe, or is it merely an evil wine that intoxicated me and blinded me from myself?"

He became silent, while his anxiety grew and his spirit exulted. Then he continued, "Oh, that which the soul reveals, and the night conceals. . . . Oh, beautiful spirit, hovering in the sky of my dream;

you have awakened in me a dormant fullness, like healthy seeds hidden under the blankets of snow; you have passed me like a frolicsome breeze carrying to my hungry self the fragrance of the flowers of heaven; you have touched my senses and agitated and quivered them like the leaves of the trees. Let me look upon you now if you are a human, or command Slumber to shut my eyes so I can view your vastness through my inner being. Let me touch you; let me hear your voice. Tear away this veil that conceals my entire purpose, and destroy this wall that hides my deity from my clearing eyes, and place upon me a pair of wings so I may fly behind you to the halls of the Supreme Universe. Or bewitch my eyes so I may follow you to the ambush of the genii if you are one of their brides. If I am worthy, place your hand upon my heart and possess me."

Ali was whispering these words into the mystic darkness, and before him crept the ghosts of night, as if they were vapour coming from his boiling tears. Upon the walls of the temple he fancied magical pictures painted with the brush of the rainbow.

Thus did one hour pass, with Ali shedding tears and reveling in his miserable plight and hearing the beats of his heart, looking beyond the objects as if he were observing the images of Life vanishing slowly and being replaced with a dream, strange in its beauty and terrible in enormity. Like a prophet who meditates the stars of heaven awaiting the Descent and Revelation, he pondered the power existing be-

yond these contemplations. He felt that his spirit left him and probed through the temples for a priceless but unknown segment of himself, lost among the ruins.

Dawn had appeared and silence roared with the passing of the breeze; the first rays of light raced through, illuminating the particles of the ether, and the sky smiled like a dreamer viewing his beloved's phantom. The birds probed from their sanctuary in the crevices of the walls and emerged into the halls of the columns, singing their morning prayers.

Ali placed his cupped hand over his forehead, looking downward with glazed eyes. Like Adam, when God opened his eyes with Almighty breath, Ali saw new objects, strange and fantastic. Then he approached his sheep and called to them, whereupon they followed him quietly toward the lush fields. He led them, as he gazed at the sky like a philosopher divining and meditating the secrets of the Universe. He reached a brook whose murmuring was soothing to the spirit, and he sat by the edge of the spring under the willow tree, whose branches dipped over the water as if drinking from the cool depths. The dew of dawn glistened upon the sheep's wool as they grazed amid flowers and green grass.

In a few moments Ali again felt that his heartbeats were increasing rapidly and his spirit commenced to vibrate violently, almost visibly. Like a mother suddenly awakened from her slumber by the scream of her child, he bolted from his position,

and as his eyes were compelled to her, he saw a beautiful maiden carrying an earthenware container upon her shoulder, slowly approaching the far side of the brook. As she reached the edge and leaned forward to fill the jar, she glanced across, and her eyes met Ali's eyes. As it in insanity she cried out, dropped the jar, and withdrew swiftly. Then she turned, gazing at Ali with anxious, agonizing disbelief.

A minute passed, whose seconds were glittering lamps illuminating their hearts and spirits, and silence brought vague remembrance, revealing to them images and scenes far away from that brook and those trees. They heard each other in the understanding silence, listening tearfully to each other's sighs of heart and soul until complete knowing prevailed between the two.

Ali, still compelled by a mysterious power, leaped across the brook and approached the maiden, embraced her and printed a long kiss upon her lips. As if the sweetness of Ali's caress had usurped her will, she did not move, and the kind touch of Ali's arms had stolen her strength. She yielded to him as the fragrance of jasmine concedes to the vibration of the breeze, carrying it into the spacious firmament.

She placed her head upon his chest like a tortured person who has found rest. She sighed deeply . . . a sigh that announced the rebirth of happiness in a torn heart and proclaimed a revolution of wings that

had ascended after having been injured and committed to earth.

She raised her head and looked at him with her soul . . . the look of a human which, in mighty silence, belittles the conventional words used amongst mankind; the expression which offers myriads of thoughts in the unspoken language of the hearts. She bore the look of a person who accepts Love not as a spirit in a body of words, but as a reunion occurring long after two souls were divided by earth and joined by God.

The enamoured couple walked amidst the willow trees, and the singleness of two selves was a speaking tongue for their unification; a seeing eye for the glory of Happiness; a silent listener to the tremendous revelation of Love.

The sheep continued grazing, and the birds of the sky still hovered above their heads, singing the song of Dawn, following the emptiness of night. As they reached the end of the valley the sun appeared, spreading a golden garment upon the knolls and the hills, and they sat by the side of a rock where the violets hid. The maiden looked into Ali's black eyes while the breeze caressed her hair, as if the shimmering wisps were fingertips craving for sweet kisses. She felt as though some magic and strong gentleness were touching her lips in spite of her will, and with a serene and charming voice she said, "Ishtar has restored both of our spirits to this life from another,

so we may not be denied the joy of Love and the glory of Youth, my beloved."

Ali closed his eyes, as if her musical voice brought to him images of a dream he had seen, and he felt an invisible pair of wings carrying him from that place and depositing him in a strange chamber by the side of a bed upon which lay the corpse of a maiden whose beauty had been claimed by Death. He cried fearfully, then opened his eyes and found that same maiden sitting by his side, and upon her lips appeared a smile. Her eyes shone with the rays of Life. Ali's face brightened and his heart was refreshed. The phantom of his vision withdrew slowly until he forgot completely the past and its cares. The two lovers embraced and drank the wine of sweet kisses together until they became intoxicated. They slumbered, wrapped between each other's arms, until the last remnant of the shadow was dispersed by the Eternal Power which had awakened them.

BETWEEN NIGHT AND MORN

B<small>E SILENT</small>, my heart, for the space cannot
Hear you; be silent, for the ether is
Laden with cries and moans, and cannot
Carry your songs and hymns.

Be silent, for the phantoms of the night
Will not give heed to the whispering of
Your secrets; nor will the processions
Of darkness halt before your dreams.

Be silent, my heart, until Dawn comes,
For he who patiently awaits the morn
Will meet him surely, and he who loves
The light will be loved by the light.

Be silent, my heart, and hearken to my
Story; in my dream I saw a nightingale
Singing over the throat of a fiery
Volcano, and I saw a lily raising her
Head above the snow, and a naked Houri
Dancing in the midst of the graves, and
An infant playing with skulls while
Laughing.

I saw all these images in my dream, and
When I opened my eyes and looked about
Me, I saw the volcano still raging, but
No longer heard the nightingale sing;
Nor did I see him hovering.

I saw the sky spreading snow upon the
Fields and valleys, and concealing under
White shrouds the stilled bodies of the
Lilies. I saw a row of graves before
The silence of the Ages, but there was
No person dancing or praying in their
Midst. I saw a heap of skulls, but no
One was there to laugh, save the wind.

In my awakeness I saw grief and sorrow;
What became of the joy and sweetness of
My dream? Where has the beauty of my
Dream gone, and in what manner did the
Images disappear?

How can the soul be patient until Slumber
Restores the happy phantoms of hope and
Desire?

Give heed, my heart, and hear my story;
Yesterday my soul was like an old and
Strong tree, whose roots grasped into the
Depths of the earth, and whose branches
Reached the Infinite. My soul blossomed
In Spring, and gave fruit in Summer, and

THE TREASURED WRITINGS OF KAHLIL GIBRAN

When Autumn came, I gathered the fruit on
A silver tray and placed it by the
Walker's portion of the street; and all
Who passed partook willingly and continued
To walk.

And when Autumn passed away, and submerged
His rejoicing under wailing and lamentation,
I looked upon my tray and found but one
Fruit remaining; I took it and placed it
Into my mouth, but found it bitter as gall,
And sour as the hard grapes, and I said to
Myself, "Woe to me, for I have placed a
Curse in the mouths of the people, and an
Ailment in their bodies. What have you
Done, my soul, with the sweet sap which
Your roots have sucked from the earth, and
The fragrance which you have drawn from
The sky?" In anger did I tear the strong
And old tree of my soul, with each of the
Struggling roots, from the depths of the
Earth.

I uprooted it from the past, and took
From it the memories of one thousand
Springs and one thousand Autumns, and I
Planted the tree of my soul in another
Place. It was now in a field afar from
The path of Time; and I tended it in day
And in night, saying within me, "Wakefulness
Will bring us closer to the stars."

I watered it with blood and tears, saying,
"There is a flavour in blood, and a
Sweetness in tears." When Spring returned,
My tree bloomed again, and in the Summer it
Bore fruit. And when Autumn came, I gathered
All the ripe fruit upon a golden plate and
Offered it in the public path, and the people
Passed but none desired my fruit.

Then I took one fruit and brought it to my
Lips, and it was sweet as the honeycomb
And exhilarating as the wine of Babylon
And fragrant as the jasmine. And I cried
Out, saying, "The people do not want a
Blessing in their mouths, nor a truth in
Their hearts, for Blessing is the daughter
Of Tears, and Truth is the son of Blood."

I left the noisome city to sit in the shadow
Of the solitary tree of my soul, in a
Field far from life's path.

Be silent, my heart, until Dawn comes;
Be silent and attend my story;
Yesterday my thoughts were a boat sailing
Amidst the waves in the sea, and moving
With the winds from one land to another.
And my boat was empty except of seven
Jars of rainbow colours; and the time
Came when I grew weary of moving about
On the face of the sea, and I said to

Myself, "I shall return with the empty
Boat of my thoughts to the harbour of the
Isle of my birth."

And I prepared by colouring my boat yellow
Like the sunset, and green like the heart
Of Spring, and blue like the sky, and red
Like the anemone. And on the masts and
On the rudder I drew strange figures that
Compelled the attention and dazzled the
Eye. And as I ended my task, the boat of
My thoughts seemed as a prophetic vision,
Sailing between the two infinities, the
Sea and the sky.

I entered the harbour of the isle of my
Birth, and the people surged to meet me
With singing and merriment. And the
Throngs invited me to enter the city;
And they were plucking their instruments
And sounding their tambourines.

Such welcome was mine because my boat
Was beautifully decorated, and none
Entered and saw the interior of the
Boat of my thoughts, nor asked what
I had brought from beyond the seas. Nor
Could they observe that I had brought
My boat back empty, for its brilliance
Had rendered them blind. Thereupon I
Said within myself, "I have led the

People astray, and with seven jars of
Colours I have cheated their eyes."

Thereafter, I embarked in the boat of
My thoughts, again to set sail. I
Visited the East Islands and gathered
Myrrh, frankincense and sandalwood, and
Placed them in my boat. . . . I roamed the
West Islands and brought ivory and ruby
And emerald and many rare gems. . . . I
Journeyed the South Islands and carried
Back with me beautiful armours and
Glittering swords and spears and all
Varieties of weapons. . . . I filled the
Boat of my thoughts with the choicest
And most precious things on earth, and
Returned to the harbour of the isle of
My birth, saying, "The people shall again
Glorify me, but with honesty, and they
Shall again invite me to enter their
City, but with merit."

And when I reached the harbour, none
Came to meet me. . . . I walked the streets
Of my earlier glory but no person looked
Upon me. . . . I stood in the market place
Shouting to the people of the treasures
In my boat, and they mocked at me and
Heeded not.

I returned to the harbour with spiritless
Heart and disappointment and confusion.

And when I gazed upon my boat, I observed
A thing which I had not seen during my
Voyage, and I exclaimed, "The waves of
The sea have done away with the colours and
The figures on my boat and caused it to look
Like a skeleton." The winds and the spray
Together with the burning sun had effaced
The brilliant hues and my boat looked now
Like tattered grey raiment. I could not
Observe these changes from amid my treasures,
For I had blinded my eyes from the inside.

I had gathered the most precious things on
Earth and placed them in a floating chest
Upon the face of the water and returned to
My people, but they cast me away and could
Not see me, for their eyes had been allured
By empty, shimmering objects.

At that hour I left the boat of my thoughts
For the City of the Dead, and sat in the
Midst of the trim graves, contemplating
Their secrets.

Be silent, my heart, until Dawn comes; be
Silent, for the raging tempest is ridiculing
Your inner whispering, and the caves of
The valleys do not echo the vibration of
Your strings.

Be silent, my heart, until Morn comes,
For he who awaits patiently the coming

Of Dawn will be embraced longingly by
Morningtide.

Dawn is breaking. Speak if you are able,
My heart. Here is the procession of
Morningtide. . . .Why do you not speak?
Has not the silence of the night left
A song in your inner depths with which
You may meet Dawn?

Here are the swarms of doves and the
Nightingales moving in the far portion
Of the valley. Are you capable of flying
With the birds, or has the horrible night
Weakened your wings? The shepherds are
Leading the sheep from their folds; has
The phantom of the night left strength
In you so you may walk behind them to
The green prairies? The young men and
Women are walking gracefully toward the
Vineyards. Will you be able to stand
And walk with them? Rise, my heart, and
Walk with Dawn, for the night has passed,
And the fear of darkness has vanished with
Its black dreams and ghastly thoughts and
Insane travels.

Rise, my heart, and raise your voice with
Music, for he who shares not Dawn with
His songs is one of the sons of ever-
Darkness.

SECRETS
OF THE HEART

SECRETS OF THE HEART

A MAJESTIC mansion stood under the wings of the silent night, as Life stands under the cover of Death. In it sat a maiden at an ivory desk, leaning her beautiful head on her soft hand, as a withering lily leans upon its petals. She looked around, feeling like a miserable prisoner, struggling to penetrate the walls of the dungeon with her eyes in order to witness Life walking in the procession of Freedom.

The hours passed like the ghosts of the night, as a procession chanting the dirge of her sorrow, and the maiden felt secure with the shedding of her tears in anguished solitude. When she could not resist the pressure of her suffering any longer, and as she felt that she was in full possession of the treasured secrets of her heart, she took the quill and commenced mingling her tears with ink upon parchment, and she inscribed:

"My Beloved Sister,
  "When the heart becomes congested with secrets,

and the eyes begin to burn from the searing tears, and the ribs are about to burst with the growing of the heart's confinement, one cannot find expression for such a labyrinth except by a surge of release.

"Sorrowful persons find joy in lamentation, and lovers encounter comfort and condolence in dreams, and the oppressed delight in receiving sympathy. I am writing to you now because I feel like a poet who fancies the beauty of objects whose impression he composes in verse while being ruled by a divine power. . . . I am like a child of the starving poor who cries for food, instigated by bitterness of hunger, disregarding the plight of his poor and merciful mother and her defeat in life.

"Listen to my painful story, my dear sister, and weep with me, for sobbing is like a prayer, and the tears of mercy are like a charity because they come forth from a living and sensitive and good soul and they are not shed in vain. It was the will of my father when I married a noble and rich man. My father was like most of the rich, whose only joy in life is to improve their wealth by adding more gold to their coffers in fear of poverty, and curry nobility with grandeur in anticipation of the attacks of the black days. . . . I find myself now, with all my love and dreams, a victim upon a golden altar which I hate, and an inherited honour which I despise.

"I respect my husband because he is generous and kind to all; he endeavours to bring happiness to me,

and spends his gold to please my heart, but I have found that the impression of all these things is not worth one moment of a true and divine love. Do not ridicule me, my sister, for I am now a most enlightened person regarding the needs of a woman's heart—that throbbing heart which is like a bird flying in the spacious sky of love. . . . It is like a vase replenished with the wine of the ages that has been pressed for the sipping souls. . . . It is like a book in whose pages one reads the chapters of happiness and misery, joy and pain, laughter and sorrow. No one can read this book except the true companion who is the other half of the woman, created for her since the beginning of the world.

"Yes, I became most knowing amongst all women as to the purpose of the soul and meaning of the heart, for I have found that my magnificent horses and beautiful carriages and glittering coffers of gold and sublime nobility are not worth one glance from the eyes of that poor young man who is patiently waiting and suffering the pangs of bitterness and misery. . . . That youth who is oppressed by the cruelty and will of my father, and imprisoned in the narrow and melancholy jail of Life. . . .

"Please, my dear, do not contrive to console me, for the calamity through which I have realized the power of my love is my great consoler. Now I am looking forward from behind my tears and awaiting the coming of Death to lead me to where I will meet

the companion of my soul and embrace him as I did before we entered this strange world.

"Do not think evil of me, for I am doing my duty as a faithful wife, and complying calmly and patiently with the laws and rules of man. I honour my husband with my sense, and respect him with my heart, and revere him with my soul, but there is a withholding, for God gave part of me to my beloved before I knew him.

"Heaven willed that I spend my life with a man not meant for me, and I am wasting my days silently according to the will of Heaven; but if the gates of Eternity do not open, I will remain with the beautiful half of my soul and look back to the Past, and that Past is this Present. . . . I shall look at life as Spring looks at Winter, and contemplate the obstacles of Life as one who has climbed the rough trail and reached the mountain top."

At that moment the maiden ceased writing and hid her face with her cupped hands and wept bitterly. Her heart declined to entrust to the pen its most sacred secrets, but resorted to the pouring of dry tears that dispersed quickly and mingled with the gentle ether, the haven of the lovers' souls and the flowers' spirits. After a moment she took the quill and added, "Do you remember that youth? Do you recollect the rays which emanated from his eyes, and the sorrowful signs upon his face? Do you recall that laughter which bespoke the tears of a mother, torn

from her only child? Can you retrace his serene voice speaking the echo of a distant valley? Do you remember him meditating and staring longingly and calmly at objects and speaking of them in strange words, and then bending his head and sighing as if fearing to reveal the secrets of his great heart? Do you recall his dreams and beliefs? Do you recollect all these things in a youth whom humanity counts as one of her children and upon whom my father looked with eyes of superiority because he is higher than earthly greed and nobler than inherited grandeur?

"You know, my dear sister, that I am a martyr in this belittling world, and a victim of ignorance. Will you sympathize with a sister who sits in the silence of the horrible night pouring down the contents of her inner self and revealing to you her heart's secrets? I am sure that you will sympathize with me, for I know that Love has visited your heart."

Dawn came, and the maiden surrendered herself to Slumber, hoping to find sweeter and more gentle dreams than those she had encountered in her awakeness. . . .

MY COUNTRYMEN

WHAT do you seek, My Countrymen?
Do you desire that I build for
You gorgeous palaces, decorated
With words of empty meaning, or
Temples roofed with dreams? Or
Do you command me to destroy what
The liars and tyrants have built?
Shall I uproot with my fingers
What the hypocrites and the wicked
Have implanted? Speak your insane
Wish!

What is it you would have me do,
My Countrymen? Shall I purr like
The kitten to satisfy you, or roar
Like the lion to please myself? I
Have sung for you, but you did not
Dance; I have wept before you, but
You did not cry. Shall I sing and
Weep at the same time?

Your souls are suffering the pangs
Of hunger, and yet the fruit of

184

Knowledge is more plentiful than
The stones of the valleys.

Your hearts are withering from
Thirst, and yet the springs of
Life are streaming about your
Homes—why do you not drink?
The sea has its ebb and flow,
The moon has its fullness and
Crescents, and the Ages have
Their winter and summer, and all
Things vary like the shadow of
An unborn God moving between
Earth and sun, but Truth cannot
Be changed, nor will it pass away;
Why, then, do you endeavour to
Disfigure its countenance?

I have called you in the silence
Of the night to point out the
Glory of the moon and the dignity
Of the stars, but you startled
From your slumber and clutched
Your swords in fear, crying,
"Where is the enemy? We must kill
Him first!" At morningtide, when
The enemy came, I called to you
Again, but now you did not wake
From your slumber, for you were
Locked in fear, wrestling with

The processions of spectres in
Your dreams.

And I said unto you, "Let us climb
To the mountain top and view the
Beauty of the world." And you
Answered me, saying, "In the depths
Of this valley our fathers lived,
And in its shadows they died, and in
Its caves they were buried. How can
We depart this place for one which
They failed to honour?"
And I said unto you, "Let us go to
The plain that gives it bounty to
The sea." And you spoke timidly to
Me, saying, "The uproar of the abyss
Will frighten our spirits, and the
Terror of the depths will deaden
Our bodies."

I have loved you, My Countrymen, but
My love for you is painful to me
And useless to you; and today I
Hate you, and hatred is a flood
That sweeps away the dry branches
And quavering houses.

I have pitied your weakness, My
Countrymen, but my pity has but
Increased your feebleness, exalting

And nourishing slothfulness which
Is vain to Life. And today I see
Your infirmity which my soul loathes
And fears.

I have cried over your humiliation
And submission; and my tears streamed
Like crystalline, but could not sear
Away your stagnant weakness; yet they
Removed the veil from my eyes.

My tears have never reached your
Petrified hearts, but they cleansed
The darkness from my inner self.
Today I am mocking at your suffering,
For laughter is a raging thunder that
Precedes the tempest and never comes
After it.

What do you desire, My Countrymen?
Do you wish for me to show you
The ghost of your countenance on
The face of still water? Come,
Now, and see how ugly you are!

Look and meditate! Fear has
Turned your hair grey as the
Ashes, and dissipation has grown
Over your eyes and made them into
Obscured hollows, and cowardice
Has touched your cheeks that now
Appear as dismal pits in the

Valley, and Death has kissed
Your lips and left them yellow
As the Autumn leaves.

What is it that you seek, My
Countrymen? What ask you from
Life, who does not any longer
Count you among her children?

Your souls are freezing in the
Clutches of the priests and
Sorcerers, and your bodies
Tremble between the paws of the
Despots and the shedders of
Blood, and your country quakes
Under the marching feet of the
Conquering enemy; what may you
Expect even though you stand
Proudly before the face of the
Sun? Your swords are sheathed
With rust, and your spears are
Broken, and your shields are
Laden with gaps; why, then, do
You stand in the field of battle?

Hypocrisy is your religion, and
Falsehood is your life, and
Nothingness is your ending; why,
Then, are you living? Is not
Death the sole comfort of the
Miserables?

Life is a resolution that
Accompanies youth, and a diligence
That follows maturity, and a
Wisdom that pursues senility; but
You, My Countrymen, were born old
And weak. And your skins withered
And your heads shrank, whereupon
You became as children, running
Into the mire and casting stones
Upon each other.

Knowledge is a light, enriching
The warmth of life, and all may
Partake who seek it out; but you,
My Countrymen, seek out darkness
And flee the light, awaiting the
Coming of water from the rock,
And your nation's misery is your
Crime. . . . I do not forgive you
Your sins, for you know what you
Are doing.

Humanity is a brilliant river
Singing its way and carrying with
It the mountains' secrets into
The heart of the sea; but you,
My Countrymen, are stagnant
Marshes infested with insects
And vipers.

The Spirit is a sacred blue
Torch, burning and devouring

The dry plants, and growing
With the storm and illuminating
The faces of the goddesses; but
You, My Countrymen . . . your souls
Are like ashes which the winds
Scatter upon the snow, and which
The tempests disperse forever in
The valleys.

Fear not the phantom of Death,
My Countrymen, for his greatness
And mercy will refuse to approach
Your smallness; and dread not the
Dagger, for it will decline to be
Lodged in your shallow hearts.

I hate you, My Countrymen, because
You hate glory and greatness. I
Despise you because you despise
Yourselves. I am your enemy, for
You refuse to realize that you are
The enemies of the goddesses.

JOHN THE MADMAN

N SUMMER John walked every morning into the field, driving his oxen and carrying his plough over his shoulder, hearkening to the soothing songs of the birds and the rustling of the leaves and the grass.

At noon he sat beside a brook in the colourful prairies for repast, leaving a few morsels upon the green grass for the birds of the sky.

At eventide he returned to his wretched hovel that stood apart from those hamlets and villages in North Lebanon. After the evening meal he sat and listened attentively to his parents, who related tales of the past ages until sleep allured and captured his eyes.

In winter he spent his days by the fireside, pondering the wailing of the winds and lamentation of the elements, meditating upon the phenomena of the seasons, and looking through the window toward the snow-laden valleys and leafless trees, symbolizing a multitude of suffering people left helpless in the jaws of biting frost and strong wind.

191

During the long winter nights he sat up until his parents retired, whereupon he opened a rough wooden closet, brought out his New Testament, and read it secretly under the dim light of a flickering lamp. The priests objected to the reading of the Good Book, and John exercised great caution during these fascinating moments of study. The fathers warned the simple-hearted people against its use, and threatened them with excommunication from the church if discovered possessing it.

Thus John spent his youth between the beautiful earth of God and the New Testament, full of light and truth. John was a youth of silence and contemplation; he listened to his parents' conversations and never spoke a word nor asked a question. When sitting with his contemporaries, he gazed steadily at the horizon, and his thoughts were as distant as his eyes. After each visit to the church he returned home with a depressed spirit, for the teachings of the priests were different from the precepts he found in the Gospel, and the life of the faithful was not the beautiful life of which Christ spoke.

Spring came and the snow melted in the fields and valleys. The snow upon the mountain tops was thawing gradually and forming many streamlets in the winding paths leading into the valleys, combining into a torrent whose roaring bespoke the awakening of Nature. The almond and apple trees were in full bloom; the willow and poplar trees were sprouting

with buds, and Nature had spread her happy and colourful garments over the countryside.

John, tired of spending his days by the fireside, and knowing that his oxen were longing for the pastures, released his animals from the sheds and led them to the fields, concealing his New Testament under his cloak for fear of detection. He reached a beautiful arbor adjacent to some fields belonging to the St. Elija Monastery * which stood majestically upon a nearby hill. As the oxen commenced grazing, John leaned upon a rock and began to read his New Testament and meditate the sadness of the children of God on earth, and the beauty of the Kingdom of Heaven.

It was the last day of Lent, and the villagers who abstained from eating meat were impatiently awaiting the coming of Easter. John, like the rest of the poor fellahin, never distinguished Lent from any other day of the year, for his whole life was an extended Lent, and his food never exceeded the simple bread, kneaded with the pain of his heart, or the fruits, purchased with the blood of his body. The only nourishment craved by John during Lent was that spiritual food—the heavenly bread that brought into his heart sad thoughts of the tragedy of the Son of Man and the end of His life on earth.

The birds were singing and hovering about him, and large flocks of doves circled in the sky, while the

* A rich abbey in North Lebanon with vast lands, occupied by scores of monks called Alepoans. (*Editor's note.*)

flowers swayed with the breeze as if exhilarated by the brilliant sunshine.

John busied himself absorbing the Book, and between these intense, light-giving sessions, he watched the domes of the churches in the nearby villages and listened to the rhythmic toll of the bells. Occasionally he would close his eyes and fly on the wings of dreams to Old Jerusalem, following Christ's steps and asking the people of the city about the Nazarene, whereupon he would receive the answer, "Here He cured the paralyzed and restored to the blind their sight; and there they braided for Him a wreath of thorns and placed it upon His head; from that portico He spoke to the multitude with beautiful parables; in that palace they tied Him to the marble columns and scourged Him; on this road He forgave the adulteress her sins, and upon that spot He fell under the weight of His Cross."

One hour passed, and John was suffering physically with God and glorifying with Him in spirit. Noon quickly came, and the oxen were beyond the reach of John's sight. He looked in every direction but could not see them, and as he reached the trail that led to the adjacent fields, he saw a man at a distance, standing amidst the orchards. As he approached and saw that the man was one of the Monastery's monks, he greeted him, bowed reverently, and asked him if he had seen the oxen. The monk appeared to be restraining anger, and he said, "Yes, I saw them.

Follow me and I will show them to you." As they reached the Monastery, John found his oxen tied with ropes in a shed. One of the monks was acting as a watchman over them, and each time an animal moved, he struck the ox across the back with a heavy club. John made a frantic attempt to unbind the helpless animals, but the monk took hold of his cloak and withheld him. At the same time he turned toward the Monastery and shouted, saying, "Here is the criminal shepherd! I have found him!" The priests and monks, preceded by the head priest, hurried to the scene and encircled John, who was bewildered, and felt like a captive. "I have done nothing to merit the treatment of a criminal," said John to the head priest. And the leader replied angrily, "Your oxen have ruined our plantation and destroyed our vineyards. Since you are responsible for the damage we will not give up your oxen until you adjust our loss."

John protested, "I am poor and have no money. Please release my oxen and I pledge my honour that I will never again bring them to these lands." The head priest took a step forward, raised his hand toward heaven, and said, "God has appointed us to be the protectors over this vast land of St. Elija, and it is our sacred duty to guard it with all of our might, for this land is holy, and, like fire, it will burn any who trespass upon it. If you refuse to account for your crime against God, the grass that your oxen

have eaten will surely turn into poison and destroy them!"

The head priest started to depart, but John touched his robe and humbly begged, "I appeal to you in the name of Jesus and all the saints, to let me and my animals free. Be kind to me, for I am poor, and the coffers of the Monastery are bursting with silver and gold. Have mercy upon my poor and aged parents, whose lives depend on me. God will forgive me if I have harmed you." The head priest looked at him with severity, and said, "Poor or rich, the Monastery cannot forgive you your debts; three denars will free your oxen." John pleaded, "I do not possess a single coin; have mercy on a poor grazier, Father." And the head priest retorted, "Then you must sell a part of your possessions and bring three denars, for it is better to enter the Kingdom of Heaven without property than to bring the wrath of St. Elija upon you and descend to hell." The other monks nodded their accord.

After a short silence, John's face brightened and his eyes shone as if fear and servility had deserted his heart. With his head high, he looked at the head priest and addressed him boldly, saying, "Do the weak poor have to sell their pitiful belongings, the source of their life's bread, in order to add more gold to the Monastery's wealth? Is it just that the poor should be oppressed and made poorer in order that St. Elija may forgive the oxen their innocent wrongs?" The head priest raised his eyes to heaven and in-

toned, "It is written in the Book of God that he who has plenty shall be given more, and he who has not shall be taken from."

When John heard these words he became furious, and like a soldier who draws his sword in the face of the enemy, he drew the New Testament from his pocket and shouted out, "This is how you twist the teachings of Christ, you hypocrite! And thus do you pervert the most sacred heritage of life in order to spread your evils. . . . Woe to you when the Son of Man comes again and destroys your Monastery and throws its debris in the valley, and burns your shrine and altars into ashes. . . . Woe to you when the wrath of the Nazarene descends upon you and throws you into the depths of the abyss. . . . Woe to you, worshippers of the idols of greed, who hide the ugliness of hatred under your black garments. . . . Woe to you, foes of Jesus, who move your lips with prayers while your hearts are laden with lusts. . . . Woe to you who kneel before the altar in body while your spirits are revolting against God! You are polluted with your own sin of punishing me for approaching your land, paid for by me and my ancestors. You ridiculed me when I asked for mercy in the name of Christ. Take this Book and show your smiling monks where the Son of God ever refused to forgive. . . . Read this heavenly tragedy and tell them where He spoke not of mercy and of kindness, be it in the Sermon of the Mount, or in the temple. Did He not forgive the adulteress her sins? Did He not part his

hands upon the Cross to embrace humanity? Look upon our wretched homes, where the sick suffer upon their hard beds. . . . Look behind the prison bars, where the innocent man is victim of oppression and injustice. . . . Look upon the beggars, stretching forth their hands for alms, humiliated in heart and broken in body. . . . Think upon your slaving followers, who are suffering the pangs of hunger while you are living a life of luxury and indifference, and enjoying the fruits of the fields and the wine of the vineyards. You have never visited a sufferer nor consoled the down-hearted nor fed the hungry; neither have you sheltered the wayfarer nor offered sympathy to the lame. Yet you are not satisfied with what you have pilfered from our fathers, but still stretch your hands like vipers' heads, grasping by threats of hell what little a widow has saved through body-breaking toil, or a miserable fellah has stored away to keep his children alive!"

John took a deep breath, then calmed his voice and quietly added, "You are numerous, and I am alone—you may do unto me what you wish; the wolves prey upon the lamb in the darkness of the night, but the blood stains remain upon the stones in the valley until the dawn comes, and the sun reveals the crime to all."

There was a magic power in John's talk that arrested their attention and injected a defensive anger into the monks' hearts. They were shaking with fury and waiting only for their superior's order to fall

upon John and bring him to submission. The brief silence was like the heavy quiet of the tempest, after laying waste the gardens. The head priest then commanded the monks, saying, "Bind this criminal and take the Book from him and drag him into a dark cell, for he who blasphemes the holy representatives of God will never be forgiven on this earth, neither in Eternity." The Monks leaped upon John and led him manacled into a narrow prison and barred him there.

The courage shown by John could not be perceived or understood by one who partakes of the submission or the deceit or the tyranny of this enslaved country, called by the Orientals "The Bride of Syria," and "The Pearl of the Sultan's Crown." And in his cell, John thought of the needless misery brought upon his countrymen by the grip of the things he had just learned. He smiled with a sad sympathy and his smile was mingled with suffering and bitterness; the kind that cuts its way through the depths of the heart; the kind that sets the soul to a choking futility; the kind which, if left unsupported, ascends to the eyes and falls down helplessly.

John then stood proudly, and looked through the window-slit facing the sunlit valley. He felt as if a spiritual joy were embracing his soul and a sweet tranquility possessing his heart. They had imprisoned his body, but his spirit was sailing freely with the breeze amidst the knolls and prairies. His love for Jesus never changed, and the torturing hands

could not remove his heart's ease, for persecution cannot harm him who stands by Truth. Did not Socrates fall proudly a victim in body? Was not Paul stoned for the sake of the Truth? It is our inner self that hurts us when we disobey and kills us when we betray.

John's parents were informed of his imprisonment and the confiscation of the oxen. His old mother came to the Monastery leaning heavily over her walking stick and she prostrated herself before the head priest, kissing his feet and begging him for mercy upon her only son. The head priest raised his head reverently toward heaven and said, "We will forgive your son for his madness, but St. Elija will not forgive any who trespass upon his land." After gazing at him with tearful eyes, the old lady took a silver locket from her neck and handed it to the head priest, saying, "This is my most precious possession, given to me as a wedding gift by my mother. . . . Will you accept it as atonement for my son's sin?"

The head priest took the locket and placed it in his pocket, whereupon he looked at John's ancient mother who was kissing his hands and expressing to him her thanks and gratitude, and he said, "Woe to this sinful age! You twist the saying of the Good Book and cause the children to eat the sour, and the parents' teeth sit on edge; go now, good woman, and

pray to God for your mad son and ask Him to restore his mind."

John left the prison, and walked quietly by the side of his mother, driving the oxen before him. When they reached their wretched hovel, he led the animals into their mangers and sat silently by the window, meditating the sunset. In a few moments he heard his father whispering to his mother, saying, "Sara, many times have I told you that John was mad, and you disbelieved. Now you will agree, after what you have seen, for the head priest has spoken to you today the very words I spoke to you in past years." John continued looking toward the distant horizon, watching the sun descend.

Easter arrived, and at that time the construction of a new church in the town of Bsherri had just been completed. This magnificent place of worship was like a prince's palace standing amidst the huts of poor subjects. The people were scurrying through the many preparations to receive a prelate who was assigned to officiate at the religious ceremonies inaugurating the new temple. The multitudes stood in rows over the roads waiting for His Grace's arrival. The chanting of the priests in unison with cymbal sounds and the hymns of the throngs filled the sky.

The prelate finally arrived, riding a magnificent horse harnessed with a gold-studded saddle, and as he dismounted, the priests and political leaders met him with the most beautiful of welcoming speeches.

He was escorted to the new altar, where he clothed himself in ecclesiastical raiment, decorated with gold threads and encrusted with sparkling gems; he wore the golden crown, and walked in a procession around the altar, carrying his jewelled staff. He was followed by the priests and the carriers of tapers and incense burners.

At that hour, John stood amongst the fellahin at the portico, contemplating the scene with bitter sighs and sorrowful eyes, for it pained him to observe the expensive robes, and precious crown, and staff, and vases and other objects of needless extravagance, while the poor fellahin who came from the surrounding villages to celebrate the occasion were suffering the gnawing pangs of poverty. Their tattered swaddles and sorrowful faces bespoke their miserable plight.

The rich dignitaries, decorated with badges and ribbons, stood aloof praying loudly, while the suffering villagers, in the rear of the scene, beat their bosoms in sincere prayer that came from the depths of their broken hearts.

The authority of those dignitaries and leaders was like the ever-green leaves of the poplar trees, and the life of those fellahin was like a boat whose pilot had met his destiny and whose rudder had been lost and whose sails had been torn by the strong wind and left at the mercy of the furious depths and the raging tempest.

Tyranny and blind submission . . . which one of

these gave birth to the other? Is tyranny a strong tree that grows not in the low earth, or is it submission, which is like a deserted field where naught but thorns can grow? Such thoughts and contemplations preyed on John's mind while the ceremonies were taking place; he braced his arms about his chest for fear his bosom would burst with agony over the people's plight in this tragedy of opposites.

He gazed upon the withering creatures of severe humanity, whose hearts were dry and whose seeds were now seeking shelter in the bosom of the earth, as destitute pilgrims seek rebirth in a new realm.

When the pageantry came to an end and the multitude was preparing to disperse, John felt that a compelling power was urging him to speak in behalf of the oppressed poor. He proceeded to an extreme end of the square, raised his hands toward the sky, and as the throngs gathered about, he opened his lips and said, "O Jesus, Who art sitting in the heart of the circle of light, give heed! Look upon this earth from behind the blue dome and see how the thorns have choked the flowers which Thy truth hast planted.

"Oh Good Shepherd, the wolves have preyed upon the weak lamb which Thou hast carried in Thy arms. Thy pure blood has been drawn into the depths of the earth which Thy feet have made sacred. This good earth has been made by Thine enemies into an arena where the strong crushes the weak. The cry of the miserable and the lamentation of the

helpless can no longer be heard by those sitting upon the thrones, preaching Thy word. The lambs which Thou hast sent to this earth are now wolves who eat the one which Thou hast carried and blessed.

"The word of light which sprang forth from Thy heart has vanished from the scripture and is replaced with an empty and terrible uproar that frightens the spirit.

"Oh Jesus, they have built these churches for the sake of their own glory, and embellished them with silk and melted gold. . . . They left the bodies of Thy chosen poor wrapped in tattered raiment in the cold night. . . . They filled the sky with the smoke of burning candles and incense and left the bodies of Thy faithful worshippers empty of bread. . . . They raised their voices with hymns of praise, but deafened themselves to the cry and moan of the widows and orphans.

"Come again, Oh Living Jesus, and drive the vendors of Thy faith from Thy sacred temple, for they have turned it into a dark cave where vipers of hypocrisy and falsehood crawl and abound."

John's words, strong and sincere, brought murmurs of approval, and the approach of the dignitaries quelled him not. With added courage, strengthened by memories of his earlier experience, he continued, "Come, Oh Jesus, and render accounts with those Caesars who usurped from the weak what is the weak's and from God what is God's. The grapevine which Thou hast planted with Thy right

hand has been eaten by worms of greed and its bunches have been trampled down. Thy sons of peace are dividing amongst themselves and fighting one with another, leaving poor souls as victims in the wintry field. Before Thy altar, they raise their voices with prayers, saying, 'Glory to God in the highest, and on earth peace, good will toward men.' Will our Father in heaven be glorified when His name is uttered by empty hearts and sinful lips and false tongues? Will peace be on earth while the sons of misery are slaving in the fields to feed the strong and fill the stomachs of the tyrants? Will ever peace come and save them from the clutches of destitution?

"What is peace? Is it in the eyes of those infants, nursing upon the dry breasts of their hungry mothers in cold huts? Or is it in the wretched hovels of the hungry who sleep upon hard beds and crave for one bite of the food which the priests and monks feed to their fat pigs?

"What is joy, Oh Beautiful Jesus? Is it manifest when the Emir buys the strong arms of men and the honour of women for threats of death or for a few pieces of silver? Or is it found in submission, and slaving of body and spirit to those who dazzle our eyes with their glittering badges and golden diadems? Upon each complaint to Thy peace makers, they reward us with their soldiers, armed with swords and spears to step upon our women and children and steal our blood.

"Oh Jesus, full of love and mercy, stretch forth

Thy strong arms and protect us from those thieves or send welcome Death to deliver us and lead us to the graves where we can rest peacefully under the watchful care of Thy Cross; there we shall wait for Thy return. Oh Mighty Jesus, this life is naught but a dark cell of enslavement. . . . It is a playing ground of horrible ghosts, and it is a pit alive with spectres of death. Our days are but sharp words concealed under the ragged quilts of our beds in the fearful darkness of the night. At dawn, these weapons rise above our heads as demons, pointing out to us our whip-driven slavery in the fields.

"Oh Jesus, have mercy upon the oppressed poor who came today to commemorate Thy Resurrection. . . . Pity them, for they are miserable and weak."

John's talk appealed to one group and displeased another. "He is telling the truth, and speaking in our behalf before heaven," one remarked. And another one said, "He is bewitched, for he speaks in the name of an evil spirit." And a third commented, "We have never heard such infamous talk, not even from our fathers! We must bring it to an end!" And a fourth one said, whispering into the next man's ears, "I felt a new spirit in me when I heard him talking." The next man added, "But the priests know our needs more so than he does; it is a sin to doubt them." As the voices grew from every direction like the roar of the sea, one of the priests approached, placed John in restraint and turned him

immediately to the law, whereupon he was taken to the Governor's palace for trial.

Upon his interrogation, John uttered not a single word, for he knew that the Nazarene resorted to silence before His persecutors. The governor ordered John to be placed in a prison, where he slept peacefully and heart-cleansed that night, leaning his head on the rock wall of the dungeon.

The next day John's father came and testified before the Governor that his son was mad, and added, sadly, "Many times have I heard him talking to himself and speaking of many strange things that none could see or understand. Many times did he sit talking in the silence of the night, using vague words. I heard him calling the ghosts with a voice like that of a sorcerer. You may ask the neighbors who talked to him and found beyond doubt that he was insane. He never answered when one spoke to him, and when he spoke, he uttered cryptic words and phrases unknown to the listener and out of the subject. His mother knows him well. Many times she saw him gazing at the distant horizon with glazed eyes and speaking with passion, like a small child, about the brooks and the flowers and the stars. Ask the monks whose teachings he ridiculed and criticized during their sacred Lent. He is insane, Your Excellency, but he is very kind to me and to his mother; he does much to help us in our old age, and he works with diligence to keep us fed and warm and alive. Pity him, and have mercy on us."

The Governor released John, and the news of his madness spread throughout the village. And when the people spoke of John they mentioned his name with humour and ridicule, and the maidens looked upon him with sorrowful eyes and said, "Heaven has its strange purpose in man. . . . God united beauty and insanity in this youth, and joined the kind brightness of his eyes with the darkness of his unseen self."

In the midst of God's fields and prairies, and by the side of the knolls, carpeted with green grass and beautiful flowers, the ghost of John, alone and restless, watches the oxen grazing peacefully, undisturbed by man's hardships. With tearful eyes he looks toward the scattered villages on both sides of the valley and repeats with deep sighs, "You are numerous and I am alone; the wolves prey upon the lambs in the darkness of the night, but the blood stains remain upon the stones in the valley until the dawn comes, and the sun reveals the crime to all."

THE ENCHANTING HOURI

Where are you leading me, Oh Enchanting
Houri, and how long shall I follow you
Upon this hispid road, planted with
Thorns? How long shall our souls ascend
And descend painfully on this twisting
And rocky path?

Like a child following his mother I am
Following you, holding the extreme end
Of your garment, forgetting my dreams
And staring at your beauty, blinding
My eyes under your spell to the
Procession of spectres hovering above
Me, and attracted to you by an inner
Force within me which I cannot deny.

Halt for a moment and let me see your
Countenance; and look upon me for a
Moment; perhaps I will learn your
Heart's secrets through your strange
Eyes. Stop and rest, for I am weary,
And my soul is trembling with fear

Upon this horrible trail. Halt, for
We have reached that terrible crossroad
Where Death embraces Life.

Oh Houri, listen to me! I was as free
As the birds, probing the valleys and
The forests, and flying in the spacious
Sky. At eventide I rested upon the
Branches of the trees, meditating the
Temples and palaces in the City of the
Colourful Clouds which the Sun builds
In the morning and destroys before
Twilight.

I was like a thought, walking alone
And at peace to the East and West of
The Universe, rejoicing with the
Beauty and joy of Life, and inquiring
Into the magnificent mystery of
Existence.

I was like a dream, stealing out under
The friendly wings of the night,
Entering through the closed windows
Into the maidens' chambers, frolicking
And awakening their hopes. . . . Then I
Sat by the youths and agitated their
Desires. . . . Then I probed the elders'
Quarters and penetrated their thoughts
Of serene contentment.

Then you captured my fancy, and since
That hypnotic moment I felt like a
Prisoner dragging his shackles and
Impelled into an unknown place. . . .
I became intoxicated with your sweet
Wine that has stolen my will, and I
Now find my lips kissing the hand
That strikes me sharply. Can you
Not see with your soul's eye the
Crushing of my heart? Halt for a
Moment; I am regaining my strength
And untying my weary feet from the
Heavy chains. I have crushed the
Cup from which I have drunk your
Tasty venom. . . . But now I am in
A strange land, and bewildered;
Which road shall I follow?

My freedom has been restored; will
You now accept me as a willing
Companion, who looks at the Sun
With glazed eyes and grasps the
Fire with untrembling fingers?

I have unbound my wings and I am
Ready to ascend; will you accompany
A youth who spends his days roaming
The mountains like the lone eagle, and
Wastes his nights wandering in the
Deserts like the restless lion?

Will you content yourself with the
Affection of one who looks upon Love
As but an entertainer, and declines
To accept her as his master?

Will you accept a heart that loves,
But never yields? And burns, but
Never melts? Will you be at ease
With a soul that quivers before the
Tempest, but never surrenders to it?
Will you accept one as a companion
Who makes not slaves, nor will become
One? Will you own me but not possess
Me, by taking my body and not my heart?

Then here is my hand—grasp it with
Your beautiful hand; and here is my
Body—embrace it with your loving
Arms; and here are my lips—bestow
Upon them a deep and dizzying kiss.

BEHIND THE GARMENT

RACHEL woke at midnight and gazed intently at something invisible in the sky of her chamber. She heard a voice more soothing than the whispers of Life, and more dismal than the moaning call of the abyss, and softer than the rustling of white wings, and deeper than the message of the waves. . . . It vibrated with hope and with futility, with joy and with misery, and with affection for life, yet with desire for death. Then Rachel closed her eyes and sighed deeply, and gasped, saying, "Dawn has reached the extreme end of the valley; we should go toward the sun and meet him." Her lips were parted, resembling and echoing a deep wound in the soul.

At that moment the priest approached her bed and felt her hand, but found it as cold as the snow; and when he grimly placed his fingers upon her heart, he determined that it was as immobile as the ages, and as silent as the secret of his heart.

The reverend father bowed his head in deep despair. His lips quivered as if wanting to utter a

divine word, repeated by the phantoms of the night in the distant and deserted valleys.

After crossing her arms upon her bosom, the priest looked toward a man sitting in an obscured corner of the room, and with a kind and merciful voice he said, "Your beloved has reached the great circle of light. Come, my brother, let us kneel and pray."

The sorrowful husband lifted his head; his eyes stared, gazing at the unseen, and his expression then changed as if he saw understanding in the ghost of an unknown God. He gathered the remnants of himself and walked reverently toward the bed of his wife, and knelt by the side of the clergyman who was praying and lamenting and making the sign of the cross.

Placing his hand upon the shoulder of the grief-stricken husband, the Father said quietly, "Go to the adjoining room, brother, for you are in great need of rest."

He rose obediently, walked to the room and threw his fatigued body upon a narrow bed, and in a few moments he was sailing in the world of sleep like a little child taking refuge in the merciful arms of his loving mother.

The priest remained standing like a statue in the center of the room, and a strange conflict gripped him. And he looked with tearful eyes first at the cold body of the young woman and then through

the parted curtain at her husband, who had surrendered himself to the allure of slumber. An hour, longer than an age and more terrible than Death, had already passed, and the priest was still standing between two parted souls. One was dreaming as a field dreams of the coming Spring after the tragedy of Winter, and the other was resting eternally.

Then the priest came close to the body of the young woman and knelt as if worshipping before the altar; he held her cold hand and placed it against his trembling lips, and looked at her face that was adorned with the soft veil of Death. His voice was at the same time calm as the night and deep as the chasm and faltering as with the hopes of man. And in voice he wept, "Oh Rachel, bride of my soul, hear me! At last I am able to talk! Death has opened my lips so that I can now reveal to you a secret deeper than Life itself. Pain has unpinioned my tongue and I can disclose to you my suffering, more painful than pain. Listen to the cry of my soul, Oh Pure Spirit, hovering between the earth and the firmament. Give heed to the youth who waited for you to come from the field, gazing upon you from behind the trees, in fear of your beauty. Hear the priest, who is serving God, calling to you unashamed, after you have reached the City of God. I have proved the strength of my love by concealing it!"

Having thus opened his soul, the Father leaned over and printed three long, warm, and mute kisses upon her forehead, eyes and throat, pouring forth

all his heart's secret of love and pain, and the anguish of the years. Then he suddenly withdrew to the dark corner and dropped in agony upon the floor, shaking like an Autumn leaf, as if the touch of her cold face had awakened within him the spirit to repent; whereupon he composed himself and knelt, hiding his face with his cupped hands, and he whispered softly, "God. . . . Forgive my sin; forgive my weakness, Oh Lord. I could no longer resist disclosing that which You knew. Seven years have I kept the deep secrets hidden in my heart from the spoken word, until Death came and tore them from me. Help me, Oh God, to hide this terrible and beautiful memory which brings sweetness from life and bitterness from You. Forgive me, My Lord, and forgive my weakness."

Without looking at the young woman's corpse, he continued suffering and lamenting until Dawn came and dropped a rosy veil upon those two still images, revealing the conflict of Love and Religion to one man; the peace of Life and Death to the other.

DEAD ARE MY PEOPLE

(Written in exile during the famine in Syria)

WORLD WAR I

Gone are my people, but I exist yet,
Lamenting them in my solitude. . . .
Dead are my friends, and in their
Death my life is naught but great
Disaster.

The knolls of my country are submerged
By tears and blood, for my people and
My beloved are gone, and I am here
Living as I did when my people and my
Beloved were enjoying life and the
Bounty of life, and when the hills of
My country were blessed and engulfed
By the light of the sun.

My people died from hunger, and he who
Did not perish from starvation was
Butchered with the sword; and I am
Here in this distant land, roaming
Amongst a joyful people who sleep

Upon soft beds, and smile at the days
While the days smile upon them.

My people died a painful and shameful
Death, and here am I living in plenty
And in peace.   This is deep tragedy
Ever-enacted upon the stage of my
Heart; few would care to witness this
Drama, for my people are as birds with
Broken wings, left behind by the flock.

If I were hungry and living amid my
Famished people, and persecuted among
My oppressed countrymen, the burden
Of the black days would be lighter
Upon my restless dreams, and the
Obscurity of the night would be less
Dark before my hollow eyes and my
Crying heart and my wounded soul.
For he who shares with his people
Their sorrow and agony will feel a
Supreme comfort created only by
Suffering in sacrifice. And he will
Be at peace with himself when he dies
Innocent with his fellow innocents.

But I am not living with my hungry
And persecuted people who are walking
In the procession of death toward
Martyrdom. . . . I am here beyond the
Broad seas living in the shadow of

Tranquility, and in the sunshine of
Peace. . . . I am afar from the pitiful
Arena and the distressed, and cannot
Be proud of aught, not even of my own
Tears.

What can an exiled son do for his
Starving people, and of what value
Unto them is the lamentation of an
Absent poet?

Were I an ear of corn grown in the earth
Of my country, the hungry child would
Pluck me and remove with my kernels
The hand of Death from his soul. Were
I a ripe fruit in the gardens of my
Country, the starving woman would
Gather me and sustain life. Were I
A bird flying in the sky of my country,
My hungry brother would hunt me and
Remove with the flesh of my body the
Shadow of the grave from his body.
But alas! I am not an ear of corn
Grown in the plains of Syria, nor a
Ripe fruit in the valleys of Lebanon;
This is my disaster, and this is my
Mute calamity which brings humiliation
Before my soul and before the phantoms
Of the night. . . . This is the painful
Tragedy which tightens my tongue and
Pinions my arms and arrests me usurped

Of power and of will and of action.
This is the curse burned upon my
Forehead before God and man.

And oftentime they say unto me,
"The disaster of your country is
But naught to the calamity of the
World, and the tears and blood shed
By your people are as nothing to
The rivers of blood and tears
Pouring each day and night in the
Valleys and plains of the earth. . . ."

Yes, but the death of my people is
A silent accusation; it is a crime
Conceived by the heads of the unseen
Serpents. . . . It is a songless and
Sceneless tragedy. . . . And if my
People had attacked the despots
And oppressors and died as rebels,
I would have said, "Dying for
Freedom is nobler than living in
The shadow of weak submission, for
He who embraces death with the sword
Of Truth in his hand will eternalize
With the Eternity of Truth, for Life
Is weaker than Death and Death is
Weaker than Truth.

If my nation had partaken in the war
Of all nations and had died in the

Field of battle, I would say that
The raging tempest had broken with
Its might the green branches; and
Strong death under the canopy of
The tempest is nobler than slow
Perishment in the arms of senility.
But there was no rescue from the
Closing jaws. . . . My people dropped
And wept with the crying angels.

If an earthquake had torn my
Country asunder and the earth had
Engulfed my people into its bosom,
I would have said, "A great and
Mysterious law has been moved by
The will of divine force, and it
Would be pure madness if we frail
Mortals endeavoured to probe its
Deep secrets. . . ."
But my people did not die as rebels;
They were not killed in the field
Of battle; nor did the earthquake
Shatter my country and subdue them.
Death was their only rescuer, and
Starvation their only spoils.

My people died on the cross. . . .
They died while their hands
Stretched toward the East and West,
While the remnants of their eyes

Stared at the blackness of the
Firmament. . . . They died silently,
For humanity had closed its ears
To their cry. They died because
They did not befriend their enemy.
They died because they loved their
Neighbours. They died because
They placed trust in all humanity.
They died because they did not
Oppress the oppressors. They died
Because they were the crushed
Flowers, and not the crushing feet.
They died because they were peace
Makers. They perished from hunger
In a land rich with milk and honey.
They died because the monsters of
Hell arose and destroyed all that
Their fields grew, and devoured the
Last provisions in their bins. . . .
They died because the vipers and
Sons of vipers spat out poison into
The space where the Holy Cedars and
The roses and the jasmine breathe
Their fragrance.

My people and your people, my Syrian
Brother, are dead. . . . What can be
Done for those who are dying? Our
Lamentations will not satisfy their
Hunger, and our tears will not quench

Their thirst; what can we do to save
Them from between the iron paws of
Hunger? My brother, the kindness
Which compels you to give a part of
Your life to any human who is in the
Shadow of losing his life is the only
Virtue which makes you worthy of the
Light of day and the peace of the
Night. . . . Remember, my brother,
That the coin which you drop into
The withered hand stretching toward
You is the only golden chain that
Binds your rich heart to the
Loving heart of God. . . .

THE AMBITIOUS VIOLET

THERE was a beautiful
and fragrant violet who lived placidly amongst her
friends, and swayed happily amidst the other flowers
in a solitary garden. One morning, as her crown was
embellished with beads of dew, she lifted her head
and looked about; she saw a tall and handsome rose
standing proudly and reaching high into space, like
a burning torch upon an emerald lamp.

The violet opened her blue lips and said, "What
an unfortunate am I among these flowers, and how
humble is the position I occupy in their presence!
Nature has fashioned me to be short and poor. . . .
I live very close to the earth and I cannot raise my
head toward the blue sky, or turn my face to the
sun, as the roses do."

And the rose heard her neighbour's words; she
laughed and commented, "How strange is your talk!
You are fortunate, and yet you cannot understand
your fortune. Nature has bestowed upon you fragrance and beauty which she did not grant to any
other. . . . Cast aside your thoughts and be con-

tented, and remember that he who humbles himself will be exalted, and he who exalts himself will be crushed."

The violet answered, "You are consoling me because you have that which I crave. . . . You seek to embitter me with the meaning that you are great. . . . How painful is the preaching of the fortunate to the heart of the miserable! And how severe is the strong when he stands as advisor among the weak!"

And Nature heard the conversation of the violet and the rose; she approached and said, "What has happened to you, my daughter violet? You have been humble and sweet in all your deeds and words. Has greed entered your heart and numbed your senses?" In a pleading voice, the violet answered her, saying, "Oh great and merciful mother, full of love and sympathy, I beg you, with all my heart and soul, to grant my request and allow me to be a rose for one day."

And Nature responded, "You know not what you are seeking; you are unaware of the concealed disaster behind your blind ambition. If you were a rose you would be sorry, and repentance would avail you but naught." The violet insisted, "Change me into a tall rose, for I wish to lift my head high with pride; and regardless of my fate, it will be my own doing." Nature yielded, saying, "Oh ignorant and rebellious violet, I will grant your request. But if

225

calamity befalls you, your complaint must be to yourself."

And Nature stretched forth her mysterious and magic fingers and touched the roots of the violet, who immediately turned into a tall rose, rising above all other flowers in the garden.

At eventide the sky became thick with black clouds, and the raging elements disturbed the silence of existence with thunder, and commenced to attack the garden, sending forth a great rain and strong winds. The tempest tore the branches and uprooted the plants and broke the stems of the tall flowers, sparing only the little ones who grew close to the friendly earth. That solitary garden suffered greatly from the belligerent skies, and when the storm calmed and the sky cleared, all the flowers were laid waste and none of them had escaped the wrath of Nature except the clan of small violets, hiding by the wall of the garden.

Having lifted her head and viewed the tragedy of the flowers and trees, one of the violet maidens smiled happily and called to her companions, saying, "See what the tempest has done to the haughty flowers!" Another violet said, "We are small, and live close to the earth, but we are safe from the wrath of the skies." And a third one added, "Because we are poor in height the tempest is unable to subdue us."

At that moment the queen of violets saw by her

side the converted violet, hurled to earth by the
storm and distorted upon the wet grass like a limp
soldier in a battle field. The queen of the violets
lifted her head and called to her family, saying,
"Look, my daughters, and meditate upon that which
Greed has done to the violet who became a proud
rose for one hour. Let the memory of this scene be
a reminder of your good fortune."

And the dying rose moved and gathered the remnants of her strength, and quietly said, "You are
contented and meek dullards; I have never feared
the tempest. Yesterday I, too, was satisfied and contented with Life, but Contentment has acted as a
barrier between my existence and the tempest of
Life, confining me to a sickly and sluggish peace and
tranquility of mind. I could have lived the same life
you are living now by clinging with fear to the earth.
. . . I could have waited for winter to shroud me
with snow and deliver me to Death, who will surely
claim all violets. . . . I am happy now because I
have probed outside my little world into the mystery of the Universe . . . something which you have
not yet done. I could have overlooked Greed, whose
nature is higher than mine, but as I hearkened to
the silence of the night, I heard the heavenly world
talking to this earthly world, saying, 'Ambition beyond existence is the essential purpose of our being.'
At that moment my spirit revolted and my heart
longed for a position higher than my limited existence. I realized that the abyss cannot hear the song

of the stars, and at that moment I commenced fighting against my smallness and craving for that which did not belong to me, until my rebelliousness turned into a great power, and my longing into a creating will. . . . Nature, who is the great object of our deeper dreams, granted my request and changed me into a rose with her magic fingers."

The rose became silent for a moment, and in a weakening voice, mingled with pride and achievement, she said, "I have lived one hour as a proud rose; I have existed for a time like a queen; I have looked at the Universe from behind the eyes of the rose; I have heard the whisper of the firmament through the ears of the rose and touched the folds of Light's garment with rose petals. Is there any here who can claim such honour?" Having thus spoken, she lowered her head, and with a choking voice she gasped, "I shall die now, for my soul has attained its goal. I have finally extended my knowledge to a world beyond the narrow cavern of my birth. This is the design of Life. . . . This is the secret of Existence." Then the rose quivered, slowly folded her petals, and breathed her last with a heavenly smile upon her lips . . . a smile of fulfillment of hope and purpose in Life . . . a smile of victory . . . a God's smile.

THE CRUCIFIED

Today, and on this same day of each year, man is startled from his deep slumber and stands before the phantoms of the Ages, looking with tearful eyes toward Mount Calvary to witness Jesus the Nazarene nailed on the Cross. . . . But when the day is over and eventide comes, human kinds return and kneel praying before the idols, erected upon every hilltop, every prairie, and every barter of wheat.

Today, the Christian souls ride on the wing of memories and fly to Jerusalem. There they will stand in throngs, beating upon their bosoms, and staring at Him, crowned with a wreath of thorns, stretching His arms before heaven, and looking from behind the veil of Death into the depths of Life. . . .

But when the curtain of night drops over the stage of the day and the brief drama is concluded, the Christians will go back in groups and lie down

in the shadow of oblivion between the quilts of ignorance and slothfulness.

On this one day of each year, the philosophers leave their dark caves, and the thinkers their cold cells, and the poets their imaginary arbors, and all stand reverently upon that silent mountain, listening to the voice of a young man saying of His killers, "Oh Father, forgive them, for they know not what they are doing."

But as dark silence chokes the voices of the light, the philosophers and the thinkers and the poets return to their narrow crevices and shroud their souls with meaningless pages of parchment.

The women who busy themselves in the splendour of Life will bestir themselves today from their cushions to see the sorrowful woman standing before the Cross like a tender sapling before the raging tempest; and when they approach near to her, they will hear a deep moaning and a painful grief.

The young men and women who are racing with the torrent of modern civilization will halt today for a moment, and look backward to see the young Magdalen washing with her tears the blood stains from the feet of a Holy Man suspended between Heaven and Earth; and when their shallow eyes weary of the scene they will depart and soon laugh.

On this day of each year, Humanity wakes with the awakening of the Spring, and stands crying below the suffering Nazarene; then she closes her eyes and surrenders herself to a deep slumber. But

230

Spring will remain awake, smiling and progressing until merged into Summer, dressed in scented golden raiment. Humanity is a mourner who enjoys lamenting the memories and heroes of the Ages. . . . If Humanity were possessed of understanding, there would be rejoicing over their glory. Humanity is like a child standing in glee by a wounded beast. Humanity laughs before the strengthening torrent which carries into oblivion the dry branches of the trees, and sweeps away with determination all things not fastened to strength.

Humanity looks upon Jesus the Nazarene as a poor-born Who suffered misery and humiliation with all of the weak. And He is pitied, for Humanity believes He was crucified painfully. . . . And all that Humanity offers to Him is crying and wailing and lamentation. For centuries Humanity has been worshipping weakness in the person of the Saviour.

The Nazarene was not weak! He was strong and is strong! But the people refuse to heed the true meaning of strength.

Jesus never lived a life of fear, nor did He die suffering or complaining. . . . He lived as a leader; He was crucified as a crusader; He died with a heroism that frightened His killers and tormentors.

Jesus was not a bird with broken wings; He was a raging tempest who broke all crooked wings. He feared not His persecutors nor His enemies. He suffered not before His killers. Free and brave and daring He was. He defied all despots and oppressors.

He saw the contagious pustules and amputated them. . . . He muted Evil and He crushed Falsehood and He choked Treachery.

Jesus came not from the heart of the circle of Light to destroy the homes and build upon their ruins the convents and monasteries. He did not persuade the strong man to become a monk or a priest, but He came to send forth upon this earth a new spirit, with power to crumble the foundation of any monarchy built upon human bones and skulls. . . . He came to demolish the majestic palaces, constructed upon the graves of the weak, and crush the idols, erected upon the bodies of the poor. Jesus was not sent here to teach the people to build magnificent churches and temples amidst the cold wretched huts and dismal hovels. . . . He came to make the human heart a temple, and the soul an altar, and the mind a priest.

These were the missions of Jesus the Nazarene, and these are the teachings for which He was crucified. And if Humanity were wise, she would stand today and sing in strength the song of conquest and the hymn of triumph.

Oh, Crucified Jesus, Who are looking sorrowfully from Mount Calvary at the sad procession of the Ages, and hearing the clamour of the dark nations, and understanding the dreams of Eternity . . . Thou art, on the Cross, more glorious and dignified than

one thousand kings upon one thousand thrones in one thousand empires. . . .

Thou art, in the agony of death, more powerful than one thousand generals in one thousand wars. . . .

With Thy sorrows, Thou art more joyous than Spring with its flowers. . . .

With Thy suffering, Thou art more bravely silent than the crying angels of heaven. . . .

Before Thy lashers, Thou art more resolute than the mountain of rock. . . .

Thy wreath of thorns is more brilliant and sublime than the crown of Bahram. . . . The nails piercing Thy hands are more beautiful than the sceptre of Jupiter. . . .

The spatters of blood upon Thy feet are more resplendent than the necklace of Ishtar.

Forgive the weak who lament Thee today, for they do not know how to lament themselves. . . .

Forgive them, for they do not know that Thou hast conquered death with death, and bestowed life upon the dead. . . .

Forgive them, for they do not know that Thy strength still awaits them. . . .

Forgive them, for they do not know that every day is Thy day.

EVENTIDE OF THE FEAST

Night had fallen and obscurity engulfed the city while the lights glittered in the palaces and the huts and the shops. The multitudes, wearing their festive raiment, crowded the streets and upon their faces appeared the signs of celebration and contentment.

I avoided the clamour of the throngs and walked alone, contemplating the Man Whose greatness they were honouring, and meditating the Genius of the Ages Who was born in poverty, and lived virtuously, and died on the Cross.

I was pondering the burning torch which was lighted in this humble village in Syria by the Holy Spirit. . . . The Holy Spirit Who hovers over all the ages, and penetrates one civilization and then another through His truth.

As I reached the public garden, I seated myself on a rustic bench and commenced looking between the naked trees toward the crowded streets; I listened to the hymns and songs of the celebrants.

After an hour of deep thinking, I looked sidewise

and was surprised to find a man sitting by me, holding a short branch with which he engraved vague figures on the ground. I was startled, for I had not seen nor heard his approach, but I said within myself, "He is solitary, as I am." And after looking thoroughly at him, I saw that in spite of his old-fashioned raiment and long hair, he was a dignified man, worthy of attention. It seemed that he detected the thoughts within me, for in a deep and quiet voice he said, "Good evening, my son."

"Good evening to you," I responded with respect.

And he resumed his drawing while the strangely soothing sound of his voice was still echoing in my ears. And I spoke to him again, saying, "Are you a stranger in this city?"

"Yes, I am a stranger in this city and every city," he replied. I consoled him, adding, "A stranger should forget that he is an outsider in these holidays, for there is kindness and generosity in the people." He replied wearily, "I am more a stranger in these days than in any other." Having thus spoken, he looked at the clear skies; his eyes probed the stars and his lips quivered as if he had found in the firmament an image of a distant country. His queer statement aroused my interest, and I said, "This is the time of the year when the people are kind to all other people. The rich remember the poor and the strong have compassion for the weak."

He returned, "Yes, the momentary mercy of the rich upon the poor is bitter, and the sympathy of

the strong toward the weak is naught but a reminder of superiority."

I affirmed, "Your words have merit, but the weak poor do not care to know what transpires in the heart of the rich, and the hungry never think of the method by which the bread he is craving is kneaded and baked."

And he responded, "The one who receives is not mindful, but the one who gives bears the burden of cautioning himself that it is with a view to brotherly love, and toward friendly aid, and not to self-esteem."

I was amazed at his wisdom, and again commenced to meditate upon his ancient appearance and strange garments. Then I returned mentally and said, "It appears that you are in need of help; will you accept a few coins from me?" And with a sad smile he answered me, saying, "Yes, I am in desperate need, but not of gold or silver."

Puzzled, I asked, "What is it that you require?"

"I am in need of shelter. I am in need of a place where I can rest my head and my thoughts."

"Please accept these two denars and go to the inn for lodging," I insisted.

Sorrowfully he answered, "I have tried every inn, and knocked at every door, but in vain. I have entered every food shop, but none cared to help me. I am hurt, not hungry; I am disappointed, not tired; I seek not a roof, but human shelter."

I said within myself, "What a strange person he

236

is! Once he talks like a philosopher and again like a madman!" As I whispered these thoughts into the ears of my inner self, he stared at me, lowered his voice to a sad level, and said, "Yes, I am a madman, but even a madman will find himself a stranger without shelter and hungry without food, for the heart of man is empty."

I apologized to him, saying, "I regret my unwitting thought. Would you accept my hospitality and take shelter in my quarters?"

"I knocked at your door and all the doors one thousand times, and received no answer," he answered severely.

Now I was convinced that he was truly a madman, and I suggested, "Let us go now, and proceed to my home."

He lifted his head slowly and said, "If you were aware of my identity you would not invite me to your home."

"Who are you?" I inquired, fearfully, slowly.

With a voice that sounded like the roar of the ocean, he thundered, bitterly, "I am the revolution who builds what the nations destroy. . . . I am the tempest who uproots the plants, grown by the ages. . . . I am the one who came to spread war on earth and not peace, for man is content only in misery!"

And, with tears coursing down his cheeks, he stood up high, and a mist of light grew about him, and he stretched forth his arms, and I saw the marks of the nails in the palms of his hands; I prostrated

myself before him convulsively and cried out, saying, "Oh Jesus, the Nazarene!"

And He continued, in anguish, "The people are
celebrating in My honour, pursuing the tradition
woven by the ages around My name, but as to Myself, I am a stranger wandering from East to West
upon this earth, and no one knows of Me. The foxes
have their holes, and the birds of the skies their
nests, but the Son of Man has no place to rest His
head."

At that moment, I opened my eyes, lifted my head,
and looked around, but found naught except a column of smoke before me, and I heard only the shivering voice of the silence of the night, coming from
the depths of Eternity. I collected myself and looked
again to the singing throngs in the distance, and a
voice within me said, "The very strength that protects the heart from injury is the strength that prevents the heart from enlarging to its intended greatness within. The song of the voice is sweet, but the
song of the heart is the pure voice of heaven."

THE GRAVE DIGGER

IN THE terrible silence of the night, as all heavenly things disappeared behind the grasping veil of thick clouds, I walked lonely and afraid in the Valley of the Phantoms of Death.

As midnight came, and the spectres leaped about me with their horrible, ribbed wings, I observed a giant ghost standing before me, fascinating me with his hypnotic ghastliness. In a thundering voice he said, "Your fear is two-fold! You fear being in fear of me! You cannot conceal it, for you are weaker than the thin thread of the spider. What is your earthly name?"

I leaned against a great rock, gathered myself from this sudden shock, and in a sickly, trembling voice replied, "My name is Abdallah, which means 'slave of God.'" For a few moments he remained silent with a frightening silence. I grew accustomed to his appearance, but was again shaken by his weird thoughts and words, his strange beliefs and contemplations.

He rumbled, "Numerous are the slaves of God,

and great are God's woes with His slaves. Why did not your father call you 'Master of Demons' instead, adding one more disaster to the huge calamity of earth? You cling with terror to the small circle of gifts from your ancestors, and your affliction is caused by your parents' bequest, and you will remain a slave of death until you become one of the dead.

"Your vocations are wasteful and deserted, and your lives are hollow. Real life has never visited you, nor will it; neither will your deceitful self realize your living death. Your illusioned eyes see the people quivering before the tempest of life and you believe them to be alive, while in truth they have been dead since they were born. There were none who would bury them, and the one good career for you is that of grave digger, and as such you may rid the few living of the corpses heaped about the homes, the paths, and the churches."

I protested, "I cannot pursue such a vocation. My wife and children require my support and companionship."

He leaned toward me, showing his braided muscles that seemed as the roots of a strong oak tree, abounding with life and energy, and he bellowed, "Give to each a spade and teach them to dig graves; your life is naught but black misery hidden behind walls of white plaster. Join us, for we genii are the only possessors of reality! The digging of graves brings a slow but positive benefit which causes the

vanishing of the dead creatures who tremble with the storm and never walk with it." He mused and then inquired, "What is your religion?"

Bravely I stated, "I believe in God and I honour His prophets; I love virtue and I have faith in eternity."

With remarkable wisdom and conviction he responded, "These empty words were placed on human lips by past ages and not by knowledge, and you actually believe in yourself only; and you honour none but yourself, and you have faith only in the eternity of your desires. Man has worshipped his own self since the beginning, calling that self by appropriate titles, until now, when he employs the word 'God' to mean that same self." Then the giant roared with laughter, the echoes reverberating through the hollows of the caverns, and he taunted, "How strange are those who worship their own selves, their real existence being naught but earthly carcasses!"

He paused, and I contemplated his sayings and meditated their meanings. He possessed a knowledge stranger than life and more terrible than death, and deeper than truth. Timidly, I ventured, "Do you have a religion or a God?"

"My name is The Mad God," he offered, "and I was born at all times, and I am the god of my own self. I am not wise, for wisdom is a quality of the weak. I am strong, and the earth moves under the steps of my feet, and when I stop, the procession of

stars stops with me. I mock at the people. . . . I accompany the giants of night. . . . I mingle with the
great kings of the genii. . . . I am in possession of
the secrets of existence and non-existence.

"In the morning I blaspheme the sun . . . at noontide I curse humanity . . . at eventide I submerge
nature . . . at night I kneel and worship myself. I
never sleep, for I am time, the sea, and myself. . . .
I eat human bodies for food, drink their blood to
quench my thirst, and use their dying gasps to draw
my breath. Although you deceive yourself, you are
my brother and you live as I do. Begone . . . hypocrite! Crawl back to earth and continue to worship
your own self amid the living dead!"

I staggered from the rocky, cavernous valley in
narcotic bewilderment, scarcely believing what my
ears had heard and my eyes had seen! I was torn in
pain by some of the truths he had spoken, and wandered trough the fields all that night in melancholy
contemplation.

I procured a spade and said within myself, "Dig
deeply the graves. . . . Go, now, and wherever you
find one of the living dead, bury him in the earth."

Since that day I have been digging graves and
burying the living dead. But the living dead are
numerous and I am alone, having none to aid me. . . .

HONEYED POISON

IT WAS a beautiful morn of dizzying brilliance in North Lebanon when the people of the village of Tula gathered around the portico of the small church that stood in the midst of their dwellings. They were discussing busily the sudden and unexplained departure of Farris Rahal, who left behind his bride of but half a year.

Farris Rahal was the Sheik and leader of the village, and he had inherited this honourable status from his ancestors who had ruled over Tula for centuries. Although he was not quite twenty-seven years of age, he possessed an outstanding ability and sincerity that won the admiration, reverence, and respect of all the fellahin. When Farris married Susan, the people commented upon him, saying, "What a fortunate man is Farris Rahal! He has attained all that man can hope for in the bounty of life's happiness, and he is but a youth!"

That morning, when all of Tula arose from slumber and learned that the Sheik had gathered his gold, mounted his steed and left the village bidding

none farewell, curiosity and concern prevailed, and inquiries were many as to the cause that prompted him to desert his wife and his home, his lands and his vineyards.

By reason of tradition and geography, life in North Lebanon is highly sociable, and the people share their joys and sorrows, provoked by humble spirit and instinctive clannishness. Upon any occurrence, the entire populace of the village convenes to inquire upon the incident, offers all possible assistance, and returns to labour until fate again offers a congregant mission.

It was such a matter that drew the people of Tula from their work that day, and caused them to gather about the church of Mar Tula discussing the departure of their Sheik and exchanging views upon its singularity.

It was at this time that Father Estephan, head of the local church, arrived, and upon his drawn countenance one could read the unmistakable signs of deep suffering, the signs of a painfully wounded spirit. He contemplated the scene for a moment and then spoke. "Do not ask . . . do not ask any question of me! Before daybreak this day, Sheik Farris knocked upon the door of my house, and I saw him holding the rein of his horse, and from his face emanated grave sorrow and agonized grief. Upon my remark as to the strangeness of the hour, he replied, 'Father, I come to bid you farewell, for I am

sailing beyond the oceans and will never again return to this land.' And he handed to me a sealed
envelope, addressed to his dearest friend Nabih
Malik, asking me to deliver it. He mounted his steed
and sped off to the east, affording me no further opportunity to understand the purpose of his unusual
departure."

One of the villagers observed, "Undoubtedly the
missive will reveal to us the secret of his going, for
Nabih is his closest friend." Another added, "Have
you seen his bride, Father?" The priest replied, saying, "I visited her after the morning prayer and
found her standing at the window, staring with unseeing eyes at something invisible, appearing as one
who has lost all senses, and when I endeavoured to
ask concerning Farris she merely said, 'I do not
know! I do not know!' Then she wept like a child
who suddenly becomes an orphan."

As the father concluded talking, the group tightened with fear at the startling report of a gunshot
coming from the east portion of the village, and it
was followed immediately by the bitter wailing of a
woman. The throng was in a dismayed trance of im-
mobility for a moment, and then, men, women and
children, all ran toward the scene, and upon their
faces there was a dark mask of fear and evil omen.
As they reached the garden that surrounded the
Sheik's residence, they became witness to a most horrible drama, portrayed with death. Nabih Malik
was lying on the ground, a stream of blood issuing

from his breast, and by him stood Susan, wife of the
Sheik Farris Rahal, tearing her hair and shredding
her raiment and flailing her arms about and shrieking wildly, "Nabih . . . Nabih . . . why did you do
it!"

The onlookers were astounded, and it was as
though the unseen hands of fate had clutched with
icy fingers at their hearts. The priest found in the
dead Nabih's right hand the note he had delivered
that morning, and he placed it deftly into his robe
without notice by the milling multitude.

Nabih was carried to his miserable mother, who,
upon seeing the lifeless body of her only son, lost her
sanity in shock and soon joined him in Eternity.
Susan was led slowly into her home, wavering between faltering life and grasping death.

As Father Estephan reached his home, under bent
shoulders, he fastened the door, adjusted his reading
glasses, and in a quivering whisper commenced reading to himself the message he had taken from the
hand of the departed Nabih.

"My Dearest Friend Nabih,
"I must leave this village of my fathers, for my
continued presence is casting misery upon you and
upon my wife and upon myself. You are noble in
spirit, and scorn the betrayal of friend or neighbour,
and although I know that Susan is innocent and
virtuous, I know also that the true love which unites
your heart and her heart is beyond your power and

beyond my hopes. I cannot struggle longer against the mighty will of God, as I cannot halt the strong flow of the great Kadeesha River.

"You have been my sincere friend, Nabih, since we played as children in the fields; and before God, believe me, you remain my friend, I beg you to ponder with good thoughts upon me in the future as you did in the past. Tell Susan that I love her and that I wronged her by taking her in empty marriage. Tell her that my heart bled in burning pain each time I turned from restless sleep in the silence of the night and observed her kneeling before the shrine of Jesus, weeping and beating upon her bosom in anguish.

"There is no punishment so severe as that suffered by the woman who finds herself imprisoned between a man she loves and another man who loves her. Susan suffered through a constant and painful conflict, but performed sorrowfully and honourably and silently her duties as a wife. She tried, but could not choke her honest love for you.

"I am leaving for distant lands and will never again return, for I can no longer act as barrier to a genuine and eternal love, embraced by the enfolded arms of God; and may God, in his inscrutable wisdom, protect and bless both of you.

FARRIS"

Father Estephan folded the letter, returned it to his pocket, and sat by the window that opened upon

the distant valley. He sailed long and deep in a great ocean of contemplation, and after wise and intense meditation, he stood suddenly, as if he had found between the plaited folds of his intricate thoughts a delicate and horrible secret, disguised with diabolical slyness, and wrapped with elaborate cunning! He cried out, "How sagacious you are, Farris! How massive, yet simple, is your crime! You sent to him honey blended with fatal poison, and enclosed death in a letter! And when Nabih pointed the weapon at his heart, it was your finger that discharged the missile, and it was your will that engulfed his will. . . . How clever you are, Farris!"

He returned quivering to his chair, shaking his head and combing his beard with his fingers, and upon his lips appeared a smile whose meaning was more terrible than the tragedy itself. He opened his prayer book and commenced reading and pondering, and at intervals he raised his head to hear the wailing and lamentation of the women, coming from the heart of the village of Tula, close by the Holy Cedars of Lebanon.

SPIRITS
REBELLIOUS

MADAME ROSE HANIE

PART ONE

ISERABLE is the man who loves a woman and takes her for a wife, pouring at her feet the sweat of his skin and the blood of his body and the life of his heart, and placing in her hands the fruit of his toil and the revenue of his diligence; for when he slowly wakes up, he finds that the heart, which he endeavoured to buy, is given freely and in sincerity to another man for the enjoyment of its hidden secrets and deepest love. Miserable is the woman who arises from the inattentiveness and restlessness of youth and finds herself in the home of a man showering her with his glittering gold and precious gifts and according her all the honors and grace of lavish entertainment but unable to satisfy her soul with the heavenly wine which God pours from the eyes of a man into the heart of a woman.

I knew Rashid Bey Namaan since I was a youngster; he was a Lebanese, born and reared in the City of Beyrouth. Being a member of an old and rich

family which preserved the tradition and glory of
his ancestry, Rashid was fond of citing incidents
that dealt mainly with the nobility of his forefathers.
In his routine life he followed their beliefs and
customs which, at that time, prevailed in the Middle
East.

Rashid Bey Namaan was generous and good-
hearted, but like many of the Syrians, looked only
at the superficial things instead of reality. He never
hearkened to the dictates of his heart, but busied
himself in obeying the voices of his environment.
He amused himself with shimmering objects that
blinded his eyes and heart to life's secrets; his soul
was diverted away from an understanding of the law
of nature, and to a temporary self-gratification. He
was one of those men who hastened to confess their
love or disgust to the people, then regretted their
impulsiveness when it was too late for recall. And
then shame and ridicule befell them, instead of pardon or sanction.

These are the characteristics that prompted
Rashid Bey Namaan to marry Rose Hanie far before her soul embraced his soul in the shadow of the
true love that makes union a paradise.

After a few years of absence, I returned to the City
of Beyrouth. As I went to visit Rashid Bey Namaan,
I found him pale and thin. On his face one could
see the spectre of bitter disappointment; his sorrowful eyes bespoke his crushed heart and melancholy

soul. I was curious to find the cause for his miserable plight; however, I did not hesitate to ask for explanation and said, "What became of you, Rashid? Where is the radiant smile and the happy countenance that accompanied you since childhood? Has death taken away from you a dear friend? Or have the black nights stolen from you the gold you have amassed during the white days? In the name of friendship, tell me what is causing this sadness of heart and weakness of body?"

He looked at me ruefully, as if I had revived to him some secluded images of beautiful days. With a distressed and faltering voice he responded, "When a person loses a friend, he consoles himself with the many other friends about him, and if he loses his gold, he meditates for a while and casts misfortune from his mind, especially when he finds himself healthy and still laden with ambition. But when a man loses the ease of his heart, where can he find comfort, and with what can he replace it? What mind can master it? When Death strikes close by, you will suffer. But when the day and night pass, you will feel the smooth touch of the soft fingers of Life; then you will smile and rejoice.

"Destiny comes suddenly, bringing concern; she stares at you with horrible eyes and clutches you at the throat with sharp fingers and hurls you to the ground and tramples upon you with ironclad feet; then she laughs and walks away, but later regrets her actions and asks you through good fortune to for-

give her. She stretches forth her silky hand and lifts you high and sings to you the Song of Hope and causes you to lose your cares. She creates in you a new zest for confidence and ambition. If your lot in life is a beautiful bird that you love dearly, you gladly feed to him the seeds of your inner self, and make your heart his cage and your soul his nest. But while you are affectionately admiring him and looking upon him with the eyes of love, he escapes from your hands and flies very high; then he descends and enters into another cage and never comes back to you. What can you do? Where can you find patience and condolence? How can you revive your hopes and dreams? What power can still your turbulent heart?"

Having uttered these words with a choking voice and suffering spirit, Rashid Bey Namaan stood shaking like a reed between the north and south wind. He extended his hands as if to grasp something with his bent fingers and destroy it. His wrinkled face was livid, his eyes grew larger as he stared a few moments, and it seemed to him as if he saw a demon appearing from nonexistence to take him away; then he fixed his eyes on mine and his appearance suddenly changed; his anger was converted into keen suffering and distress, and he cried out saying, "It is the woman whom I rescued from between the deathly paws of poverty; I opened my coffers to her and made her envied by all women for the beautiful raiment and precious gems and magnificent carriages drawn by spirited horses; the woman whom

my heart has loved and at whose feet I poured my affection; the woman, to whom I was a true friend, sincere companion and a faithful husband; the woman who betrayed me and departed me for another man to share with him destitution and partake his evil bread, kneaded with shame and mixed with disgrace. The woman I loved; the beautiful bird whom I fed, and to whom I made my heart a cage, and my soul a nest, has escaped from my hands and entered into another cage; that pure angel, who resided in the paradise of my affection and love, now appears to me as a horrible demon, descended into the darkness to suffer for her sin and cause me to suffer on earth for her crime."

He hid his face with his hands as if wanting to protect himself from himself, and became silent for a moment. Then he sighed and said, "This is all I can tell you; please do not ask anything further. Do not make a crying voice of my calamity, but let it rather be mute misfortune; perhaps it will grow in silence and deaden me away so that I may rest at last with peace."

I rose with tears in my eyes and mercy in my heart, and silently bade him goodbye; my words had no power to console his wounded heart, and my knowledge had no torch to illuminate his gloomy self.

PART TWO

A few days thereafter I met Madame Rose Hanie for the first time, in a poor hovel, surrounded by

flowers and trees. She had heard of me through Rashid Bey Namaan, the man whose heart she had crushed and stamped upon and left under the terrible hoofs of Life. As I looked at her beautiful bright eyes, and heard her sincere voice, I said to myself, "Can this be the sordid woman? Can this clear face hide an ugly soul and a criminal heart? Is this the unfaithful wife? Is this the woman of whom I have spoken evil and imagined as a serpent disguised in the form of a beautiful bird?" Then I whispered again to myself saying, "Is it this beautiful face that made Rashid Bey Namaan miserable? Haven't we heard that obvious beauty is the cause of many hidden distresses and deep suffering? Is not the beautiful moon, that inspires the poets, the same moon that angers the silence of the sea with a terrible roar?"

As we seated ourselves, Madame Hanie seemed to have heard and read my thoughts and wanted not to prolong my doubts. She leaned her beautiful head upon her hands and with a voice sweeter than the sound of the lyre, she said, "I have never met you, but I heard the echoes of your thoughts and dreams from the mouths of the people, and they convinced me that you are merciful and have understanding for the oppressed woman—the woman whose heart's secrets you have discovered and whose affections you have known. Allow me to reveal to you the full contents of my heart so you may know that Rose Hanie never was an unfaithful woman.

"I was scarcely eighteen years of age when fate led me to Rashid Bey Namaan, who was then forty years old. He fell in love with me, according to what the people say, and took me for a wife and put me in his magnificent home, placing at my disposal servants and maids and dressing me with expensive clothes and precious gems. He exhibited me as a strange rarity at the homes of his friends and family; he smiled with triumph when he saw his contemporaries looking upon me with surprise and admiration; he lifted his chin high with pride when he heard the ladies speak of me with praise and affection. But never could he hear the whispers, 'Is this the wife of Rashid Bey Namaan, or his adopted daughter?' And another one commenting, 'If he had married at the proper age, his first born would have been older than Rose Hanie.'

"All that happened before my life had awakened from the deep swoon of youth, and before God inflamed my heart with the torch of love, and before the growth of the seeds of my affections. Yes, all this transpired during the time when I believed that real happiness came through beautiful clothes and magnificent mansions. When I woke up from the slumber of childhood, I felt the flames of sacred fire burning in my heart, and a spiritual hunger gnawing at my soul, making it suffer. When I opened my eyes, I found my wings moving to the right and left, trying to ascend into the spacious firmament of love, but shivering and dropping under the gusts of the

shackles of laws that bound my body to a man before I knew the true meaning of that law. I felt all these things and knew that a woman's happiness does not come through man's glory and honour, nor through his generosity and affection, but through love that unites both of their hearts and affections, making them one member of life's body and one word upon the lips of God. When Truth showed herself to me, I found myself imprisoned by law in the mansion of Rashid Bey Nemaan, like a thief stealing his bread and hiding in the dark and friendly corners of the night. I knew that every hour spent with him was a terrible lie written upon my forehead with letters of fire before heaven and earth. I could not give him my love and affection in reward for his generosity and sincerity. I tried in vain to love him, but love is a power that makes our hearts, yet our hearts cannot make that power. I prayed and prayed in the silence of the night before God to create in the depths of my heart a spiritual attachment that would carry me closer to the man who had been chosen for me as a companion through life.

"My prayers were not granted, because Love descends upon our souls by the will of God and not by the demand or the plea of the individual. Thus I remained for two years in the home of that man, envying the birds of the field their freedom while my friends envied me my painful chains of gold. I was like a woman who is torn from her only child; like a lamenting heart, existing without attachment;

like an innocent victim of the severity of human law. I was close to death from spiritual thirst and hunger.

"One dark day, as I looked behind the heavy skies, I saw a gentle light pouring from the eyes of a man who was walking forlornly on the path of life; I closed my eyes to that light and said to myself, 'Oh, my soul, darkness of the grave is thy lot, do not be greedy for the light.' Then I heard a beautiful melody from heaven that revived my wounded heart with its purity, but I closed my ears and said, 'Oh, my soul, the cry of the abyss is thy lot, do not be greedy for heavenly songs.' I closed my eyes again so I could not see, and shut my ears so I could not hear, but my closed eyes still saw that gentle light, and my ears still heard that divine sound. I was frightened for the first time and felt like the beggar who found a precious jewel near the Emir's palace and could not pick it up on account of fear, or leave it because of poverty. I cried—a cry of a thirsty soul who sees a brook surrounded by wild beasts, and falls upon the ground waiting and watching fearfully."

Then she turned her eyes away from me as if she remembered the past that made her ashamed to face me, but she continued, "Those people who go back to eternity before they taste the sweetness of real life are unable to understand the meaning of a woman's suffering. Especially when she devotes her soul to a man she loves by the will of God, and her body to another whom she caresses by the enforce-

ment of earthly law. It is a tragedy written with the woman's blood and tears which the man reads with ridicule because he cannot understand it; yet, if he does understand, his laughter will turn into scorn and blasphemy that act like fire upon her heart. It is a drama enacted by the black nights upon the stage of a woman's soul, whose body is tied up into a man, known to her as husband, ere she perceives God's meaning of marriage. She finds her soul hovering about the man whom she adores by all agencies of pure and true love and beauty. It is a terrible agony that began with the existence of weakness in a woman and the commencement of strength in a man. It will not end unless the days of slavery and superiority of the strong over the weak are abolished. It is a horrible war between the corrupt law of humanity and the sacred affections and holy purpose of the heart. In such a battlefield I was lying yesterday, but I gathered the remnants of my strength, and unchained my irons of cowardice, and untied my wings from the swaddles of weakness and arose into the spacious sky of love and freedom.

"Today I am one with the man I love; he and I sprang out as one torch from the hand of God before the beginning of the world. There is no power under the sun that can take my happiness from me, because it emanated from two embraced spirits, engulfed by understanding, radiated by Love, and protected by heaven."

She looked at me as if she wanted to penetrate

my heart with her eyes in order to discover the
impression of her words upon me, and to hear the
echo of her voice from within me; but I remained
silent and she continued. Her voice was full of
bitterness of memory and sweetness of sincerity and
freedom when she said, "The people will tell you
that Rose Hanie is an heretic and unfaithful woman
who followed her desires by leaving the man who
elated her into him and made her the elegance of
his home. They will tell you that she is an adulteress
and prostitute who destroyed with her filthy hands
the wreath of a sacred marriage and replaced it with
a besmirched union woven of the thorns of hell.
She took off the garment of virtue and put on the
cloak of sin and disgrace. They will tell you more
than that, because the ghosts of their fathers are still
living in their bodies. They are like the deserted
caves of the mountains that echo voices whose meanings are not understood. They neither understand
the law of God, nor comprehend the true intent of
veritable religion, nor distinguish between a sinner
and an innocent. They look only at the surface of
objects without knowing their secrets. They pass
their verdicts with ignorance, and judge with blindness, making the criminal and the innocent, the
good and the bad, equal. Woe to those who prosecute and judge the people. . . .

"In God's eyes I was unfaithful and an adulteress
only while at the home of Rashid Bey Namaan,
because he made me his wife according to the cus-

toms and traditions and by the force of haste, before heaven had made him mine in conformity with the spiritual law of Love and Affection. I was a sinner in the eyes of God and myself when I ate his bread and offered him my body in reward for his generosity. Now I am pure and clean because the law of Love has freed me and made me honourable and faithful. I ceased selling my body for shelter and my days for clothes. Yes, I was an adulteress and a criminal when the people viewed me as the most honourable and faithful wife; today I am pure and noble in spirit, but in their opinion I am polluted, for they judge the soul by the outcome of the body and measure the spirit by the standard of matter."

Then she looked through the window and pointed out with her right hand toward the city as if she had seen the ghost of corruption and the shadow of shame among its magnificent buildings. She said pityingly, "Look at those majestic mansions and sublime palaces where hypocrisy resides; in those edifices and between their beautifully decorated walls resides Treason beside Putridity; under the ceiling painted with melted gold lives Falsehood beside Pretension. Notice those gorgeous homes that represent happiness, glory and domination; they are naught but caverns of misery and distress. They are plastered graves in which Treason of the weak woman hides behind her kohled eyes and crimsoned lips; in their corners selfishness exists, and the ani-

mality of man through his gold and silver rules supreme.

"If those high and impregnable buildings scented the odor of hatred, deceit and corruption, they would have cracked and fallen. The poor villager looks upon those residences with tearful eyes, but when he finds that the hearts of the occupants are empty of that pure love that exists in the heart of his wife and fills its domain, he will smile and go back to his fields contented."

And then she took hold of my hand and led me to the side of the window and said, "Come, I will show you the unveiled secrets of those people whose path I refused to follow. Look at that palace with giant columns. In it lives a rich man who inherited his gold from his father. After having led a life of filth and putrefaction, he married a woman about whom he knew nothing except that her father was one of the Sultan's dignitaries. As soon as the wedding trip was over he became disgusted and commenced associations with women who sell their bodies for pieces of silver. His wife was left alone in that palace like an empty bottle left by a drunkard. She cried and suffered for the first time; then she realized that her tears were more precious than her degenerate husband. Now she is busying herself in the love and devotion of a young man upon whom she showers her joyous hours, and into whose heart she pours her sincere love and affection.

"Let me take you now to that gorgeous home sur-

rounded by beautiful gardens. It is the home of a man who comes from a noble family which ruled the country for many generations, but whose standards, wealth, and prestige have declined due to their indulgence in mad spending and slothfulness. A few years ago this man married an ugly but rich woman. After he acquired her fortune, he ignored her completely and commenced devoting himself to an attractive young woman. His wife today is devoting her time to curling her hair, painting her lips and perfuming her body. She wears the most expensive clothes and hopes that some young man will smile and come to visit her, but it is all in vain, for she cannot succeed except in receiving a smile from her ugly self in the mirror.

"Observe that big manor, encircled with marble statuary; it is the home of a beautiful woman who possesses strange character. When her first husband died, she inherited all his money and estates; then she selected a man with a weak mind and feeble body and became his wife to protect herself from the evil tongues, and to use him as a shield for her abominations. She is now among her admirers like a bee that sucks the sweetest and most delicious flowers.

"That beautiful home next to it was built by the greatest architect in the province; it belongs to a greedy and substantial man who devotes all of his time to amassing gold and grinding the faces of the poor. He has a wife of supernatural beauty, bodily

and spiritually, but she is like the rest, a victim of early marriage. Her father committed a crime by giving her away to a man before she attained understanding age, placing on her neck the heavy yoke of corrupt marriage. She is thin and pale now, and cannot find an outlet for her imprisoned affection. She is sinking slowly and craving for death to free her from the mesh of slavery and deliver her from a man who spends his life gathering gold and cursing the hour he married a barren woman who could not bring him a child to carry on his name and inherit his money.

"In that home among those orchards lives an ideal poet; he married an ignorant woman who ridicules his works because she cannot understand them, and laughs at his conduct because she cannot adjust herself to his sublime way of life. That poet found freedom from despair in his love for a married woman who appreciates his intelligence and inspires him by kindling in his heart the torch of affections, and revealing to him the most beautiful and eternal sayings by means of her charm and beauty."

Silence prevailed for a few moments, and Madame Hanie seated herself on a sofa by the window as if her soul were tired of roaming those quarters. Then she slowly continued, "These are the residences in which I refused to live; these are the graves in which I, too, was spiritually buried. Those people from whom I have freed myself are the ones who become attracted by the body and repelled by the spirit, and

who know naught of Love and Beauty. The only mediator between them and God is God's pity for their ignorance of the law of God. I cannot judge, for I was one of them, but I sympathize with all my heart. I do not hate them, but I hate their surrender to weakness and falsehood. I have said all these things to show you the reality of people from whom I have escaped against their will. I was trying to explain to you the life of persons who speak every evil against me because I have lost their friendship and finally gained my own. I emerged from their dark dungeon and directed my eyes towards the light where sincerity, truth and justice prevail. They have exiled me now from their society and I am pleased, because humanity does not exile except the one whose noble spirit rebels against despotism and oppression. He who does not prefer exile to slavery is not free by any measure of freedom, truth and duty.

"Yesterday I was like a tray containing all kinds of palatable food, and Rashid Bey Namaan never approached me unless he felt a need for that food; yet both of our souls remained far apart from us like two humble, dignified servants. I have tried to reconcile myself to what people call misfortune, but my spirit refused to spend all its life kneeling with me before a horrible idol erected by the dark ages and called Law. I kept my chains until I heard Love calling me and saw my spirit preparing to embark. Then I broke them and walked out from Rashid Bey Namaan's home like a bird freed from his iron cage and

leaving behind me all the gems, clothes and servants. I came to live with my beloved, for I knew that what I was doing was honest. Heaven does not want me to weep and suffer. Many times at night I prayed for dawn to come and when dawn came, I prayed for the day to be over. God does not want me to lead a miserable life, for He placed in the depths of my heart a desire for happiness; His glory rests in the happiness of my heart.

"This is my story and this my protest before heaven and earth; this is what I sing and repeat while the people are closing their ears for fear of hearing me and leading their spirits into rebellion that would crumble the foundation of their quavering society.

"This is the rough pathway I have carved until I reached the mountain peak of my happiness. Now if death comes to take me away, I will be more than willing to offer myself before the Supreme Throne of Heaven without fear or shame. I am ready for the day of judgment and my heart is white as the snow. I have obeyed the will of God in everything I have done and followed the call of my heart while listening to the angelic voice of heaven. This is my drama which the people of Beyrouth call 'A curse upon the lips of life,' and 'An ailment in the body of society.' But one day love will arouse their hearts like the sun rays that bring forth the flowers even from contaminated earth. One day the wayfarers will stop by my grave and greet the earth that enfolds my body and say, 'Here lies Rose Hanie who freed herself

from the slavery of decayed human laws in order to comply with God's law of pure love. She turned her face toward the sun so she would not see the shadow of her body amongst the skulls and thorns.' "

The door was opened and a man entered. His eyes were shining with magic rays and upon his lips appeared a wholesome smile. Madame Hanie rose, took the young man's arm and introduced him to me, then gave him my name with flattering words. I knew that he was the one for whose sake she denied the whole world and violated all earthly laws and customs.

As we sat down, silence controlled. Each one of us was engrossed in deep thought. One minute worthy of silence and respect had passed when I looked at the couple sitting side by side. I saw something I had never seen before, and realized instantly the meaning of Madame Hanie's story. I comprehended the secret of her protest against the society which persecutes those who rebel against confining laws and customs before determining the cause for the rebellion. I saw one heavenly spirit before me, composed of two beautiful and united persons, in the midst of which stood the god of Love stretching his wings over them to protect them from evil tongues. I found a complete understanding emanating from two smiling faces, illuminated by sincerity and surrounded by virtue. For the first time in my life I found the phantom of happiness standing between a man and

a woman, cursed by religion and opposed by the law. I rose and bade them goodbye and left that poor hovel which Affection had erected as an altar to Love and Understanding. I walked past the buildings which Madame Hanie pointed out to me. As I reached the end of these quarters I remembered Rashid Bey Namaan and meditated his miserable plight and said to myself, "He is oppressed; will heaven ever listen to him if he complains about Madame Hanie? Had that woman done wrong when she left him and followed the freedom of her heart? Or did he commit a crime by subduing her body in marriage before subduing her heart in love? Which of the two is the oppressed and which is the oppressor? Who is the criminal and who is the innocent?"

Then I resumed talking to myself after a few moments of deep thinking. "Many times deception had tempted woman to leave her husband and follow wealth, because her love for riches and beautiful raiment blinds her and leads her into shame. Was Madame Hanie deceitful when she left her rich husband's palace for a poor man's hut? Many times ignorance kills a woman's honour and revives her passion; she grows tired and leaves her husband, prompted by her desires, and follows a man to whom she lowers herself. Was Madame Hanie an ignorant woman following her physical desires when she declared publicly her independence and joined her beloved young man? She could have satisfied herself

secretly while at her husband's home, for many men were willing to be the slaves of her beauty and martyrs of her love. Madame Hanie was a miserable woman. She sought only happiness, found it, and embraced it. This is the very truth which society disrespects." Then I whispered through the ether and inquired of myself, "Is it permissible for a woman to buy her happiness with her husband's misery?" And my soul added, "Is it lawful for a man to enslave his wife's affection when he realizes he will never possess it?"

I continued walking and Madame Hanie's voice was still sounding in my ears when I reached the extreme end of the city. The sun was disappearing and silence ruled the fields and prairies while the birds commenced singing their evening prayers. I stood there meditating, and then I sighed and said, "Before the throne of Freedom, the trees rejoice with the frolicsome breeze and enjoy the rays of the sun and the beams of the moon. Through the ears of Freedom these birds whisper and around Freedom they flutter to the music of the brooks. Throughout the sky of Freedom these flowers breathe their fragrance and before Freedom's eyes they smile when dawn comes.

"Everything on earth lives according to the law of nature, and from that law emerges the glory and joy of liberty; but man is denied this fortune, because he set for the God-given soul a limited and earthly

law of his own. He made for himself strict rules. Man built a narrow and painful prison in which he secluded his affections and desires. He dug out a deep grave in which he buried his heart and its purpose. If an individual, through the dictates of his soul, declares his withdrawal from society and violates the law, his fellowmen will say he is a rebel worthy of exile, or an infamous creature worthy only of execution. Will man remain a slave of self-confinement until the end of the world? Or will he be freed by the passing of time and live in the Spirit for the Spirit? Will man insist upon staring downward and backward at the earth? Or will he turn his eyes toward the sun so he will not see the shadow of his body amongst the skulls and thorns?"

THE CRY OF THE GRAVES

PART ONE

THE EMIR walked into the court room and took the central chair while at his right and left sat the wise men of the country. The guards, armed with swords and spears, stood in attention, and the people who came to witness the trial rose and bowed ceremoniously to the Emir whose eyes emanated a power that revealed horror to their spirits and fear to their hearts. As the court came to order and the hour of judgment approached, the Emir raised his hand and shouted saying, "Bring forth the criminals singly and tell me what crimes they have committed." The prison door opened like the mouth of a ferocious yawning beast. In the obscure corners of the dungeon one could hear the echo of shackles rattling in unison with the moaning and lamentations of the prisoners. The spectators were eager to see the prey of Death emerging from the depths of that inferno. A few moments later, two soldiers came out leading a young man with his arms pinioned behind his back. His stern

face bespoke nobility of spirit and strength of the heart. He was halted in the middle of the court room and the soldiers marched a few steps to the rear. The Emir stared at him steadily and said, "What crime has this man, who is proudly and triumphantly standing before me, committed?" One of the courtmen responded, "He is a murderer; yesterday he slew one of the Emir's officers who was on an important mission in the surrounding villages; he was still grasping the bloody sword when he was arrested." The Emir retorted with anger, "Return the man to the dark prison and tie him with heavy chains, and at dawn cut off his head with his own sword and throw his body in the woods so that the beasts may eat the flesh, and the air may carry its remindful odor into the noses of his family and friends." The youth was returned to prison while the people looked upon him with sorrowful eyes, for he was a young man in the spring of life.

The soldiers returned back again from the prison leading a young woman of natural and frail beauty. She looked pale and upon her face appeared the signs of oppression and disappointment. Her eyes were soaked with tears and her head was bent under the burden of grief. After eyeing her thoroughly, the Emir exclaimed, "And this emaciated woman, who is standing before me like the shadow beside a corpse, what has she done?" One of the soldiers answered him, saying, "She is an adulteress; last night her husband discovered her in the arms of another.

After her lover escaped, her husband turned her over to the law." The Emir looked at her while she raised her face without expression, and he ordered, "Take her back to the dark room and stretch her upon a bed of thorns so she may remember the resting place which she polluted with her fault; give her vinegar mixed with gall to drink so she may remember the taste of those sweet kisses. At dawn drag her naked body outside the city and stone her. Let the wolves enjoy the tender meat of her body and the worms pierce her bones." As she walked back to the dark cell, the people looked upon her with sympathy and surprise. They were astonished with the Emir's justice and grieved over her fate. The soldiers reappeared, bringing with them a sad man with shaking knees and trembling like a tender sapling before the north wind. He looked powerless, sickly and frightened, and he was miserable and poor. The Emir stared at him loathfully and inquired, "And this filthy man, who is like dead amongst the living; what has he done?" One of the guards returned, "He is a thief who broke into the monastery and stole the sacred vases which the priests found under his garment when they arrested him."

As a hungry eagle who looks at a bird with broken wings, the Emir looked at him and said, "Take him back to the jail and chain him, and at dawn drag him into a lofty tree and hang him between heaven and earth so his sinful hands may perish and the members of his body may be turned into particles and

scattered by the wind." As the thief stumbled back into the depths of the prison, the people commenced whispering one to another saying, "How dare such a weak and heretic man steal the sacred vases of the monastery?"

At this time the court adjourned and the Emir walked out accompanied by all his wise men, guarded by the soldiers, while the audience scattered and the place became empty except of the moaning and wailing of the prisoners. All this happened while I was standing there like a mirror before passing ghosts. I was meditating the laws, made by man for man, contemplating what the people call "justice," and engrossing myself with deep thoughts of the secrets of life. I tried to understand the meaning of the universe. I was dumbfounded in finding myself lost like a horizon that disappears beyond the cloud. As I left the place I said to myself, "The vegetable feeds upon the elements of the earth, the sheep eats the vegetable, the wolf preys upon the sheep, and the bull kills the wolf while the lion devours the bull; yet Death claims the lion. Is there any power that will overcome Death and make these brutalities an eternal justice? Is there a force that can convert all the ugly things into beautiful objects? Is there any might that can clutch with its hands all the elements of life and embrace them with joy as the sea joyfully engulfs all the brooks into its depths? Is there any power that can arrest the murdered and the murderer, the adulteress and the adulterer, the robber

and the robbed, and bring them to a court loftier and more supreme than the court of the Emir?"

PART TWO

The next day I left the city for the fields where silence reveals to the soul that which the spirit desires, and where the pure sky kills the germs of despair, nursed in the city by the narrow streets and obscured places. When I reached the valley, I saw a flock of crows and vultures soaring and descending, filling the sky with cawing, whistling and rustling of the wings. As I proceeded I saw before me a corpse of a man hanged high in a tree, the body of a dead naked woman in the midst of a heap of stones, and a carcass of a youth with his head cut off and soaked with blood mixed with earth. It was a horrible sight that blinded my eyes with a thick, dark veil of sorrows. I looked in every direction and saw naught except the spectre of Death standing by those ghastly remains. Nothing could be heard except the wailing of non-existence, mingled with the cawing of crows hovering about the victims of human laws. Three human beings, who yesterday were in the lap of Life, today fell as victims to Death because they broke the rules of human society. When a man kills another man, the people say he is a murderer, but when the Emir kills him, the Emir is just. When a man robs a monastery, they say he is a thief, but when the Emir robs him of his life, the Emir is honourable. When a woman betrays her husband, they say she is an

adulteress, but when the Emir makes her walk naked in the streets and stones her later, the Emir is noble. Shedding of blood is forbidden, but who made it lawful for the Emir? Stealing one's money is a crime, but taking away one's life is a noble act. Betrayal of a husband may be an ugly deed, but stoning of living souls is a beautiful sight. Shall we meet evil with evil and say this is the Law? Shall we fight corruption with greater corruption and say this is the Rule? Shall we conquer crimes with more crimes and say this is Justice? Had not the Emir killed an enemy in his past life? Had he not robbed his weak subjects of money and property? Had he not committed adultery? Was he infallible when he killed the murderer and hanged the thief and stoned the adulteress? Who are those who hanged the thief in the tree? Are they angels descended from heaven, or men looting and usurping? Who cut off the murderer's head? Are they divine prophets, or soldiers shedding blood wherever they go? Who stoned that adulteress? Were they virtuous hermits who came from their monasteries, or humans who loved to commit atrocities with glee, under the protection of ignorant Law? What is Law? Who saw it coming with the sun from the depths of heaven? What human saw the heart of God and found its will or purpose? In what century did the angels walk among the people and preach to them, saying, "Forbid the weak from enjoying life, and kill the outlaws with the sharp edge of the sword, and step upon the sinners with iron feet?"

As my mind suffered in this fashion, I heard a rustling of feet in the grass close by. I took heed and say a young woman coming from behind the trees; she looked carefully in every direction before she approached the three carcasses that were there. As she glanced, she saw the youth's head that was cut off. She cried fearfully, knelt, and embraced it with her trembling arms; then she commenced shedding tears and touching the blood-matted, curly hair with her soft fingers, crying in a voice that came from the remnants of a shattered heart. She could bear the sight no longer. She dragged the body to a ditch and placed the head gently between the shoulders, covered the entire body with earth, and upon the grave she planted the sword with which the head of the young man had been cut off.

As she started to leave, I walked toward her. She trembled when she saw me, and her eyes were heavy with tears. She sighed and said, "Turn me over to the Emir if you wish. It is better for me to die and follow the one who saved my life from the grip of disgrace than to leave his corpse as food for the ferocious beasts." Then I responded, "Fear me not, poor girl, I have lamented the young man before you did. But tell me, how did he save you from the grip of disgrace?" She replied with a choking and fainting voice, "One of the Emir's officers came to our farm to collect the tax; when he saw me, he looked upon me as a wolf looks upon a lamb. He imposed on my father a heavy tax that even a rich man could not

pay. He arrested me as a token to take to the Emir in ransom for the gold which my father was unable to give. I begged him to spare me, but he took no heed, for he had no mercy. Then I cried for help, and this young man, who is dead now, came to my help and saved me from a living death. The officer attempted to kill him, but this man took an old sword that was hanging on the wall of our home and stabbed him. He did not run away like a criminal, but stood by the dead officer until the law came and took him into custody." Having uttered these words which would make any human heart bleed with sorrow, she turned her face and walked away.

In a few moments I saw a youth coming and hiding his face with a cloak. As he approached the corpse of the adulteress, he took off the garment and placed it upon her naked body. Then he drew a dagger from under the cloak and dug a pit in which he placed the dead girl with tenderness and care, and covered her with earth upon which he poured his tears. When he finished his task, he plucked some flowers and placed them reverently upon the grave. As he started to leave, I halted him saying, "What kin are you to this adulteress? And what prompted you to endanger your life by coming here to protect her naked body from the ferocious beasts?" When he stared at me, his sorrowful eyes bespoke his misery, and he said, "I am the unfortunate man for whose love she was stoned; I loved her and she loved me since childhood; we grew together; Love, whom

we served and revered, was the lord of our hearts. Love joined both of us and embraced our souls. One day I absented myself from the city, and upon my return I discovered that her father obliged her to marry a man she did not love. My life became a perpetual struggle, and all my days were converted into one long and dark night. I tried to be at peace with my heart, but my heart would not be still. Finally I went to see her secretly and my sole purpose was to have a glimpse of her beautiful eyes and hear the sound of her serene voice. When I reached her house I found her lonely, lamenting her unfortunate self. I sat by her; silence was our important conversation and virtue our companion. One hour of understanding quiet passed, when her husband entered. I cautioned him to contain himself but he dragged her with both hands into the street and cried out saying, "Come, come and see the adulteress and her lover!" All the neighbours rushed about and later the law came and took her to the Emir, but I was not touched by the soldiers. The ignorant Law and sodden customs punished the woman for her father's fault and pardoned the man."

Having thus spoken, the man turned toward the city while I remained pondering the corpse of the thief hanging in that lofty tree and moving slightly every time the wind shook the branches, waiting for someone to bring him down and stretch him upon the bosom of the earth beside the Defender of Honour and Martyr of Love. An hour later, a frail

and wretched woman appeared, crying. She stood before the hanged man and prayer reverently. Then she struggled up into the tree and gnawed with her teeth on the linen rope until it broke and the dead fell on the ground like a huge wet cloth; whereupon she came down, dug a grave, and buried the thief by the side of the other two victims. After covering him with earth, she took two pieces of wood and fashioned a cross and placed it over the head. When she turned her face to the city and started to depart, I stopped her saying, "What incited you to come and bury this thief?" She looked at me miserably and said, "He is my faithful husband and merciful companion; he is the father of my children—five young ones starving to death; the oldest is eight years of age, and the youngest is still nursing. My husband was not a thief, but a farmer working in the monastery's land, making our living on what little food the priests and monks gave him when he returned home at eventide. He had been farming for them since he was young, and when he became weak, they dismissed him, advising him to go back home and send his children to take his place as soon as they grew older. He begged them in the name of Jesus and the angels of heaven to let him stay, but they took no heed to his plea. They had no mercy on him nor on his starving children who were helplessly crying for food. He went to the city seeking employment, but in vain, for the rich did not employ except the strong and the healthy. Then he sat on the dusty

street stretching his hand toward all who passed, begging and repeating the sad song of his defeat in life, while suffering from hunger and humiliation, but the people refused to help him, saying that lazy people did not deserve alms. One night, hunger gnawed painfully at our children, especially the youngest, who tried hopelessly to nurse on my dry breast. My husband's expression changed and he left the house under the cover of night. He entered the monastery's bin and carried out a bushel of wheat. As he emerged, the monks woke up from their slumber and arrested him after beating him mercilessly. At dawn they brought him to the Emir and complained that he came to the monastery to steal the golden vases of the altar. He was placed in prison and hanged the second day. He was trying to fill the stomachs of his little hungry one with the wheat he had raised by his own labour, but the Emir killed him and used his flesh as food to fill the stomachs of the birds and the beasts." Having spoken in this manner, she left me alone in a sorrowful plight and departed.

I stood there before the graves like a speaker suffering wordlessness while trying to recite a eulogy. I was speechless, but my falling tears substituted for my words and spoke for my soul. My spirit rebelled when I attempted to meditate a while, because the soul is like a flower that folds its petals when dark comes, and breathes not its fragrance into the phan-

toms of the night. I felt as if the earth that enfolded the victims of oppression in that lonely place were filling my ears with sorrowful tunes of suffering souls, and inspiring me to talk. I resorted to silence, but if the people understood what silence reveals to them, they would have been as close to God as the flowers of the valleys. If the flames of my sighing soul had touched the trees, they would have moved from their places and marched like a strong army to fight the Emir with their branches and tear down the monastery upon the heads of those priests and monks. I stood there watching, and felt that the sweet feeling of mercy and the bitterness of sorrow were pouring from my heart upon the newly dug graves—a grave of a young man who sacrificed his life in defending a weak maiden, whose life and honour he had saved from between the paws and teeth of a savage human; a youth whose head was cut off in reward for his bravery; and his sword was planted upon his grave by the one he saved, as a symbol of heroism before the face of the sun that shines upon an empire laden with stupidity and corruption. A grave of a young woman whose heart was inflamed with love before her body was taken by greed, usurped by lust, and stoned by tyranny. . . . She kept her faith until death; her lover placed flowers upon her grave to speak through their withering hours of those souls whom Love had selected and blessed among a people blinded by earthly substance and muted by ignorance. A grave of a miserable

man, weakened by hard labour in the monastery's land, who asked for bread to feed his hungry little ones, and was refused. He resorted to begging, but the people took no heed. When his soul led him to restore a small part of the crop which he had raised and gathered, he was arrested and beaten to death. His poor widow erected a cross upon his head as a witness in the silence of the night before the stars of heaven to testify against those priests who converted the kind teaching of Christ into sharp swords by which they cut the people's necks and tore the bodies of the weak.

The sun disappeared behind the horizon as if tiring of the world's troubles and loathing the people's submission. At that moment the evening began to weave a delicate veil from the sinews of silence and spread it upon Nature's body. I stretched my hand toward the graves, pointing at their symbols, lifted my eyes toward heaven and cried out, "Oh, Bravery, this is your sword, buried now in the earth! Oh, Love, these are your flowers, scorched by fire! Oh, Lord Jesus, this is Thy Cross, submerged in the obscurity of the night!"

KHALIL THE HERETIC

PART ONE

SHEIK ABBAS was looked
upon as a prince by the people of a solitary village
in North Lebanon. His mansion stood in the midst
of those poor villagers' huts like a healthy giant
amidst sickly dwarfs. He lived amid luxury while
they pursued an existence of penury. They obeyed
him and bowed reverently before him as he spoke to
them. It seemed as though the power of mind had
appointed him its official interpreter and spokesman.
His anger would make them tremble and scatter like
autumn leaves before a strong wind. If he were to
slap one's face, it would be heresy on the individual's
part to move or lift his head or make any attempt to
discover why the blow had come. If he smiled at a
man, the villagers would consider the person thus
honoured as the most fortunate. The people's fear
and surrender to Sheik Abbas were not due to weakness; however, their poverty and need of him had
brought about this state of continual humiliation.
Even the huts they lived in and the fields they culti-

vated were owned by Sheik Abbas who had inherited them from his ancestors.

The farming of the land and the sowing of the seeds and the gathering of wheat were all done under the supervision of the Sheik who, in reward for their toil, compensated them with a small portion of the crop which barely kept them from falling as victims of gnawing starvation.

Often many of them were in need of bread before the crop was reaped, and they came to Sheik Abbas and asked him with pouring tears to advance them a few piastres or a bushel of wheat, and the Sheik gladly granted their request for he knew that they would pay their debts doubly when harvest time came. Thus those people remained obligated all their lives, left a legacy of debts to their children and were submissive to their master whose anger they had always feared and whose friendship and good will they had constantly but unsuccessfully endeavoured to win.

PART TWO

Winter came and brought heavy snow and strong winds; the valleys and the fields became empty of all things except leafless trees which stood as spectres of death above the lifeless plains.

Having stored the products of the land in the Sheik's bins and filled his vases with the wine of the vineyards, the villagers retreated to their huts to spend a portion of their lives idling by the fireside

and commemorating the glory of the past ages and relating to one another the tales of weary days and long nights.

The old year had just breathed its last into the grey sky. The night had arrived during which the New Year would be crowned and placed upon the throne of the Universe. The snow began to fall heavily and the whistling winds were racing from the lofty mountains down to the abyss and blowing the snow into heaps to be stored away in the valleys.

The trees were shaking under the heavy storms and the fields and knolls were covered with a white floor upon which Death was writing vague lines and effacing them. The mists stood as partitions between the scattered villages by the sides of the valleys. The lights that flickered through the windows of those wretched huts disappeared behind the thick veil of Nature's wrath.

Fear penetrated the fellahin's hearts and the animals stood by their mangers in the sheds, while the dogs were hiding in the corners. One could hear the voices of the screaming winds and thundering of the storms resounding from the depths of the valleys. It seemed as if Nature were enraged by the passing of the old year and trying to wrest revenge from those peaceful souls by fighting with weapons of cold and frost.

That night under the raging sky, a young man was attempting to walk the winding trail that con-

nected Deir Kizhaya * with Sheik Abbas' village. The youth's limbs were numbed with cold, while pain and hunger usurped him of his strength. The black raiment he wore was bleached with the falling snow, as if he were shrouded in death before the hour of his death had come. He was struggling against the wind. His progress was difficult, and he took but a few steps forward with each effort. He called for help and then stood silent, shivering in the cold night. He had slim hope, withering between great despair and deep sorrow. He was like a bird with a broken wing, who fell in a stream whose whirlpools carried him down to the depths.

The young man continued walking and falling until his blood stopped circulating and he collapsed. He uttered a terrible sound . . . the voice of a soul who encountered the hollow face of Death . . . a voice of dying youth, weakened by man and trapped by nature . . . a voice of the love of existence in the space of nothingness.

PART THREE

On the north side of that village, in the midst of the wind-torn fields, stood the solitary home of a woman named Rachel, and her daughter Miriam who had not then attained the age of eighteen. Rachel was the

---

* One of the richest and most famous convents in Lebanon. Kizhaya is a Syriac word meaning "Paradise of Life." (*Editor's note.*)

widow of Samaan Ramy, who was found slain six years earlier, but the law of man did not find the murderer.

Like the rest of the Lebanese widows, Rachel sustained life through long, hard work. During the harvest season, she would look for ears of corn left behind by others in the field, and in Autumn she gathered the remnants of some forgotten fruits in the gardens. In Winter she spun wool and made raiment for which she received a few piastres or a bushel of grain. Miriam, her daughter, was a beautiful girl who shared with her mother the burden of toil.

That bitter night the two women were sitting by the fireplace whose warmth was weakened by the frost and whose firebrands were buried beneath the ashes. By their side was a flickering lamp that sent its yellow, dimmed rays into the heart of darkness like prayer that sends phantoms of hope into the hearts of the sorrowful.

Midnight had come and they were listening to the wailing winds outside. Every now and then Miriam would get up, open the small transom and look toward the obscured sky, and then she would return to her chair worried and frightened by the raging elements. Suddenly Miriam started, as if she had awakened from a swoon of deep slumber. She looked anxiously toward her mother and said, "Did you hear that, Mother? Did you hear a voice calling for help?" The mother listened a moment and said,

"I hear nothing except the crying wind, my daughter." Then Miriam exclaimed, "I heard a voice deeper than the thundering heaven and more sorrowful than the wailing of the tempest."

Having uttered these words, she stood up and opened the door and listened for a moment. Then she said, "I hear it again, Mother!" Rachel hurried toward the frail door and after a moment's hesitation she said, "And I hear it, too. Let us go and see."

She wrapped herself with a long robe, opened the door and walked out cautiously, while Miriam stood at the door, the wind blowing her long hair.

Having forced her way a short distance through the snow, Rachel stopped and shouted out, "Who is calling . . . where are you?" There was no answer; then she repeated the same words again and again, but she heard naught except thunder. Then she courageously advanced forward, looking in every direction. She had walked for some time, when she found some deep footprints upon the snow; she followed them fearfully and in a few moments found a human body lying before her on the snow, like a patch on a white dress. As she approached him and leaned his head over her knees, she felt his pulse that bespoke his slowing heart beats and his slim chance in life. She turned her face toward the hut and called, "Come, Miriam, come and help me, I have found him!" Miriam rushed out and followed her mother's footprints, while shivering with cold and trembling with fear. As she reached the place and

saw the youth lying motionless, she cried with an aching voice. The mother put her hands under his armpits, calmed Miriam and said, "Fear not, for he is still living; hold the lower edge of his cloak and let us carry him home."

Confronted with the strong wind and heavy snow, the two women carried the youth and started toward the hut. As they reached the little haven, they laid him down by the fireplace. Rachel commenced rubbing his numbed hands and Miriam drying his hair with the end of her dress. The youth began to move after a few minutes. His eyelids quivered and he took a deep sigh—a sigh that brought the hope of his safety into the hearts of the merciful women. They removed his shoes and took off his black robe. Miriam looked at her mother and said, "Observe his raiment, Mother; these clothes are worn by the monks." After feeding the fire with a bundle of dry sticks, Rachel looked at her daughter with perplexity and said, "The monks do not leave their convent on such a terrible night." And Miriam inquired, "But he has no hair on his face; the monks wear beards." The mother gazed at him with eyes full of mercy and maternal love; then she turned to her daughter and said, "It makes no difference whether he is a monk or a criminal; dry his feet well, my daughter." Rachel opened a closet, took from it a jar of wine and poured some in an earthenware bowl. Miriam held his head while the mother gave him some of it to stimulate his heart. As he sipped

the wine he opened his eyes for the first time and gave his rescuers a sorrowful look mingled with tears of gratitude—the look of a human who felt the smooth touch of life after having been gripped in the sharp claws of death—a look of great hope after hope had died. Then he bent his head, and his lips trembled when he uttered the words, "May God bless both of you." Rachel placed her hand upon his shoulder and said, "Be calm, brother. Do not tire yourself with talking until you gain strength." And Miriam added, "Rest your head on this pillow, brother, and we will place you closer to the fire." Rachel refilled the bowl with wine and gave it to him. She looked at her daughter and said, "Hang his robe by the fire so it will dry." Having executed her mother's command, she returned and commenced looking at him mercifully, as if she wanted to help him by pouring into his heart all the warmth of her soul. Rachel brought two loaves of bread with some preserves and dry fruits; she sat by him and began to feed him small morsels, as a mother feeds her little child. At this time he felt stronger and sat up on the hearth mat while the red flames of fire reflected upon his sad face. His eyes brightened and he shook his head slowly, saying, "Mercy and cruelty are both wrestling in the human heart like the mad elements in the sky of this terrible night, but mercy shall overcome cruelty because it is divine, and the terror alone, of this night, shall pass away when daylight comes." Silence prevailed for a minute and

then he added with a whispering voice, "A human hand drove me into desperation and a human hand rescued me; how severe man is, and how merciful man is!" And Rachel inquired, "How ventured you, brother, to leave the convent on such a terrible night, when even the beasts do not venture forth?"

The youth shut his eyes as if he wanted to restore his tears back into the depths of his heart, whence they came, and he said, "The animals have their caves, and the birds of the sky their nests, but the son of man has no place to rest his head." Rachel retorted, "That is what Jesus said about himself." And the young man resumed, "This is the answer for every man who wants to follow the Spirit and the Truth in this age of falsehood, hypocrisy and corruption."

After a few moments of contemplation, Rachel said, "But there are many comfortable rooms in the convent, and the coffers are full of gold, and all kinds of provisions. The sheds of the convent are stocked with fat calves and sheep; what made you leave such haven in this deathly night?" The youth sighed deeply and said, "I left that place because I hated it." And Rachel rejoined, "A monk in a convent is like a soldier in the battlefield who is required to obey the orders of his leader regardless of their nature. I heard that a man could not become a monk unless he did away with his will, his thoughts, his desires, and all that pertains to the mind. But a good head priest does not ask his monks to do unrea-

sonable things. How could the head priest of Deir Kizhaya ask you to give up your life to the storms and snow?" And he remarked, "In the opinion of the head priest, a man cannot become a monk unless he is blind and ignorant, senseless and dumb. I left the convent because I am a sensible man who can see, feel, and hear."

Miriam and Rachel stared at him as if they had found in his face a hidden secret; after a moment of meditation the mother said, "Will a man who sees and hears go out on a night that blinds the eyes and deafens the ears?" And the youth stated quietly, "I was expelled from the convent." "Expelled!" exclaimed Rachel; and Miriam repeated the same word in unison with her mother.

He lifted his head, regretting his words, for he was afraid lest their love and sympathy be converted into hatred and disrespect; but when he looked at them and found the rays of mercy still emanating from their eyes, and their bodies vibrating with anxiety to learn further, his voice choked and he continued, "Yes, I was expelled from the convent because I could not dig my grave with my own hands, and my heart grew weary of lying and pilfering. I was expelled from the convent because my soul refused to enjoy the bounty of a people who surrendered themselves to ignorance. I was driven away because I could not find rest in the comfortable rooms, built with the money of the poor fellahin. My stomach could not hold bread baked with the

tears of orphans. My lips could not utter prayers sold for gold and food by the heads to the simple and faithful people. I was expelled from the convent like a filthy leper because I was repeating to the monks the rules that qualified them to their present position."

Silence prevailed while Rachel and Miriam were contemplating his words and gazing at him, when they asked, "Are your father and mother living?" And he responded, "I have no father or mother nor a place that is my home." Rachel drew a deep sigh and Miriam turned her face toward the wall to hide her merciful and loving tears.

As a withering flower is brought back to life by dew drops that dawn pours into its begging petals, so the youth's anxious heart was enlivened by his benefactors' affection and kindness. He looked at them as a soldier looks upon his liberators who rescue him from the grip of the enemy, and he resumed, "I lost my parents before I reached the age of seven. The village priest took me to Deir Kizhaya and left me at the disposal of the monks who were happy to take me in and put me in charge of the cows and sheep, which I led each day to the pasture. When I attained the age of fifteen, they put on me this black robe and led me into the altar whereupon the head priest addressed me saying, "Swear by the name of God and all saints, and make a vow to live a virtuous life of poverty and obedience." I repeated the words before I realized their significance or com-

prehended his own interpretation of poverty, virtue and obedience.

"My name was Khalil, and since that time the monks addressed me as Brother Mobaarak,* but they never did treat me as a brother. They ate the most palatable foods and drank the finest wine, while I lived on dry vegetables and water, mixed with tears. They slumbered in soft beds while I slept on a stone slab in a dark and cold room by the shed. Oftentimes I asked myself, 'When will I become a monk and share with those fortunate priests their bounty? When will my heart stop craving for the food they eat and the wine they drink? When will I cease to tremble with fear before my superiors?' But all my hopes were in vain, for I was kept in the same state; and in addition to caring for the cattle, I was obliged to move heavy stones on my shoulders and to dig pits and ditches. I sustained life on a few morsels of bread given to me in reward for my toil. I knew of no other place to which I might go, and the clergymen at the convent had caused me to abhor everything they were doing. They had poisoned my mind until I commenced to think that the whole world was an ocean of sorrows and miseries and that the convent was the only port of salvation. But when I discovered the source of their food and gold, I was happy that I did not share it."

* Coincidentally, Mobaarak was the name of the Right Reverend Maronite Archbishop who officiated at Kahlil Gibran's last rites. (*Editor's note.*)

Khalil straightened himself and looked about with wonder, as if he had found something beautiful standing before him in that wretched hut. Rachel and Miriam remained silent and he proceeded, "God, who took my father and exiled me as an orphan to the convent, did not want me to spend all my life walking blindly toward a dangerous jungle; nor did He wish me to be a miserable slave for the rest of my life. God opened my eyes and ears and showed me the bright light and made me hear Truth when Truth was talking."

Rachel thought aloud, "Is there any light, other than the sun, that shines over all the people? Are human beings capable of understanding the Truth?" Khalil returned, "The true light is that which emanates from within man, and reveals the secrets of the heart to the soul, making it happy and contented with life. Truth is like the stars; it does not appear except from behind obscurity of the night. Truth is like all beautiful things in the world; it does not disclose its desirability except to those who first feel the influence of falsehood. Truth is a deep kindness that teaches us to be content in our everyday life and share with the people the same happiness."

Rachel rejoined, "Many are those who live according to their goodness, and many are those who believe that compassion to others is the shadow of the law of God to man; but still, they do not rejoice in life, for they remain miserable until death." Khalil

replied, "Vain are the beliefs and teachings that make man miserable, and false is the goodness that leads him into sorrow and despair, for it is man's purpose to be happy on this earth and lead the way to felicity and preach its gospel wherever he goes. He who does not see the kingdom of heaven in this life will never see it in the coming life. We came not into this life by exile, but we came as innocent creatures of God, to learn how to worship the holy and eternal spirit and seek the hidden secrets within ourselves from the beauty of life. This is the truth which I have learned from the teachings of the Nazarene. This is the light that came from within me and showed me the dark corners of the convent that threatened my life. This is the deep secret which the beautiful valleys and fields revealed to me when I was hungry, sitting lonely and weeping under the shadow of the trees.

"This is the religion as the convent should impart it; as God wished it; as Jesus taught it. One day, as my soul became intoxicated with the heavenly intoxication of Truth's beauty, I stood bravely before the monks who were gathering in the garden, and criticized their wrong deeds saying, 'Why do you spend your days here and enjoy the bounty of the poor, whose bread you eat was made with the sweat of their bodies and the tears of their hearts? Why are you living in the shadow of parasitism, segregating yourselves from the people who are in need of knowledge? Why are you depriving the country of

your help? Jesus has sent you as lambs amongst the wolves; what has made you as wolves amongst the lambs? Why are you fleeing from mankind and from God who created you? If you are better than the people who walk in the procession of life, you should go to them and better their lives; but if you think they are better than you, you should desire to learn from them. How do you take an oath and vow to live in poverty, then forget what you have said and live in luxury? How do you swear an obedience to God and then revolt against all that religion means? How do you adopt virtue as your rule when your hearts are full of lusts? You pretend that you are killing your bodies, but in fact you are killing your souls. You feign to abhor the earthly things, but your hearts are swollen with greed. You have the people believe in you as religious teachers; truly speaking you are like busy cattle who divert themselves from knowledge by grazing in a green and beautiful pasture. Let us restore to the needy the vast land of the convent and give back to them the silver and gold we took from them. Let us disperse from our aloofness and serve the weak who made us strong, and cleanse the country in which we live. Let us teach this miserable nation to smile and rejoice with heaven's bounty and glory of life and freedom.

" 'The people's tears are more beautiful and God-joined than the ease and tranquillity to which you have accustomed yourselves in this place. The sympathy that touches the neighbour's heart is more

supreme than the hidden virtue in the unseen corners of the convent. A word of compassion to the
weak criminal or prostitute is nobler than the long
prayer which we repeat emptily every day in the
temple.' "

At this time Khalil took a deep breath. Then he
lifted his eyes toward Rachel and Miriam saying,
"I was saying all of these things to the monks and
they were listening with an air of perplexity, as if
they could not believe that a young man would dare
stand before them and utter such bold words. When
I finished, one of the monks approached and angrily
said to me, 'How dare you talk in such fashion in
our presence?' And another one came laughing and
added, 'Did you learn all this from the cows and pigs
you tended in the fields?' And a third one stood up
and threatened me saying, 'You shall be punished,
heretic!' Then they dispersed as though running
away from a leper. Some of them complained to the
head priest who summoned me before him at eventide. The monks took delight in anticipation of my
suffering, and there was glee on their faces when I
was ordered to be scourged and put into prison for
forty days and nights. They led me into the dark cell
where I spent the time lying in that grave without
seeing the light. I could not tell the end of the night
from the beginning of the day, and could feel nothing but crawling insects and the earth under me. I
could hear naught save the tramping of their feet
when my morsel of bread and dish of water mixed

with vinegar were brought to me at great intervals.

"When I came out of the prison I was weak and frail, and the monks believed that they had cured me of thinking, and that they had killed my soul's desire. They thought that hunger and thirst had choked the kindness which God placed in my heart. In my forty days of solitude I endeavoured to find a method by which I could help these monks to see the light and hear the true song of life, but all of my ponderings were in vain, for the thick veil which the long ages had woven around their eyes could not be torn away in a short time; and the mortar with which ignorance had cemented their ears was hardened and could not be removed by the touch of soft fingers."

Silence prevailed for a moment, and then Miriam looked at her mother as if asking permission to speak. She said, "You must have talked to the monks again, if they selected this terrible night in which to banish you from the convent. They should learn to be kind even to their enemies."

Khalil returned, "This evening, as the thunder storms and warring elements raged in the sky, I withdrew myself from the monks who were crouching about the fire, telling tales and humourous stories. When they saw me alone they commenced to place their wit at my expense. I was reading my Gospel and contemplating the beautiful sayings of Jesus that made me forget for the time the enraged nature and belligerent elements of the sky, when they approached me with a new spirit of ridicule.

I ignored them by occupying myself and looking through the window, but they became furious because my silence dried the laughter of their hearts and the taunting of their lips. One of them said, 'What are you reading, GreatReformer?' In response to his inquiry, I opened my book and read aloud the following passage, 'But when he saw many of the Pharisees and Saducees come to his baptism, he said unto them, "O generation of vipers, who hath warned you to flee from the wrath to come? Bring forth therefore fruits for repentance; And think not to say within yourselves, 'We have Abraham to our father;' " 'for I say unto you, that God is able of these stones to raise children unto Abraham. And now also the axe is laid unto the root of the trees; therefore every tree which bringeth not forth good fruit is hewn down, and cast into the fire.'

"As I read to them these words of John the Baptist, the monks became silent as if an invisible hand strangled their spirits, but they took false courage and commenced laughing. One of them said, 'We have read these words many times, and we are not in need of a cow grazier to repeat them to us.'

"I protested, 'If you had read these words and comprehended their meaning, these poor villagers would not have frozen or starved to death.' When I said this, one of the monks slapped my face as if I had spoken evil of the priests; another kicked me and a third took the book from me and a fourth one called the head priest who hurried to the scene

shaking with anger. He cried out, 'Arrest this rebel and drag him from this sacred place, and let the storm's fury teach him obedience. Take him away and let nature do unto him the will of God, and then wash your hands of the poisonous germs of heresy infesting his raiment. If he should return pleading for forgiveness, do not open the door for him, for the viper will not become a dove if placed in a cage, nor will the briar bear figs if planted in the vineyards.'

"In accordance with the command, I was dragged out by the laughing monks. Before they locked the door behind me, I heard one saying, 'Yesterday you were king of cows and pigs, and today you are dethroned, Oh Great Reformer; go now and be the king of wolves and teach them how to live in their lairs.' "

Khalil sighed deeply, then turned his face and looked toward the flaming fire. With a sweet and loving voice, and with a pained countenance he said, "Thus was I expelled from the convent, and thus did the monks deliver me over to the hands of Death. I fought through the night blindly; the heavy wind was tearing my robe and the piling snow was trapping my feet and pulling me down until I fell, crying desperately for help. I felt that no one heard me except Death, but a power which is all knowledge and mercy had heard my cry. That power did not want me to die before I had learned what is left of life's secrets. That power sent you

both to me to save my life from the depth of the abyss and non-existence."

Rachel and Miriam felt as if their spirits understood the mystery of his soul, and they became his partners in feeling and understanding. Notwithstanding her will, Rachel stretched forth and gently touched his hand while tears coursed down from her eyes, and she said, "He who has been chosen by heaven as a defender of Truth will not perish by heaven's own storms and snow." And Miriam added, "The storms and snow may kill the flowers, but cannot deaden the seeds, for the snow keeps them warm from the killing frost."

Khalil's face brightened upon hearing those words of encouragement, and he said, "If you do not look upon me as a rebel and an heretic as the monks did, the persecution which I have sustained in the convent is the symbol of an oppressed nation that has not yet attained knowledge; and this night in which I was on the verge of death is like a revolution that precedes full justice. And from a sensitive woman's heart springs the happiness of mankind, and from the kindness of her noble spirit comes mankind's affection."

He closed his eyes and leaned down on the pillow; the two women did not bother him with further conversation for they knew that the weariness caused by long exposure had allured and captured his eyes. Khalil slept like a lost child who had finally found safety in his mother's arms.

Rachel and her daughter slowly walked to their bed and sat there watching him as if they had found in his trouble-torn face an attraction bringing their souls and hearts closer to him. And the mother whispered, saying, "There is a strange power in his closed eyes that speaks in silence and stimulates the soul's desires."

And Miriam rejoined, "His hands, Mother, are like those of Christ in the Church." The mother replied, "His face possesses at the same time a woman's tenderness and a man's boldness."

And the wings of slumber carried the women's spirits into the world of dream, and the fire went down and turned into ashes, while the light of the oil lamp dimmed gradually and disappeared. The fierce tempest continued its roar, and the obscured sky spread layers of snow, and the strong wind scattered them to the right and left.

PART FOUR

Five days passed, and the sky was still heavy with snow, burying the mountains and prairies relentlessly. Khalil made three attempts to resume his journey toward the plains, but Rachel restrained him each time, saying, "Do not give up your life to the blind elements, brother; remain here, for the bread that suffices two will also feed three, and the fire will still be burning after your departure as it was before your arrival. We are poor, brother, but like the rest of the people, we live our lives before

the face of the sun and mankind, and God gives us our daily bread."

And Miriam was begging him with her kind glances, and pleading with her deep sighs, for since he entered the hut she felt the presence of a divine power in her soul sending forth life and light into her heart and awakening new affection in the Holy of Holies of her spirit. For the first time she experienced the feeling which made her heart like a white rose that sips the dew drops from the dawn and breathes its fragrance into the endless firmament.

There is no affection purer and more soothing to the spirit than the one hidden in the heart of a maiden who awakens suddenly and fills her own spirit with heavenly music that makes her days like poets' dreams and her nights prophetic. There is no secret in the mystery of life stronger and more beautiful than that attachment which converts the silence of a virgin's spirit into a perpetual awareness that makes a person forget the past, for it kindles fiercely in the heart the sweet and overwhelming hope of the coming future.

The Lebanese woman distinguishes herself from the woman of other nations by her simplicity. The manner in which she is trained restricts her progress educationally, and stands as a hindrance to her future. Yet for this reason, she finds herself inquiring of herself as to the inclination and mystery of her heart. The Lebanese young woman is like a spring that comes out from the heart of the earth

and follows its course through winding depressions, but since it cannot find an outlet to the sea, it turns into a calm lake that reflects upon its growing surface the glittering stars and the shining moon. Khalil felt the vibration of Miriam's heart twining steadily about his soul, and he knew that the divine torch that illuminated his heart had also touched her heart. He rejoiced for the first time, like a parched brook greeting the rain, but he blamed himself for his haste, believing that this spiritual understanding would pass like a cloud when he departed from that village. He often spoke to himself saying, "What is this mystery that plays so great a part in our lives? What is this Law that drives us into a rough road and stops us just before we reach the face of the sun where we might rejoice? What is this power that elevates our spirits until we reach the mountain top, smiling and glorying, then suddenly we are cast to the depths of the valley, weeping and suffering? What is this life that embraces us like a lover one day, and fights us like an enemy the second day? Was I not persecuted yesterday? Did I not survive hunger and thirst and suffering and mockery for the sake of the Truth which heaven had awakened in my heart? Did I not tell the monks that happiness through Truth is the will and the purpose of God in man? Then what is this fear? And why do I close my eyes to the light that emanates from that young woman's eyes? I am expelled and she is poor, but is it on bread only that man can

live? Are we not, between famine and plenty, like trees between winter and summer? But what would Rachel say if she knew that my heart and her daughter's heart came to an understanding in silence, and approached close to each other and neared the circle of the Supreme Light? What would she say if she discovered that the young man whose life she saved longed to gaze upon her daughter? What would the simple villagers say if they knew that a young man, reared in the convent, came to their village by necessity and expulsion, and desired to live near a beautiful maiden? Will they listen to me if I tell them that he who leaves the convent to live amongst them is like a bird that flies from the bruising walls of the cage to the light of freedom? What will Sheik Abbas say if he hears my story? What will the priest of the village do if he learns of the cause of my expulsion?"

Khalil was talking to himself in this fashion while sitting by the fireplace, meditating the flames, symbol of his love; and Miriam was stealing a glance now and then at his face and reading his dreams through his eyes, and hearing the echo of his thoughts, and feeling the touch of his love, even though no word was uttered.

One night, as he stood by the small transom that faced the valleys where the trees and rocks were shrouded with white coverings, Miriam came and stood by him, looking at the sky. As their eyes turned and met, he drew a deep sigh and shut his

eyes as if his soul were sailing in the spacious sky looking for a word. He found no word necessary, for the silence spoke for them. Miriam ventured, "Where will you go when the snow meets the stream and the paths are dry?" His eyes opened, looking beyond the horizon, and he explained, "I shall follow the path to wherever my destiny and my mission for Truth shall take me." Miriam sighed sadly and offered, "Why will you not remain here and live close to us? Is it that you are obliged to go elsewhere?" He was moved by her kindness and sweet words, but protested, "The villagers here will not accept an expelled monk as their neighbour, and will not permit him to breathe the air they breathe because they believe that the enemy of the convent is an infidel, cursed by God and His saints." Miriam resorted to silence, for the Truth that pained her prevented further talk. Then Khalil turned aside and explained, "Miriam, these villagers are taught by those in authority to hate everyone who thinks freely; they are trained to remain afar from those whose minds soar aloft; God does not like to be worshipped by an ignorant man who imitates someone else; if I remained in this village and asked the people to worship as they please, they would say that I am an infidel disobeying the authority that was given to the priest by God. If I asked them to listen and hear the voices of their hearts and do according to the will of the spirit within, they would say that I am an evil man who

wants them to do away with the clergy that God placed between heaven and earth." Khalil looked straight into Miriam's eyes, and with a voice that bespoke the sound of silver strings said, "But, Miriam, there is a magic power in this village that possesses me and engulfs my soul; a power so divine that it causes me to forget my pain. In this village I met Death to his very face, and in this place my soul embraced God's spirit. In this village there is a beautiful flower grown over the lifeless grass; its beauty attracts my heart and its fragrance fills its domain. Shall I leave this important flower and go out preaching the ideas that caused my expulsion from the convent, or shall I remain by the side of that flower and dig a grave and bury my thoughts and truths among its neighbouring thorns? What shall I do, Miriam?" Upon hearing these words, she shivered like a lily before the frolicsome breeze of the dawn. Her heart glowed through her eyes when she faltered, "We are both in the hands of a mysterious and merciful power. Let it do its will."

At that moment the two hearts joined and thereafter both spirits were one burning torch illuminating their lives.

PART FIVE

Since the beginning of the creation and up to our present time, certain clans, rich by inheritance, in co-operation with the clergy, had appointed themselves the administrators of the people. It is an old,

gaping wound in the heart of society that cannot be removed except by intense removal of ignorance.

The man who acquires his wealth by inheritance builds his mansion with the weak poor's money. The clergyman erects his temple upon the graves and bones of the devoted worshippers. The prince grasps the fellah's arms while the priest empties his pocket; the ruler looks upon the sons of the fields with frowning face, and the bishop consoles them with his smile, and between the frown of the tiger and the smile of the wolf the flock is perished; the ruler claims himself as king of the law, and the priest as the representative of God, and between these two, the bodies are destroyed and the souls wither into nothing.

In Lebanon, that mountain rich in sunlight and poor in knowledge, the noble and the priest joined hands to exploit the farmer who ploughed the land and reaped the crop in order to protect himself from the sword of the ruler and the curse of the priest. The rich man in Lebanon stood proudly by his palace and shouted at the multitudes saying, "The Sultan had appointed me as your lord." And the priest stands before the altar saying, "God has delegated me as an executive of your souls." But the Lebanese resorted to silence, for the dead could not talk.

Sheik Abbas had friendship in his heart for the clergymen, because they were his allies in choking

the people's knowledge and reviving the spirit of stern obedience among his workers.

That evening, when Khalil and Miriam were approaching the throne of Love, and Rachel was looking upon them with the eyes of affection, Father Elias informed Sheik Abbas that the head priest had expelled a rebellious young man from the convent and that he had taken refuge at the house of Rachel, the widow of Samaan Ramy. And the priest was not satisfied with the little information he gave the Sheik, but commented, "The demon they chased out of the convent cannot become an angel in this village, and the fig tree which is hewn and cast into the fire, does not bear fruit while burning. If we wish to clean this village of the filth of this beast, we must drive him away as the monks did." And the Sheik inquired, "Are you certain that the young man will be a bad influence upon our people? Is it not better for us to keep him and make him a worker in our vineyards? We are in need of strong men."

The priest's face showed his disagreement. Combing his beard with his fingers, he said shrewdly, "If he were fit to work, he would not have been expelled from the convent. A student who works in the convent, and who happened to spend last night at my house, informed me that this young man had violated the rules of the head priest by preaching danger-ridden ideas among the monks, and he quoted him as saying, 'Restore the fields and the vineyards and the silver of the convent to the poor

312

and scatter it in all directions; and help the people
who are in need of knowledge; by thus doing, you
will please your Father in Heaven.' "

On hearing these words, Sheik Abbas leaped to
his feet, and like a tiger making ready to strike the
victim, he walked to the door and called to the servants, ordering them to report immediately. Three
men entered, and the Sheik commanded, "In the
house of Rachel, the widow of Samaan Ramy, there
is a young man wearing a monk's raiment. Tie him
and bring him here. If that woman objects to his
arrest, drag her out by her braided hair over the
snow and bring her with him, for he who helps evil
is evil himself." The men bowed obediently and
hurried to Rachel's home while the priest and the
Sheik discussed the type of punishment to be
awarded to Khalil and Rachel.

PART SIX

The day was over and the night had come spreading
its shadow over those wretched huts, heavily laden
with snow. The stars finally appeared in the sky,
like hopes in the coming eternity after the suffering
of death's agony. The doors and windows were
closed and the lamps were lighted. The fellahin
sat by the fireside warming their bodies. Rachel,
Miriam and Khalil were seated at a rough wooden
table eating their evening meal when there was a
knock at the door and three men entered. Rachel
and Miriam were frightened, but Khalil remained

calm, as if he awaited the coming of those men. One of the Sheik's servants walked toward Khalil, laid his hand upon his shoulder and asked, "Are you the one who was expelled from the convent?" And Khalil responded, "Yes, I am the one, what do you want?" The man replied, "We are ordered to arrest you and take you with us to Sheik Abbas' home, and if you object we shall drag you out like a butchered sheep over the snow."

Rachel turned pale as she exclaimed, "What crime has he committed, and why do you want to tie him and drag him out?" The two women pleaded with tearful voices, saying, "He is one individual in the hands of three and it is cowardly of you to make him suffer." The men became enraged and shouted, "Is there any woman in this village who opposes the Sheik's order?" And he drew forth a rope and started to tie Khalil's hands. Khalil lifted his head proudly, and a sorrowful smile appeared on his lips when he said, "I feel sorry for you men, because you are a strong and blind instrument in the hands of a man who oppresses the weak with the strength of your arms. You are slaves of ignorance. Yesterday I was a man like you, but tomorrow you shall be free in mind as I am now. Between us there is a deep precipice that chokes my calling voice and hides my reality from you, and you cannot hear or see. Here I am, tie my hands and do as you please." The three men were moved by his talk and it seemed that his voice had awakened in them a new spirit, but the

voice of Sheik Abbas still rang in their minds, warning them to complete the mission. They bound his
hands and led him out silently with a heavy conscience. Rachel and Miriam followed them to the
Sheik's home, like the daughters of Jerusalem who
followed Christ to Mount Calvary.

PART SEVEN

Regardless of its import, news travels swiftly among
the fellahin in the small villages, because their absence from the realm of society makes them anxious
and busy in discussing the happenings of their limited environs. In winter, when the fields are slumbering under the quilts of snow, and when human
life is taking refuge and warming itself by the fireside, the villagers become most inclined to learn of
current news in order to occupy themselves.

It was not long after Khalil was arrested, when
the story spread like a contagious disease amongst
the villagers. They left their huts and hurried like
an army from every direction into the home of
Sheik Abbas. When Khalil's feet stepped into the
Sheik's home, the residence was crowded with men,
women and children who were endeavouring for a
glance at the infidel who was expelled from the
convent. They were also anxious to see Rachel and
her daughter, who had helped Khalil in spreading
the hellish disease of heresy in the pure sky of their
village.

The Sheik took the seat of judgment and beside

him sat Father Elias, while the throng was gazing at the pinioned youth who stood bravely before them. Rachel and Miriam were standing behind Khalil and trembling with fear. But what could fear do to the heart of a woman who found Truth and followed him? What could the scorn of the crowd do to the soul of a maiden who had been awakened by Love? Sheik Abbas looked at the young man, and with a thundering voice he interrogated him saying, "What is your name, man?" "Khalil is my name," answered the youth. The Sheik returned, "Who are your father and mother and relatives, and where were you born?" Khalil turned toward the fellahin, who looked upon him with hateful eyes, and said, "The oppressed poor are my clan and my relatives, and this vast country is my birthplace."

Sheik Abbas, with an air of ridicule, said, "Those people whom you claim as kin demand that you be punished, and the country you assert as your birthplace objects to your being a member of its people." Khalil replied, "The ignorant nations arrest their good men and turn them into their despots; and a country, ruled by a tyrant, persecutes those who try to free the people from the yoke of slavery. But will a good son leave his mother if she is ill? Will a merciful man deny his brother who is miserable? Those poor men who arrested me and brought me here today are the same ones who surrendered their lives to you yesterday. And this vast earth that dis-

approves my existence is the one that does not yawn and swallow the greedy despots."

The Sheik uttered a loud laugh, as if wanting to depress the young man's spirit and prevent him from influencing the audience. He turned to Khalil and said impressively, "You cattle grazier, do you think that we will show more mercy than did the monks, who expelled you from the convent? Do you think that we feel pity for a dangerous agitator?" Khalil responded, "It is true that I was a cattle grazier, but I am glad that I was not a butcher. I led my herds to the rich pastures and never grazed them on arid land. I led my animals to pure springs and kept them from contaminated marshes. At eventide I brought them safely to their shed and never left them in the valleys as prey for the wolves. Thus I have treated the animals; and if you had pursued my course and treated human beings as I treated my flock, these poor people would not live in wretched huts and suffer the pangs of poverty, while you are living like Nero in this gorgeous mansion."

The Sheik's forehead glittered with drops of perspiration, and his smirk turned into anger, but he tried to show only calm by pretending that he did not heed Khalil's talk, and he expostulated, pointing at Khalil with his finger, "You are a heretic, and we shall not listen to your ridiculous talk; we summoned you to be tried as a criminal, and you realize that you are in the presence of the Lord of this village who is empowered to represent his Excellency

Emir Ameen Shebab. You are standing before Father Elias, the representative of the Holy Church whose teachings you have opposed. Now, defend yourself, or kneel down before these people and we will pardon you and make you a cattle grazier, as you were in the convent." Khalil calmly returned, "A criminal is not to be tried by another criminal, as an atheist will not defend himself before sinners." And Khalil looked at the audience and spoke to them saying, "My brethren, the man whom you call the Lord of your fields, and to whom you have yielded thus long, has brought me to be tried before you in this edifice which he built upon the graves of your forefathers. And the man who became a pastor of your church through your faith, has come to judge me and help you to humiliate me and increase my sufferings. You have hurried to this place from every direction to see me suffer and hear me plead for mercy. You have left your huts in order to witness your pinioned son and brother. You have come to see the prey trembling between the paws of a ferocious beast. You came here tonight to view an infidel standing before the judges. I am the criminal and I am the heretic who has been expelled from the convent. The tempest brought me into your village. Listen to my protest, and do not be merciful, but be just, for mercy is bestowed upon the guilty criminal, while justice is all that an innocent man requires.

"I select you now as my jury, because the will of

the people is the will of God. Awaken your hearts and listen carefully and then prosecute me according to the dictates of your conscience. You have been told that I am an infidel, but you have not been informed of what crime or sin I have committed. You have seen me tied like a thief, but you have not yet heard about my offenses, for wrongdoings are not revealed in this court, while punishment comes out like thunder. My crime, dear fellowmen, is my understanding of your plight, for I felt the weight of the irons which have been placed upon your necks. My sin is my heartfelt sorrows for your women; it is my sympathy for your children who suck life from your breast mixed with the shadow of death. I am one of you, and my forefathers lived in these valleys and died under the same yoke which is bending your heads now. I believe in God who listens to the call of your suffering souls, and I believe in the Book that makes all of us brothers before the face of heaven. I believe in the teachings that make us all equal, and that render us unpinioned upon this earth, the stepping place of the careful feet of God.

"As I was grazing my cows at the convent, and contemplating the sorrowful condition you tolerate, I heard a desperate cry coming from your miserable homes—a cry of oppressd souls—a cry of broken hearts which are locked in your bodies as slaves to the lord of these fields. As I looked, I found me in the convent and you in the fields, and I saw you as a

flock of lambs following a wolf to the lair; and as I stopped in the middle of the road to aid the lambs, I cried for help and the wolf snapped me with his sharp teeth.

"I have sustained imprisonment, thirst, and hunger for the sake of Truth that hurts only the body. I have undergone suffering beyond endurance because I turned your sad sighs into a crying voice that rang and echoed in every corner of the convent. I never felt fear, and my heart never tired, for your painful cry was injecting a new strength into me every day, and my heart was healthy. You may ask yourself now saying, 'When did we ever cry for help, and who dares open his lips?' But I say unto you, your souls are crying every day, and pleading for help every night, but you cannot hear them, for the dying man cannot hear his own heart rattling, while those who are standing by his bedside can surely hear. The slaughtered bird, in spite of his will, dances painfully and unknowingly, but those who witness the dance know what caused it. In what hour of the day do you sigh painfully? Is it in the morning, when love of existence cries at you and tears the veil of slumber off your eyes and leads you like slaves into the fields? Is it at noon, when you wish to sit under a tree to protect yourself from the burning sun? Or at eventide, when you return home hungry, wishing for sustaining food instead of a meagre morsel and impure water? Or at night when fatigue throws you upon your rough bed, and as

soon as slumber closes your eyes, you sit up with open eyes, fearing that the Sheik's voice is ringing in your ears?

"In what season of the year do you not lament yourselves? Is it in Spring, when nature puts on her beautiful dress and you go to meet her with tattered raiment? Or in Summer, when you harvest the wheat and gather the sheaves of corn and fill the shelves of your master with the crop, and when the reckoning comes you receive naught but hay and tare? Is it in Autumn, when you pick the fruits and carry the grapes into the wine-press, and in reward for your toil you receive a jar of vinegar and a bushel of acorns? Or in Winter, when you are confined to your huts laden with snow, do you sit by the fire and tremble when the enraged sky urges you to escape from your weak minds?

"This is the life of the poor; this is the perpetual cry I hear. This is what makes my spirit revolt against the oppressors and despise their conduct. When I asked the monks to have mercy upon you, they thought that I was an atheist, and expulsion was my lot. Today I came here to share this miserable life with you, and to mix my tears with yours. Here I am now, in the grip of your worst enemy. Do you realize that this land you are working like slaves was taken from your fathers when the law was written on the sharp edge of the sword? The monks deceived your ancestors and took all their fields and vineyards when the religious rules were written on

the lips of the priests. Which man or woman is not influenced by the lord of the fields to do according to the will of the priests? God said, 'With the sweat of thy brow, thou shall eat thy bread.' But Sheik Abbas is eating his bread baked in the years of your lives and drinking his wine mixed with your tears. Did God distinguish this man from the rest of you while in his mother's womb? Or is it your sin that made you his property? Jesus said, 'Gratis you have taken and gratis you shall give. . . . Do not possess gold, nor silver, neither copper.' Then what teachings allow the clergymen to sell their prayers for pieces of gold and silver? In the silence of the night you pray saying, 'Give us today our daily bread.' God has given you this land from which to draw your daily bread, but what authority has He given the monks to take this land and this bread away from you?

"You curse Judas because he sold his Master for a few pieces of silver, but you bless those who sell Him every day. Judas repented and hanged himself for his wrongdoing, but these priests walk proudly, dressed with beautiful robes, resplendent with shining crosses hanging over their chests. You teach your children to love Christ and at the same time you instruct them to obey those who oppose His teachings and violate His law.

"The apostles of Christ were stoned to death in order to revive in you the Holy Spirit, but the monks and the priests are killing that spirit in you

so they may live on your pitiful bounty. What persuades you to live such a life in this universe, full of misery and oppression? What prompts you to kneel before that horrible idol which has been erected upon the bones of your fathers? What treasure are you reserving for your posterity?

"Your souls are in the grip of the priests, and your bodies are in the closing jaws of the rulers. What thing in life can you point at and say 'this is mine!' My fellowmen, do you know the priest you fear? He is a traitor who uses the Gospel as a threat to ransom your money . . . a hypocrite wearing a cross and using it as a sword to cut your veins . . . a wolf disguised in lambskin . . . a glutton who respects the tables more than the altars . . . a gold-hungry creature who follows the Denar to the farthest land . . . a cheat pilfering from widows and orphans. He is a queer being, with an eagle's beak, a tiger's clutches, a hyena's teeth and a viper's clothes. Take the Book away from him and tear his raiment off and pluck his beard and do whatever you wish unto him; then place in his hand one Denar, and he will forgive you smilingly.

"Slap his face and spit on him and step on his neck; then invite him to sit at your board. He will immediately forget and untie his belt and gladly fill his stomach with your food.

"Curse him and ridicule him; then send him a jar of wine or a basket of fruit. He will forgive you your sins. When he sees a woman, he turns his face,

saying, 'Go from me, Oh, daughter of Babylon.' Then he whispers to himself saying, 'Marriage is better than coveting.' He sees the young men and women walking in the procession of Love, and he lifts his eyes toward heaven and says, 'Vanity of vanities, all is vanity.' And in his solitude he talks to himself saying, 'May the laws and traditions that deny me the joys of life, be abolished.'

"He preaches to the people saying, 'Judge not, lest ye be judged.' But he judges all those who abhor his deeds and sends them to hell before Death separates them from this life.

"When he talks he lifts his head toward heaven, but at the same time, his thoughts are crawling like snakes through your pockets.

"He addresses you as beloved children, but his heart is empty of paternal love, and his lips never smile at a child, nor does he carry an infant between his arms.

"He tells you, while shaking his head, 'Let us keep away from earthly things, for life passes like a cloud.' But if you look thoroughly at him, you will find that he is gripping on to life, lamenting the passing of yesterday, condemning the speed of today, and waiting fearfully for tomorrow.

"He asks you for charity when he has plenty to give; if you grant his request, he will bless you publicly, and if you refuse him, he will curse you secretly.

"In the temple he asks you to help the needy, and

about his house the needy are begging for bread, but he cannot see or hear.

"He sells his prayers, and he who does not buy is an infidel, excommunicated from Paradise.

"This is the creature of whom you are afraid. This is the monk who sucks your blood. This is the priest who makes the sign of the Cross with the right hand, and clutches your throat with the left hand.

"This is the pastor whom you appoint as your servant, but he appoints himself as your master.

"This is the shadow that embraces your souls from birth until death.

"This is the man who came to judge me tonight because my spirit revolted against the enemies of Jesus the Nazarene Who loved all and called us brothers, and Who died on the Cross for us."

Khalil felt that there was understanding in the villagers' hearts; his voice brightened and he resumed his discourse saying, "Brethren, you know that Sheik Abbas has been appointed as Master of this village by Emir Shehab, the Sultan's representative and Governor of the Province, but I ask you if anyone has seen that power appoint the Sultan as the god of this country. That Power, my fellowmen, cannot be seen, nor can you hear it talk, but you can feel its existence in the depths of your hearts. It is that Power which you worship and pray for every day saying, 'Our Father which art in heaven.' Yes, your Father Who is in heaven is the one Who appoints kings and princes, for He is powerful and

above all. But do you think that your Father, Who loved you and showed you the right path through His prophets, desires for you to be oppressed? Do you believe that God, Who brings forth the rain from heaven, and the wheat from the hidden seeds in the heart of the earth, desires for you to be hungry in order that but one man will enjoy His bounty? Do you believe that the Eternal Spirit Who reveals to you the wife's love, the children's pity and the neighbor's mercy, would have upon you a tyrant to enslave you through your life? Do you believe that the Eternal Law that made life beautiful, would send you a man to deny you of that happiness and lead you into the dark dungeon of painful Death? Do you believe that your physical strength, provided you by nature, belongs beyond your body to the rich?

"You cannot believe in all these things, because if you do you will be denying the justice of God who made us all equal, and the light of Truth that shines upon all peoples of the earth. What makes you struggle against yourselves, heart against body, and help those who enslave you while God has created you free on this earth?

"Are you doing yourselves justice when you lift your eyes towards Almighty God and call him Father, and then turn around, bow your heads before a man, and call him Master?

"Are you contented, as sons of God, with being slaves of man? Did not Christ call you brethren?

Yet Sheik Abbas calls you servants. Did not Jesus make you free in Truth and Spirit? Yet the Emir made you slaves of shame and corruption. Did not Christ exalt you to heaven? Then why are you descending to hell? Did He not enlighten your hearts? Then why are you hiding your souls in darkness? God has placed a glowing torch in your hearts that glows in knowledge and beauty, and seeks the secrets of the days and nights; it is a sin to extinguish that torch and bury it in ashes. God has created your spirits with wings to fly in the spacious firmament of Love and Freedom; it is pitiful that you cut your wings with your own hands and suffer your spirits to crawl like insects upon the earth."

Sheik Abbas observed in dismay the attentiveness of the villagers, and attempted to interrupt, but Khalil, inspired, continued, "God has sown in your hearts the seeds of Happiness; it is a crime that you dig those seeds out and throw them wilfully on the rocks so the wind will scatter them and the birds will pick them. God has given you children to rear, to teach them the truth and fill their hearts with the most precious things of existence. He wants you to bequeath upon them the joy of Life and the bounty of Life; why are they now strangers to their place of birth and cold creatures before the face of the Sun? A father who makes his son a slave is the father who gives his child a stone when he asks for bread. Have you not seen the birds of the sky training their young ones to fly? Why, then, do you teach your

children to drag the shackles of slavery? Have you not seen the flowers of the valleys deposit their seeds in the sun-heated earth? Then why do you commit your children to the cold darkness?"

Silence prevailed for a moment, and it seemed as if Khalil's mind were crowded with pain. But now with a low and compelling voice he continued, "The words which I utter tonight are the same expressions that caused my expulsion from the convent. If the lord of your fields and the pastor of your church were to prey upon me and kill me tonight, I will die happy and in peace because I have fulfilled my mission and revealed to you the Truth which demons consider a crime. I have now completed the will of Almighty God."

There had been a magic message in Khalil's voice that forced the villagers' interest. The women were moved by the sweetness of his words and looked upon him as a messenger of peace, and their eyes were rich with tears.

Sheik Abbas and Father Elias were shaking with anger. As Khalil finished, he walked a few steps and stopped near Rachel and Miriam. Silence dominated the courtroom, and it seemed as if Khalil's spirit hovered in that vast hall and diverted the souls of the multitude from fearing Sheik Abbas and Father Elias, who sat trembling in annoyance and guilt.

The Sheik stood suddenly and his face was pale. He looked toward the men who were standing about

him as he said, "What has become of you, dogs? Have your hearts been poisoned? Has your blood stopped running and weakened you so that you cannot leap upon this criminal and cut him to pieces? What awful thing has he done to you?" Having finished reprimanding the men, he raised a sword and started toward the fettered youth, whereupon a strong villager walked to him, gripped his hand and said, "Lay down your weapon, Master, for he who draws the sword to kill, shall, by the sword, be killed!"

The Sheik trembled visibly and the sword fell from his hand. He addressed the man saying, "Will a weak servant oppose his Master and benefactor?" And the man responded, "The faithful servant does not share his Master in the committing of crimes; this young man has spoken naught but the truth." Another man stepped forward and assured, "This man is innocent and is worthy of honour and respect." And a woman raised her voice saying, "He did not swear at God or curse any saint; why do you call him heretic?" And Rachel asked, "What is his crime?" The Sheik shouted, "You are rebellious, you miserable widow; have you forgotten the fate of your husband who turned rebel six years ago?" Upon hearing these impulsive words, Rachel shivered with painful anger, for she had found the murderer of her husband. She choked her tears and looked upon the throng and cried out, "Here is the criminal you have been trying for six years to find; you hear him now confessing his guilt. He is the killer

who has been hiding his crime. Look at him and read his face; study him well and observe his fright; he shivers like the last leaf on winter's tree. God has shown you that the Master whom you have always feared is a murderous criminal. He caused me to be a widow amongst these women, and my daughter an orphan amidst these children." Rachel's utterance fell like thunder upon the Sheik's head, and the uproar of men and exaltation of women fell like firebrands upon him.

The priest assisted the Sheik to his seat. Then he called the servants and ordered them saying, "Arrest this woman who has falsely accused your Master of killing her husband; drag her and this young man into a dark prison, and any who oppose you will be criminals, excommunicated as he was from the Holy Church." The servants gave no heed to his command, but remained motionless staring at Khalil who was still bound with rope. Rachel stood at his right and Miriam at his left like a pair of wings ready to soar aloft into the spacious sky of Freedom.

His beard shaking with anger, Father Elias said, "Are you denying your Master for the sake of an infidel criminal and a shameless adulteress?" And the oldest one of the servants answered him saying, "We have served Sheik Abbas long for bread and shelter, but we have never been his slaves." Having thus spoken, the servant took off his cloak and turban and threw them before the Sheik and added, "I shall no longer require this raiment, nor do I wish

my soul to suffer in the narrow house of a criminal."
And all the servants did likewise and joined the
crowd whose faces radiated with joy, symbol of
Freedom and Truth. Father Elias finally saw that
his authority had declined, and he left the place
cursing the hour that brought Khalil to the village.
A strong man strode to Khalil and untied his hands,
looked at Sheik Abbas who fell like a corpse upon
his seat, and boldly addressed him saying, "This
fettered youth, whom you have brought here tonight to be tried as a criminal, has lifted our depressed spirits and enlightened our hearts with
Truth and Knowledge. And this poor widow whom
Father Elias referred to as a false accuser has revealed to us the crime you committed six years past.
We came here tonight to witness the trial of an innocent youth and a noble soul. Now, heaven has
opened our eyes and has shown us your atrocity; we
shall leave you and ignore you and allow heaven to
do its will."

Many voices were raised in that hall, and one
could hear a certain man saying, "Let us leave this
ill-famed residence for our homes." And another
one remarking, "Let us follow this young man to
Rachel's home and listen to his wise sayings and
consoling wisdom." And a third one saying, "Let
us seek his advice, for he knows our needs." And a
fourth one calling out, "If we are seeking justice,
let us complain to the Emir and tell him of Abbas'
crime." And many were saying, "Let us petition the

Emir to appoint Khalil as our Master and ruler, and tell the Bishop that Father Elias was a partner in these crimes." While the voices were rising and falling upon the Sheik's ears like sharp arrows, Khalil lifted his hands and calmed the villagers saying, "My brethren, do not seek haste, but rather listen and meditate. I ask you, in the name of my love and friendship for you, not to go to the Emir, for you will not find justice. Remember that a ferocious beast does not snap another one like him, neither should you go to the Bishop, for he knows well that the house cloven amid itself shall be ruined. Do not ask the Emir to appoint me as the Sheik in this village, for the faithful servant does not like to be an aid to the evil Master. If I deserve your kindness and love, let me live amongst you and share with you the happiness and sorrows of Life. Let me join hands and work with you at home and in the fields, for if I could not make myself one of you, I would be a hypocrite who does not live according to his sermon. And now, as the axe is laid unto the root of the tree, let us leave Sheik Abbas alone in the courtroom of his conscience and before the Supreme Court of God whose sun shines upon the innocent and the criminal."

Having thus spoken, he left the place, and the multitude followed him as if there were a divine power in him that attracted their hearts. The Sheik remained alone with the terrible silence, like a destroyed ·tower, suffering his defeat quietly like

a surrendering commander. When the multitude reached the church yard and the moon was just showing from behind the cloud, Khalil looked at them with the eyes of love like a good shepherd watching over his herd. He was moved with sympathy upon those villagers who symbolized an oppressed nation; and he stood like a prophet who saw all the nations of the East walking in those valleys and dragging empty souls and heavy hearts.

He raised both hands toward heaven and said, "From the bottom of these depths we call thee, Oh, Liberty. Give heed to us! From behind the darkness we raise our hands to thee, Oh, Liberty. Look upon us! Upon the snow, we worship before thee, Oh, Liberty. Have mercy on us! Before thy great throne we stand, hanging on our bodies the blood-stained garments of our forefathers, covering our heads with the dust of the graves mixed with their remains, carrying the swords that stabbed their hearts, lifting the spears that pierced their bodies, dragging the chains that slowed their feet, uttering the cry that wounded their throats, lamenting and repeating the song of our failure that echoed throughout the prison, and repeating the prayers that came from the depths of our fathers' hearts. Listen to us, Oh Liberty, and hear us. From the Nile to the Euphrates comes the wailing of the suffering souls, in unison with the cry of the abyss; and from the end of the East to the mountains of Lebanon, hands are stretched to you, trembling with the presence of

Death. From the shores of the sea to the end of the desert, tear-flooded eyes look beseechingly toward you. Come, Oh Liberty, and save us.

"In the wretched huts standing in the shadow of poverty and oppression, they beat at their bosoms, soliciting thy mercy; watch us, Oh Liberty, and have mercy on us. In the pathways and in the houses miserable youth calls thee; in the churches and the mosques, the forgotten Book turns to thee; in the courts and in the palaces the neglected Law appeals to thee. Have mercy on us, Oh Liberty, and save us. In our narrow streets the merchant sells his days in order to make tribute to the exploiting thieves of the West, and none would give him advice. In the barren fields the fellah tills the soil and sows the seeds of his heart and nourishes them with his tears, but he reaps naught except thorns, and none would teach him the true path. In our arid plains the Bedouin roams barefoot and hungry, but none would have mercy on him; speak, Oh Liberty, and teach us! Our sick lambs are grazing upon the grassless prairie, our calves are gnawing on the roots of the trees, and our horses are feeding on dry plants. Come, Oh Liberty, and help us. We have been living in darkness since the beginning, and like prisoners they take us from one prison to another, while time ridicules our plight. When will dawn come? Until when shall we bear the scorn of the ages? Many a stone have we been dragging, and many a yoke has been placed upon our necks. Until

when shall we bear this human outrage? The Egyptian slavery, the Babylonian exile, the tyranny of Persia, the despotism of the Romans, and the greed of Europe . . . all these things we have suffered. Where are we going now, and when shall we reach the sublime end of the rough roadway? From the clutches of Pharaoh to the paws of Nebuchadnezzar, to the iron hands of Alexander, to the swords of Herod, to the talons of Nero, and the sharp teeth of Demon . . . into whose hands are we now to fall, and when will Death come and take us, so we may rest at last?

"With the strength of our arms we lifted the columns of the temple, and upon our backs we carried the mortar to build the great walls and the impregnable pyramids for the sake of glory. Until when shall we continue building such magnificent palaces and living in wretched huts? Until when shall we continue filling the bins of the rich with provisions, while sustaining weak life on dry morsels? Until when shall we continue weaving silk and wool for our lords and masters while we wear naught except tattered swaddles?

"Through their wickedness we were divided amongst ourselves; and the better to keep their thrones and be at ease, they armed the Druze to fight the Arab, and stirred up the Shiite to attack the Sunnite, and encouraged the Kurdish to butcher the Bedouin, and cheered the Mohammedan to dispute with the Christian. Until when shall a brother

continue killing his own brother upon his mother's bosom? Until when shall the Cross be kept apart from the Crescent * before the eyes of God? Oh Liberty, hear us, and speak in behalf of but one individual, for a great fire is started with a small spark. Oh Liberty, awaken but one heart with the rustling of thy wings, for from one cloud alone comes the lightning which illuminates the pits of the valleys and the tops of the mountains. Disperse with thy power these black clouds and descend like thunder and destroy the thrones that were built upon the bones and skulls of our ancestors."

"Hear us, Oh Liberty;
Bring mercy, Oh Daughter of Athens;
Rescue us, Oh Sister of Rome;
Advise us, Oh Companion of Moses;
Help us, Oh Beloved of Mohammed;
Teach us, Oh Bride of Jesus;
Strengthen our hearts so we may live,
Or harden our enemies so we may perish
And live in peace eternally."

As Khalil was pouring forth his sentiment before heaven, the villagers were gazing at him in reverence, and their love was springing forth in unison with the song of his voice until they felt that he became part of their hearts. After a short silence,

* The crescent is the emblem of the Mohammedan flag, flown over Syria during the Turkish rule. (Editor's note.)

Khalil brought his eyes upon the multitude and quietly said, "Night has brought us to the house of Sheik Abbas in order to realize the daylight; oppression has arrested us before the cold Space, so we may understand one another and gather like chicks under the wings of the Eternal Spirit. Now let us go to our homes and sleep until we meet again tomorrow."

Having thus spoken, he walked away, following Rachel and Miriam to their poor hovel. The throng departed and each went to his home, contemplating what he had seen and heard that memorable night. They felt that a burning torch of a new spirit had scoured their inner selves and led them into the right path. In an hour all the lamps were extinguished and Silence engulfed the whole village while Slumber carried the fellahin's souls into the world of strong dreams; but Sheik Abbas found no sleep all night, as he watched the phantoms of darkness and the horrible ghosts of his crimes in procession.

PART EIGHT

Two months had already passed and Khalil was still preaching and pouring his sentiments in the villagers' hearts, reminding them of their usurped rights and showing them the greed and oppression of the rulers and the monks. They listened to him with care, for he was a source of pleasure; his words fell upon their hearts like rain upon thirsty land.

In their solitude, they repeated Khalil's sayings as they did their daily prayers. Father Elias commenced fawning upon them to regain their friendship; he became docile since the villagers found out that he was the Sheik's ally in crime, and the fellahin ignored him.

Sheik Abbas had a nervous suffering, and walked through his mansion like a caged tiger. He issued commands to his servants, but no one answered except the echo of his voice inside the marble walls. He shouted at his men, but no one came to his aid except his poor wife who suffered the pang of his cruelty as much as the villagers did. When Lent came and Heaven announced the coming of Spring, the days of the Sheik expired with the passing of Winter. He died after a long agony, and his soul was carried away on the carpet of his deeds to stand naked and shivering before that high Throne whose existence we feel, but cannot see. The fellahin heard various tales about the manner of Sheik Abbas' death; some of them related that the Sheik died insane, while others insisted that disappointment and despair drove him to death by his own hand. But the women who went to offer their sympathies to his wife reported that he died from fear, because the ghost of Samaan Ramy hunted him and drove him every midnight out to the place where Rachel's husband was found slain six years before.

The month of Nisan proclaimed to the villagers the love secrets of Khalil and Miriam. They rejoiced

the good tidings which assured them that Khalil would thereby remain in their village. As the news reached all the inhabitants of the huts, they congratulated one another upon Khalil's becoming their beloved neighbour.

When harvest time came, the fellahin went to the fields and gathered the sheaves of corn and bundles of wheat to the threshing floor. Sheik Abbas was not there to take the crop and have it carried to his bins. Each fellah harvested his own crop; the villagers' huts where filled with wheat and corn; their vessels were replenished with good wine and oil. Khalil shared with them their toils and happiness; he helped them in gathering the crop, pressing the grapes and picking the fruits. He never distinguished himself from any one of them except by his excess of love and ambition. Since that year and up to our present time, each fellah in that village commenced to reap with joy the crop which he sowed with toil and labour. The land which the fellahin tilled and the vineyards they cultivated became their own property.

Now, half a century has passed since this incident, and the Lebanese have awakened.

On his way to the Holy Cedars of Lebanon, a traveller's attention is caught by the beauty of that village, standing like a bride at the side of the valley. The wretched huts are now comfortable and happy homes surrounded by fertile fields and blooming orchards. If you ask any one of the resi-

dents about Sheik Abbas' history, he will answer you, pointing with his finger to a heap of demolished stones and destroyed walls saying, "This is the Sheik's palace, and this is the history of his life." And if you inquire about Khalil, he will raise his hand toward heaven saying, "There resides our beloved Khalil, whose life's history was written by God with glittering letters upon the pages of our hearts, and they cannot be effaced by the ages."

THE BROKEN
WINGS

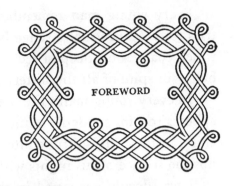

FOREWORD

WAS EIGHTEEN
years of age when love opened my eyes with its magic
rays and touched my spirit for the first time with its
fiery fingers, and Selma Karamy was the first woman
who awakened my spirit with her beauty and led me
into the garden of high affection, where days pass
like dreams and nights like weddings.

Selma Karamy was the one who taught me to
worship beauty by the example of her own beauty
and revealed to me the secret of love by her affection;
she was the one who first sang to me the poetry of
real life.

343

Every young man remembers his first love and tries to recapture that strange hour, the memory of which changes his deepest feeling and makes him so happy in spite of all the bitterness of its mystery.

In every young man's life there is a "Selma" who appears to him suddenly while in the spring of life and transforms his solitude into happy moments and fills the silence of his nights with music.

I was deeply engrossed in thought and contemplation and seeking to understand the meaning of nature and the revelation of books and scriptures when I heard LOVE whispered into my ears through Selma's lips. My life was a coma, empty like that of Adam's in Paradise, when I saw Selma standing before me like a column of light. She was the Eve of my heart who filled it with secrets and wonders and made me understand the meaning of life.

The first Eve led Adam out of Paradise by her own will, while Selma made me enter willingly into the paradise of pure love and virtue by her sweetness and love; but what happened to the first man also happened to me, and the fiery sword which chased Adam out of Paradise was like the one which frightened me by its glittering edge and forced me away from the paradise of my love without having disobeyed any order or tasted the fruit of the forbidden tree.

Today, after many years have passed, I have nothing left out of that beautiful dream except painful memories flapping like invisible wings around me, filling the depths of my heart with sorrow, and bringing tears to my eyes; and my beloved, beautiful Selma, is dead and nothing is left to commemorate her except my broken heart and a tomb surrounded by cypress trees. That tomb and this heart are all that is left to bear witness of Selma.

The silence that guards the tomb does not reveal God's secret in the obscurity of the coffin, and the rustling of the branches whose roots suck the body's elements do not tell the mysteries of the grave, but the agonized sighs of my heart announce to the living the drama which love, beauty, and death have performed.

Oh, friends of my youth who are scattered in the city of Beirut, when you pass by that cemetery near the pine forest, enter it silently and walk slowly so the tramping of your feet will not disturb the slumber of the dead, and stop humbly by Selma's tomb and greet the earth that encloses her corpse and mention my name with a deep sigh and say to yourself, "Here, all the hopes of Gibran, who is living as a prisoner of love beyond the seas, were buried. On this spot he lost his happiness, drained his tears, and forgot his smile."

By that tomb grows Gibran's sorrow together with the cypress trees, and above the tomb his spirit flickers every night commemorating Selma, joining the branches of the trees in sorrowful wailing, mourning and lamenting the going of Selma, who, yesterday, was a beautiful tune on the lips of life and today is a silent secret in the bosom of the earth.

Oh, comrades of my youth! I appeal to you in the names of those virgins whom your hearts have loved, to lay a wreath of flowers on the forsaken tomb of my beloved, for the flowers you lay on Selma's tomb are like falling drops of dew from the eyes of dawn on the leaves of a withering rose.

1

SILENT SORROW

Y NEIGHBORS,
you remember the dawn of youth with pleasure and
regret its passing; but I remember it like a prisoner
who recalls the bars and shackles of his jail. You
speak of those years between infancy and youth as a
golden era free from confinement and cares, but I
call those years an era of silent sorrow which dropped
as a seed into my heart and grew with it and could
find no outlet to the world of knowledge and wisdom
until love came and opened the heart's doors and
lighted its corners. Love provided me with a tongue

347

and tears. You people remember the gardens and orchids and the meeting places and street corners that witnessed your games and heard your innocent whispering; and I remember, too, the beautiful spot in North Lebanon. Every time I close my eyes I see those valleys full of magic and dignity and those mountains covered with glory and greatness trying to reach the sky. Every time I shut my ears to the clamor of the city I hear the murmur of the rivulets and the rustling of the branches. All those beauties which I speak of now and which I long to see, as a child longs for his mother's breast, wounded my spirit, imprisoned in the darkness of youth, as a falcon suffers in its cage when it sees a flock of birds flying freely in the spacious sky. Those valleys and hills fired my imagination, but bitter thoughts wove round my heart a net of hopelessness.

Every time I went to the fields I returned disappointed, without understanding the cause of my disappointment. Every time I looked at the gray sky I felt my heart contract. Every time I heard the singing of the birds and babbling of the spring I suffered without understanding the reason for my suffering. It is said that unsophistication makes a man empty and that emptiness makes him carefree. It may be true among those who were born dead and who exist like frozen corpses; but the sensitive boy

who feels much and knows little is the most unfortunate creature under the sun, because he is torn by two forces. The first force elevates him and shows him the beauty of existence through a cloud of dreams; the second ties him down to the earth and fills his eyes with dust and overpowers him with fears and darkness.

Solitude has soft, silky hands, but with strong fingers it grasps the heart and makes it ache with sorrow. Solitude is the ally of sorrow as well as a companion of spiritual exaltation.

The boy's soul undergoing the buffeting of sorrow is like a white lily just unfolding. It trembles before the breeze and opens its heart to daybreak and folds its leaves back when the shadow of night comes. If that boy does not have diversion or friends or companions in his games, his life will be like a narrow prison in which he sees nothing but spiderwebs and hears nothing but the crawling of insects.

That sorrow which obsessed me during my youth was not caused by lack of amusement, because I could have had it; neither from lack of friends, because I could have found them. That sorrow was caused by an inward ailment which made me love solitude. It killed in me the inclination for games and amusement. It removed from my shoulders the wings of youth and made me like a pond of water

between mountains which reflects in its calm surface the shadows of ghosts and the colors of clouds and trees, but cannot find an outlet by which to pass singing to the sea.

Thus was my life before I attained the age of eighteen. That year is like a mountain peak in my life, for it awakened knowledge in me and made me understand the vicissitudes of mankind. In that year I was reborn and unless a person is born again his life will remain like a blank sheet in the book of existence. In that year, I saw the angels of Heaven looking at me through the eyes of a beautiful woman. I also saw the devils of hell raging in the heart of an evil man. He who does not see the angels and devils in the beauty and malice of life will be far removed from knowledge, and his spirit will be empty of affection.

THE HAND OF DESTINY

 N THE SPRING OF
that wonderful year, I was in Beirut. The gardens
were full of Nisan flowers and the earth was carpeted with green grass, all like a secret of earth revealed to Heaven. The orange trees and apple trees,
looking like houris or brides sent by nature to inspire
poets and excite the imagination, were wearing white
garments of perfumed blossoms.

Spring is beautiful everywhere, but it is most
beautiful in Lebanon. It is a spirit that roams round
the earth but hovers over Lebanon, conversing with

kings and prophets, singing with the rivers the songs of Solomon, and repeating with the Holy Cedars of Lebanon the memory of ancient glory. Beirut, free from the mud of winter and the dust of summer, is like a bride in the spring, or like a mermaid sitting by the side of a brook drying her smooth skin in the rays of the sun.

One day, in the month of Nisan, I went to visit a friend whose home was at some distance from the glamorous city. As we were conversing, a dignified man of about sixty-five entered the house. As I rose to greet him, my friend introduced him to me as Farris Effandi Karamy and then gave him my name with flattering words. The old man looked at me a moment, touching his forehead with the ends of his fingers as if he were trying to regain his memory. Then he smilingly approached me, saying, "You are the son of a very dear friend of mine, and I am happy to see that friend in your person."

Much affected by his words, I was attracted to him like a bird whose instinct leads him to his nest before the coming of the tempest. As we sat down, he told us about his friendship with my father, recalling the time which they spent together. An old man likes to return in memory to the days of his youth like a stranger who longs to go back to his own country. He delights to tell stories of the past like a

poet who takes pleasure in reciting his best poem. He lives spiritually in the past because the present passes swiftly, and the future seems to him an approach to the oblivion of the grave. An hour full of old memories passed like the shadows of the trees over the grass. When Farris Effandi started to leave, he put his left hand on my shoulder and shook my right hand, saying, "I have not seen your father for twenty years. I hope you will take his place in frequent visits to my house." I promised gratefully to do my duty toward a dear friend of my father.

When the old man left the house, I asked my friend to tell me more about him. He said, "I do not know any other man in Beirut whose wealth has made him kind and whose kindness has made him wealthy. He is one of the few who come to this world and leave it without harming any one, but people of that kind are usually miserable and oppressed because they are not clever enough to save themselves from the crookedness of others. Farris Effandi has one daughter whose character is similar to his and whose beauty and gracefulness are beyond description, and she will also be miserable because her father's wealth is placing her already at the edge of a horrible precipice."

As he uttered these words, I noticed that his face clouded. Then he continued, "Farris Effandi is a

good old man with a noble heart, but he lacks will power. People lead him like a blind man. His daughter obeys him in spite of her pride and intelligence, and this is the secret which lurks in the life of father and daughter. This secret was discovered by an evil man who is a bishop and whose wickedness hides in the shadow of his Gospel. He makes the people believe that he is kind and noble. He is the head of religion in this land of the religious. The people obey and worship him. He leads them like a flock of lambs to the slaughter house. This bishop has a nephew who is full of hatefulness and corruption. The day will come sooner or later when he will place his nephew on his right and Farris Effandi's daughter on his left, and, holding with his evil hand the wreath of matrimony over their heads, will tie a pure virgin to a filthy degenerate, placing the heart of the day in the bosom of night.

"That is all I can tell you about Farris Effandi and his daughter, so do not ask me any more questions."

Saying this, he turned his head toward the window as if he were trying to solve the problems of human existence by concentrating on the beauty of the universe.

As I left the house, I told my friend that I was going to visit Farris Effandi in a few days for the

purpose of fulfilling my promise and for the sake of the friendship which had joined him and my father. He stared at me for a moment, and I noticed a change in his expression as if my few simple words had revealed to him a new idea. Then he looked straight through my eyes in a strange manner, a look of love, mercy, and fear—the look of a prophet who foresees what no one else can divine. Then his lips trembled a little, but he said nothing when I started toward the door. That strange look followed me, the meaning of which I could not understand until I grew up in the world of experience, where hearts understand each other intuitively and where spirits are mature with knowledge.

ENTRANCE TO THE SHRINE

I N A FEW DAYS,
loneliness overcame me; and I tired of the grim faces
of books; I hired a carriage and started for the house
of Farris Effandi. As I reached the pine woods where
people went for picnics, the driver took a private
way, shaded with willow trees on each side. Passing
through, we could see the beauty of the green grass,
the grapevines, and the many colored flowers of
Nisan just blossoming.

In a few minutes the carriage stopped before a
solitary house in the midst of a beautiful garden. The

scent of roses, gardenia, and jasmine filled the air. As I dismounted and entered the spacious garden, I saw Farris Effandi coming to meet me. He ushered me into his house with a hearty welcome and sat by me, like a happy father when he sees his son, showering me with questions on my life, future and education. I answered him, my voice full of ambition and zeal; for I heard ringing in my ears the hymn of glory, and I was sailing the calm sea of hopeful dreams. Just then a beautiful young woman, dressed in a gorgeous white silk gown, appeared from behind the velvet curtains of the door and walked toward me. Farris Effandi and I rose from our seats.

"This is my daughter Selma," said the old man. Then he introduced me to her, saying, "Fate has brought back to me a dear old friend of mine in the person of his son." Selma stared at me a moment as if doubting that a visitor could have entered their house. Her hand, when I touched it, was like a white lily, and a strange pang pierced my heart.

We all sat silent as if Selma had brought into the room with her a heavenly spirit worthy of mute respect. As she felt the silence she smiled at me and said, "Many a time my father has repeated to me the stories of his youth and of the old days he and your father spent together. If your father spoke to you in

the same way, then this meeting is not the first one between us."

The old man was delighted to hear his daughter talking in such a manner and said, "Selma is very sentimental. She sees everything through the eyes of the spirit." Then he resumed his conversation with care and tact as if he had found in me a magic charm which took him on the wings of memory to the days of the past.

As I considered him, dreaming of my own later years, he looked upon me, as a lofty old tree that has withstood storms and sunshine throws its shadow upon a small sapling which shakes before the breeze of dawn.

But Selma was silent. Occasionally, she looked first at me and then at her father as if reading the first and last chapters of life's drama. The day passed fast in that garden, and I could see through the window the ghostly yellow kiss of sunset on the mountains of Lebanon. Farris Effandi continued to recount his experiences and I listened entranced and responded with such enthusiasm that his sorrow was changed to happiness.

Selma sat by the window, looking on with sorrowful eyes and not speaking, although beauty has its own heavenly language, loftier than the voices of

tongues and lips. It is a timeless language, common to all humanity, a calm lake that attracts the singing rivulets to its depth and makes them silent.

Only our spirits can understand beauty, or live and grow with it. It puzzles our minds; we are unable to describe it in words; it is a sensation that our eyes cannot see, derived from both the one who observes and the one who is looked upon. Real beauty is a ray which emanates from the holy of holies of the spirit, and illuminates the body, as life comes from the depths of the earth and gives color and scent to a flower.

Real beauty lies in the spiritual accord that is called love which can exist between a man and a woman.

Did my spirit and Selma's reach out to each other that day when we met, and did that yearning make me see her as the most beautiful woman under the sun? Or was I intoxicated with the wine of youth which made me fancy that which never existed?

Did my youth blind my natural eyes and make me imagine the brightness of her eyes, the sweetness of her mouth, and the grace of her figure? Or was it that her brightness, sweetness, and grace opened my eyes and showed me the happiness and sorrow of love?

It is hard to answer these questions, but I say truly that in that hour I felt an emotion that I had never felt before, a new affection resting calmly in my heart, like the spirit hovering over the waters at the creation of the world, and from that affection was born my happiness and my sorrow. Thus ended the hour of my first meeting with Selma, and thus the will of Heaven freed me from the bondage of youth and solitude and let me walk in the procession of love.

Love is the only freedom in the world because it so elevates the spirit that the laws of humanity and the phenomena of nature do not alter its course.

As I rose from my seat to depart, Farris Effandi came close to me and said soberly, "Now my son, since you know your way to this house, you should come often and feel that you are coming to your father's house. Consider me as a father and Selma as a sister." Saying this, he turned to Selma as if to ask confirmation of his statement. She nodded her head positively and then looked at me as one who has found an old acquaintance.

Those words uttered by Farris Effandi Karamy placed me side by side with his daughter at the altar of love. Those words were a heavenly song which started with exaltation and ended with sorrow; they

raised our spirits to the realm of light and searing flame; they were the cup from which we drank happiness and bitterness.

I left the house. The old man accompanied me to the edge of the garden, while my heart throbbed like the trembling lips of a thirsty man.

THE WHITE TORCH

HE MONTH OF NISAN
had nearly passed. I continued to visit the home of
Farris Effendi and to meet Selma in that beautiful
garden, gazing upon her beauty, marveling at her
intelligence, and hearing the stillness of sorrow. I felt
an invisible hand drawing me to her.

Every visit gave me a new meaning to her beauty
and a new insight into her sweet spirit, until she became a book whose pages I could understand and
whose praises I could sing, but which I could never
finish reading. A woman whom Providence has pro-

vided with beauty of spirit and body is a truth, at the same time both open and secret, which we can understand only by love, and touch only by virtue; and when we attempt to describe such a woman she disappears like a vapor.

Selma Karamy had bodily and spiritual beauty, but how can I describe her to one who never knew her? Can a dead man remember the singing of a nightingale and the fragrance of a rose and the sigh of a brook? Can a prisoner who is heavily loaded with shackles follow the breeze of the dawn? Is not silence more painful than death? Does pride prevent me from describing Selma in plain words since I cannot draw her truthfully with luminous colors? A hungry man in a desert will not refuse to eat dry bread if Heaven does not shower him with manna and quails.

In her white silk dress, Selma was slender as a ray of moonlight coming through the window. She walked gracefully and rhythmically. Her voice was low and sweet; words fell from her lips like drops of dew falling from the petals of flowers when they are disturbed by the wind.

But Selma's face! No words can describe its expression, reflecting first great internal suffering, then heavenly exaltation.

The beauty of Selma's face was not classic; it

was like a dream of revelation which cannot be meas-
ured or bound or copied by the brush of a painter,
or the chisel of a sculptor. Selma's beauty was not in
her golden hair, but in the virtue and purity which
surrounded it; not in her large eyes, but in the light
which emanated from them; not in her red lips, but
in the sweetness of her words; not in her ivory neck,
but in its slight bow to the front. Nor was it in her
perfect figure, but in the nobility of her spirit, burning like a white torch between earth and sky. Her
beauty was like a gift of poetry. But poets are unhappy people, for, no matter how high their spirits
reach, they will still be enclosed in an envelope of
tears.

Selma was deeply thoughtful rather than talka-
tive, and her silence was a kind of music that carried
one to a world of dreams and made him listen to the
throbbing of his heart, and see the ghosts of his
thoughts and feelings standing before him, looking
him in the eyes.

She wore a cloak of deep sorrow through her life,
which increased her strange beauty and dignity, as a
tree in blossom is more lovely when seen through the
mist of dawn.

Sorrow linked her spirit and mine, as if each saw
in the other's face what the heart was feeling and
heard the echo of a hidden voice. God had made two

bodies in one, and separation could be nothing but agony.

The sorrowful spirit finds rest when united with a similar one. They join affectionately, as a stranger is cheered when he sees another stranger in a strange land. Hearts that are united through the medium of sorrow will not be separated by the glory of happiness. Love that is cleansed by tears will remain eternally pure and beautiful.

THE TEMPEST

NE DAY FARRIS
Effandi invited me to dinner at his home. I accepted,
my spirit hungry for the divine bread which Heaven
placed in the hands of Selma, the spiritual bread
which makes our hearts hungrier the more we eat of
it. It was this bread which Kais, the Arabian poet,
Dante, and Sappho tasted and which set their hearts
afire; the bread which the Goddess prepares with the
sweetness of kisses and the bitterness of tears.

As I reached the home of Farris Effandi, I saw
Selma sitting on a bench in the garden resting her

head against a tree and looking like a bride in her white silk dress, or like a sentinel guarding that place.

Silently and reverently I approached and sat by her. I could not talk; so I resorted to silence, the only language of the heart, but I felt that Selma was listening to my wordless call and watching the ghost of my soul in my eyes.

In a few minutes the old man came out and greeted me as usual. When he stretched his hand toward me, I felt as if he were blessing the secrets that united me and his daughter. Then he said, "Dinner is ready, my children; let us eat." We rose and followed him, and Selma's eyes brightened; for a new sentiment had been added to her love by her father's calling us his children.

We sat at the table enjoying the food and sipping the old wine, but our souls were living in a world far away. We were dreaming of the future and its hardships.

Three persons were separated in thoughts, but united in love; three innocent people with much feeling but little knowledge; a drama was being performed by an old man who loved his daughter and cared for her happiness, a young woman of twenty looking into the future with anxiety, and a young man, dreaming and worrying, who had tasted neither

the wine of life nor its vinegar, and trying to reach
the height of love and knowledge but unable to lift
himself up. We three sitting in twilight were eating
and drinking in that solitary home, guarded by
Heaven's eyes, but at the bottoms of our glasses were
hidden bitterness and anguish.

As we finished eating, one of the maids announced the presence of a man at the door who
wished to see Farris Effandi. "Who is he?" asked the
old man. "The Bishop's messenger," said the maid.
There was a moment of silence during which Farris
Effandi stared at his daughter like a prophet who
gazes at Heaven to divine its secret. Then he said to
the maid, "Let the man in."

As the maid left, a man, dressed in oriental uniform and with a big mustache curled at the ends,
entered and greeted the old man, saying, "His Grace,
the Bishop, has sent me for you with his private carriage; he wishes to discuss important business with
you." The old man's face clouded and his smile disappeared. After a moment of deep thought he came
close to me and said in a friendly voice, "I hope to
find you here when I come back, for Selma will enjoy
your company in this solitary place."

Saying this, he turned to Selma and, smiling,
asked her if she agreed. She nodded her head, but
her cheeks became red, and with a voice sweeter than

the music of a lyre she said, "I will do my best, Father, to make our guest happy."

Selma watched the carriage that had taken her father and the Bishop's messenger until it disappeared. Then she came and sat opposite me on a divan covered with green silk. She looked like a lily bent to the carpet of green grass by the breeze of dawn. It was the will of Heaven that I should be with Selma alone, at night, in her beautiful home surrounded by trees, where silence, love, beauty, and virtue dwelt together.

We were both silent, each waiting for the other to speak, but speech is not the only means of understanding between two souls. It is not the syllables that come from the lips and tongues that bring hearts together.

There is something greater and purer than what the mouth utters. Silence illuminates our souls, whispers to our hearts, and brings them together. Silence separates us from ourselves, makes us sail the firmament of spirit, and brings us closer to Heaven; it makes us feel that bodies are no more than prisons and that this world is only a place of exile.

Selma looked at me and her eyes revealed the secret of her heart. Then she quietly said, "Let us go to the garden and sit under the trees and watch the

moon come up behind the mountains." Obediently
I rose from my seat, but I hesitated.

"Don't you think we had better stay here until
the moon has risen and illuminates the garden?" And
I continued, "The darkness hides the trees and
flowers. We can see nothing."

Then she said, "If darkness hides the trees and
flowers from our eyes, it will not hide love from our
hearts."

Uttering these words in a strange tone, she turned
her eyes and looked through the window. I remained
silent, pondering her words, weighing the true meaning of each syllable. Then she looked at me as if she
regretted what she had said and tried to take away
those words from my ears by the magic of her eyes.
But those eyes, instead of making me forget what
she had said, repeated through the depths of my heart
more clearly and effectively the sweet words which
had already become graven in my memory for eternity.

Every beauty and greatness in this world is
created by a single thought or emotion inside a man.
Every thing we see today, made by past generations,
was, before its appearance, a thought in the mind of
a man or an impulse in the heart of a woman. The
revolutions that shed so much blood and turned

men's minds toward liberty were the idea of one man who lived in the midst of thousands of men. The devastating wars which destroyed empires were a thought that existed in the mind of an individual. The supreme teachings that changed the course of humanity were the ideas of a man whose genius separated him from his environment. A single thought built the Pyramids, founded the glory of Islam, and caused the burning of the library at Alexandria.

One thought will come to you at night which will elevate you to glory or lead you to the asylum. One look from a woman's eye makes you the happiest man in the world. One word from a man's lips will make you rich or poor.

That word which Selma uttered that night arrested me between my past and future, as a boat which is anchored in the midst of the ocean. That word awakened me from the slumber of youth and solitude and set me on the stage where life and death play their parts.

The scent of flowers mingled with the breeze as we came into the garden and sat silently on a bench near a jasmine tree, listening to the breathing of sleeping nature, while in the blue sky the eyes of heaven witnessed our drama.

The moon came out from behind Mount Sunnin

and shone over the coast, hills, and mountains; and we could see the villages fringing the valley like apparitions which have suddenly been conjured from nothing. We could see the beauty of all Lebanon under the silver rays of the moon.

Poets of the West think of Lebanon as a legendary place, forgotten since the passing of David and Solomon and the Prophets, as the Garden of Eden became lost after the fall of Adam and Eve. To those Western Poets, the word "Lebanon" is a poetical expression associated with a mountain whose sides are drenched with the incense of the Holy Cedars. It reminds them of the temples of copper and marble standing stern and impregnable and of a herd of deer feeding in the valleys. That night I saw Lebanon dream-like with the eyes of a poet.

Thus, the appearance of things changes according to the emotions, and thus we see magic and beauty in them, while the magic and beauty are really in ourselves.

As the rays of the moon shone on the face, neck, and arms of Selma, she looked like a statue of ivory sculptured by the fingers of some worshiper of Ishtar, goddess of beauty and love. As she looked at me, she said, "Why are you silent? Why do you not tell me something about your past?" As I gazed at her, my

muteness vanished, and I opened my lips and said, "Did you not hear what I said when we came to this orchard? The spirit that hears the whispering of flowers and the singing of silence can also hear the shrieking of my soul and the clamor of my heart."

She covered her face with her hands and said in a trembling voice, "Yes, I heard you—I heard a voice coming from the bosom of night and a clamor raging in the heart of the day."

Forgetting my past, my very existence—everything but Selma—I answered her, saying, "And I heard you, too, Selma. I heard exhilarating music pulsing in the air and causing the whole universe to tremble."

Upon hearing these words, she closed her eyes and on her lips I saw a smile of pleasure mingled with sadness. She whispered softly, "Now I know that there is something higher than heaven and deeper than the ocean and stranger than life and death and time. I know now what I did not know before."

At that moment Selma became dearer than a friend and closer than a sister and more beloved than a sweetheart. She became a supreme thought, a beautiful dream, an overpowering emotion living in my spirit.

It is wrong to think that love comes from long

companionship and persevering courtship. Love is the offspring of spiritual affinity and unless that affinity is created in a moment, it will not be created in years or even generations.

Then Selma raised her head and gazed at the horizon where Mount Sunnin meets the sky, and said, "Yesterday you were like a brother to me, with whom I lived and by whom I sat calmly under my father's care. Now, I feel the presence of something stranger and sweeter than brotherly affection, an unfamiliar commingling of love and fear that fills my heart with sorrow and happiness."

I responded, "This emotion which we fear and which shakes us when it passes through our hearts is the law of nature that guides the moon around the earth and the sun around God."

She put her hand on my head and wove her fingers through my hair. Her face brightened and tears came out of her eyes like drops of dew on the leaves of a lily, and she said, "Who would believe our story—who would believe that in this hour we have surmounted the obstacles of doubt? Who would believe that the month of Nisan which brought us together for the first time, is the month that halted us in the Holy of Holies of life?"

Her hand was still on my head as she spoke, and

I would not have preferred a royal crown or a wreath of glory to that beautiful smooth hand whose fingers were twined in my hair.

Then I answered her: "People will not believe our story because they do not know that love is the only flower that grows and blossoms without the aid of seasons, but was it Nisan that brought us together for the first time, and is it this hour that has arrested us in the Holy of Holies of life? Is it not the hand of God that brought our souls close together before birth and made us prisoners of each other for all the days and nights? Man's life does not commence in the womb and never ends in the grave; and this firmament, full of moonlight and stars, is not deserted by loving souls and intuitive spirits."

As she drew her hand away from my head, I felt a kind of electrical vibration at the roots of my hair mingled with the night breeze. Like a devoted worshiper who receives his blessing by kissing the altar in a shrine, I took Selma's hand, placed my burning lips on it, and gave it a long kiss, the memory of which melts my heart and awakens by its sweetness all the virtue of my spirit.

An hour passed, every minute of which was a year of love. The silence of the night, moonlight, flowers, and trees made us forget all reality except love, when suddenly we heard the galloping of horses and rat-

tling of carriage wheels. Awakened from our pleasant swoon and plunged from the world of dreams into the world of perplexity and misery, we found that the old man had returned from his mission. We rose and walked through the orchard to meet him.

When the carriage reached the entrance of the garden, Farris Effandi dismounted and slowly walked towards us, bending forward slightly as if he were carrying a heavy load. He approached Selma and placed both of his hands on her shoulders and stared at her. Tears coursed down his wrinkled cheeks and his lips trembled with sorrowful smile. In a choking voice, he said, "My beloved Selma, very soon you will be taken away from the arms of your father to the arms of another man. Very soon fate will carry you from this lonely home to the world's spacious court, and this garden will miss the pressure of your footsteps, and your father will become a stranger to you. All is done; may God bless you."

Hearing these words, Selma's face clouded and her eyes froze as if she felt a premonition of death. Then she screamed, like a bird shot down, suffering, and trembling, and in a choked voice said, "What do you say? What do you mean? Where are you sending me?"

Then she looked at him searchingly, trying to discover his secret. In a moment she said, "I understand.

I understand everything. The Bishop has demanded me from you and has prepared a cage for this bird with broken wings. Is this your will, Father?"

His answer was a deep sigh. Tenderly he led Selma into the house while I remained standing in the garden, waves of perplexity beating upon me like a tempest upon autumn leaves. Then I followed them into the living room, and to avoid embarrassment, shook the old man's hand, looked at Selma, my beautiful star, and left the house.

As I reached the end of the garden I heard the old man calling me and turned to meet him. Apologetically he took my hand and said, "Forgive me, my son. I have ruined your evening with the shedding of tears, but please come to see me when my house is deserted and I am lonely and desperate. Youth, my dear son, does not combine with senility, as morning does not meet the night; but you will come to me and call to my memory the youthful days which I spent with your father, and you will tell me the news of life which does not count me as among its sons any longer. Will you not visit me when Selma leaves and I am left here in loneliness?"

While he said these sorrowful words and I silently shook his hand, I felt the warm tears falling from his eyes upon my hand. Trembling with sorrow and filial affection, I felt as if my heart were choked with

grief. When I raised my head and he saw the tears in my eyes, he bent toward me and touched my forehead with his lips. "Good-bye, son, Good-bye."

An old man's tear is more potent than that of a young man because it is the residuum of life in his weakening body. A young man's tear is like a drop of dew on the leaf of a rose, while that of an old man is like a yellow leaf which falls with the wind at the approach of winter.

As I left the house of Farris Effandi Karamy, Selma's voice still rang in my ears, her beauty followed me like a wraith, and her father's tears dried slowly on my hand.

My departure was like Adam's exodus from Paradise, but the Eve of my heart was not with me to make the whole world an Eden. That night, in which I had been born again, I felt that I saw death's face for the first time.

Thus the sun enlivens and kills the fields with its heat.

The Lake of Fire

VERYTHING THAT
a man does secretly in the darkness of night will be
clearly revealed in daylight. Words uttered in pri
vacy will become unexpectedly common conversation. Deeds which we hide today in the corners of
our lodgings will be shouted on every street tomorrow.

Thus the ghosts of darkness revealed the purpose
of Bishop Bulos Galib's meeting with Farris Effandi
Karamy, and his conversation was repeated all over
the neighborhood until it reached my ears.

The discussion that took place between Bishop Bulos Galib and Farris Effandi that night was not over the problems of the poor or the widows and orphans. The main purpose for sending after Farris Effandi and bringing him in the Bishop's private carriage was the betrothal of Selma to the Bishop's nephew, Mansour Bey Galib.

Selma was the only child of the wealthy Farris Effandi, and the Bishop's choice fell on Selma, not on account of her beauty and noble spirit, but on account of her father's money which would guarantee Mansour Bey a good and prosperous fortune and make him an important man.

The heads of religion in the East are not satisfied with their own munificence, but they must strive to make all members of their families superiors and oppressors. The glory of a prince goes to his eldest son by inheritance, but the exaltation of a religious head is contagious among his brothers and nephews. Thus the Christian bishop and the Moslem imam and the Brahman priest become like sea reptiles who clutch their prey with many tentacles and suck their blood with numerous mouths.

When the Bishop demanded Selma's hand for his nephew, the only answer that he received from her father was deep silence and falling tears, for he hated to lose his only child. Any man's soul trembles

when he is separated from his only daughter whom he has reared to young womanhood.

The sorrow of parents at the marriage of a daughter is equal to their happiness at the marriage of a son, because a son brings to the family a new member, while a daughter, upon her marriage, is lost to them.

Farris Effandi perforce granted the Bishop's request, obeying his will unwillingly, because Farris Effandi knew the Bishop's nephew very well, knew that he was dangerous, full of hate, wickedness, and corruption.

In Lebanon, no Christian could oppose his bishop and remain in good standing. No man could disobey his religious head and keep his reputation. The eye could not resist a spear without being pierced, and the hand could not grasp a sword without being cut off.

Suppose that Farris Effandi had resisted the Bishop and refused his wish; then Selma's reputation would have been ruined and her name would have been blemished by the dirt of lips and tongues. In the opinion of the fox, high bunches of grapes that can't be reached are sour.

Thus destiny seized Selma and led her like a humiliated slave in the procession of miserable oriental woman, and thus fell that noble spirit into the

trap after having flown freely on the white wings of love in a sky full of moonlight scented with the odor of flowers.

In some countries, the parent's wealth is a source of misery for the children. The wide strong box which the father and mother together have used for the safety of their wealth becomes a narrow, dark prison for the souls of their heirs. The Almighty Dinar* which the people worship becomes a demon which punishes the spirit and deadens the heart. Selma Karamy was one of those who were victims of their parents' wealth and bridegrooms' cupidity. Had it not been for her father's wealth, Selma would still be living happily.

A week had passed. The love of Selma was my sole entertainer, singing songs of happiness for me at night and waking me at dawn to reveal the meaning of life and the secrets of nature. It is a heavenly love that is free from jealousy, rich and never harmful to the spirit. It is a deep affinity that bathes the soul in contentment; a deep hunger for affection which, when satisfied, fills the soul with bounty; a tenderness that creates hope without agitating the soul, changing earth to paradise and life to a sweet and beautiful dream. In the morning, when I walked in the fields, I saw the token of Eternity in the awakening of

* Kind of money used in the Near East.

nature, and when I sat by the seashore I heard the waves singing the song of Eternity. And when I walked in the streets I saw the beauty of life and the splendor of humanity in the appearance of passers-by and movements of workers.

Those days passed like ghosts and disappeared like clouds, and soon nothing was left for me but sorrowful memories. The eyes with which I used to look at the beauty of spring and the awakening of nature, could see nothing but the fury of the tempest and the misery of winter. The ears with which I formerly heard with delight the song of the waves, could hear only the howling of the wind and the wrath of the sea against the precipice. The soul which had observed happily the tireless vigor of mankind and the glory of the universe, was tortured by the knowledge of disappointment and failure. Nothing was more beautiful than those days of love, and nothing was more bitter than those horrible nights of sorrow.

When I could no longer resist the impulse, I went, on the weekend, once more to Selma's home—the shrine which Beauty had erected and which Love had blessed, in which the spirit could worship and the heart kneel humbly and pray. When I entered the garden I felt a power pulling me away from this world and placing me in a sphere supernaturally

free from struggle and hardship. Like a mystic who receives a revelation of Heaven, I saw myself amid the trees and flowers, and as I approached the entrance of the house I beheld Selma sitting on the bench in the shadow of a jasmine tree where we both had sat the week before, on that night which Providence had chosen for the beginning of my happiness and sorrow.

She neither moved nor spoke as I approached her. She seemed to have known intuitively that I was coming, and when I sat by her she gazed at me for a moment and sighed deeply, then turned her head and looked at the sky. And, after a moment full of magic silence, she turned back toward me and tremblingly took my hand and said in a faint voice, "Look at me, my friend; study my face and read in it that which you want to know and which I can not recite. Look at me, my beloved . . . look at me, my brother."

I gazed at her intently and saw that those eyes, which a few days ago were smiling like lips and moving like the wings of a nightingale, were already sunken and glazed with sorrow and pain. Her face, that had resembled the unfolding, sunkissed leaves of a lily, had faded and become colorless. Her sweet lips were like two withering roses that autumn has left on their stems. Her neck, that had been a column

of ivory, was bent forward as if it no longer could support the burden of grief in her head.

All these changes I saw in Selma's face, but to me they were like a passing cloud that covered the face of the moon and makes it more beautiful. A look which reveals inward stress adds more beauty to the face, no matter how much tragedy and pain it bespeaks; but the face which, in silence, does not announce hidden mysteries is not beautiful, regardless of the symmetry of its features. The cup does not entice our lips unless the wine's color is seen through the transparent crystal.

Selma, on that evening, was like a cup full of heavenly wine concocted of the bitterness and sweetness of life. Unaware, she symbolized the oriental woman who never leaves her parents' home until she puts upon her neck the heavy yoke of her husband, who never leaves her loving mother's arms until she must live as a slave, enduring the harshness of her husband's mother.

I continued to look at Selma and listen to her depressed spirit and suffer with her until I felt that time had ceased and the universe had faded from existence. I could see only her two large eyes staring fixedly at me and could feel only her cold, trembling hand holding mine.

I woke from my swoon hearing Selma saying

quietly, "Come, my beloved, let us discuss the horrible future before it comes. My father has just left the house to see the man who is going to be my companion until death. My father, whom God chose for the purpose of my existence, will meet the man whom the world has selected to be my master for the rest of my life. In the heart of this city, the old man who accompanied me during my youth will meet the young man who will be my companion for the coming years. Tonight the two families will set the marriage date. What a strange and impressive hour! Last week at this time, under this jasmine tree, Love embraced my soul for the first time, while Destiny was writing the first word of my life's story at the Bishop's mansion. Now, while my father and my suitor are planning the day of marriage, I see your spirit quivering around me as a thirsty bird flickers above a spring of water guarded by a hungry serpent. Oh, how great this night is! And how deep is its mystery!"

Hearing these words, I felt that the dark ghost of complete despondency was seizing our love to choke it in its infancy, and I answered her, "That bird will remain flickering over that spring until thirst destroys him or falls into the grasp of a serpent and becomes its prey."

She responded, "No, my beloved, this nightin-

gale should remain alive and sing until dark comes, until spring passes, until the end of the world, and keep on singing eternally. His voice should not be silenced, because he brings life to my heart, his wings should not be broken, because their motion removes the cloud from my heart."

Then I whispered, "Selma, my beloved, thirst will exhaust him; and fear will kill him."

She replied immediately with trembling lips, "The thirst of soul is sweeter than the wine of material things, and the fear of spirit is dearer than the security of the body. But listen, my beloved, listen carefully, I am standing today at the door of a new life which I know nothing about. I am like a blind man who feels his way so that he will not fall. My father's wealth has placed me in the slave market, and this man has bought me. I neither know nor love him, but I shall learn to love him, and I shall obey him, serve him, and make him happy. I shall give him all that a weak woman can give a strong man.

"But you, my beloved, are still in the prime of life. You can walk freely upon life's spacious path, carpeted with flowers. You are free to traverse the world, making of your heart a torch to light your way. You can think, talk, and act freely; you can write your name on the face of life because you are a man; you can live as a master because your father's

wealth will not place you in the slave market to be bought and sold; you can marry the woman of your choice and, before she lives in your home, you can let her reside in your heart and can exchange confidences without hindrance."

Silence prevailed for a moment, and Selma continued, "But, is it now that Life will tear us apart so that you may attain the glory of a man and I the duty of a woman? Is it for this that the valley swallows the song of the nightingale in its depths, and the wind scatters the petals of the rose, and the feet tread upon the wine cup? Were all those nights we spent in the moonlight by the jasmine tree, where our souls united, in vain? Did we fly swiftly toward the stars until our wings tired, and are we descending now into the abyss? Or was Love asleep when he came to us, and did he, when he woke, become angry and decide to punish us? Or did our spirits turn the night's breeze into a wind that tore us to pieces and blew us like dust to the depth of the valley? We disobeyed no commandment, nor did we taste of forbidden fruit, so what is making us leave this paradise? We never conspired or practised mutiny, then why are we descending to hell? No, no, the moments which united us are greater than centuries, and the light that illuminated our spirits is stronger than the dark; and if the tempest separates us on this rough

ocean, the waves will unite us on the calm shore; and if this life kills us, death will unite us. A woman's heart will not change with time or season; even if it dies eternally, it will never perish. A woman's heart is like a field turned into a battleground; after the trees are uprooted and the grass is burned and the rocks are reddened with blood and the earth is planted with bones and skulls, it is calm and silent as if nothing has happened; for the spring and autumn come at their intervals and resume their work.

"And now, my beloved, what shall we do? How shall we part and when shall we meet? Shall we consider love a strange visitor who came in the evening and left us in the morning? Or shall we suppose this affection a dream that came in our sleep and departed when we awoke?

"Shall we consider this week an hour of intoxication to be replaced by soberness? Raise your head and let me look at you, my beloved; open your lips and let me hear your voice. Speak to me! Will you remember me after this tempest has sunk the ship of our love? Will you hear the whispering of my wings in the silence of the night? Will you hear my spirit fluttering over you? Will you listen to my sighs? Will you see my shadow approach with the shadows of dusk and disappear with the flush of dawn? Tell me, my beloved, what will you be after having been

magic ray to my eyes, sweet song to my ears, and wings to my soul? What will you be?"

Hearing these words, my heart melted, and I answered her, "I will be as you want me to be, my beloved."

Then she said, "I want you to love me as a poet loves his sorrowful thoughts. I want you to remember me as a traveler remembers a calm pool in which his image was reflected as he drank its water. I want you to remember me as a mother remembers her child that died before it saw the light, and I want you to remember me as a merciful king remembers a prisoner who died before his pardon reached him. I want you to be my companion, and I want you to visit my father and console him in his solitude because I shall be leaving him soon and shall be a stranger to him."

I answered her, saying, "I will do all you have said and will make my soul an envelope for your soul, and my heart a residence for your beauty and my breast a grave for your sorrows. I shall love you, Selma, as the prairies love the spring, and I shall live in you the life of a flower under the sun's rays. I shall sing your name as the valley sings the echo of the bells of the village churches; I shall listen to the language of your soul as the shore listens to the story of the waves. I shall remember you as a stranger remembers his beloved country, and as a hungry man

remembers a banquet, and as a dethroned king remembers the days of his glory, and as a prisoner remembers the hours of ease and freedom. I shall remember you as a sower remembers the bundles of wheat on his threshing floor, and as a shepherd remembers the green prairies and sweet brooks."

Selma listened to my words with palpitating heart, and said, "Tomorrow the truth will become ghostly and the awakening will be like a dream. Will a lover be satisfied embracing a ghost, or will a thirsty man quench his thirst from the spring of a dream?"

I answered her, "Tomorrow, destiny will put you in the midst of a peaceful family, but it will send me into the world of struggle and warfare. You will be in the home of a person whom chance has made most fortunate through your beauty and virtue, while I shall be living a life of suffering and fear. You will enter the gate of life, while I shall enter the gate of death. You will be received hospitably, while I shall exist in solitude, but I shall erect a statue of love and worship it in the valley of death. Love will be my sole comforter, and I shall drink love like wine and wear it like a garment. At dawn, Love will wake me from slumber and take me to the distant field, and at noon will lead me to the shadows of trees, where I will find shelter with the birds from the heat of the sun. In

the evening, it will cause me to pause before sunset to hear nature's farewell song to the light of day and will show me ghostly clouds sailing in the sky. At night, Love will embrace me, and I shall sleep, dreaming of the heavenly world where the spirits of lovers and poets abide. In the Spring I shall walk side by side with love among violets and jasmines and drink the remaining drops of winter in the lily cups. In Summer we shall make the bundles of hay our pillows and the grass our bed, and the blue sky will cover us as we gaze at the stars and moon.

"In Autumn, Love and I will go to the vineyard and sit by the wine press and watch the grapevines being denuded of their golden ornaments, and the migrating flocks of birds will wing over us. In Winter we shall sit by the fireside reciting stories of long ago and chronicles of far countries. During my youth, Love will be my teacher; in middle age, my help; and in old age, my delight. Love, my beloved Selma, will stay with me to the end of my life, and after death the hand of God will unite us again."

All these words came from the depths of my heart like flames of fire which leap raging from the hearth and then disappear in the ashes. Selma was weeping as if her eyes were lips answering me with tears.

Those whom love has not given wings cannot fly behind the cloud of appearances to see the magic

world in which Selma's spirit and mine existed together in that sorrowfully happy hour. Those whom
Love has not chosen as followers do not hear when
Love calls. This story is not for them. Even if they
should comprehend these pages, they would not be
able to grasp the shadowy meanings which are not
clothed in words and do not reside on paper, but
what human being is he who has never sipped the
wine from the cup of love, and what spirit is it that
has never stood reverently before that lighted altar in
the temple whose pavement is the hearts of men and
women and whose ceiling is the secret canopy of
dreams? What flower is that on whose leaves the
dawn has never poured a drop of dew; what streamlet is that which lost its course without going to the
sea?

Selma raised her face toward the sky and gazed at
the heavenly stars which studded the firmament. She
stretched out her hands; her eyes widened, and her
lips trembled. On her pale face, I could see the signs
of sorrow, oppression, hopelessness, and pain. Then
she cried, "Oh, Lord, what has a woman done that
hath offended Thee? What sin has she committed to
deserve such a punishment? For what crime has she
been awarded everlasting castigation? Oh, Lord,
Thou art strong, and I am weak. Why hast Thou
made me suffer pain? Thou art great and almighty,

while I am nothing but a tiny creature crawling before Thy throne. Why hast Thou crushed me with Thy foot? Thou art a raging tempest, and I am like dust; why, my Lord, hast Thou flung me upon the cold earth? Thou art powerful, and I am helpless; why art Thou fighting me? Thou art considerate, and I am prudent; why art Thou destroying me? Thou hast created woman with love, and why, with love, dost Thou ruin her? With Thy right hand dost Thou lift her, and with Thy left hand dost Thou strike her into the abyss, and she knows not why. In her mouth Thou blowest the breath of life, and in her heart Thou sowest the seeds of death. Thou dost show her the path of happiness, but Thou leadest her in the road of misery; in her mouth Thou dost place a song of happiness, but then Thou dost close her lips with sorrow and dost fetter her tongue with agony. With Thy mysterious fingers dost Thou dress her wounds, and with Thine hands Thou drawest the dread of pain round her pleasures. In her bed Thou hidest pleasure and peace, but beside it Thou dost erect obstacles and fear. Thou dost excite her affection through Thy will, and from her affection does shame emanate. By Thy will Thou showest her the beauty of creation, but her love for beauty becomes a terrible famine. Thou dost make her drink life in the cup of death, and death in the cup of life.

Thou purifiest her with tears, and in tears her life streams away. Oh, Lord, Thou hast opened my eyes with love, and with love Thou hast blinded me. Thou hast kissed me with Thy lips and struck me with Thy strong hand. Thou hast planted in my heart a white rose, but around the rose a barrier of thorns. Thou hast tied my present with the spirit of a young man whom I love, but my life with the body of an unknown man. So help me, my Lord, to be strong in this deadly struggle and assist me to be truthful and virtuous until death. Thy will be done, Oh, Lord God."

Silence continued. Selma looked down, pale and frail; her arms dropped, and her head bowed and it seemed to me as if a tempest had broken a branch from a tree and cast it down to dry and perish.

I took her cold hand and kissed it, but when I attempted to console her, it was I who needed consolation more than she did. I kept silent, thinking of our plight and listening to my heartbeats. Neither of us said more.

Extreme torture is mute, and so we sat silent, petrified, like columns of marble buried under the sand of an earthquake. Neither wished to listen to the other because our heart-threads had become weak and even breathing would have broken them.

It was midnight, and we could see the crescent

moon rising from behind Mt. Sunnin, and it looked, in the midst of the stars, like the face of a corpse, in a coffin surrounded by the dim lights of candles. And Lebanon looked like an old man whose back was bent with age and whose eyes were a haven for insomnia, watching the dark and waiting for dawn, like a king sitting on the ashes of his throne in the debris of his palace.

The mountains, trees, and rivers change their appearance with the vicissitudes of times and seasons, as a man changes with his experiences and emotions. The lofty poplar that resembles a bride in the daytime, will look like a column of smoke in the evening; the huge rock that stands impregnable at noon, will appear to be a miserable pauper at night, with earth for his bed and the sky for his cover; and the rivulet that we see glittering in the morning and hear singing the hymn of Eternity, will, in the evening, turn to a stream of tears wailing like a mother bereft of her child, and Lebanon, that had looked dignified a week before, when the moon was full and our spirits were happy, looked sorrowful and lonesome that night.

We stood up and bade each other farewell, but love and despair stood between us like two ghosts, one stretching his wings with his fingers over our

throats, one weeping and the other laughing hideously.

As I took Selma's hand and put it to my lips, she came close to me and placed a kiss on my forehead, then dropped on the wooden bench. She shut her eyes and whispered softly, "Oh, Lord God, have mercy on me and mend my broken wings!"

As I left Selma in the garden, I felt as if my senses were covered with a thick veil, like a lake whose surface is concealed by fog.

The beauty of trees, the moonlight, the deep silence, everything about me looked ugly and horrible. The true light that had showed me the beauty and wonder of the universe was converted to a great flame of fire that seared my heart; and the Eternal music I used to hear became a clamor, more frightening than the roar of a lion.

I reached my room, and like a wounded bird shot down by a hunter, I fell on my bed, repeating the words of Selma: "Oh, Lord God, have mercy on me and mend my broken wings!"

ARRIAGE IN these days is a mockery whose management is in the hands of young men and parents. In most countries the young men win while the parents lose. The woman is looked upon as a commodity, purchased and delivered from one house to another. In time her beauty fades and she becomes like an old piece of furniture left in a dark corner.

Modern civilization has made woman a little wiser, but it has increased her suffering because of man's covetousness. The woman of yesterday was a

happy wife, but the woman of today is a miserable mistress. In the past she walked blindly in the light, but now she walks open-eyed in the dark. She was beautiful in her ignorance, virtuous in her simplicity, and strong in her weakness. Today she has become ugly in her ingenuity, superficial and heartless in her knowledge. Will the day ever come when beauty and knowledge, ingenuity and virtue, and weakness of body and strength of spirit will be united in a woman?

I am one of those who believe that spiritual progress is a rule of human life, but the approach to perfection is slow and painful. If a woman elevates herself in one respect and is retarded in another, it is because the rough trail that leads to the mountain peak is not free of ambushes of thieves and lairs of wolves.

This strange generation exists between sleeping and waking. It holds in its hands the soil of the past and the seeds of the future. However, we find in every city a woman who symbolizes the future.

In the city of Beirut, Selma Karamy was the symbol of the future Oriental woman, but, like many who live ahead of their time, she became the victim of the present; and like a flower snatched from its stem and carried away by the current of a river, she walked in the miserable procession of the defeated.

Mansour Bey Galib and Selma were married, and lived together in a beautiful house at Ras Beyrouth, where all the wealthy dignitaries resided. Farris Effandi Karamy was left in his solitary home in the midst of his garden and orchards like a lonely shepherd amid his flock.

The days and merry nights of the wedding passed, but the honeymoon left memories of times of bitter sorrow, as wars leave skulls and dead bones on the battlefield. The dignity of an Oriental wedding inspires the hearts of young men and women, but its termination may drop them like millstones to the bottom of the sea. Their exhilaration is like footprints on sand which remain only till they are washed away by the waves.

Spring departed, and so did summer and autumn, but my love for Selma increased day by day until it became a kind of mute worship, the feeling that an orphan has toward the soul of his mother in Heaven. My yearning was converted to blind sorrow that could see nothing but itself, and the passion that drew tears from my eyes was replaced by perplexity that sucked the blood from my heart, and my sighs of affection became a constant prayer for the happiness of Selma and her husband and peace for her father.

My hopes and prayers were in vain, because

Selma's misery was an internal malady that nothing but death could cure.

Mansour Bey was a man to whom all the luxuries of life came easily; but, in spite of that, he was dissatisfied and rapacious. After marrying Selma, he neglected her father in his loneliness and prayed for his death so that he could inherit what was left of the old man's wealth.

Mansour Bey's character was similar to his uncle's; the only difference between the two was that the Bishop got everything he wanted secretly, under the protection of his ecclesiastical robe and the golden cross which he wore on his chest, while his nephew did everything publicly. The Bishop went to church in the morning and spent the rest of the day pilfering from the widows, orphans, and simple-minded people. But Mansour Bey spent his days in pursuit of sexual satisfaction. On Sunday, Bishop Bulos Galib preached his Gospel; but during weekdays he never practiced what he preached, occupying himself with the political intrigues of the locality. And, by means of his uncle's prestige and influence, Mansour Bey made it his business to secure political plums for those who could offer a sufficient bribe.

Bishop Bulos was a thief who hid himself under the cover of night, while his nephew, Mansour Bey, was a swindler who walked proudly in daylight.

However, the people of Oriental nations place trust in such as they—wolves and butchers who ruin their country through covetousness and crush their neighbors with an iron hand.

Why do I occupy these pages with words about the betrayers of poor nations instead of reserving all the space for the story of a miserable woman with a broken heart? Why do I shed tears for oppressed peoples rather than keep all my tears for the memory of a weak woman whose life was snatched by the teeth of death?

But my dear readers, don't you think that such a woman is like a nation that is oppressed by priests and rulers? Don't you believe that thwarted love which leads a woman to the grave is like the despair which pervades the people of the earth? A woman is to a nation as light is to a lamp. Will not the light be dim if the oil in the lamp is low?

Autumn passed, and the wind blew the yellow leaves from the trees, making way for winter, which came howling and crying. I was still in the City of Beirut without a companion save my dreams, which would lift my spirit to the sky and then bury it deep in the bosom of the earth.

The sorrowful spirit finds relaxation in solitude. It abhors people, as a wounded deer deserts the herd and lives in a cave until it is healed or dead.

One day I heard that Farris Effandi was ill. I left my solitary abode and walked to his home, taking a new route, a lonely path between olive trees, avoiding the main road with its rattling carriage wheels.

Arriving at the old man's house, I entered and found Farris Effandi lying on his bed, weak and pale. His eyes were sunken and looked like two deep, dark valleys haunted by the ghosts of pain. The smile which had always enlivened his face was choked with pain and agony; and the bones of his gentle hands looked like naked branches trembling before the tempest. As I approached him and inquired as to his health, he turned his pale face toward me, and on his trembling lips appeared a smile, and he said in a weak voice, "Go—go, my son, to the other room and comfort Selma and bring her to sit by the side of my bed."

I entered the adjacent room and found Selma lying on a divan, covering her head with her arms and burying her face in a pillow so that her father would not hear her weeping. Approaching slowly, I pronounced her name in a voice that seemed more like sighing than whispering. She moved fearfully, as if she had been interrupted in a terrible dream, and sat up, looking at me with glazed eyes, doubting whether I was a ghost or a living being. After a deep silence which took us back on the wings of memory

to that hour when we were intoxicated with the wine of love, Selma wiped away her tears and said, "See how time has changed us! See how time has changed the course of our lives and left us in these ruins. In this place spring united us in a bond of love, and in this place has brought us together before the throne of death. How beautiful was spring, and how terrible is this winter!"

Speaking thus, she covered her face again with her hands as if she were shielding her eyes from the spectre of the past standing before her. I put my hand on her head and said, "Come, Selma, come and let us be as strong towers before the tempest. Let us stand like brave soldiers before the enemy and face his weapons. If we are killed, we shall die as martyrs; and if we win, we shall live as heroes. Braving obstacles and hardships is nobler than retreat to tranquility. The butterfly that hovers around the lamp until it dies is more admirable than the mole that lives in a dark tunnel. Come, Selma, let us walk this rough path firmly, with our eyes toward the sun so that we may not see the skulls and serpents among the rocks and thorns. If fear should stop us in the middle of the road, we would hear only ridicule from the voices of the night, but if we reach the mountain peak bravely we shall join the heavenly spirits in songs of triumph and joy. Cheer up, Selma, wipe

away your tears and remove the sorrow from your face. Rise, and let us sit by the bed of your father, because his life depends on your life, and your smile is his only cure."

Kindly and affectionately she looked at me and said, "Are you asking me to have patience, while you are in need of it yourself? Will a hungry man give his bread to another hungry man? Or will a sick man give medicine to another which he himself needs badly?"

She rose, her head bent slightly forward, and we walked to the old man's room and sat by the side of his bed. Selma forced a smile and pretended to be patient, and her father tried to make her believe that he was feeling better and getting stronger; but both father and daughter were aware of each other's sorrow and heard the unvoiced sighs. They were like two equal forces, wearing each other away silently. The father's heart was melting because of his daughter's plight. They were two pure souls, one departing and the other agonized with grief, embracing in love and death; and I was between the two with my own troubled heart. We were three people, gathered and crushed by the hands of destiny; an old man like a dwelling ruined by flood, a young woman whose symbol was a lily beheaded by the sharp edge of a sickle, and a young man who was a weak sapling,

bent by a snowfall; and all of us were toys in the hands of fate.

Farris Effandi moved slowly and stretched his weak hand toward Selma, and in a loving and tender voice said, "Hold my hand, my beloved." Selma held his hand; then he said, "I have lived long enough, and I have enjoyed the fruits of life's seasons. I have experienced all its phases with equanimity. I lost your mother when you were three years of age, and she left you as a precious treasure in my lap. I watched you grow, and your face reproduced your mother's features as stars reflected in a calm pool of water. Your character, intelligence, and beauty are your mother's, even your manner of speaking and gestures. You have been my only consolation in this life because you were the image of your mother in every deed and word. Now, I grow old, and my only resting place is between the soft wings of death. Be comforted, my beloved daughter, because I have lived long enough to see you as a woman. Be happy because I shall live in you after my death. My departure today would be no different from my going tomorrow or the day after, for our days are perishing like the leaves of autumn. The hour of my death approaches rapidly, and my soul is desirous of being united with your mother's."

As he uttered these words sweetly and lovingly,

his face was radiant. Then he put his hand under his pillow and pulled out a small picture in a gold frame. With his eyes on the little photograph, he said, "Come, Selma, come and see your mother in this picture."

Selma wiped away her tears, and after gazing long at the picture, she kissed it repeatedly and cried, "Oh, my beloved mother! Oh, mother!" Then she placed her trembling lips on the picture as if she wished to pour her soul into that image.

The most beautiful word on the lips of mankind is the word "Mother," and the most beautiful call is the call of "My mother." It is a word full of hope and love, a sweet and kind word coming from the depths of the heart. The mother is every thing—she is our consolation in sorrow, our hope in misery, and our strength in weakness. She is the source of love, mercy, sympathy, and forgiveness. He who loses his mother loses a pure soul who blesses and guards him constantly.

Every thing in nature bespeaks the mother. The sun is the mother of earth and gives it its nourishment of heat; it never leaves the universe at night until it has put the earth to sleep to the song of the sea and the hymn of birds and brooks. And this earth is the mother of trees and flowers. It produces them, nurses them, and weans them. The trees and

flowers become kind mothers of their great fruits and seeds. And the mother, the prototype of all existence, is the eternal spirit, full of beauty and love.

Selma Karamy never knew her mother because she had died when Selma was an infant, but Selma wept when she saw the picture and cried, "Oh, mother!" The word mother is hidden in our hearts, and it comes upon our lips in hours of sorrow and happiness as the perfume comes from the heart of the rose and mingles with clear and cloudy air.

Selma stared at her mother's picture, kissing it repeatedly, until she collapsed by her father's bed.

The old man placed both hands on her head and said, "I have shown you, my dear child, a picture of your mother on paper. Now listen to me and I shall let you hear her words."

She lifted her head like a little bird in the nest that hears its mother's wing, and looked at him attentively.

Farris Effandi opened his mouth and said, "Your mother was nursing you when she lost her father; she cried and wept at his going, but she was wise and patient. She sat by me in this room as soon as the funeral was over and held my hand and said, 'Farris, my father is dead now and you are my only consolation in this world. The heart's affections are divided like the branches of the cedar tree; if the tree

loses one strong branch, it will suffer but it does not die. It will pour all its vitality into the next branch so that it will grow and fill the empty place.' This is what your mother told me when her father died, and you should say the same thing when death takes my body to its resting place and my soul to God's care."

Selma answered him with falling tears and broken heart, "When Mother lost her father, you took his place; but who is going to take yours when you are gone? She was left in the care of a loving and truthful husband; she found consolation in her little daughter, and who will be my consolation when you pass away? You have been my father and mother and the companion of my youth."

Saying these words, she turned and looked at me, and, holding the side of my garment, said, "This is the only friend I shall have after you are gone, but how can he console me when he is suffering also? How can a broken heart find consolation in a disappointed soul? A sorrowful woman cannot be comforted by her neighbor's sorrow, nor can a bird fly with broken wings. He is the friend of my soul, but I have already placed a heavy burden of sorrow upon him and dimmed his eyes with my tears till he can see nothing but darkness. He is a brother whom I dearly love, but he is like all brothers who share my

sorrow and help me shed tears which increase my bitterness and burn my heart."

Selma's words stabbed my heart, and I felt that I could bear no more. The old man listened to her with depressed spirit, trembling like the light of a lamp before the wind. Then he stretched out his hand and said, "Let me go peacefully, my child. I have broken the bars of this cage; let me fly and do not stop me, for your mother is calling me. The sky is clear and the sea is calm and the boat is ready to sail; do not delay its voyage. Let my body rest with those who are resting; let my dream end and my soul awaken with the dawn; let your soul embrace mine and give me the kiss of hope; let no drops of sorrow or bitterness fall upon my body lest the flowers and grass refuse their nourishment. Do not shed tears of misery upon my hand, for they may grow thorns upon my grave. Do not draw lines of agony upon my forehead, for the wind may pass and read them and refuse to carry the dust of my bones to the green prairies . . . I loved you, my child, while I lived, and I shall love you when I am dead, and my soul shall always watch over you and protect you."

Then Farris Effandi looked at me with his eyes half closed and said, "My son, be a real brother to Selma as your father was to me. Be her help and

friend in need, and do not let her mourn, because mourning for the dead is a mistake. Repeat to her pleasant tales and sing for her the songs of life so that she may forget her sorrows. Remember me to your father; ask him to tell you the stories of our youth and tell him that I loved him in the person of his son in the last hour of my life."

Silence prevailed, and I could see the pallor of death on the old man's face. Then he rolled his eyes and looked at us and whispered, "Don't call the physician, for he might extend my sentence in this prison by his medicine. The days of slavery are gone, and my soul seeks the freedom of the skies. And do not call the priest to my bedside, because his incantations would not save me if I were a sinner, nor would it rush me to Heaven if I were innocent. The will of humanity cannot change the will of God, as an astrologer cannot change the course of the stars. But after my death let the doctors and priest do what they please, for my ship will continue sailing until it reaches its destination."

At midnight Farris Effandi opened his tired eyes for the last time and focused them on Selma, who was kneeling by his bedside. He tried to speak, but could not, for death had already choked his voice; but he finally managed to say, "The night has passed

. . . Oh, Selma . . . Oh . . . Oh, Selma . . ." Then he bent his head, his face turned white, and I could see a smile on his lips as he breathed his last.

Selma felt her father's hand. It was cold. Then she raised her head and looked at his face. It was covered with the veil of death. Selma was so choked that she could not shed tears, nor sigh, nor even move. For a moment she stared at him with fixed eyes like those of a statue; then she bent down until her forehead touched the floor, and said, "Oh, Lord, have mercy and mend our broken wings."

Farris Effandi Karamy died; his soul was embraced by Eternity, and his body was returned to the earth. Mansour Bey Galib got possession of his wealth, and Selma became a prisoner for life—a life of grief and misery.

I was lost in sorrow and reverie. Days and nights preyed upon me as the eagle ravages its victim. Many a time I tried to forget my misfortune by occupying myself with books and scriptures of past generations, but it was like extinguishing fire with oil, for I could see nothing in the procession of the past but tragedy and could hear nothing but weeping and wailing. The Book of Job was more fascinating to me than the Psalms and I preferred the Elegies of Jeremiah to the Song of Solomon. *Hamlet* was closer to my

heart than all other dramas of western writers. Thus despair weakens our sight and closes our ears. We can see nothing but spectres of doom, and can hear only the beating of our agitated hearts.

8

BETWEEN CHRIST AND ISHTAR

N THE MIDST OF
the gardens and hills which connect the city of Beirut
with Lebanon there is a small temple, very ancient,
dug out of white rock, surrounded by olive, almond,
and willow trees. Although this temple is a half mile
from the main highway, at the time of my story very
few people interested in relics and ancient ruins had
visited it. It was one of many interesting places hidden and forgotten in Lebanon. Due to its seclusion,
it had become a haven for worshipers and a shrine for
lonely lovers.

As one enters this temple he sees on the wall at
the east side an old Phoenician picture, carved in the

rock, depicting Ishtar, goddess of love and beauty, sitting on her throne, surrounded by seven nude virgins standing in different poses. The first one carries a torch; the second, a guitar; the third, a censer; the fourth, a jug of wine; the fifth, a branch of roses; the sixth, a wreath of laurel; the seventh, a bow and arrow; and all of them look at Ishtar reverently.

On the second wall there is another picture, more modern than the first one, symbolizing Christ nailed to the cross, and at His side stand His sorrowful mother and Mary Magdalene and two other women weeping. This Byzantine picture shows that it was carved in the fifteenth or sixteenth century.*

On the west side wall there are two round transits through which the sun's rays enter the temple and strike the pictures and make them look as if they were painted with gold water color. In the middle of the temple there is a square marble with old paintings on its sides, some of which can hardly be seen under the petrified lumps of blood which show that the ancient people offered sacrifices on this rock and poured perfume, wine, and oil upon it.

There is nothing else in that little temple except deep silence, revealing to the living the secrets of the

---

* It is known by the students of relics that most of the Christian churches in the East were temples for the old Phoenician and Greek gods. In Damascus, Antioch and Constantinople, there are many edifices, the walls of which echoed heathen hymns; these places were converted into churches and then into mosques.

goddess and speaking wordlessly of past generations and the evolution of religions. Such a sight carries the poet to a world far away from the one in which he dwells and convinces the philosopher that men were born religious; they felt a need for that which they could not see and drew symbols, the meaning of which divulged their hidden secrets and their desires in life and death.

In that unknown temple, I met Selma once every month and spent the hours with her, looking at those strange pictures, thinking of the crucified Christ and pondering upon the young Phoenician men and women who lived, loved and worshipped beauty in the person of Ishtar by burning incense before her statue and pouring perfume on her shrine, people for whom nothing is left to speak except the name, repeated by the march of time before the face of Eternity.

It is hard to write down in words the memories of those hours when I met Selma—those heavenly hours, filled with pain, happiness, sorrow, hope, and misery.

We met secretly in the old temple, remembering the old days, discussing our present, fearing our future, and gradually bringing out the hidden secrets in the depths of our hearts and complaining to each other of our misery and suffering, trying to console

ourselves with imaginary hopes and sorrowful dreams. Every now and then we would become calm and wipe our tears and start smiling, forgetting everything except Love; we embraced each other until our hearts melted; then Selma would print a pure kiss on my forehead and fill my heart with ecstasy; I would return the kiss as she bent her ivory neck while her cheeks became gently red like the first ray of dawn on the forehead of hills. We silently looked at the distant horizon where the clouds were colored with the orange ray of sunset.

Our conversation was not limited to love; every now and then we drifted on to current topics and exchanged ideas. During the course of conversation Selma spoke of woman's place in society, the imprint that the past generation had left on her character, the relationship between husband and wife, and the spiritual diseases and corruption which threatened married life. I remember her saying: "The poets and writers are trying to understand the reality of woman, but up to this day they have not understood the hidden secrets of her heart, because they look upon her from behind the sexual veil and see nothing but externals; they look upon her through a magnifying glass of hatefulness and find nothing except weakness and submission."

On another occasion she said, pointing to the

carved pictures on the walls of the temple, "In the heart of this rock there are two symbols depicting the essence of a woman's desires and revealing the hidden secrets of her soul, moving between love and sorrow—between affection and sacrifice, between Ishtar sitting on the throne and Mary standing by the cross. The man buys glory and reputation, but the woman pays the price."

No one knew about our secret meetings except God and the flock of birds which flew over the temple. Selma used to come in her carriage to a place named Pasha Park and from there she walked to the temple, where she found me anxiously waiting for her.

We feared not the observer's eyes, neither did our consciences bother us; the spirit which is purified by fire and washed by tears is higher than what the people call shame and disgrace; it is free from the laws of slavery and old customs against the affections of the human heart. That spirit can proudly stand unashamed before the throne of God.

Human society has yielded for seventy centuries to corrupted laws until it cannot understand the meaning of the superior and eternal laws. A man's eyes have become accustomed to the dim light of candles and cannot see the sunlight. Spiritual disease is inherited from one generation to another until it has become a part of the people, who look upon it, not as a disease, but as a natural gift, showered by God upon Adam. If those people found someone free from the germs of this disease, they would think of him with shame and disgrace.

Those who think evil of Selma Karamy because she left her husband's home and met me in the temple are the diseased and weak-minded kind who look upon the healthy and sound as rebels. They are like insects crawling in the dark for fear of being stepped upon by the passers-by.

The oppressed prisoner, who can break away from his jail and does not do so, is a coward. Selma, an innocent and oppressed prisoner, was unable to free herself from slavery. Was she to blame because she looked through the jail window upon the green fields and spacious sky? Will the people count her as being untruthful to her husband because she came from his home to sit by me between Christ and Ishtar? Let the people say what they please; Selma had passed the marshes which submerge other spirits and had landed in a world that could not be reached by the howling of wolves and rattling of snakes. People may say what they want about me, for the spirit who has seen the spectre of death cannot be scared by the faces of thieves; the soldier who has seen the swords glittering over his head and streams of blood under his feet does not care about rocks thrown at him by the children on the streets.

THE SACRIFICE

ONE DAY IN THE LATE part of June, as the people left the city for the mountain to avoid the heat of summer, I went as usual to the temple to meet Selma, carrying with me a little book of Andalusian poems. As I reached the temple I sat there waiting for Selma, glancing at intervals at the pages of my book, reciting those verses which filled my heart with ecstasy and brought to my soul the memory of the kings, poets, and knights who bade farewell to Granada, and left, with tears in their eyes and sorrow in their hearts, their palaces, institutions and hopes behind. In an hour I saw Selma walking in the midst of the gardens and approaching the temple, leaning on her parasol as if

she were carrying all the worries of the world upon her shoulders. As she entered the temple and sat by me, I noticed some sort of change in her eyes and I was anxious to inquire about it.

Selma felt what was going on in my mind, and she put her hand on my head and said, "Come close to me, come my beloved, come and let me quench my thirst, for the hour of separation has come."

I asked her, "Did your husband find out about our meetings here?" She responded, "My husband does not care about me, neither does he know how I spend my time, for he is busy with those poor girls whom poverty has driven into the houses of ill fame; those girls who sell their bodies for bread, kneaded with blood and tears."

I inquired, "What prevents you from coming to this temple and sitting by me reverently before God? Is your soul requesting our separation?"

She answered with tears in her eyes, "No, my beloved, my spirit did not ask for separation, for you are a part of me. My eyes never get tired of looking at you, for you are their light; but if destiny ruled that I should walk the rough path of life loaded with shackles, would I be satisfied if your fate should be like mine?" Then she added, "I cannot say everything, because the tongue is mute with pain and cannot talk; the lips are sealed with misery and can-

not move; all I can say to you is that I am afraid you may fall in the same trap I fell in."

Then I asked, "What do you mean, Selma, and of whom are you afraid?" She covered her face with her hands and said, "The Bishop has already found out that once a month I have been leaving the grave which he buried me in."

I inquired, "Did the Bishop find out about our meetings here?" She answered, "If he did, you would not see me here sitting by you; but he is getting suspicious and he informed all his servants and guards to watch me closely. I am feeling that the house I live in and the path I walk on are all eyes watching me, and fingers pointing at me, and ears listening to the whisper of my thoughts."

She was silent for a while, and then she added, with tears pouring down her cheeks, "I am not afraid of the Bishop, for wetness does not scare the drowned, but I am afraid you might fall into the trap and become his prey; you are still young and free as the sunlight. I am not frightened of fate which has shot all its arrows in my breast, but I am afraid the serpent might bite your feet and detain you from climbing the mountain peak where the future awaits you with its pleasure and glory."

I said, "He who has not been bitten by the serpents of light and snapped at by the wolves of dark-

ness will always be deceived by the days and nights. But listen, Selma, listen carefully; is separation the only means of avoiding people's evils and meanness? Has the path of love and freedom been closed and is nothing left except submission to the will of the slaves of death?"

She responded, "Nothing is left save separation and bidding each other farewell."

With rebellious spirit I took her hand and said excitedly, "We have yielded to the people's will for a long time; since the time we met until this hour we have been led by the blind and have worshipped with them before their idols. Since the time I met you we have been in the hands of the Bishop like two balls which he has thrown around as he pleased. Are we going to submit to his will until death takes us away? Did God give us the breath of life to place it under death's feet? Did He give us liberty to make it a shadow for slavery? He who extinguishes his spirit's fire with his own hands is an infidel in the eyes of Heaven, for Heaven set the fire that burns in our spirits. He who does not rebel against oppression is doing himself injustice. I love you, Selma, and you love me, too; and Love is a precious treasure, it is God's gift to sensitive and great spirits. Shall we throw this treasure away and let the pigs scatter it and trample on it? This world is full of

wonder and beauty. Why are we living in this narrow tunnel which the Bishop and his assistants have dug out for us? Life is full of happiness and freedom; why don't we take this heavy yoke off our shoulders and break the chains tied to our feet, and walk freely toward peace? Get up and let us leave this small temple for God's great temple. Let us leave this country and all its slavery and ignorance for another country far away and unreached by the hands of the thieves. Let us go to the coast under the cover of night and catch a boat that will take us across the oceans, where we can find a new life full of happiness and understanding. Do not hesitate, Selma, for these minutes are more precious to us than the crowns of kings and more sublime than the thrones of angels. Let us follow the column of light that leads us from this arid desert into the green fields where flowers and aromatic plants grow."

She shook her head and gazed at something invisible on the ceiling of the temple; a sorrowful smile appeared on her lips; then she said, "No, no my beloved. Heaven placed in my hand a cup, full of vinegar and gall; I forced myself to drink it in order to know the full bitterness at the bottom until nothing was left save a few drops, which I shall drink patiently. I am not worthy of a new life of love and peace; I am not strong enough for life's

pleasure and sweetness, because a bird with broken wings cannot fly in the spacious sky. The eyes that are accustomed to the dim light of a candle are not strong enough to stare at the sun. Do not talk to me of happiness; its memory makes me suffer. Mention not peace to me; its shadow frightens me; but look at me and I will show you the holy torch which Heaven has lighted in the ashes of my heart —you know that I love you as a mother loves her only child, and Love only taught me to protect you even from myself. It is Love, purified with fire, that stops me from following you to the farthest land. Love kills my desires so that you may live freely and virtuously. Limited love asks for possession of the beloved, but the unlimited asks only for itself. Love that comes between the naiveté and awakening of youth satisfies itself with possessing, and grows with embraces. But Love which is born in the firmament's lap and has descended with the night's secrets is not contented with anything but Eternity and immortality; it does not stand reverently before anything except deity.

"When I knew that the Bishop wanted to stop me from leaving his nephew's house and to take my only pleasure away from me, I stood before the window of my room and looked toward the sea, thinking of the vast countries beyond it and the real freedom

and personal independence which can be found there. I felt that I was living close to you, surrounded by the shadow of your spirit, submerged in the ocean of your affection. But all these thoughts which illuminate a woman's heart and make her rebel against old customs and live in the shadow of freedom and justice, made me believe that I am weak and that our love is limited and feeble, unable to stand before the sun's face. I cried like a king whose kingdom and treasures have been usurped, but immediately I saw your face through my tears and your eyes gazing at me and I remembered what you said to me once (*Come, Selma, come and let us be strong towers before the tempest. Let us stand like brave soldiers before the enemy and face his weapons. If we are killed, we shall die as martyrs; and if we win, we shall live as heroes. Braving obstacles and hardships is nobler than retreat to tranquility.*) These words, my beloved, you uttered when the wings of death were hovering around my father's bed; I remembered them yesterday when the wings of despair were hovering above my head. I strengthened myself and felt, while in the darkness of my prison, some sort of precious freedom easing our difficulties and diminishing our sorrows. I found out that our love was as deep as the ocean and as high as the stars and as spacious as the sky. I came here to see you, and in my

weak spirit there is a new strength, and this strength is the ability to sacrifice a great thing in order to obtain a greater one; it is the sacrifice of my happiness so that you may remain virtuous and honorable in the eyes of the people and be far away from their treachery and persecution . . .

"In the past, when I came to this place I felt as if heavy chains were pulling down on me, but today I came here with a new determination that laughs at the shackles and shortens the way. I used to come to this temple like a scared phantom, but today I came like a brave woman who feels the urgency of sacrifice and knows the value of suffering, a woman who likes to protect the one she loves from the ignorant people and from her hungry spirit. I used to sit by you like a trembling shadow, but today I came here to show you my true self before Ishtar and Christ.

"I am a tree, grown in the shade, and today I stretched my branches to tremble for a while in the daylight. I came here to tell you good-bye, my beloved, and it is my hope that our farewell will be great and awful like our love. Let our farewell be like fire that bends the gold and makes it more resplendent."

Selma did not allow me to speak or protest, but she looked at me, her eyes glittering, her face retaining its dignity, seeming like an angel worthy of silence and respect. Then she flung herself upon me, something which she had never done before, and put

her smooth arms around me and printed a long, deep, fiery kiss on my lips.

As the sun went down, withdrawing its rays from those gardens and orchards, Selma moved to the middle of the temple and gazed long at its walls and corners as if she wanted to pour the light of her eyes on its pictures and symbols. Then she walked forward and reverently knelt before the picture of Christ and kissed His feet, and she whispered, "Oh, Christ, I have chosen Thy Cross and deserted Ishtar's world of pleasure and happiness; I have worn the wreath of thorns and discarded the wreath of laurel and washed myself with blood and tears instead of perfume and scent; I have drunk vinegar and gall from a cup which was meant for wine and nectar; accept me, my Lord, among Thy followers and lead me toward Galilee with those who have chosen Thee, contented with their sufferings and delighted with their sorrows."

Then she rose and looked at me and said, "Now I shall return happily to my dark cave, where horrible ghosts reside. Do not sympathize with me, my beloved, and do not feel sorry for me, because the soul that sees the shadow of God once will never be frightened, thereafter, of the ghosts of devils. And the eye that looks on Heaven once will not be closed by the pains of the world."

Uttering these words, Selma left the place of wor-

ship; and I remained there lost in a deep sea of thoughts, absorbed in the world of revelation where God sits on the throne and the angels write down the acts of human beings, and the souls recite the tragedy of life, and the brides of Heaven sing the hymns of love, sorrow and immortality.

Night had already come when I awakened from my swoon and found myself bewildered in the midst of the gardens, repeating the echo of every word uttered by Selma and remembering her silence, her actions, her movements, her expressions and the touch of her hands, until I realized the meaning of farewell and the pain of lonesomeness. I was depressed and heart-broken. It was my first discovery of the fact that men, even if they are born free, will remain slaves of strict laws enacted by their forefathers; and that the firmament, which we imagine as unchanging, is the yielding of today to the will of tomorrow and submission of yesterday to the will of today—Many a time, since that night, I have thought of the spiritual law which made Selma prefer death to life, and many a time I have made a comparison between nobility of sacrifice and happiness of rebellion to find out which one is nobler and more beautiful; but until now I have distilled only one truth out of the whole matter, and this truth is *sincerity,* which makes all our deeds beautiful and honorable. And this *sincerity* was in Selma Karamy.

10

THE RESCUER

IVE YEARS OF SELMA'S
marriage passed without bringing children to
strengthen the ties of spiritual relation between her
and her husband and bind their repugnant souls
together.

A barren woman is looked upon with disdain
everywhere because of most men's desire to perpetuate themselves through posterity.

The substantial man considers his childless wife
as an enemy; he detests her and deserts her and
wishes her death. Mansour Bey Galib was that kind

of man; materially, he was like earth, and hard like steel and greedy like a grave. His desire of having a child to carry on his name and reputation made him hate Selma in spite of her beauty and sweetness.

A tree grown in a cave does not bear fruit; and Selma, who lived in the shade of life, did not bear children. . . .

The nightingale does not make his nest in a cage lest slavery be the lot of its chicks. . . . Selma was a prisoner of misery and it was Heaven's will that she would not have another prisoner to share her life. The flowers of the field are the children of sun's affection and nature's love; and the children of men are the flowers of love and compassion. . . .

The spirit of love and compassion never dominated Selma's beautiful home at Ras Beyrouth; nevertheless, she knelt down on her knees every night before Heaven and asked God for a child in whom she would find comfort and consolation. . . . She prayed successively until Heaven answered her prayers. . . .

The tree of the cave blossomed to bear fruit at last. The nightingale in the cage commenced making its nest with the feathers of its wings.

Selma stretched her chained arms toward Heaven to receive God's precious gift and nothing in the

world could have made her happier than becoming a potential mother. . . .

She waited anxiously, counting the days and looking forward to the time when Heaven's sweetest melody, the voice of her child, should ring in her ears. . . .

She commenced to see the dawn of a brighter future through her tears. . . .

It was in the month of Nisan when Selma was stretched on the bed of pain and labor, where life and death were wrestling. The doctor and the midwife were ready to deliver to the world a new guest. Late at night Selma started her successive cry . . . a cry of life's partition from life . . . a cry of continuance in the firmament of nothingness . . . a cry of a weak force before the stillness of great forces . . . the cry of poor Selma who was lying down in despair under the feet of life and death.

At dawn Selma gave birth to a baby boy. When she opened her eyes she saw smiling faces all over the room, then she looked again and saw life and death still wrestling by her bed. She closed her eyes and cried, saying for the first time, "Oh, my son." The midwife wrapped the infant with silk swaddles and placed him by his mother, but the doctor kept looking at Selma and sorrowfully shaking his head.

The voices of joy woke the neighbors, who rushed into the house to felicitate the father upon the birth of his heir, but the doctor still gazed at Selma and her infant and shook his head. . . .

The servants hurried to spread the good news to Mansour Bey, but the doctor stared at Selma and her child with a disappointed look on his face.

As the sun came out, Selma took the infant to her breast; he opened his eyes for the first time and looked at his mother; then he quivered and closed them for the last time. The doctor took the child from Selma's arms, and on his cheeks fell tears; then he whispered to himself, "He is a departing guest."

The child passed away while the neighbors were celebrating with the father in the big hall at the house and drinking to the health of the heir; and Selma looked at the doctor, and pleaded, "Give me my child and let me embrace him."

Though the child was dead, the sounds of the drinking cups increased in the hall. . . .

He was born at dawn and died at sunrise. . . .

He was born like a thought and died like a sigh and disappeared like a shadow.

He did not live to console and comfort his mother.

His life began at the end of the night and ended at the beginning of the day, like a drop of dew

poured by the eyes of the dark and dried by the touch of the light.

A pearl brought by the tide to the coast and returned by the ebb into the depth of the sea. . . .

A lily that has just blossomed from the bud of life and is mashed under the feet of death.

A dear guest whose appearance illuminated Selma's heart and whose departure killed her soul.

This is the life of men, the life of nations, the life of suns, moons and stars.

And Selma focused her eyes upon the doctor and cried, "Give me my child and let me embrace him; give me my child and let me nurse him."

Then the doctor bent his head. His voice choked and he said, "Your child is dead, Madame, be patient."

Upon hearing the doctor's announcement, Selma uttered a terrible cry. Then she was quiet for a moment and smiled happily. Her face brightened as if she had discovered something, and quietly she said, "Give me my child; bring him close to me and let me see him dead."

The doctor carried the dead child to Selma and placed him between her arms. She embraced him, then turned her face toward the wall and addressed the dead infant saying, "You have come to take me

away, my child; you have come to show me the way that leads to the coast. Here I am, my child; lead me and let us leave this dark cave."

And in a minute the sun's ray penetrated the window curtains and fell upon two calm bodies lying on a bed, guarded by the profound dignity of silence and shaded by the wings of death. The doctor left the room with tears in his eyes, and as he reached the big hall the celebration was converted into a funeral, but Mansour Bey Galib never uttered a word or shed a tear. He remained standing motionless like a statue, holding a drinking cup with his right hand.

. . . . .

The second day Selma was shrouded with her white wedding dress and laid in a coffin; the child's shroud was his swaddle; his coffin was his mother's arms; his grave was her calm breast. Two corpses were carried in one coffin, and I walked reverently with the crowd accompanying Selma and her infant to their resting place.

Arriving at the cemetery, Bishop Galib commenced chanting while the other priests prayed, and on their gloomy faces appeared a veil of ignorance and emptiness.

As the coffin went down, one of the bystanders whispered, "This is the first time in my life I have

seen two corpses in one coffin." Another one said, "It seems as if the child had come to rescue his mother from her pitiless husband."

A third one said, "Look at Mansour Bey: he is gazing at the sky as if his eyes were made of glass. He does not look like he has lost his wife and child in one day." A fourth one added, "His uncle, the Bishop, will marry him again tomorrow to a wealthier and stronger woman."

The Bishop and the priests kept on singing and chanting until the grave digger was through filling the ditch. Then, the people, individually, approached the Bishop and his nephew and offered their respects to them with sweet words of sympathy, but I stood lonely aside without a soul to console me, as if Selma and her child meant nothing to me.

The farewell-bidders left the cemetery; the grave digger stood by the new grave holding a shovel with his hand.

As I approached him, I inquired, "Do you remember where Farris Effandi Karamy was buried?"

He looked at me for a moment, then pointed at Selma's grave and said, "Right here; I placed his daughter upon him and upon his daughter's breast rests her child, and upon all I put the earth back with this shovel."

Then I said, "In this ditch you have also buried my heart."

As the grave digger disappeared behind the poplar trees, I could not resist any more; I dropped down on Selma's grave and wept.

THE VOICE
OF THE MASTER

I

The Master and the Disciple

I

The Master's Journey to Venice

AND IT CAME TO PASS that the Disciple saw the Master walking silently to and fro in the garden, and signs of deep sorrow showed upon his pale face. The Disciple greeted the Master in the name of Allah, and inquired after the cause of his grief. The Master motioned with his staff, and bade the Disciple seat himself on the rock by the fish pond. The Disciple did so, and made ready to listen to the Master's story.

Said the Master:

"You desire me to tell you of the tragedy which Memory reenacts every day and night upon the stage of my heart. You are weary of my long silence and my unspoken secret, and you are troubled by my sighs and lamentations. To yourself you say, 'If the Master will not admit me into the temple of his sorrows, how shall I ever enter into the house of his affections?'

"Hearken to my story . . . Listen, but do not pity me;

441

for pity is intended for the weak—and I am still strong in my affliction.

"From the days of my youth, I have been haunted, waking and sleeping, by the phantom of a strange woman. I see her when I am alone at night, sitting by my bedside. In the midnight silence I hear her heavenly voice. Often, when I close my eyes, I feel the touch of her gentle fingers upon my lips; and when I open my eyes, I am overcome with dread, and suddenly begin listening intently to the whispered sounds of Nothingness. . . .

"Often I wonder, saying to myself, 'Is it my fancy that sets me spinning until I seem to lose myself in the clouds? Have I fashioned from the sinews of my dreams a new divinity with a melodious voice and a gentle touch? Have I lost my senses, and in my madness have I created this dearly loved companion? Have I withdrawn myself from the society of men and the clamor of the city so that I might be alone with the object of my adoration? Have I shut my eyes and ears to Life's forms and accents so that I might the better see her and hear her divine voice?'

"Often I wonder: 'Am I a madman who is content to be alone, and from the phantoms of his loneliness fashions a companion and spouse for his soul?'

"I speak of a *Spouse*, and you marvel at that word. But how often are we puzzled by some strange experience, which we reject as impossible, but whose reality we cannot efface from our minds, try as we will?

"This visionary woman has indeed been my spouse,

sharing with me all the joys and sorrows of life. When I awake in the morning, I see her bending over my pillow, gazing at me with eyes glowing with kindness and maternal love. She is with me when I plan some undertaking, and she helps me bring it to fulfilment. When I sit down to my repast, she sits with me, and we exchange thoughts and words. In the evening, she is with me again, saying, 'We have tarried too long in this place. Let us walk in the fields and meadows.' Then I leave my work, and follow her into the fields, and we sit on a high rock and gaze at the distant horizon. She points to the golden cloud; and makes me aware of the song the birds sing before they retire for the night, thanking the Lord for the gift of freedom and peace.

"Many a time she comes to my room when I am anxious and troubled. But no sooner do I spy her, than all care and worry are turned to joy and calm. When my spirit rebels against man's injustice to man, and I see her face amidst those other faces I would flee from, the tempest in my heart subsides and is replaced by the heavenly voice of peace. When I am alone, and the bitter darts of life stab at my heart, and I am chained to the earth by life's shackles, I behold my companion gazing at me with love in her eyes, and sorrow turns to joy, and Life seems an Eden of happiness.

"You may ask, how can I be content with such a strange existence, and how can a man, like myself, in the spring-time of life, find joy in phantoms and dreams? But I say to you, the years I have spent in this state are the cornerstone of

all that I have come to know about Life, Beauty, Happiness, and Peace.

"For the companion of my imagination and I have been like thoughts freely hovering before the face of the sun, or floating on the surface of the waters, singing a song in the moonlight—a song of peace that soothes the spirit and leads it toward ineffable beauty.

"Life is that which we see and experience through the spirit; but the world around us we come to know through our understanding and reason. And such knowledge brings us great joy or sorrow. It was sorrow I was destined to experience before I reached the age of thirty. Would that I had died before I attained the years that drained my heart's blood and my life's sap, and left me a withered tree with branches that no longer move in the frolicsome breeze, and where birds no longer build their nests."

The Master paused, and then, seating himself by his Disciple, continued:

"Twenty years ago, the Governor of Mount Lebanon sent me to Venice on a scholarly mission, with a letter of recommendation to the Mayor of the city, whom he had met in Constantinople. I left Lebanon on an Italian vessel in the month of Nisan. The spring air was fragrant, and the white clouds hung above the horizon like so many lovely paintings. How shall I describe to you the exultation I felt during the journey? Words are too poor and too scant to express the inmost feeling in the heart of man.

"The years I spent with my ethereal companion were filled with contentment, joy, and peace. I never suspected

that Pain lay in wait for me, or that Bitterness lurked at the bottom of my cup of Joy.

"As the carriage bore me away from my native hills and valleys, and toward the coast, my companion sat by my side. She was with me during the three joyful days I spent in Beirut, roaming the city with me, stopping where I stopped, smiling when a friend accosted me.

"When I sat on the balcony of the inn, overlooking the city, she joined me in my reveries.

"But when I was about to embark, a great change swept over me. I felt a strange hand seizing hold of me and pulling me back; and I heard a voice within me whispering, 'Turn back! Do not go! Turn back to the shore before the ship sets sail!'

"I did not heed that voice. But when the ship hoisted sail, I felt like a tiny bird that had suddenly been snatched between the claws of a hawk and was being borne aloft into the sky.

"In the evening, as the mountains and hills of Lebanon receded on the horizon, I found myself alone at the prow of the ship. I looked around for the woman of my dreams, the woman my heart loved, the spouse of my days, but she was no longer at my side. The beautiful maiden whose face I saw whenever I gazed at the sky, whose voice I heard in the stillness of the night, whose hand I held whenever I walked the streets of Beirut—was no longer with me.

"For the first time in my life I found myself utterly alone on a boat sailing the deep ocean. I paced the deck, calling to her in my heart, gazing on the waves in the hope

445

of seeing her face. But all in vain. At midnight, when all the other passengers had retired, I remained on deck, alone, troubled, and anxious.

"Suddenly I looked up, and I saw her, the companion of my life, above me, in a cloud, a short distance from the prow. I leaped with joy, opened my arms wide, and cried out, 'Why have you forsaken me, my beloved! Where have you gone? Where have you been? Be near me now, and never leave me alone again!'

"She did not move. On her face I descried signs of sorrow and pain, something I had never seen before. Speaking softly and in sad tones she said, 'I have come from the depths of the ocean to see you once more. Now go down to your cabin, and give yourself over to sleep and dreams.'

"And having uttered these words, she became one with the clouds, and vanished. Like a hungry child I called to her frantically. I opened my arms in all directions, but all they embraced was the night air, heavy with dew.

"I went down to my berth, feeling within me the ebb and flow of the raging elements. It was as if I were on another boat altogether, being tossed on the rough seas of Bewilderment and Despair.

"Strangely enough, as soon as I touched my pillow, I fell fast asleep.

"I dreamt, and in my dream I saw an apple tree shaped like a cross, and hanging from it, as if crucified, was the companion of my life. Drops of blood fell from her hands and feet upon the falling blossoms of the tree.

"The ship sailed on, day and night, but I was as though lost in a trance, not certain whether I was a human being sailing to a distant clime or a ghost moving across a cloudy sky. In vain I implored Providence for the sound of her voice, or a glimpse of her shadow, or the soft touch of her fingers on my lips.

"Fourteen days passed and I was still alone. On the fifteenth day, at noon, we sighted the coast of Italy at a distance, and at dusk we entered the harbor. A throng of people in gaily decorated gondolas came to greet the ship and convey the passengers to the city.

"The City of Venice is situated on many small islands, close to one another. Its streets are canals and its numerous palaces and residences are built on water. Gondolas are the only means of transportation.

"My gondolier asked where I was going, and when I told him to the Mayor of Venice, he looked at me with awe. As we moved through the canals, night was spreading her black cloak over the city. Lights gleamed from the open windows of palaces and churches, and their reflection in the water gave the city the appearance of something seen in a poet's dream, at once charming and enchanting.

"When the gondola reached the junction of two canals, I suddenly heard the mournful ringing of church bells. Though I was in a spiritual trance, and far removed from all reality, the sounds penetrated my heart and depressed my spirits.

"The gondola docked, and tied up at the foot of marble

steps that led to a paved street. The gondolier pointed to a magnificent palace set in the middle of a garden and said: 'Here is your destination.' Slowly I climbed the steps leading to the palace, followed by the gondolier carrying my belongings. When I reached the gate, I paid him and dismissed him with my thanks.

"I rang, and the door was opened. As I entered I was greeted by sounds of wailing and weeping. I was startled and amazed. An elderly servant came toward me, and in a sorrowful voice asked what was my pleasure. 'Is this the palace of the Mayor?' I inquired. He bowed and nodded, and I handed him the missive given me by the Governor of Lebanon. He looked at it and solemnly walked toward the door leading to the reception room.

"I turned to a young servant and asked the cause of the sorrow that pervaded the room. He said that the Mayor's daughter had died that day, and as he spoke, he covered his face and wept bitterly.

"Imagine the feelings of a man who has crossed an ocean, all the while hovering between hope and despair, and at the end of his journey stands at the gate of a palace inhabited by the cruel phantoms of grief and lamentation. Imagine the feelings of a stranger seeking entertainment and hospitality in a palace, only to find himself welcomed by white-winged Death.

"Soon the old servant returned, and bowing, said, 'The Mayor awaits you.'

"He led me to a door at the extreme end of a corridor, and motioned to me to enter. In the reception room I found

a throng of priests and other dignitaries, all sunk in deep silence. In the center of the room, I was greeted by an elderly man with a long white beard, who shook my hand and said, 'It is our unhappy lot to welcome you, who come from a distant land, on a day that finds us bereft of our dearest daughter. Yet I trust our bereavement will not interfere with your mission, which, rest assured, I shall do all in my power to advance.'

"I thanked him for his kindness and expressed my deepest grief. Whereupon he led me to a seat, and I joined the rest of the silent throng.

"As I gazed at the sorrowful faces of the mourners, and listened to their painful sighs, I felt my heart contracting with grief and misery.

"Soon one after the other of the mourners took his departure, and only the grief-stricken father and I remained. When I, too, made a movement to leave, he held me back, and said, 'I beg you, my friend, do not go. Be our guest, if you can bear with us in our sorrow.'

"His words touched me deeply, and I bowed in acquiescence, and he continued, 'You men of Lebanon are most open-handed toward the stranger in your land. We should be seriously remiss in our duties were we to be less kind and courteous to our guest from Lebanon.' He rang, and in response to his summons a chamberlain appeared, attired in a magnificent uniform.

" 'Show our guest to the room in the east wing,' he said, 'and take good care of him while he is with us.'

"The chamberlain conducted me to a spacious and lavishly appointed room. As soon as he was gone, I sank down on the couch, and began reflecting on my situation in this foreign land. I reviewed the first few hours I had spent here, so far away from the land of my birth.

"Within a few minutes, the chamberlain returned, bringing my supper on a silver tray. After I had eaten, I began pacing the room, stopping now and then at the window to look out upon the Venetian sky, and to listen to the shouts, of the gondoliers and the rhythmic beat of their oars. Before long I became drowsy, and dropping my wearied body on the bed, I gave myself over to an oblivion, in which was mingled the intoxication of sleep and the sobriety of wakefulness.

"I do not know how many hours I spent in this state, for there are vast spaces of life which the spirit traverses, and which we are unable to measure with time, the invention of man. All that I felt then, and feel now, is the wretched condition in which I found myself.

"Suddenly I became aware of a phantom hovering above me, of some ethereal spirit calling to me, but without any sensible signs. I stood up, and made my way toward the hall, as though prompted and drawn by some divine force. I walked, will-less, as if in a dream, feeling as though I were journeying in a world that was beyond time and space.

"When I reached the end of the hall, I threw open a door and found myself in a vast chamber, in the center of which stood a coffin surrounded by flickering candles and

wreaths of white flowers. I knelt by the side of the bier and looked upon the departed. There before me, veiled by death, was the face of my beloved, my life-long companion. It was the woman I worshipped, now cold in death, white-shrouded, surrounded by white flowers, and guarded by the silence of the ages.

"O Lord of Love, of Life, and of Death! Thou art the creator of our souls. Thou leadest our spirits toward light and darkness. Thou calmest our hearts and makest them to quicken with hope and pain. Now Thou hast shown me the companion of my youth in this cold and lifeless form.

"Lord, Thou hast plucked me from my land and hast placed me in another, and revealed to me the power of Death over Life, and of Sorrow over Joy. Thou hast planted a white lily in the desert of my broken heart, and hast removed me to a distant valley to show me a withered one.

"Oh friends of my loneliness and exile: God has willed that I must drink the bitter cup of life. His will be done. We are naught but frail atoms in the heaven of the infinite; and we cannot but obey and surrender to the will of Providence.

"If we love, our love is neither from us, nor is it for us. If we rejoice, our joy is not in us, but in Life itself. If we suffer, our pain lies not in our wounds, but in the very heart of Nature.

"I do not complain, as I tell this tale; for he who complains doubts Life, and I am a firm believer. I believe in

the worth of the bitterness mingled in each potion that I drink from the cup of Life. I believe in the beauty of the sorrow that penetrates my heart. I believe in the ultimate mercy of these steel fingers that crush my soul.

"This is my story. How can I end it, when in truth it has no ending?

"I remained on my knees before that coffin, lost in silence, and I stared at that angelic face until dawn came. Then I stood up and returned to my room, bowed under the heavy weight of Eternity, and sustained by the pain of suffering humanity.

"Three weeks later I left Venice and returned to Lebanon. It was as though I had spent aeons of years in the vast and silent depths of the past.

"But the vision remained. Though I had found her again only in death, in me she was still alive. In her shadow I have labored and learned. What those labors were, you, my disciple, know well.

"The knowledge and wisdom I have acquired I strove to bring to my people and their rulers. I brought to Al-Haris, Governor of Lebanon, the cry of the oppressed, who were being crushed under the injustices and evils of his State and Church officials.

"I counseled him to follow the path of his forefathers and to treat his subjects as they had done, with clemency, charity, and understanding. And I said to him, 'The people are the glory of our kingdom and the source of its wealth.' And I said further, 'There are four things a ruler should

banish from his realm: Wrath, Avarice, Falsehood, and Violence.

"For this and other teachings I was chastised, sent into exile, and excommunicated by the Church.

"There came a night when Al-Haris, troubled in heart, was unable to sleep. Standing at his window, he contemplated the firmament. Such marvels! So many heavenly bodies lost in the infinite! Who created this mysterious and admirable world? Who directs these stars in their courses? What relation have these distant planets to ours? Who am I and why am I here? All these things Al-Haris said to himself.

"Then he remembered my banishment and repented of the harsh treatment he had meted out to me. At once he sent for me, imploring my pardon. He honored me with an official robe and proclaimed me before all the people as his advisor, placing a golden key in my hand.

"For my years in exile I regret nothing. He who would seek Truth and proclaim it to mankind is bound to suffer. My sorrows have taught me to understand the sorrows of my fellow men; neither persecution nor exile have dimmed the vision within me.

"And now I am tired . . ."

Having finished his story, the Master dismissed his Disciple, whose name was Almuhtada, which means "the Convert," and went up to his retreat to rest body and soul from the fatigues of ancient memories.

2

The Death of the Master

TWO WEEKS LATER, the Master fell ill, and a multitude of admirers came to the hermitage to inquire after his health. When they reached the gate of the garden, they saw coming out of the Master's quarters a priest, a nun, a doctor, and Almuhtada. The beloved Disciple announced the death of the Master. The crowd began to wail and lament, but Almuhtada neither wept nor spoke a word.

For a time the Disciple pondered within himself, then he stood upon the rock by the fish pond, and spoke:

"Brothers and countrymen: You have just heard the news of the Master's death. The immortal Prophet of Lebanon has given himself over to eternal sleep, and his blessed soul is hovering over us in the heavens of the spirit, high beyond all sorrow and mourning. His soul has cast off the servitude of the body and the fever and burdens of this earthly life.

"The Master has left this world of matter, attired in the garments of glory, and has gone to another world free of hardships and afflictions. He is now where our eyes cannot see him and our ears cannot hear him. He dwells in the world of the spirit, whose inhabitants sorely need him. He is now gathering knowledge in a new cosmos, whose history and beauty have always fascinated him and whose speech he has always striven to learn.

"His life on this earth was one long chain of great deeds. It was a life of constant thought; for the Master knew no rest except in work. He loved work, which he defined as *Visible Love.*

"His was a thirsty soul that could not rest except in the lap of wakefulness. His was a loving heart that overflowed with kindness and zeal.

"Such was the life he led on this earth. . . .

"He was a spring of knowledge that issued from the bosom of Eternity, a pure stream of wisdom that waters and refreshes the mind of Man.

"And now that river has reached the shores of Eternal Life. Let no intruder lament for him or shed tears at his departure!

"Remember, only those who have stood before the Temple of Life, and never fructified the earth with one drop of the sweat of their brow are deserving your tears and lamentations when they leave it.

"But as for the Master—did he not spend all the days of his life laboring for the benefit of Mankind? Is there any

among you who has not drunk from the pure fountain of his wisdom? And so, if you wish to honor him, offer his blessed soul a hymn of praise and thanksgiving, and not your mournful dirges and laments. If you wish to pay him due reverence, assert your claim to a portion of the knowledge in the books of wisdom he has left as a legacy to the world.

"Do not *give* to genius, but *take* from him! Thus only shall you be honoring him. Do not mourn for him, but be merry, and drink deeply of his wisdom. Only thus will you be paying him the tribute rightly his."

After hearing the words of the Disciple, the multitude returned to their homes, with smiles upon their lips, and songs of thanksgiving in their hearts.

Almuhtada was left alone in this world; but loneliness never possessed his heart, for the voice of the Master always resounded in his ears, urging him to carry on his work and sow the words of the Prophet in the hearts and minds of all who would listen of their own free will. He spent many hours alone in the garden meditating upon the scrolls which the Master had bequeathed to him, and in which he had set down his words of wisdom.

After forty days of meditation, Almuhtada left his Master's retreat and began his wanderings through the hamlets, villages, and cities of Ancient Phoenicia.

One day, as he was crossing the market place of the city of Beirut, a multitude followed him. He stopped at a public

walk, and the throng gathered around him, and he spoke to them with the voice of the Master, saying:

"The tree of my heart is heavy with fruit; come, ye hungry ones, and gather it. Eat and be satisfied. . . . Come and receive from the bounty of my heart and lighten my burden. My soul is weary under the weight of gold and silver. Come, ye seekers after hidden treasures, fill your purses and relieve me of my burden. . . .

"My heart overflows with the wine of the ages. Come, all ye thirsty ones, drink and quench your thirst.

"The other day I saw a rich man standing at the temple door, stretching out his hands, which were full of precious stones, toward all passers-by, and calling to them, saying: 'Have pity on me. Take these jewels from me. For they have made my soul sick and hardened my heart. Pity me, take them, and make me whole again.'

"But none of the passers-by paid heed to his pleas.

"And I looked at the man, and I said to myself, 'Surely it were better for him to be a pauper, roaming the streets of Beirut, stretching out a trembling hand for alms, and returning home at eventide empty-handed.'

"I have seen a wealthy and open-handed sheik of Damascus, pitching his tents in the wilderness of the Arabian desert, and by the sides of the mountains. In the evening he sent his slaves out to waylay travelers and bring them to his tents to be sheltered and entertained. But the rough roads were deserted, and the servants brought him no guests.

"And I pondered the plight of the lonely sheik, and my

heart spoke to me, saying: 'Surely it is better for him to be a straggler, with a staff in his hand and an empty bucket hanging from his arm, sharing at noontide the bread of friendship with his companions by the refuse heaps at the edge of the city. . . .'

"In Lebanon I saw the Governor's daughter rising from her slumber, attired in a precious gown. Her hair was sprinkled with musk and her body was anointed with perfume. She walked into the garden of her father's palace, seeking a lover. The dewdrops upon the carpeted grass moistened the hem of her garment. But alas! Among all her father's subjects there was no one who loved her.

"As I meditated upon the wretched state of the Governor's daughter, my soul admonished me, saying, 'Were it not better for her to be the daughter of a simple peasant, leading her father's flocks to pasture and bringing them back to the fold in the evening, with the fragrance of the earth and of the vineyards in her coarse shepherd's gown? At the very least, she could steal away from her father's hut, and in the silence of the night walk toward her beloved, waiting for her by the murmuring brook!'

"The tree of my heart is heavy with fruit. Come, ye hungry souls, gather it, eat and be satisfied. My spirit overflows with aged wine. Come, oh ye thirsty hearts, drink and quench your thirst. . . .

"Would that I were a tree that neither blossoms nor bears fruit; for the pain of fertility is harsher than the

bitterness of barrenness; and the ache of the open-handed rich is more terrible than the misery of the wretched poor. . . .

"Would that I were a dry well, so people might throw stones into my depths. For it is better to be an empty well than a spring of pure water untouched by thirsty lips.

"Would I were a broken reed, trampled by the foot of man, for that is better than to be a lyre in the house of one whose fingers are blistered and whose household is deaf to sound.

"Hear me, Oh ye sons and daughters of my motherland; meditate upon these words that come to you through the voice of the Prophet. Make room for them in the precincts of your heart, and let wisdom's seed blossom in the garden of your soul. For that is the precious gift of the Lord."

And the fame of Almuhtada spread all over the land, and many people came to him from other countries to do him reverence and to listen to the spokesman of the Master.

Physicians, men-of-law, poets, philosophers overwhelmed him with questions whenever they would meet him, whether in the street, in the church, in the mosque, or in the synagogue, or any other place where men foregather. Their minds were enriched by his beautiful words, which passed from lips to lips.

He spoke to them of Life and the Reality of Life, saying:

"Man is like the foam of the sea, that floats upon the

surface of the water. When the wind blows, it vanishes, as if it had never been. Thus are our lives blown away by Death. . . .

"The Reality of Life is Life itself, whose beginning is not in the womb, and whose ending is not in the grave. For the years that pass are naught but a moment in eternal life; and the world of matter and all in it is but a dream compared to the awakening which we call the terror of Death.

"The ether carries every sound of laughter, every sigh that comes from our hearts, and preserves their echo, which responds to every kiss whose source is joy.

"The angels keep count of every tear shed by Sorrow; and they bring to the ears of the spirits hovering in the heavens of the Infinite each song of Joy wrought from our affections.

"There, in the world to come, we shall see and feel all the vibrations of our feelings and the motions of our hearts. We shall understand the meaning of the divinity within us, whom we contemn because we are prompted by Despair.

"That deed which in our guilt we today call weakness, will appear tomorrow as an essential link in the complete chain of Man.

"The cruel tasks for which we received no reward will live with us, and show forth in splendor, and declare our glory; and the hardships we have sustained shall be as a wreath of laurel on our honored heads . . ."

Having uttered these words, the Disciple was about to withdraw from the crowds and repose his body from the labors of the day, when he spied a young man gazing at a lovely girl, with eyes that reflected bewilderment.

And the Disciple addressed him, saying:

"Are you troubled by the many faiths that Mankind professes? Are you lost in the valley of conflicting beliefs? Do you think that the freedom of heresy is less burdensome than the yoke of submission, and the liberty of dissent safer than the stronghold of acquiescence?

"If such be the case, then make Beauty your religion, and worship her as your godhead; for she is the visible, manifest and perfect handiwork of God. Cast off those who have toyed with godliness as if it were a sham, joining together greed and arrogance; but believe instead in the divinity of beauty that is at once the beginning of your worship of Life, and the source of your hunger for Happiness.

"Do penance before Beauty, and atone for your sins, for Beauty brings your heart closer to the throne of woman, who is the mirror of your affections and the teacher of your heart in the ways of Nature, which is your life's home."

And before dismissing the assembled throng, he added:

"In this world there are two sorts of men: the men of yesterday and the men of tomorrow. To which of these do you belong, my brethren? Come, let me gaze at you, and learn whether you are of those entering into the world

of light, or of those going forth into the land of darkness. Come, tell me who you are and what you are.

"Are you a politician who says to himself: 'I will use my country for my own benefit'? If so, you are naught but a parasite living on the flesh of others. Or are you a devoted patriot, who whispers into the ear of his inner self: 'I love to serve my country as a faithful servant.' If so, you are an oasis in the desert, ready to quench the thirst of the wayfarer.

"Or are you a merchant, drawing advantage from the needs of the people, engrossing goods so as to resell them at an exorbitant price? If so, you are a reprobate; and it matters naught whether your home is a palace or a prison.

"Or are you an honest man, who enables farmer and weaver to exchange their products, who mediates between buyer and seller, and through his just ways profits both himself and others?

"If so, you are a righteous man; and it matters not whether you are praised or blamed.

"Are you a leader of religion, who weaves out of the simplicity of the faithful a scarlet robe for his body; and of their kindness a golden crown for his head; and while living on Satan's plenty, spews forth his hatred of Satan? If so, you are a heretic; and it matters not that you fast all day and pray all night.

"Or are you the faithful one who finds in the goodness of people a groundwork for the betterment of the whole nation; and in whose soul is the ladder of perfection lead-

ing to the Holy Spirit? If you are such, you are like a lily in the garden of Truth; and it matters not if your fragrance is lost upon men, or dispersed into the air, where it will be eternally preserved.

"Or are you a journalist who sells his principles in the markets of slaves and who fattens on gossip and misfortune and crime? If so, you are like a ravenous vulture preying upon rotting carrion.

"Or are you a teacher standing upon the raised stage of history, who, inspired by the glories of the past, preaches to mankind and acts as he preaches? If so, you are a restorative to ailing humanity and a balm for the wounded heart.

"Are you a governor looking down on those you govern, never stirring abroad except to rifle their pockets or to exploit them for your own profit? If so, you are like tares upon the threshing floor of the nation.

"Are you a devoted servant who loves the people and is ever watchful over their welfare, and zealous for their success? If so, you are as a blessing in the granaries of the land.

"Or are you a husband who regards the wrongs he has committed as lawful, but those of his wife as unlawful? If so, you are like those extinct savages who lived in caves and covered their nakedness with hides.

"Or are you a faithful companion, whose wife is ever at his side, sharing his every thought, rapture, and victory? If so, you are as one who at dawn walks at the head of a nation toward the high noon of justice, reason and wisdom.

"Are you a writer who holds his head high above the crowd, while his brain is deep in the abyss of the past, that is filled with the tatters and useless cast-offs of the ages? If so, you are like a stagnant pool of water.

"Or are you the keen thinker, who scrutinizes his inner self, discarding that which is useless, outworn and evil, but preserving that which is useful and good? If so, you are as manna to the hungry, and as cool, clear water to the thirsty.

"Are you a poet full of noise and empty sounds? If so, you are like one of those mountebanks that make us laugh when they are weeping, and make us weep, when they laugh.

"Or are you one of those gifted souls in whose hands God has placed a viol to soothe the spirit with heavenly music, and bring his fellow men close to Life and the Beauty of Life? If so, you are a torch to light us on our way, a sweet longing in our hearts, and a revelation of the divine in our dreams.

"Thus is mankind divided into two long columns, one composed of the aged and bent, who support themselves on crooked staves, and as they walk on the path of Life, they pant as if they were climbing toward a mountaintop, while they are actually descending into the abyss.

"And the second column is composed of youth, running as with winged feet, singing as if their throats were strung with silver strings, and climbing toward the mountaintop as though drawn by some irresistible, magic power.

"In which of these two processions do you belong, my brethren? Ask yourselves this question, when you are alone in the silence of the night.

"Judge for yourselves whether you belong with the Slaves of Yesterday or the Free Men of Tomorrow."

And Almuhtada returned to his retreat, and kept himself in seclusion for many months, while he read and pondered the words of wisdom the Master had set down in the scrolls bequeathed to him. He learned much; but there were many things he found he had not learned, nor ever heard from the lips of the Master. He vowed that he would not leave the hermitage until he had thoroughly studied and mastered all that the Master had left behind, so that he might deliver it to his countrymen. In this way Almuhtada became engrossed in the perusal of his Master's words, oblivious of himself and all around him, and forgetting all those who had hearkened to him in the market places and streets of Beirut.

In vain his admirers tried to reach him, having become concerned about him. Even when the Governor of Mount Lebanon summoned him with a request that he address the officials of the state, he declined, saying, "I shall come back to you soon, with a special message for all the people."

The Governor decreed that on the day Almuhtada was to appear all citizens should receive and welcome him with honor in their homes, and in the churches, mosques, synagogues, and houses of learning, and they should hearken

THE TREASURED WRITINGS OF KAHLIL GIBRAN

with reverence to his words, for his was the voice of the Prophet.

The day when Almuhtada finally emerged from his retreat to begin his mission became a day of rejoicing and festivity for all. Almuhtada spoke freely and without hindrance; he preached the gospel of love and brotherhood. No one dared threaten him with exile from the country or excommunication from the Church. How unlike the fate of his Master, whose portion had been banishment and excommunication, before eventual pardon and recall!

Almuhtada's words were heard all over Lebanon. Later they were printed in a book, in the form of epistles, and distributed in Ancient Phoenicia and other Arabic lands. Some of the epistles are in the Master's own words; others were culled by Master and Disciple from ancient books of wisdom and lore.

II

The Words of the Master

I

Of Life

LIFE IS AN ISLAND in an ocean of loneliness, an island whose rocks are hopes, whose trees are dreams, whose flowers are solitude, and whose brooks are thirst.

Your life, my fellow men, is an island separated from all other islands and regions. No matter how many are the ships that leave your shores for other climes, no matter how many are the fleets that touch your coast, you remain a solitary island, suffering the pangs of loneliness and yearning for happiness. You are unknown to your fellow men and far removed from their sympathy and understanding.

My brother, I have seen you sitting on your hillock of gold rejoicing over your riches—proud of your treasures and secure in your belief that each handful of gold you have amassed is an invisible link that joins other men's desires and thoughts with yours.

I have seen you in my mind's eye as a great conqueror

leading your troops, intent on the destruction of your enemies' strongholds. But when I looked again, I saw naught but a solitary heart pining behind your coffers of gold, a thirsty bird in a golden cage, with its water tray empty.

I have seen you, my brother, sitting upon the throne of glory, and around you stood your people acclaiming your majesty, and singing praises of your great deeds, extolling your wisdom, and gazing upon you as though in the presence of a prophet, their spirits exulting even to the canopy of heaven.

And as you gazed upon your subjects, I saw in your face the marks of happiness and power and triumph, as if you were the soul of their body.

But when I looked again, behold I found you alone in your loneliness, standing by the side of your throne, an exile stretching his hand in every direction, as if pleading for mercy and kindness from invisible ghosts—begging for shelter, even such as has naught in it but warmth and friendliness.

I have seen you, my brother, enamoured of a beautiful woman, laying down your heart at the altar of her loveliness. When I saw her gazing upon you with tenderness and maternal love, I said to myself, "Long live Love that has done away with this man's loneliness and joined his heart with another's."

Yet, when I looked again, I saw within your loving heart another solitary heart, crying out in vain to reveal

its secrets to a woman; and behind your love-filled soul, another lonely soul that was like a wandering cloud, wishing in vain that it might turn into teardrops in the eyes of your beloved. . . .

Your life, my brother, is a solitary habitation separated from other men's dwellings. It is a house into whose interior no neighbor's gaze can penetrate. If it were plunged into darkness, your neighbor's lamp could not illumine it. If it were emptied of provisions, the stores of your neighbors could not fill it. If it stood in a desert, you could not move it into other men's gardens, tilled and planted by other hands. If it stood on a mountaintop, you could not bring it down into the valley trod by other men's feet.

Your spirit's life, my brother, is encompassed by loneliness, and were it not for that loneliness and solitude, you would not be *you*, nor would I be *I*. Were it not for this loneliness and solitude, I would come to believe on hearing your voice that it was my voice speaking; or seeing your face, that it was myself looking into a mirror.

2

Of the Martyrs to Man's Law

ARE YOU ONE who was born in the cradle of sorrow, and reared in the lap of misfortune and in the house of oppression? Are you eating a dry crust, moistened with tears? Are you drinking the turbid water in which are mingled blood and tears?

Are you a soldier compelled by the harsh law of man to forsake wife and children, and go forth into the field of battle for the sake of *Greed*, which your leaders mis-call *Duty?*

Are you a poet content with your crumbs of life, happy in the possession of parchment and ink, and sojourning in your land as a stranger, unknown to your fellow men?

Are you a prisoner, pent up in a dark dungeon for some petty offence and condemned by those who seek to reform man by corrupting him?

Are you a young woman on whom God has bestowed

beauty, but who has fallen prey to the base lust of the rich, who deceived you and bought your body but not your heart, and abandoned you to misery and distress?

If you are one of these, you are a martyr to man's law. You are wretched, and your wretchedness is the fruit of the iniquity of the strong and the injustice of the tyrant, the brutality of the rich, and the selfishness of the lewd and the covetous.

Comfort ye, my beloved weak ones, for there is a Great Power behind and beyond this world of Matter, a Power that is all Justice, Mercy, Pity and Love.

You are like a flower that grows in the shade; the gentle breeze comes and bears your seed into the sunlight, where you will live again in beauty.

You are like the bare tree bowed with winter's snow; Spring shall come and spread her garments of green over you; and Truth shall rend the veil of tears that hides your laughter. I take you unto me, my afflicted brothers, I love you, and I contemn your oppressors.

3

Thoughts and Meditations

LIFE TAKES US UP and bears us from one place to another; Fate moves us from one point to another. And we, caught up between these twain, hear dreadful voices and see only that which stands as a hindrance and obstacle in our path.

Beauty reveals herself to us as she sits on the throne of glory; but we approach her in the name of Lust, snatch off her crown of purity, and pollute her garment with our evil-doing.

Love passes by us, robed in meekness; but we flee from her in fear, or hide in the darkness; or else pursue her, to do evil in her name.

Even the wisest among us bows under the heavy weight

of Love; but in truth she is as light as the frolicsome breeze of Lebanon.

Freedom bids us to her table where we may partake of her savory food and rich wine; but when we sit down at her board, we eat ravenously and glut ourselves.

Nature reaches out to us with welcoming arms, and bids us enjoy her beauty; but we dread her silence and rush into the crowded cities, there to huddle like sheep fleeing from a ferocious wolf.

Truth calls to us, drawn by the innocent laughter of a child, or the kiss of a loved one; but we close the doors of affection in her face and deal with her as with an enemy.

The human heart cries out for help; the human soul implores us for deliverance; but we do not heed their cries, for we neither hear nor understand. But the man who hears and understands we call mad, and flee from him.

Thus the nights pass, and we live in unawareness; and the days greet us and embrace us. But we live in constant dread of day and night.

We cling to the earth, while the gate of the Heart of the Lord stands wide open. We trample upon the bread of Life, while hunger gnaws at our hearts. How good is Life to Man; yet how far removed is Man from Life!

4

Of the First Look

IT IS THAT MOMENT that divides the intoxication of Life from the awakening. It is the first flame that lights up the inner domain of the heart. It is the first magic note plucked on the silver string of the heart. It is that brief moment that unfolds before the soul the chronicles of time, and reveals to the eyes the deeds of the night, and the works of conscience. It opens Eternity's secrets of the future. It is the seed cast by Ishtar, goddess of Love, and sown by the eyes of the beloved in the field of Love, brought forth by affection, and reaped by the Soul.

The first glance from the eyes of the beloved is like the spirit that moved upon the face of the waters, giving birth to heaven and earth, when the Lord spoke and said, "Let there be."

Of the First Kiss

IT IS THE FIRST SIP from the cup filled by the goddess with the nectar of Life. It is the dividing line between Doubt that beguiles the spirit and saddens the heart, and Certitude that floods the inner self with joy. It is the beginning of the song of Life and the first act in the drama of the Ideal Man. It is the bond that unites the strangeness of the past with the brightness of the future; the link between the silence of the feelings and their song. It is a word uttered by four lips proclaiming the heart a throne, Love a king, and fidelity a crown. It is the gentle touch of the delicate fingers of the breeze on the lips of the rose—uttering a long sigh of relief and a sweet moan.

It is the beginning of that magic vibration that carries the lovers from the world of weights and measures into the world of dreams and revelations.

It is the union of two fragrant flowers; and the mingling of their fragrance toward the creation of a third soul.

As the first glance is like a seed sown by the goddess in the field of the human heart, so the first kiss is the first flower at the tip of the branch of the Tree of Life.

Of Marriage

HERE LOVE BEGINS to render the prose of Life into hymns and canticles of praise, with music that is set by night, to

be sung in the day. Here Love's longing draws back the veil, and illumines the recesses of the heart, creating a happiness that no other happiness can surpass but that of the Soul when she embraces God.

Marriage is the union of two divinities that a third might be born on earth. It is the union of two souls in a strong love for the abolishment of separateness. It is that higher unity which fuses the separate unities within the two spirits. It is the golden ring in a chain whose beginning is a glance, and whose ending is Eternity. It is the pure rain that falls from an unblemished sky to fructify and bless the fields of divine Nature.

As the first glance from the eyes of the beloved is like a seed sown in the human heart, and the first kiss of her lips like a flower upon the branch of the Tree of Life, so the union of two lovers in marriage is like the first fruit of the first flower of that seed.

5

Of the Divinity of Man

SPRING CAME, and Nature began speaking in the murmur of brooks and rivulets and in the smiles of the flowers; and the soul of Man was made happy and content.

Then suddenly Nature waxed furious and laid waste the beautiful city. And man forgot her laughter, her sweetness, and her kindness.

In one hour a frightful, blind force had destroyed what it had taken generations to build. Terrifying death seized man and beast in his claws and crushed them.

Ravaging fires consumed man and his goods; a deep and terrifying night hid the beauty of life under a shroud of ashes. The fearful elements raged and destroyed man, his habitations, and all his handiwork.

Amidst this frightful thunder of Destruction from the bowels of the Earth, amidst all ·this misery and ruin, stood

the poor Soul, gazing upon all this from a distance, and meditating sorrowfully upon the weakness of Man and the omnipotence of God. She reflected upon the enemy of Man hidden deep beneath the layers of the earth and among the atoms of the ether. She heard the wailing of the mothers and of the hungry children and she shared their suffering. She pondered the savagery of the elements and the smallness of Man. And she recalled how only yesterday the children of Man had slept safely in their homes—but today they were homeless fugitives, bewailing their beautiful city as they gazed upon it from a distance, their hope turned to despair, their joy to sorrow, their life of peace to warfare. She suffered with the brokenhearted, who were caught in the iron claws of Sorrow, Pain, and Despair.

And as the Soul stood there pondering, suffering, doubting the justice of the Divine Law that binds all of the world's forces, she whispered into the ear of Silence:

"Behind all this creation there is eternal Wisdom that brings forth wrath and destruction, but which will yet bring forth unpredictable beauty.

"For fire, thunder, and tempests are to the Earth what hatred, envy and evil are to the human heart. While the afflicted nation was filling the firmament with groans and lamentations, Memory brought to my mind all the warnings and calamities and tragedies that have been enacted on the stage of Time.

"I saw Man, throughout history, erecting towers, palaces, cities, temples on the face of the earth; and I saw

478

the earth turn in her fury upon them and snatch them back into her bosom.

"I saw strong men building impregnable castles and I observed artists embellishing their walls with paintings; then I saw the earth gape, open wide her mouth, and swallow all that the skilful hand and the luminous mind of genius had shaped.

"And I knew that the earth is like a beautiful bride who needs no man-made jewels to heighten her loveliness but is content with the green verdure of her fields, and the golden sands of her seashores, and the precious stones on her mountains.

"But man in his Divinity I saw standing like a giant in the midst of Wrath and Destruction, mocking the anger of the earth and the raging of the elements.

"Like a pillar of light Man stood amidst the ruins of Babylon, Nineveh, Palmyra and Pompeii, and as he stood he sang the song of Immortality:

> *Let the Earth take*
> *That which is hers,*
> *For I, Man, have no ending."*

6

Of Reason and Knowledge

WHEN REASON SPEAKS TO YOU, hearken to what she says, and you shall be saved. Make good use of her utterances, and you shall be as one armed. For the Lord has given you no better guide than Reason, no stronger arm than Reason. When Reason speaks to your inmost self, you are proof against Desire. For Reason is a prudent minister, a loyal guide, and a wise counsellor. Reason is light in darkness, as anger is darkness amidst light. Be wise—let Reason, not Impulse, be your guide.

Yet be mindful that even if Reason be at your side, she is helpless without the aid of Knowledge. Without her blood-sister, Knowledge, Reason is like houseless poverty; and Knowledge without Reason is like a house unguarded. And even Love, Justice, and Goodness avail little if Reason be not there too.

The learned man who has not judgment is like an un-armed soldier proceeding into battle. His wrath will poison

the pure spring of the life of his community and he will be like the grain of aloes in a pitcher of pure water.

Reason and learning are like body and soul. Without the body, the soul is nothing but empty wind. Without the soul, the body is but a senseless frame.

Reason without learning is like the untilled soil, or like the human body that lacks nourishment.

Reason is not like the goods sold in the market places— the more plentiful they are, the less they are worth. Reason's worth waxes with her abundance. But were she sold in the market, it is only the wise man who would understand her true value.

The fool sees naught but folly; and the madman only madness. Yesterday I asked a foolish man to count the fools among us. He laughed and said, "This is too hard a thing to do, and it will take too long. Were it not better to count only the wise?"

Know your own true worth, and you shall not perish. Reason is your light and your beacon of Truth. Reason is the source of Life. God has given you Knowledge, so that by its light you may not only worship him, but also see yourself in your weakness and strength.

If you do not descry the mote in your own eye, surely you will not see it in your neighbor's.

Each day look into your conscience and amend your faults; if you fail in this duty you will be untrue to the Knowledge and Reason that are within you.

Keep a watchful eye over yourself as if you were your own enemy; for you cannot learn to govern yourself, unless you first learn to govern your own passions and obey the dictates of your conscience.

I once heard a learned man say, "Every evil has its remedy, except folly. To reprimand an obstinate fool or to preach to a dolt is like writing upon the water. Christ healed the blind, the halt, the palsied, and the leprous. But the fool He could not cure.

"Study a question from all sides, and you will be sure to discover where error has crept in.

"When the portal of your house is wide, see to it that the postern-gate be not too narrow.

"He who tries to seize an opportunity after it has passed him by is like one who sees it approach but will not go to meet it."

God does not work evil. He gives us Reason and Learning so that we may ever be on our guard against the pitfalls of Error and Destruction.

Blessed are they on whom God has conferred the gift of Reason.

7

Of Music

I SAT BY ONE whom my heart loves, and I listened to her words. My soul began to wander in the infinite spaces where the universe appeared like a dream, and the body like a narrow prison.

The enchanting voice of my Beloved entered my heart.

This is Music, oh friends, for I heard her through the sighs of the one I loved, and through the words, half-uttered between her lips.

With the eyes of my hearing I saw my Beloved's heart.

My friends: Music is the language of spirits. Its melody is like the frolicsome breeze that makes the strings quiver with love. When the gentle fingers of Music knock at the door of our feelings, they awaken memories that have long lain hidden in the depths of the Past. The sad strains of Music bring us mournful recollections; and her quiet

strains bring us joyful memories. The sound of strings makes us weep at the departure of a dear one, or makes us smile at the peace God has bestowed upon us.

The soul of Music is of the Spirit, and her mind is of the Heart.

When God created Man, he gave him Music as a language different from all other languages. And early man sang her glory in the wilderness; and she drew the hearts of kings and moved them from their thrones.

Our souls are like tender flowers at the mercy of the winds of Destiny. They tremble in the morning breeze, and bend their heads under the falling dews of heaven.

The song of the bird awakens Man from his slumber, and invites him to join in the psalms of glory to Eternal Wisdom that has created the song of the bird.

Such music makes us ask ourselves the meaning of the mysteries contained in ancient books.

When the birds sing, do they call to the flowers in the fields, or are they speaking to the trees, or are they echoing the murmur of the brooks? For Man with his understanding cannot know what the bird is saying, nor what the brook is murmuring, nor what the waves whisper when they touch the beaches slowly and gently.

Man with his understanding cannot know what the rain is saying when it falls upon the leaves of the trees or when it taps at the window panes. He cannot know what the breeze is saying to the flowers in the fields.

But the Heart of Man can feel and grasp the meaning of

these sounds that play upon his feelings. Eternal Wisdom often speaks to him in a mysterious language; Soul and Nature converse together, while Man stands speechless and bewildered.

Yet has not Man wept at the sounds? And are not his tears eloquent understanding?

Divine Music!
Daughter of the Soul of Love

Vase of bitterness and of
Love

Dream of the human heart, fruit
of sorrow

Flower of joy, fragrance and
bloom of feeling

Tongue of lovers, revealer of
secrets

Mother of the tears of hidden love

Inspirer of poets, composers,
architects

Unity of thoughts within fragments
of words

485

Designer of love out of beauty
Wine of the exulting heart in
a world of dreams

Heartener of warriors, and strengthener
of souls
Ocean of mercy and sea of tenderness

O Music
In your depths we deposit our hearts
and souls
Thou hast taught us to see with our
ears
And hear with our hearts.

8

Of Wisdom

THE WISE MAN is he who loves and reveres God. A man's merit lies in his knowledge and in his deeds, not in his color, faith, race, or descent. For remember, my friend, the son of a shepherd who possesses knowledge is of greater worth to a nation than the heir to the throne, if he be ignorant. Knowledge is your true patent of nobility, no matter who your father or what your race may be.

Learning is the only wealth tyrants cannot despoil. Only death can dim the lamp of knowledge that is within you. The true wealth of a nation lies not in its gold or silver but in its learning, wisdom, and in the uprightness of its sons.

The riches of the spirit beautify the face of man and

give birth to sympathy and respect. The spirit in every being is made manifest in the eyes, the countenance, and in all bodily movements and gestures. Our appearance, our words, our actions are never greater than ourselves. For the soul is our house; our eyes its windows; and our words its messengers.

Knowledge and understanding are life's faithful companions who will never prove untrue to you. For knowledge is your crown, and understanding your staff; and when they are with you, you can possess no greater treasures.

He who understands you is greater kin to you than your own brother. For even your own kindred may neither understand you nor know your true worth.

Friendship with the ignorant is as foolish as arguing with a drunkard.

God has bestowed upon you intelligence and knowledge. Do not extinguish the lamp of Divine Grace and do not let the candle of wisdom die out in the darkness of lust and error. For a wise man approaches with his torch to light up the path of mankind.

Remember, one just man causes the Devil greater affliction than a million blind believers.

A little knowledge that *acts* is worth infinitely more than much knowledge that is idle.

If your knowledge teaches you not the value of things, and frees you not from the bondage to matter, you shall never come near the throne of Truth.

If your knowledge teaches you not to rise above human weakness and misery and lead your fellow man on the right path, you are indeed a man of little worth and will remain such till Judgment Day.

Learn the words of wisdom uttered by the wise and apply them in your own life. Live them—but do not make a show of reciting them, for he who repeats what he does not understand is no better than an ass that is loaded with books.

9

Of Love and Equality

MY POOR FRIEND, if you only knew that the Poverty which causes you so much wretchedness is the very thing that reveals the knowledge of Justice and the understanding of Life, you would be contented with your lot.

I say knowledge of Justice: for the rich man is too busy amassing wealth to seek this knowledge.

And I say understanding of Life: for the strong man is too eager in his pursuit of power and glory to keep to the straight path of truth.

Rejoice then, my poor friend, for you are the mouth of Justice and the book of Life. Be content, for you are the source of virtue in those who rule over you and the pillar of integrity of those who guide you.

If you could see, my sorrowful friend, that the misfortune which has defeated you in life is the very power that illumines your heart and raises your soul from the pit of

490

derision to the throne of reverence, you would be content with your share and you would look upon it as a legacy to instruct you and make you wise.

For Life is a chain made up of many diverse links. Sorrow is one golden link between submission to the present and the promised hope of the future.

It is the dawn between slumber and awakening.

My fellow poor, Poverty sets off the nobility of the spirit, while wealth discloses its evil. Sorrow softens the feelings, and Joy heals the wounded heart. Were Sorrow and Poverty abolished, the spirit of man would be like an empty tablet, with naught inscribed save the signs of selfishness and greed.

Remember that Divinity is the true self of Man. It cannot be sold for gold; neither can it be heaped up as are the riches of the world today. The rich man has cast off his Divinity, and has clung to his gold. And the young today have forsaken their Divinity and pursue self-indulgence and pleasure.

My beloved poor, the hour you spend with your wife and your children when you return home from the field is the earnest of all human families to come; it is the emblem of the happiness that will be the lot of all coming generations.

But the life that the rich man spends in heaping up gold is in truth like the life of the worms in the grave. It is a sign of fear.

The tears you shed, my sorrowful friend, are purer than

the laughter of him that seeks to forget and sweeter than the mockery of the scoffer. These tears cleanse the heart of the blight of hatred, and teach man to share the pain of the brokenhearted. They are the tears of the Nazarene.

The strength you sow for the rich you shall reap in time to come, for all things return to their source, according to the Law of Nature.

And the sorrow you have borne shall be turned to gladness by the will of Heaven.

And generations to come shall learn of Sorrow and Poverty a lesson of Love and Equality.

IO

Further Sayings of the Master

I HAVE BEEN HERE since the beginning, and I shall be until the end of days; for there is no ending to my existence. The human soul is but a part of a burning torch which God separated from Himself at Creation.

My brothers, seek counsel of one another, for therein lies the way out of error and futile repentance. The wisdom of the many is your shield against tyranny. For when we turn to one another for counsel we reduce the number of our enemies.

He who does not seek advice is a fool. His folly blinds him to Truth and makes him evil, stubborn, and a danger to his fellow man.

When you have grasped a problem clearly, face it with resolution, for that is the way of the strong.

Seek ye counsel of the aged, for their eyes have looked on the faces of the years and their ears have hearkened to the voices of Life. Even if their counsel is displeasing to you, pay heed to them.

Do not expect good counsel from a tyrant, or a wrong-doer, or a presumptuous man, or a deserter from honor. Woe to him who conspires with the wrongdoer who comes seeking advice. For to agree with the wrongdoer is infamy, and to hearken to that which is false is treachery.

Unless I be endowed with wide knowledge, keen judgment and great experience, I cannot account myself a counsellor of men.

Make haste slowly, and do not be slothful when opportunity beckons. Thus you will avoid grave errors.

My friend, be not like him who sits by his fireside and watches the fire go out, then blows vainly upon the dead ashes. Do not give up hope or yield to despair because of that which is past, for to bewail the irretrievable is the worst of human frailties.

Yesterday I repented of my deed, and today I understand my error and the evil I brought upon myself when I broke my bow and destroyed my quiver.

I love you, my brother, whoever you are—whether you worship in your church, kneel in your temple, or pray in your mosque. You and I are all children of one faith, for the divers paths of religion are fingers of the loving hand of one Supreme Being, a hand extended to all, offering completeness of spirit to all, eager to receive all.

God has given you a spirit with wings on which to soar into the spacious firmament of Love and Freedom. Is it not pitiful then that you cut your wings with your own hands and suffer your soul to crawl like an insect upon the earth?

My soul, living is like a courser of the night; the swifter its flight, the nearer the dawn.

II

The Listener

OH WIND, you who pass by us, now singing sweetly and softly, now sighing and lamenting: we hear you, but we cannot see you. We feel your touch, but we cannot descry your shape. You are like an ocean of love that engulfs our spirits, but does not drown them.

You ascend with the hills, and descend with the valleys, diffusing yourself over field and meadow. There is strength in your ascent and gentleness in your descent; and grace in your dispersion. You are like a merciful king, gracious toward the oppressed, but stern toward the arrogant and strong.

In Autumn you moan through the valleys, and the trees echo your wailing. In Winter you break your chains, and all Nature rebels with you.

In Spring you stir from your slumbers, still weak and infirm, and through your faint stirrings the fields begin to awake.

In Summer you hide behind the veil of Silence as if you had died, smitten by the shafts of the sun and the spears of heat.

Were you indeed lamenting in the late Autumn days, or were you laughing at the blushes of the naked trees? Were you angry in Winter, or were you dancing around the snow-decked tomb of Night?

Were you indeed languishing in the Spring, or were you grieving for the loss of your beloved, the Youth of all Seasons?

Were you perchance dead in those Summer days, or were you only asleep in the heart of the fruits, in the eyes of the vineyards, or in the ears of the wheat upon the threshing floors?

From the streets of the cities you raise up and bear the seeds of plagues; and from the hills you waft the fragrant breath of flowers. Thus the great Soul sustains the sorrow of Life and silently meets its joys.

Into the ears of the rose you whisper a secret whose meaning she grasps; often she is troubled—then she rejoices. Such is the way of God with the soul of Man.

Now you tarry. Now you hasten here and yonder, moving ceaselessly. Such too is the mind of Man, who lives when he acts and dies when he is idle.

You write your songs on the face of the waters; then you erase them. So does the poet when he is creating.

From the South you come as warm as Love; and from the North as cold as Death. From the East as gentle as the

touch of the Soul; and from the West as fierce as Wrath and Fury. Are you as fickle as Age, or are you the courier of weighty tidings from the four points of the compass?

You rage through the desert, you trample the innocent caravans underfoot and bury them in mountains of sand. Are you that same frolicsome breeze that trembles with the dawn among the leaves and branches and flits like a dream through the windings of the valleys where the flowers bow in greeting and where the grass droops heavy-lidded with the intoxication of your breath?

You rise from the oceans and shake their silent depths from your tresses, and in your rage you lay waste ships and crews. Are you that selfsame gentle breeze that caresses the locks of children as they play around their homes?

Whither do you carry our hearts, our sighs, our breaths, our smiles? What do you do with the flying torches of our souls? Do you bear them beyond the horizon of Life? Do you drag them like sacrificial victims to distant and horrible caves to destroy them?

In the still night, hearts reveal their secrets to you. And at dawn, eyes open at your gentle touch. Are you mindful of what the heart has felt or the eyes have seen?

Between your wings the anguished lays the echo of his mournful songs, the orphan the fragments of his broken heart, and the oppressed his painful sighs. Within the folds of your mantle the stranger lays his longing, the forsaken his burden, and the fallen woman her despair.

Do you preserve all these in safekeeping for the humble?

Or are you like Mother Earth, who entombs all that she brings forth?

Do you hear these cries and lamentations? Do you hear these moans and sighs? Or are you like the proud and mighty who do not see the outstretched hand or hear the cries of the poor?

O Life of all Listeners, do you hear?

I2

Love and Youth

A YOUTH IN THE DAWN OF LIFE sat at his desk in a solitary house. Now he looked through the window at the sky that was studded with glittering stars, now he turned his gaze toward a maiden's picture, which he held in his hand. Its lines and colors were worthy of a master; they became reflected in the youth's mind, and opened to him the secrets of the World and the mystery of Eternity.

The picture of the woman called to the youth, and at that moment turned his eyes into ears, so that he understood the language of the spirits that hovered over the room, and his heart became seared with love.

Thus the hours passed as if they were only a moment of some beautiful dream, or only a year in a life of Eternity.

Then the youth set the picture before him, took up his pen, and poured out his heart's feelings upon the parchment:

"Beloved: Great truth that transcends Nature does not pass from one being to another by way of human speech. Truth chooses Silence to convey her meaning to loving souls.

"I know that the silence of the night is the worthiest messenger between our two hearts, for she bears Love's message and recites the psalms of our hearts. Just as God has made our souls prisoners of our bodies, so Love has made me a prisoner of words and speech.

"They say, O Beloved, that Love is a devouring flame in the heart of man. I knew at our first meeting that I had known you for ages, and I knew at the time of parting that nothing was strong enough to keep us apart.

"My first glimpse of you was not in truth the first. The hour in which our hearts met confirmed in me the belief in Eternity and in the immortality of the Soul.

"At such a moment Nature lifts the veil from him who believes himself oppressed, and reveals her everlasting justice.

"Do you recall the brook by which we sat and gazed at each other, Beloved? Do you know your eyes told me at that moment that your love was not born of pity but of justice? And now I can proclaim to myself and to the world that the gifts which derive from justice are greater than those that spring from charity.

"And I can say too that Love which is the child of chance is like the stagnant waters of the marshes.

"Beloved, before me stretches a life which I can fashion

into greatness and beauty—a life that began with our first meeting, and which will last to eternity.

"For I know that it is within you to bring forth the power that God has bestowed upon me, to be embodied in great words and deeds, even as the sun brings to life the fragrant flowers of the field.

"And thus, my love for you shall endure for ever."

The youth rose and walked slowly and reverently across the room. He looked through the window and saw the moon rising above the horizon and filling the spacious sky with her gentle radiance.

Then he returned to his desk and wrote:

"Forgive me, my Beloved, for speaking to you in the second person. For you are my other, beautiful, half, which I have lacked ever since we emerged from the sacred hand of God. Forgive me, my Beloved!"

13

Wisdom and I

IN THE SILENCE OF THE NIGHT, Wisdom came into my chamber and stood by my bed. She gazed upon me like a loving mother, dried my tears, and said:

"I have heard the cries of your soul, and have come here to comfort you. Open your heart to me and I shall fill it with light. Ask, and I shall show you the path of Truth."

I complied with her bidding, and asked:

"Who am I, Wisdom, and how came I to this place of horrors? What are these mighty hopes, these mountains of books, and these strange figures? What are these thoughts that come and go like a flock of doves? What are these words we compose with desire and write down in joy? What are these sorrowful and joyous conclusions that embrace my soul and envelop my heart? Whose are these eyes that stare at me and pierce the very inmost recesses of my soul, and yet are oblivious of my grief? What are these

503

voices that lament the passing of my days and chant the praises of my childhood? Who is this youth that toys with my desires and mocks my feelings, forgetting the deeds of yesterday, contenting himself with the littleness of today, and arming himself against the slow approach of tomorrow?

"What is this dreadful world that moves me and to what unknown land?

"What is this earth that opens wide her jaws to swallow our bodies and prepares an everlasting shelter for greed? Who is this Man who contents himself with the favors of Fortune and craves a kiss from the lips of Life while Death smites him in the face? Who is this Man who buys a moment of pleasure with a year of repentance and gives himself over to sleep, while dreams call to him? Who is this Man who swims on the waves of Ignorance toward the gulf of Darkness?

"Tell me, Wisdom, what are all these things?"

And Wisdom opened her lips and spoke:
"You, Man, would see the world with the eyes of God, and would grasp the secrets of the hereafter by means of human thought. Such is the fruit of ignorance.

"Go into the field, and see how the bee hovers over the sweet flowers and the eagle swoops down on its prey. Go into your neighbor's house and see the infant child bewitched by the firelight, while the mother is busied at her tasks. Be like the bee, and do not waste your spring days

gazing on the doings of the eagle. Be like the child rejoicing at the firelight and let the mother be. All that you see was, and still is, yours.

"The many books and strange figures and the lovely thoughts around you are ghosts of the spirits that have been before you. The words your lips utter are the links in the chain that binds you and your fellow men. The sorrowful and joyful conclusions are the seeds sown by the past in the field of your soul to be reaped by the future.

"The youth that toys with your desires is he who will open the gate of your heart for Light to enter. The earth that opens wide her mouth to swallow man and his works is the redeemer of our souls from bondage to our bodies.

"The world that moves with you is your heart, which is the world itself. And Man, whom you deem so small and ignorant, is God's messenger who has come to learn the joy of life through sorrow and gain knowledge from ignorance."

Thus spoke Wisdom, and laid a hand upon my burning brow, saying:

"March on. Do not tarry. To go forward is to move toward perfection. March on, and fear not the thorns or the sharp stones on Life's path."

I4

The Two Cities

LIFE TOOK ME UP ON HER WINGS and bore me to the top of Mount Youth. Then she beckoned and pointed behind her. I looked back and saw a strange city, from which rose dark smoke of many hues moving slowly like phantoms. A thin cloud almost hid the city from my gaze.

After a moment of silence, I exclaimed: "What is this I see, Life?"

And Life answered: "This is the City of the Past. Look upon it and ponder."

And I gazed upon this wonderful scene and I saw many objects and sights: halls built for action, standing giant-like beneath the wings of Slumber; temples of talk around which hovered spirits at once crying in despair, and singing songs of hope. I saw churches built by Faith and destroyed by Doubt. I spied minarets of Thought, lifting their spires like the upraised arms of beggars; I saw avenues of Desire

stretching like rivers through valleys; storehouses of secrets guarded by sentinels of Concealment and pillaged by thieves of Disclosure; towers of strength raised by Valor and demolished by Fear; shrines of Dreams, embellished by Slumber and destroyed by Wakefulness; slight huts inhabited by Weakness; mosques of Solitude and Self-Denial; institutions of learning lighted by Intelligence and darkened by Ignorance; taverns of Love, where lovers became drunk and Emptiness mocked at them; theatres upon whose boards Life acted out its play, and Death rounded out Life's tragedies.

Such is the City of the Past—in appearance far away, though in reality nearby—visible, though barely, through the dark clouds.

Then Life beckoned to me and said, "Follow me. We have tarried here too long." And I replied, "Whither are we going, Life?"

And Life said, "We are going to the City of the Future."

And I said, "Have pity on me, Life. I am weary, and my feet are bruised and the strength is gone out of me."

But Life replied, "March on, my friend. Tarrying is cowardice. To remain forever gazing upon the City of the Past is Folly. Behold, the City of the Future beckons. . . ."

15

Nature and Man

AT DAYBREAK I sat in a field, holding converse with Nature, while Man rested peacefully under coverlets of slumber. I lay in the green grass and meditated upon these questions: "Is Truth Beauty? Is Beauty Truth?"

And in my thoughts I found myself carried far from mankind, and my imagination lifted the veil of matter that hid my inner self. My soul expanded and I was brought closer to Nature and her secrets, and my ears were opened to the language of her wonders.

As I sat thus deep in thought, I felt a breeze passing through the branches of the trees, and I heard a sighing like that of a strayed orphan.

"Why do you sigh, gentle breeze?" I asked.

And the breeze replied, "Because I have come from the city that is aglow with the heat of the sun, and the seeds of plagues and contaminations cling to my pure garments. Can you blame me for grieving?"

Then I looked at the tear-stained faces of the flowers, and heard their soft lament. And I asked, "Why do you weep, my lovely flowers?"

One of the flowers raised her gentle head and whispered, "We weep because Man will come and cut us down, and offer us for sale in the markets of the city."

And another flower added, "In the evening, when we are wilted, he will throw us on the refuse heap. We weep because the cruel hand of Man snatches us from our native haunts."

And I heard the brook lamenting like a widow mourning her dead child and I asked, "Why do you weep, my pure brook?"

And the brook replied, "Because I am compelled to go to the city where Man contemns me and spurns me for stronger drinks and makes of me a scavenger for his offal, pollutes my purity, and turns my goodness to filth."

And I heard the birds grieving, and I asked, "Why do you cry, my beautiful birds?" And one of them flew near, and perched at the tip of a branch and said, "The sons of Adam will soon come into this field with their deadly weapons and make war upon us as if we were their mortal enemies. We are now taking leave of one another, for we know not which of us will escape the wrath of Man. Death follows us wherever we go."

Now the sun rose from behind the mountain peaks, and gilded the treetops with coronals. I looked upon this beauty and asked myself, "Why must Man destroy what Nature has built?"

16

The Enchantress

THE WOMAN WHOM MY HEART HAS LOVED sat yesterday in this lonely room and rested her lovely body upon this velvet couch. From these crystal goblets she sipped the aged wine.

This is yesterday's dream; for the woman my heart has loved is gone to a distant place—the Land of Oblivion and Emptiness.

The print of her fingers is yet upon my mirror; and the fragrance of her breathing is still within the folds of my garments; and the echo of her sweet voice can be heard in this room.

But the woman my heart has loved is gone to a distant place called the Valley of Exile and Forgetfulness.

By my bed hangs a portrait of this woman. The love-

letters she wrote to me I have kept in a silver case, studded with emeralds and coral. And all these things will remain with me till tomorrow, when the wind will blow them away into oblivion, where only mute silence reigns.

The woman I have loved is like the women to whom you have given your hearts. She is strangely beautiful, as if fashioned by a god; as meek as the dove, as wily as the serpent, as proudly graceful as the peacock, as fierce as the wolf, as lovely as the white swan, and as fearful as the black night. She is compounded of a handful of earth and a beakerful of sea-foam.

I have known this woman since childhood. I have followed her into the fields and laid hold of the hem of her garments as she walked in the streets of the city. I have known her since the days of my youth, and I have seen the shadow of her face in the pages of the books I have read. I have heard her heavenly voice in the murmur of the brook.

To her I opened my heart's discontents and the secrets of my soul.

The woman whom my heart has loved is gone to a cold, desolate and distant place—the Land of Emptiness and Oblivion.

The woman my heart has loved is called *Life*. She is beautiful, and draws all hearts to herself. She takes our lives in pawn and buries our yearnings in promises.

Life is a woman bathing in the tears of her lovers and anointing herself with the blood of her victims. Her

raiments are white days, lined with the darkness of night. She takes the human heart to lover, but denies herself in marriage.

> *Life is an enchantress*
> *Who seduces us with her beauty—*
> *But he who knows her wiles*
> *Will flee her enchantments.*

17

Youth and Hope

YOUTH WALKED BEFORE ME and I followed him until we came to a distant field. There he stopped, and gazed at the clouds that drifted over the horizon like a flock of white lambs. Then he looked at the trees whose naked branches pointed toward the sky as if praying to Heaven for the return of their foliage.

And I said, "Where are we now, Youth?"

And he replied, "We are in the field of Bewilderment. Take heed."

And I said, "Let us go back at once, for this desolate place affrights me, and the sight of the clouds and the naked trees saddens my heart."

And he replied, "Be patient. Perplexity is the beginning of knowledge."

Then I looked around me and saw a form moving gracefully toward us and I asked, "Who is this woman?"

513

And Youth replied, "This is Melpomene, daughter of Zeus, and Muse of Tragedy."

"Oh, happy Youth!" I exclaimed, "what does Tragedy want of me, while you are at my side?"

And he answered, "She has come to show you the earth and its sorrows; for he who has not looked on Sorrow will never see Joy."

Then the spirit laid a hand upon my eyes. When she withdrew it, Youth was gone, and I was alone, divested of my earthly garments, and I cried, "Daughter of Zeus, where is Youth?"

Melpomene did not answer; but took me up under her wings, and carried me to the summit of a high mountain. Below me I saw the earth and all in it, spread out like the pages of a book, upon which were inscribed the secrets of the universe. I stood in awe beside the maiden, pondered the mystery of Man, and struggled to decipher Life's symbols.

And I saw woeful things: The Angels of Happiness warring with the Devils of Misery, and standing between them was Man, now drawn one way by Hope and now another by Despair.

I saw Love and Hate dallying with the human heart; Love concealing Man's guilt and besotting him with the wine of submission, praise and flattery; while Hatred provoked him, and sealed his ears and blinded his eyes to Truth.

And I beheld the city crouching like a child of its slums and snatching at the garment of the son of Adam. From afar I saw the lovely fields weeping over man's sorrow.

I beheld priests foaming like sly foxes; and false messiahs contriving and conspiring against Man's happiness.

And I saw Man calling upon Wisdom for deliverance; but Wisdom did not hearken to his cries, for he had contemned her when she spoke to him in the streets of the city.

And I saw preachers gazing in adoration toward the heavens, while their hearts were interred in the pits of Greed.

I saw a youth winning a maiden's heart with sweet speech; but their true feelings were asleep, and their divinity was far away.

I saw the lawmakers chattering idly, selling their wares in the market places of Deceit and Hypocrisy.

I saw physicians toying with the souls of the simple-hearted and trustful. I saw the ignorant sitting with the wise, exalting their past to the throne of glory, adorning their present with the robes of plenty, and preparing a couch of luxury for the future.

I saw the wretched poor sowing the seed, and the strong reaping; and oppression, miscalled Law, standing guard.

I saw the thieves of Ignorance despoiling the treasures of Knowledge, while the sentinels of Light lay drowned in the deep sleep of inaction.

And I saw two lovers; but the woman was like a lute in the hand of a man who cannot play, but understands only harsh sounds.

And I beheld the forces of Knowledge laying siege to the

city of Inherited Privilege; but they were few in number and were soon dispersed.

And I saw Freedom walking alone, knocking at doors, and asking for shelter, but no one heeded her pleas. Then I saw Prodigality striding in splendor, and the multitude acclaiming her as Liberty.

I saw Religion buried in books, and Doubt stood in her place.

And I saw Man wearing the garments of Patience as a cloak for Cowardice and calling Sloth Tolerance, and Fear Courtesy.

I saw the intruder sitting at the board of Knowledge, uttering folly, but the guests were silent.

I saw gold in the hands of the wasteful, a means of evil-doing; and in the hands of the miserly as a bait for hatred. But in the hands of the wise I saw no gold.

When I beheld all these things, I cried out in pain, "Oh Daughter of Zeus, is this indeed the Earth? Is this Man?"

In a soft and anguished voice she replied, "What you see is the Soul's path, and it is paved with sharp stones and carpeted with thorns. This is only the shadow of Man. This is Night. But wait! Morning will soon be here!"

Then she laid a gentle hand upon my eyes, and when she withdrew it, behold! there was Youth walking slowly by my side, and ahead of us, leading the way, marched Hope.

18

Resurrection

YESTERDAY, MY BELOVED, I was almost alone in the world, and my solitude was as pitiless as death. I was like a flower that grows in the shadow of a huge rock, of whose existence Life is not aware, and which is not aware of Life.

But today my soul awakened, and I beheld you standing by my side. I rose to my feet and rejoiced; then I knelt in reverence and worshipped before you.

Yesterday the touch of the frolicsome breeze seemed harsh, my beloved, and the sun's beams seemed weak, a mist hid the face of the earth, and the waves of the ocean roared like a tempest.

I looked all about me, but saw naught but my own suffering self standing by my side, while the phantoms of darkness rose and fell around me like ravenous vultures.

But today Nature is bathed in light, and the roaring waves are calm and the fogs are dispersed. Wherever I look I see Life's secrets lying open before me.

THE TREASURED WRITINGS OF KAHLIL GIBRAN

Yesterday I was a soundless word in the heart of the Night; today I am a song on the lips of Time.

And all this has come to pass in a moment, and was fashioned by a glance, a word, a sigh, and a kiss.

That moment, my beloved, has blended my soul's past readiness with my heart's hopes of the future. It was like a white rose that bursts from the bosom of the earth into the light of day.

That moment was to my life what the birth of Christ has been to the ages of Man, for it was filled with love and goodness. It turned darkness into light, sorrow into joy, and despair to bliss.

Beloved, the fires of Love descend from heaven in many shapes and forms, but their impress on the world is one. The tiny flame that lights up the human heart is like a blazing torch that comes down from heaven to light up the paths of mankind.

For in one soul are contained the hopes and feelings of all Mankind.

The Jews, my beloved, awaited the coming of a Messiah, who had been promised them, and who was to deliver them from bondage.

And the Great Soul of the World sensed that the worship of Jupiter and Minerva no longer availed, for the thirsty hearts of men could not be quenched with that wine.

In Rome men pondered the divinity of Apollo, a god

without pity, and the beauty of Venus already fallen into decay.

For deep in their hearts, though they did not understand it, these nations hungered and thirsted for the supreme teaching that would transcend any to be found on the earth. They yearned for the spirit's freedom that would teach man to rejoice with his neighbor at the light of the sun and the wonder of living. For it is this cherished freedom that brings man close to the Unseen, which he can approach without fear or shame.

All this took place two thousand years ago, my beloved, when the heart's desires hovered around visible things, fearful of approaching the eternal spirit—while Pan, Lord of Forests, filled the hearts of shepherds with terror, and Baal, Lord of the Sun, pressed with the merciless hands of priests upon the souls of the poor and lowly.

And in one night, in one hour, in one moment of time, the lips of the spirit parted and spoke the sacred word, "Life"; and it became flesh in an infant lying asleep in the lap of a virgin, in a stable where shepherds guarded their flocks against the assault of wild beasts of the night and looked with wonder upon that humble infant, asleep in the manger.

The Infant King, swaddled in his mother's wretched garments, sat upon a throne of burdened hearts and hungry souls, and through his humility wrested the sceptre of power from the hands of Jove and gave it to the poor shepherd watching over his flock.

And from Minerva he took Wisdom, and set it in the heart of a poor fisherman who was mending his fishing net.

From Apollo he drew Joy through his own sorrows and bestowed it upon the brokenhearted beggar by the wayside.

From Venus he took Beauty and poured it into the soul of the fallen woman trembling before her cruel oppressor.

He dethroned Baal and set in his place the humble plowman, who sowed his seed and tilled the soil by the sweat of his brow.

Beloved, was not my soul yesterday like unto the tribes of Israel? Did I not wait in the silence of the night for the coming of my Savior to deliver me from the bondage and evils of Time? Did I not feel the great thirst and the spirit's hunger as did those nations of the past? Did I not walk the road of Life like a child lost in some wilderness, and was not my life like a seed cast upon a stone, that no bird would seek, nor the elements split and bring to life?

All this came to pass yesterday, my beloved, when my dreams crouched in the dark, and feared the approach of the day.

All this came to pass when Sorrow tore my heart, and Hope strove to mend it.

In one night, in one hour, in one moment of time, the Spirit descended from the center of the circle of divine light and looked at me with your heart's eyes. From that glance Love was born, and found a dwelling in my heart.

This great Love, swaddled in the robes of my feelings,

has turned sorrow to joy, despair to bliss, aloneness to paradise.

Love, the great King, has restored life to my dead self; returned light to my tear-blinded eyes; raised me up from the pit of despair to the celestial kingdom of Hope.

For all my days were as nights, my beloved. But behold! the dawn has come; soon the sun will rise. For the breath of the Infant Jesus has filled the firmament and is mingled with the ether. Life, once full of woe, is now overflowing with joy, for the arms of the Infant are around me and embrace my soul.

THOUGHTS AND
MEDITATIONS

The Poet from Baalbek

Sarkis Effandi, one of Gibran's closest friends, was highly regarded among the intelligentsia of Lebanon. He owned a publishing house and a daily Arabic newspaper called Lisan-Ul-Hal. In the year 1912, the Arab League of Progress, organized for the promotion of Arab unity and culture, decided to honor the great Lebanese poet Khalil Effandi Mutran.

Since Sarkis was the head of the committee honoring the poet, he extended an invitation to his friend Gibran, now settled in New York, to join them in Beirut on that occasion. Gibran could not make the trip, but he sent Sarkis a story with instructions to read it in his behalf before the poet. In the story, which eulogises the poet, Gibran expresses his belief in the transmigration of souls and praises the great soul reincarnated in the honored poet.

IN THE CITY OF BAALBEK, THE YEAR 112 B. C.

The Emir sat on his golden throne surrounded by glittering lamps and gilded censers. The aromatic scent of the latter filled the palace. At his right and left sides were the

525

high priests and the chiefs; the slaves and guards stood immobile before him like statues of bronze erected before the face of the sun.

After the cantors had chanted echoing hymns, an elderly vizier stood before the Emir, and in a voice modulated in the serenity of age, said, "Oh great and merciful Prince, yesterday there arrived in our city a sage from India who believes in a diversity of religions and speaks of strange things difficult to understand. He preaches the doctrine of the transmigration of souls and the incarnation of spirits which move from one generation to another seeking more and more perfect avatars until they become godlike. This sage seeks an audience with you to explain his dogma."

The Emir shook his head, smiled, and said, "From India come many strange and wonderful things. Call in the sage that we may hear his words of wisdom."

As soon as he uttered these words, a dark-hued, aged man walked in with dignity and stood before the Emir. His large brown eyes spoke, without words, of deep secrets. He bowed, raised his head, his eyes glittered, and he commenced to speak.

He explained how the spirits pass from one body to another, elevated by the good acts of the medium which they choose, and influenced by their experience in each existence; aspiring toward a splendor that exalts them and strengthens their growth by Love that makes them both happy and miserable. . . .

Then the philosopher dwelt on the manner in which the

spirits move from place to place in their quest for perfection, atoning in the present for sins committed in the past, and reaping in one existence what they had sown in another.

Observing signs of restlessness and weariness on the Emir's countenance, the old vizier whispered to the sage, "You have preached enough at present; please postpone the rest of your discourse until our next meeting."

Thereupon the sage withdrew from the Emir's presence and sat among the priests and chiefs, closing his eyes as if weary of gazing into the deeps of Existence.

After a profound silence, similar to the trance of a prophet, the Emir looked to the right and to the left and inquired, "Where is our poet, we have not seen him for many days. What became of him? He always attended our meeting."

A priest responded, saying, "A week ago I saw him sitting in the portico of Ishtar's temple, staring with glazed and sorrowful eyes at the distant evening twilight as if one of his poems had strayed among the clouds."

And a chief added, "I saw him yesterday standing beneath the shade of the willow and cypress trees. I greeted him but he gave no heed to my greeting, and remained submerged in the deep sea of his thoughts and meditations."

Then the Grand Eunuch said, "I saw him today in the palace garden, with pale and haggard face, sighing, and his eyes full of tears."

"Go seek out this unhappy soul, for his absence from our midst troubles us," ordered the Emir.

At this command, the slaves and the guards left the hall to seek the poet, while the Emir and his priests and chiefs remained in the assembly hall awaiting their return. It seemed as if their spirits had felt his invisible presence among them.

Soon the Grand Eunuch returned and prostrated himself at the feet of the Emir like a bird shot by the arrow of an archer. Whereupon the Emir shouted at him saying, "What happened . . . what have you to say?" The slave raised his head and said in a trembling voice, "We found the poet dead in the palace garden."

Then the Emir rose and hastened sorrowfully to the palace garden, preceded by his torchbearers and followed by the priests and the chiefs. At the end of the garden close by the almond and pomegranate trees, the yellow light of the torches brought the dead youth into their sight. His corpse lay upon the green grass like a withered rose.

"Look how he embraced his viol as if the two were lovers pledged to die together!" said one of the Emir's aides.

Another one said, "He still stares, as in life, at the heart of space; he still seems to be watching the invisible movements of an unknown god among the planets."

And the high priest addressed the Emir, saying, "Tomorrow let us bury him, as a great poet, in the shade of Ishtar's temple, and let the townspeople march in his

funeral procession, while youths sing his poems and virgins strew flowers over his sepulchre. Let it be a commemoration worthy of his genius."

The Emir nodded his head without diverting his eyes from the young poet's face, pale with the veil of Death. "We have neglected this pure soul when he was alive, filling the Universe with the fruit of his brilliant intellect and spreading throughout space the aromatic scent of his soul. If we do not honor him now, we will be mocked and reviled by the gods and the nymphs of the prairies and valleys.

"Bury him in this spot where he breathed his last and let his viol remain between his arms. If you wish to honor him and pay him tribute, tell your children that the Emir had neglected him and was the cause of his miserable and lonely death." Then the monarch asked, "Where is the sage from India?" And the sage walked forth and said, "Here, oh great Prince."

And the Emir inquired, saying, "Tell us, oh sage, will the gods ever restore me to this world as a prince and bring back the deceased poet to life? Will my spirit become incarnated in a body of a great king's son, and will the poet's soul transmigrate into the body of another genius? Will the sacred Law make him stand before the face of Eternity that he may compose poems of Life? Will he be restored that I may honor him and pay him tribute by showering upon him precious gifts and rewards that will enliven his heart and inspire his soul?"

And the sage answered the Emir, saying, *"Whatever the soul longs for, will be attained by the spirit.* Remember, oh great Prince, that the sacred Law which restores the sublimity of Spring after the passing of Winter will reinstate you a prince and him a genius poet."

The Emir's hopes were revived and signs of joy appeared on his face. He walked toward his palace thinking and meditating upon the words of the sage: *"Whatever the soul longs for, will be attained by the spirit."*

IN CAIRO, EGYPT, THE YEAR 1912 A. D.

The full moon appeared and spread her silver garment upon the city. The Prince of the land stood at the balcony of his palace gazing at the clear sky and pondering upon the ages that have passed along the bank of the Nile. He seemed to be reviewing the processions of the nations that marched, together with Time, from the Pyramid to the palace of Abedine.

As the circle of the Prince's thoughts widened and extended into the domain of his dreams, he looked at his boon companion sitting by his side and said, "My soul is thirsty; recite a poem for me tonight."

And the boon companion bowed his head and began a pre-Islamic poem. But before he had recited many stanzas, the Prince interrupted him saying, "Let us hear a modern poem . . . a more recent one."

And, bowing, the boon companion began to recite verses

composed by a Hadramout poet. The Prince stopped him again, saying, "More recent . . . a more recent poem."

The singer raised his hand and touched his forehead as if trying to recall to memory all the poems composed by contemporary poets. Then his eyes glittered, his face brightened, and he began to sing lovely verses in soothing rhythm, full of enchantment.

Intoxicated and seeming to feel the movement of hidden hands beckoning him from his palace to a distant land, the Prince fervently inquired, "Who composed these verses?" And the singer answered, "The Poet from Baalbek."

The Poet from Baalbek is an ancient name and it brought into the Prince's memory images of forgotten days. It awakened in the depth of his heart phantoms of remembrance, and drew before his eyes, with lines formed by the mist, a picture of a dead youth embracing his viol and surrounded by priests, chiefs, and ministers.

Like dreams dissipated by the light of Morn, the vision soon left the Prince's eyes. He stood up and walked toward his palace with crossed arms repeating the words of Mohammed, "*You were dead and He brought you back to life, and He will return you to the dead and then restore you to life. Whereupon you shall go back to Him.*"

Then he looked at his boon companion and said, "We are fortunate to have the Poet from Baalbek in our land, and shall make it our paramount duty to honor and befriend him." After a few moments worthy of silence and

respect, the Prince added in a low voice, "The poet is a bird of strange moods. He descends from his lofty domain to tarry among us, singing; if we do not honor him he will unfold his wings and fly back to his dwelling place."

The night was over, and the skies doffed their garments studded with stars, and put on raiment woven from the sinews of the rays of Morn. And the Prince's soul swayed between the wonders and strangeness of Existence and the concealed mysteries of Life.

The Return of the Beloved

By nightfall the enemy fled with slashes of the sword and wounds of lance tips scarring their backs. Our heroes waved banners of triumph and chanted songs of victory to the cadence of their horses' hoofs that drummed upon the stones of the valley.

The moon had already risen from behind Fam El Mizab. The mighty and lofty rocks seemed to ascend with the spirits of the people, and the forest of cedars to lie like a medal of honor upon the bosom of Lebanon.

They continued their march, and the moon shone upon their weapons. The distant caves echoed their songs of praise and victory, until they reached the foot of a slope. There they were arrested by the neighing of a horse standing among gray rocks as though carved from them.

Near the horse they found a corpse, and the earth on which he lay was stained with his blood. The leader of the

troop shouted, "Show me the man's sword and I will tell you who the owner is."

Some of the horsemen dismounted and surrounded the dead man and then one said to the chief, "His fingers have taken too strong a hold on the hilt. It would be a shame to undo them."

Another said, "The sword has been sheathed with escaping life that hides its metal."

A third one added. "The blood has congealed on both the hand and the hilt and made them one piece."

Whereupon the chief dismounted and walked to the corpse and said, "Raise his head and let the moon shine on his face so we may identify him." The men did as ordered, and the face of the slain man appeared from behind the veil of Death showing the marks of valor and nobility. It was the face of a strong horseman, and it bespoke manhood. It was the face of a sorrowing and rejoicing man; the face of one who had met the enemy courageously and faced death smilingly; the face of a Lebanese hero who, on that day, had witnessed the triumph but had not lived to march and sing and celebrate the victory with his comrades.

As they removed the silk head-wrapper and cleaned the dust of battle from his pale face, the chief cried out, in agony, "This is the son of Assaaby, what a great loss!" And the men repeated that name, sighing. Then silence fell upon them, and their hearts, intoxicated with the wine of victory, sobered. For they had seen something greater than the glory of triumph, in the loss of a hero.

Like statues of marble they stood in that scene of dread, and their taut tongues were mute and voiceless. This is what death does to the souls of heroes. Weeping and lamentation are for women; and moans and cries for children. Nothing befits the sorrow of men of the sword save silence which grips the strong heart as the eagle's talons grip the throat of its prey. It is that silence which rises above tears and wailing which, in its majesty, adds more awe and anguish to the misfortune; that silence which causes the soul to descend from the mountain-top into the abyss. It is the silence which proclaims the coming tempest. And when the tempest makes not its appearance, it is because the silence is stronger than the tempest.

They removed the raiment of the young hero to see where death had placed its iron claws. And the wounds appeared in his breast like speaking lips proclaiming, in the calmness of the night, the bravery of men.

The chief approached the corpse and dropped on his knees. Taking a closer look at the slain warrior, he found a scarf embroidered with gold threads tied around the arm. He recognized the hand that had spun its silk and the fingers that had woven its thread. He hid it under his raiment and withdrew slowly, hiding his stricken face with a trembling hand. Yet this trembling hand, with its might, had disjoined the heads of the enemy. Now it trembled because it had touched the edge of a scarf tied by loving fingers around the arm of a slain hero, who would return to her lifeless, borne upon the shoulders of his comrades.

While the leader's spirit wavered, considering both the

535

tyranny of death and the secrets of love, one of the men suggested, "Let us dig a grave for him under that oak tree so that its roots may drink from his blood and its branches may receive nourishment from his remains. It will gain strength and become immortal and stand as a sign declaring to the hills and valleys his bravery and his might."

Another man said, "Let us carry him to the forest of the cedars and bury him by the church. There his bones will be eternally guarded by the shadow of the Cross."

And another said, "Bury him here where his blood is mingled with the earth. And let his sword remain in his right hand; plant his lance by his side and slay his horse over his grave and let his weapons be his cheer in his solitude."

But another objected, "Do not bury a sword stained with the enemy blood, nor slay a steed that has withstood death in the battle field. Do not leave in the wilderness weapons accustomed to action and strength, but carry them to his relatives as a great and good inheritance."

"Let us kneel down by his side and pray the Nazarene's prayers that God might forgive him and bless our victory," said another.

"Let us raise him upon our shoulders and make our shields and lances a bier for him and circle again this valley of our victory singing the songs of triumph so that the lips of his wounds will smile before they are muffled by the earth of the grave," said a comrade.

And another: "Let us mount him upon his charger and support him with the skulls of the dead enemy and gird him with his lance and bring him to the village a victor. He never yielded to death until he burdened it with the enemy's souls."

Another one said, "Come, let us bury him at the foot of this mountain. The echo of the caves shall be his companion and the murmur of the brook his minstrel. His bones shall rest in a wilderness where the tread of the silenced night is light and gentle."

Another objected, "No. Do not leave him in this place, for here dwells tedium and solitude. But let us carry him to the burial-ground of the village. The spirits of our forefathers will be his comrades and will speak to him in the silenced night and relate to him tales of their wars and sagas of their glory."

Then the chief walked to the center and motioned them to silence. He sighed and said, "Do not annoy him with memories of war or repeat to the ears of his soul, that hovers over us, the tales of swords and lances. Rather come and let us carry him calmly and silently to his birth-place, where a loving soul awaits his homecoming . . . a soul of a maiden awaiting his return from the battlefield. Let us return him to her so she may not be denied the sight of his face and the printing of a last kiss upon his forehead."

So they carried him upon their shoulders and walked silently with bent heads and downcast eyes. His sorrow-

ful horse plodded behind them dragging its reins on the ground, uttering from time to time a desolate neighing echoed by the caves as if those caves had hearts and shared their grief.

Through the thorny path of the valley illuminated by a full moon, the procession of victory walked behind the cavalcade of Death and the spirit of Love led the way dragging his broken wings.

Union

In this poem the prophet of Lebanon appears to have previsioned the union of Egypt and Syria.

When the night had embellished heaven's garment with the stars' gems, there rose a houri from the Valley of the Nile and hovered in the sky on invisible wings. She sat upon a throne of mist hung between heaven and the sea. Before her passed a host of angels chanting in unison, "Holy, holy, holy the daughter of Egypt whose grandeur fills the globe."

Then on the summit of Fam el Mizab, girdled by the forest of the cedars, a phantom youth was raised by the hands of the seraphim, and he sat upon the throne beside the houri. The spirits circled them singing, "Holy, holy, holy the youth of Lebanon, whose magnificence fills the ages."

And when the suitor held the hands of his beloved and

539

gazed into her eyes, the wave and wind carried their communion to all the universe:

How faultless is your radiance, Oh daughter of Isis, and how great my adoration for you!

How graceful you are among the youths, Oh son of Astarte, and how great my yearning for you!

My love is as strong as your Pyramids, and the ages shall not destroy it.

My love is as staunch as your Holy Cedars, and the elements shall not prevail over it.

The wise men of all the nations come from East and West to discern your wisdom and to interpret your signs.

The scholars of the world come from all the kingdoms to intoxicate themselves with the nectar of your beauty and the magic of your voice.

Your palms are fountains of abundance.

Your arms are springs of pure water, and your breath is a refreshing breeze.

The palaces and temples of the Nile announce your glory, and the Sphinx narrates your greatness.

The cedars upon your bosom are like a medal of honor, and the towers about you speak your bravery and might.

Oh how sweet is your love and how wonderful is the hope that you foster.

Oh what a generous partner you are, and how faithful a spouse you have proved to be. How sublime are your gifts, and how precious your sacrifice!

You sent to me young men who were as an awakening

after deep slumber. You gave me men of daring to conquer the weakness of my people, and scholars to exalt them, and geniuses to enrich their powers.

From the seeds I sent you you wrought flowers; from saplings you raised trees. For you are a virgin meadow on which roses and lilies grow and the cypresses and the cedar trees rise.

I see sorrow in your eyes, my beloved; do you grieve while you are at my side?

I have sons and daughters who emigrated beyond the seas and left me weeping and longing for their return.

Are you afraid, oh daughter of the Nile, and dearest of all nations?

I fear a tyrant approaching me with a sweet voice so that he may later rule me with the strength of his arms.

The life of the nations, my love, is like the life of individuals; a life cheered by Hope and married to Fear, beset by desires and frowned upon by Despair.

And the lovers embraced and kissed and drank from the cups of love the scented wine of the ages; and the host of spirits chanted, "Holy, holy, holy, Love's glory fills heaven and earth."

My Soul Preached to Me

My soul preached to me and taught me to love that which the people abhor and befriend him whom they revile.

My soul showed me that Love prides itself not only in the one who loves, but also in the beloved.

Ere my soul preached to me, Love was in my heart as a tiny thread fastened between two pegs.

But now Love has become a halo whose beginning is its end, and whose end is its beginning. It surrounds every being and extends slowly to embrace all that shall be.

My soul advised me and taught me to perceive the hidden beauty of the skin, figure, and hue. She instructed me to meditate upon that which the people call ugly until its true charm and delight appear.

Ere my soul counselled me, I saw Beauty like a trembling

torch between columns of smoke. Now since the smoke has vanished, I see naught save the flame.

My soul preached to me and taught me to listen to the voices which the tongue and the larynx and the lips do not utter.

Ere my soul preached to me, I heard naught but clamor and wailing. But now I eagerly attend Silence and hear its choirs singing the hymns of the ages and the songs of the firmament announcing the secrets of the Unseen.

My soul preached to me and instructed me to drink the wine that cannot be pressed and cannot be poured from cups that hands can lift or lips can touch.

Ere my soul preached to me, my thirst was like a dim spark hidden under the ashes that can be extinguished by a swallow of water.

But now my longing has become my cup, my affections my wine, and my loneliness my intoxication; yet, in this unquenchable thirst there is eternal joy.

My soul preached to me and taught me to touch that which has not become incarnate; my soul revealed to me that whatever we touch is part of our desire.

But now my fingers have turned into mist penetrating that which is seen in the universe and mingling with the Unseen.

My soul instructed me to inhale the scent that no myrtle or incense emits. Ere my soul preached to me, I

543

craved the scent of perfume in the gardens or in flasks or in censers.

But now I can savor the incense that is not burnt for offering or sacrifice. And I fill my heart with a fragrance that has never been wafted by the frolicsome breeze of space.

My soul preached to me and taught me to say, "I am ready" when the Unknown and Danger call on me.

Ere my soul preached to me, I answered no voice save the voice of the crier whom I knew, and walked not save upon the easy and smooth path.

Now the Unknown has become a steed that I can mount in order to reach the Unknown; and the plain has turned into a ladder on whose steps I climb to the summit.

My soul spoke to me and said, "Do not measure Time by saying, 'There was yesterday, and there shall be to-morrow.' "

And ere my soul spoke to me, I imagined the Past as an epoch that never returned, and the Future as one that could never be reached.

Now I realize that the present moment contains all time and within it is all that can be hoped for, done and realized.

My soul preached to me exhorting me not to limit space by saying, "Here, there, and yonder."

Ere my soul preached to me, I felt that wherever I walked was far from any other space.

Now I realize that wherever I am contains all places; and the distance that I walk embraces all distances.

My soul instructed me and advised me to stay awake while others sleep. And to surrender to slumber when others are astir.

Ere my soul preached to me, I saw not their dreams in my sleep, neither did they observe my vision.

Now I never sail the vessel of my dreams unless they watch me, and they never soar into the sky of their vision unless I rejoice in their freedom.

My soul preached to me and said, "Do not be delighted because of praise, and do not be distressed because of blame."

Ere my soul counselled me, I doubted the worth of my work.

Now I realize that the trees blossom in Spring and bear fruit in Summer without seeking praise; and they drop their leaves in Autumn and become naked in Winter without fearing blame.

My soul preached to me and showed me that I am neither more than the pygmy, nor less than the giant.

Ere my soul preached to me, I looked upon humanity as two men: one weak, whom I pitied, and the other strong, whom I followed or resisted in defiance.

But now I have learned that I was as both are and made from the same elements. My origin is their origin, my

conscience is their conscience, my contention is their contention, and my pilgrimage is their pilgrimage.

If they sin, I am also a sinner. If they do well, I take pride in their well-doing. If they rise, I rise with them. If they stay inert, I share their slothfulness.

My soul spoke to me and said, "The lantern which you carry is not yours, and the song that you sing was not composed within your heart, for even if you bear the light, you are not the light, and even if you are a lute fastened with strings, you are not the lute player."

My soul preached to me, my brother, and taught me much. And your soul has preached and taught as much to you. For you and I are one, and there is no variance between us save that I urgently declare that which is in my inner self, while you keep as a secret that which is within you. But in your secrecy there is a sort of virtue.

The Sons of the Goddess
And the Sons of the Monkeys

How strange Time is, and how queer we are! Time has really changed, and lo, it has changed us too. It walked one step forward, unveiled its face, alarmed us and then elated us.

Yesterday we complained about Time and trembled at its terrors. But today we have learned to love it and revere it, for we now understand its intents, its natural disposition, its secrets, and its mysteries.

Yesterday we crawled in fright like shuddering ghosts between the fears of the night and the menaces of the day. But today we walk joyously towards the mountain peak, the dwelling place of the raging tempest and the birthplace of thunder.

Yesterday we ate our bread kneaded with blood, and we drank our water mixed with tears. But today we began to

receive the manna from the hands of the morning brides and drank the aged wine scented with the sweet breath of Spring.

Yesterday we were a toy in the hands of Destiny. But today Destiny has awakened from her intoxication to play and laugh and walk with us. We do not follow her but she follows us.

Yesterday we burned incense before the idols and offered sacrifices to the angry gods. But today we burn incense and offer sacrifices to our own being, for the greatest and most beautiful of all gods has raised his temple in our hearts.

Yesterday we bowed to the kings and bent our necks to the sultans. But today we do not pay reverence save to Right and we follow no one except Beauty and Love.

Yesterday we honored false prophets and sorcerers. But today Time has changed, and lo, it has changed us too. We can now stare at the face of the sun and listen to the songs of the sea, and nothing can shake us except a cyclone.

Yesterday we tore down the temples of our souls and from their debris we built tombs for our forefathers. But today our souls have turned into sacred altars that the ghosts of the Past cannot approach, that the fleshless fingers of the dead cannot touch.

We were a silent thought hidden in the corners of Oblivion. Today we are a strong voice that can make the firmament reverberate.

We were a tiny spark buried under the ashes. Today we are a raging fire burning at the head of the valley.

We spent many a night awake, with the earth as our pillow and the snow as our blanket.

Like sheep without a shepherd we flocked together many nights grazing on our thoughts, and chewing the cud of our emotions; yet we remained hungry and athirst.

Oftentime we stood between a passing day and a coming night lamenting our withering youth and longing for someone unknown, and gazing at the void and dark sky listening to the moaning of Silence and the shrieking of nothingness.

Those ages passed like wolves among the graves. But today the skies are clear, and we can rest peacefully upon divine beds and welcome our thoughts and dreams, and embrace our desires. Grasping with untrembling fingers the torches that sway around us, we can talk to the genii with explicit meaning. As the choirs of angels pass us, they become intoxicated with the longing of our hearts and the hymns of our souls.

Yesterday we were, and today we are! This is the will of the goddess among the sons of the goddess. What is your will, oh sons of the monkeys? Have you walked a single step forward since you came forth from the crevices of the earth? Have you gazed toward heaven since Satan opened your eyes? Have you uttered a word from the book of Right since the lips of vipers kissed your lips? Or have you listened a moment to the song of Life since Death closed your ears?

Seventy thousand years ago I passed by and saw you moving like insects inside the caves; and seven minutes ago

I glanced at you through the crystal glass of my window and saw you walking through the alleys fettered by slavery while the wings of Death hovered over you. You look the same today as you looked yesterday; and tomorrow, and the day after it, you shall look as I saw you in the beginning.

Yesterday we were, and today we are! This is the will of the goddess among the sons of the goddess; what is your will, oh sons of the monkeys?

Decayed Teeth

I had a decayed tooth in my mouth that troubled me. It stayed dormant during the day. But in the tranquility of the night, when the dentists were asleep and drug stores closed, it began to ache.

One day, as I grew impatient, I went to the dentist and told him to extract that damned tooth that dealt me misery and denied me the joy of slumber by converting the silence of my night into moaning and uproar.

The dentist shook his head and said, "It is foolish to have your tooth extracted if we can cure it."

Then he started to drill its sides and clean its cavities and used every means to restore it and free it from decay. Having finished drilling, he filled it with pure gold and said boastfully, "Your bad tooth now is stronger and more solid than your good ones." I believed him and paid him and departed from the place.

But before the week was over, the cursed tooth returned

to its diseased condition and the torture it inflicted converted the beautiful songs of my soul into wailing and agony.

So I went to another dentist and said to him, "Extract this damned tooth without asking me any question, for the person who receives the blows is not like the one who counts them."

Obeying my command, he extracted the tooth. Looking at it he said, "You have done well to have this rotten tooth extracted."

In the mouth of Society are many diseased teeth, decayed to the bones of the jaws. But Society makes no efforts to have them extracted and be rid of the affliction. It contents itself with gold fillings. Many are the dentists who treat the decayed teeth of Society with glittering gold.

Numerous are those who yield to the enticements of such reformers, and pain, sickness, and death are their lot.

In the mouth of the Syrian nation are many rotten, black, and dirty teeth that fester and stink. The doctors have attempted cures with gold fillings instead of extraction. And the disease remains.

A nation with rotten teeth is doomed to have a sick stomach. Many are the nations afflicted with such indigestion.

If you wish to take a look at the decayed teeth of Syria, visit its schools where the sons and daughters of today are preparing to become the men and women of tomorrow.

Visit the courts and witness the acts of the crooked

and corrupted purveyors of justice. See how they play with the thoughts and minds of the simple people as a cat plays with a mouse.

Visit the homes of the rich where conceit, falsehood, and hypocrisy reign.

But don't neglect to go through the huts of the poor as well, where dwell fear, ignorance, and cowardice.

Then visit the nimble-fingered dentists, possessors of delicate instruments, dental plasters and tranquilizers, who spend their days filling the cavities in the rotten teeth of the nation to mask the decay.

Talk to those reformers who pose as the intelligentsia of the Syrian nation and organize societies, hold conferences, and deliver public speeches. When you talk to them you will hear tunes that perhaps sound more sublime than the grinding of a millstone, and nobler than the croaking of frogs on a June night.

When you tell them the Syrian nation gnaws its bread with decayed teeth and each morsel it chews is mixed with poisoned saliva that spreads diseases in the nation's stomach, they answer, "Yes, but we are seeking better tooth fillings and tranquilizers."

And if you suggest "extraction" to them, they will laugh at you because you have not yet learned the noble art of dentistry that conceals disease.

If you were to insist, they would go off and shun you, saying to themselves:

"Many are the idealists in this world, and weak are their dreams."

Mister Gabber

I am bored with gabbers and their gab; my soul abhors them.

When I wake up in the morning to peruse the letters and magazines placed by my bedside, I find them full of gab; all I see is loose talk empty of meaning but stuffed with hypocrisy.

When I sit by the window to lower the veil of slumber from my eyes and sip my Turkish coffee, Mister Gabber appears before me, hopping, crying, and grumbling. He condescends to sip my coffee and smoke my cigarettes.

When I go to work Mister Gabber follows, whispering in my ears and tickling my sensitive brain. When I try to get rid of him he giggles and is soon midstream again, in his flood of meaningless talk.

When I go to the market, Mister Gabber stands at the door of every shop passing judgment on people. I see him even upon the faces of the silent for he accompanies them

too. They are unaware of his presence, yet he disturbs them.

If I sit down with a friend Mister Gabber, uninvited, makes a third. If I elude him, he manages to remain so close that the echo of his voice irritates me and upsets my stomach like spoiled meat.

When I visit the courts and the institutions of learning, I find him and his father and mother dressing Falsehood in silky garments and Hypocrisy in a magnificent cloak and a beautiful turban.

When I call at factory offices, there too, to my surprise, I find Mister Gabber, in the midst of his mother, aunt, and grandfather chattering and flapping his thick lips. And his kinfolks applaud him and mock me.

On my visit to the temples and other places of worship, there he is, seated on a throne, his head crowned and a gleaming sceptre in his hand.

Returning home at eventide, I find him there, too. From the ceiling he hangs like a snake; or crawls like a boa in the four corners of my house.

In short, Mister Gabber is found everywhere; within and beyond the skies, on land and underground, on the wings of the ether and upon the waves of the sea, in the forests, in the caves, and on the mountaintops.

Where can a lover of silence and tranquility find rest from him? Will God ever have mercy on my soul and grant me the grace of dumbness so I may reside in the paradise of Silence?

Is there in this universe a nook where I can go and live happily by myself?

Is there any place where there is no traffic in empty talk?

Is there on this earth one who does not worship himself talking?

Is there any person among all persons whose mouth is not a hiding place for the knavish Mister Gabber?

If there were but one kind of gabber, I would be resigned. But gabbers are innumerable. They can be divided into clans and tribes:

There are those who live in marshes all day long, but when night comes, they move to the banks and raise their heads out of the water and the slime, and fill the silent night with horrible croaking that bursts the eardrums.

There are those who belong to the family of gnats. It is they who hover around our heads and make tiny devilish noises out of spite and hatred.

There is the clan whose members swill brandy and beer and stand at the street corners and fill the ether with a bellowing thicker than a buffalo's wallow.

We see also a queer tribe of people who pass their time at the tombs of Life converting silence into a sort of wailing more lugubrious than the screeching of the owl.

Then there is the gang of gabbers who imagine life as a piece of lumber from which they try to shape something for themselves, raising as they do so, a screeching sound uglier than the din of a sawmill.

Following this gang is a denomination of creatures who pound themselves with mallets to produce hollow tones more awful than the tomtoms of jungle savages.

Supporting these creatures is a sect whose members have nothing to do save to sit down, whenever a seat is available, and there chew words instead of uttering them.

Once in a while we find a party of gabbers who weave air from air, but remain without a garment.

Oftentime we run across a unique order of gabbers whose representatives are like starlings but deem themselves eagles when they soar in the currents of their words.

And what of those gabbers who are like ringing bells calling the people to worship but who never enter the church.

There are still more tribes and clans of gabbers, but they are too many to enumerate. Of these the strangest, in my opinion, is a sleeping denomination whose members trouble the universe with their snoring and awaken themselves, from time to time, to say, "How erudite we are!"

Having expressed my abhorrence of Mister Gabber and his comrades, I find myself like the doctor who cannot heal himself, or like a convict preaching to his cellmates. I have satirized Mister Gabber and his gabbing friends— with my own gabbing. I have fled from gabbers but I am one of them.

Will God ever forgive my sins before He blesses me and places me in the world of Thought, Truth, and Affection, where gabbers do not exist?

In the Dark Night

Written in World War I during the famine in Lebanon

In the dark night we call to one another and cry for help, while the ghost of Death stands in our midst stretching his black wings over us and, with his iron hands, pushes our souls into the abyss.

In the dark night Death strides on and we follow him frightened and moaning. Not one of us is capable of halting the fateful procession or even nourishing a hope of its end.

In the dark night Death walks and we walk behind him. And when he looks backward, hundreds of souls fall down on both sides of the road. And he who falls, sleeps and never awakens. And he who keeps his footing marches on fearfully in the dread certainty of falling later and joining those who have yielded to Death and entered the eternal sleep. But Death marches on, gazing at the distant Evening Twilight.

In the dark night the brother calls his brother, the father his son, and the mother her children; but the pangs and torments of hunger afflict us equally.

But Death does not hunger or thirst. He devours our souls and bodies, drinks our blood and tears and is never sated.

During the first part of the night the child calls his mother saying, "I am hungry, mother," and the mother replies, "Wait a while, my child."

In the second part of the night the child repeats, "I am hungry, mother, give me some bread," and the mother answers him, saying, "I have no bread, my beloved child."

In the third part of the night Death arrives and smites both the mother and the child with his wings and they both sleep eternally by the side of the road. And Death marches on, gazing at the distant Evening Twilight.

In the morn the husband goes to the field in search of nourishment, but he finds naught in it save dust and stones.

At noontide he returns to his wife and children pale, weak, and empty-handed.

And at eventide Death arrives and the husband, his wife, and children lie in eternal sleep. And he laughs and marches on toward the distant Evening Twilight.

In the morn the farmer leaves his hut for the city, carrying in his pocket his mother's and sisters' jewelry to exchange for bread. At eventide he returns without bread and without jewels, to find his mother and sisters sunk into eternal sleep, their eyes staring at nothingness. Where-

upon he lifts his arms toward heaven and drops like a bird shot by a merciless hunter.

And Death, seeing the farmer, his mother and sisters beguiled to eternal sleep by the evil angel, laughs again and marches on toward the distant Evening Twilight.

Oh, you who walk in the light of the day, we call you from the endless dark of the night. Do you hear our cries?

We have sent to you the spirits of our dead as our apostles. Have you heeded the apostles' word?

We have burdened the East Wind with our gasps. Has the Wind reached your distant shores to unload his burden in your hands? Are you aware of our misery? Have you thought of coming to our rescue? Or have you hugged to yourselves your peace and comfort, saying, "What can the sons of the light do for the sons of the dark? Let the dead bury their dead and God's will be done."

Yes, let God's will be done. But can you not raise yourselves above yourselves so that God may make you instruments of His will and use you for our aid?

In the dark night we call one another.

The brother calls his brother, the mother her daughter, the man his wife, and the lover his beloved.

And when our voices mingle together and reach the heart of heaven, Death pauses and laughs, then mocks us and marches on, gazing at the distant Evening Twilight.

The Silver-Plated Turd

SILMAN EFFANDI is a well-dressed man, tall and handsome, thirty-five years of age. He curls his mustaches and wears silk socks and patent-leather shoes. In his soft and delicate hand he carries a gold-headed and bejewelled walking stick. He eats in the most expensive restaurants where the fashionable forgather. In his magnificent carriage, drawn by thoroughbreds, he rides through the upper-class boulevards.

Silman Effandi's wealth was not inherited from his father, who (may his soul rest in peace) was a poor man. Neither did Silman Effandi amass wealth by shrewd and persevering business activities. He is lazy and hates to work, regarding any form of labor as degrading.

Once we heard him say, "My physique and temperament unfit me for work; work is meant for those with sluggish character and brutish body."

561

Then how did Silman attain his riches? By what magic was the dirt in his hands transformed into gold and silver? This is a secret hidden in a silver-plated turd which Azrael, the angel of Death, has revealed to us, and we in turn shall reveal it to you:

Five years ago Silman Effandi married the lady Faheema, widow of Betros Namaan, famous for his honesty, perseverence, and hard work.

Faheema was then forty-five years of age, but only sweet sixteen in her thoughts and behavior. She now dyes her hair and by the use of cosmetics deludes herself that she remains young and beautiful. She does not see Silman, her young husband, except after midnight when he vouchsafes her a scornful look and some vulgarities and abuse by way of conversation. This entitles him, he believes, to spend the money which her first husband earned by the sweat of his brow.

ADEEB EFFANDI is a young man, twenty-seven years of age, blessed with a big nose, small eyes, dirty face and ink-spotted hands with filth-encrusted fingernails. His clothes are frayed and adorned with oil, grease and coffee stains.

His ugly appearance is not due to Adeeb Effandi's poverty but to his preoccupation with spiritual and theological ideas. He often quotes Ameen El Jundy's saying that a scholar cannot be both clean and intelligent.

In his incessant talk Adeeb Effandi has nothing to say except to deliver judgment on others. On investigation, we

found that Adeeb Effandi had spent two years in a school at Beirut studying rhetoric. He wrote poems, essays, and articles, which never saw print. His reasons for failing to achieve publication are the degeneration of the Arabic press and the ignorance of the Arabic reading public.

Recently Adeeb Effandi has been occupying himself with the study of the old and new philosophy. He admires Socrates and Nietzsche, and relishes the sayings of Saint Augustine as well as Voltaire and Rousseau. At a wedding party we heard him discussing Hamlet; but his talk was a soliloquy, for the others preferred to drink and sing.

On another occasion, at a funeral, the subjects of his talk were the love poems of Ben Al Farid and the wine-ism' of Abi Nawaas. But the mourners ignored him, being oppressed by grief.

Why, we often wonder, does Adeeb Effandi exist? What use are his rotting books and his parchments falling into dust? Would it not be better for him to buy himself an ass and become a healthy and useful ass-driver?

This is a secret hidden in the silver-plated turd revealed to us by Baal-Zabul and we in turn shall now reveal it to you:

Three years ago Adeeb Effandi composed a poem in praise of His Excellency, Bishop Joseph Shamoun. His Excellency placed his hand on the shoulder of Adeeb Effandi, smiled and said, "Bravo, my son, God bless you! I have no doubt about your intelligence; some day you will be among the great men of the East."

FAREED BEY DAVIS is a man in his late thirties, tall, with a small head and large mouth, narrow forehead and a bald pate. He walks with a pompous rolling gait, swelling his chest and stretching his long neck like a camel.

From his loud voice and his haughty manner you might imagine him (provided you had not met him before) the minister of a great empire, absorbed in public affairs.

But Fareed has nothing to do aside from enumerating and glorifying the deeds of his ancesters. He is fond of citing exploits of famous men, and deeds of heroes such as Napoleon and Antar. He is a collector of weapons of which he has never learned the use.

One of his sayings is that God created two different classes of people: the leaders and those who serve them. Another is that the people are like stubborn asses who do not stir unless you whip them. Another, that the pen was meant for the weak and the sword for the strong.

What prompts Fareed to boast of his ancestry and behave as he does? This is a secret hidden in the silver-plated turd which Satanael has revealed to us, and we, in turn, reveal to you:

In the third decade of the nineteenth century when Emeer Basheer, the great Governor of Mount Lebanon, was passing with his retinue through the Lebanese valleys, they approached the village in which Mansour Davis, Fareed's grandfather lived. It was an exceedingly hot day, and the Emeer dismounted from his horse and ordered his men to rest in the shadow of an oak tree.

Mansour Davis, discovering the Emeer's presence, called the neighboring farmers, and the good news spread through the village. Led by Mansour the villagers brought baskets of grapes and figs, and jars of honey, wine and milk for the Emeer. When they reached the oak tree, Mansour kneeled before the Emeer and kissed the hem of his robe. Then he stood up and killed a sheep in the Emeer's honor, saying, "The sheep is from thy bounty, oh Prince and protector of our lives." The Emeer, pleased with such hospitality, said to him, "Henceforth you shall be the mayor of this village which I will exempt from taxes for this year."

That night, after the Emeer had left, the villagers met at the house of "Sheik" Mansour Davis and vowed loyalty to the newly appointed Sheik. May God have mercy on their souls.

There are too many secrets contained in the silver-plated turd to enumerate them all. The devils and satans reveal some to us every day and night, which we shall share with you before the angel of death wraps us under his wings and takes us into the Great Beyond.

Since it is now midnight and our eyes are getting heavy, permit us to surrender ourselves to Slumber and perhaps the beautiful bride of dreams will carry our souls into a world cleaner than this one.

Martha

I

Her father died when she was in the cradle, and she lost her mother before reaching the age of ten. As an orphan, Martha was left in the care of a poor peasant whose servant she became. They lived in an obscure hamlet on a slope of the beautiful mountains of North Lebanon.

At his death, her father had left his family only his good name and a hut standing amidst willow and walnut trees. It was the death of her mother which truly orphaned her. It left an emptiness in her heart which could not be filled. She became a stranger in her birthplace. Every day she walked barefoot leading a cow to pasture. While the cow grazed she sat under a tree, singing with the birds, weeping with the stream, envying the cow her serenity, and gazing at the flowers over which the butterflies hovered.

At night she returned home to a simple dinner of bread,

olives, and dried fruit. She slept in a bed of straw, with her arms for a pillow; and it was her prayer that her whole life might be uninterrupted slumber. At dawn her master would wake her so that she would get the housework done before she led the cow to pasture. She trembled and did as she was ordered.

Thus the gloomy and puzzling years passed, and Martha grew like a sapling. In her heart there developed a quiet affection of which she herself was unaware . . . like fragrance born in the heart of a flower. She followed her fancy as sheep follow a stream to quench their thirst. Her mind was like virgin land where knowledge had sown no seeds and upon which no feet had trod.

We who live amid the excitements of the city know nothing of the life of the mountain villagers. We are swept into the current of urban existence, until we forget the peaceful rhythms of simple country life, which smiles in the spring, toils in summer, reaps in autumn, rests in winter, imitating nature in all her cycles. We are wealthier than the villagers in silver or gold, but they are richer in spirit. What we sow we reap not; they reap what they sow. We are slaves of gain, and they the children of contentment. Our draught from the cup of life is mixed with bitterness and despair, fear and weariness; but they drink the pure nectar of life's fulfillment.

At sixteen, Martha's soul was like a clear mirror that reflects a beautiful landscape; her heart like a primeval valley that echoes all voices.

One day in autumn she sat by the spring, gazing at the falling yellow leaves, stripped from the trees by the breeze that moved between the branches as death moves into a man's soul. She looked at the withering flowers whose hearts were dry and whose seeds sought shelter in earth's bosom like refugees seeking a new life.

While thus engrossed, she heard hoofbeats upon the ground. Turning, she observed a horseman approaching. As he reached the spring he dismounted and greeted her with kind words, such as she had not heard from a man before. Then he went on to say, "Young lady, I have lost my way. Will you please direct me to the road to the coast?"

Looking like a tender branch, there by the spring, she replied, "I regret, sir, that I am unable to direct you, never having been away from home; but if you will ask my master I am sure he can help you." Her flushed face, as she spoke, made her look more gentle and beautiful. As she started away he stopped her. His expression became soft as he said, "Please do not go."

And a strange power in the man's voice held her immobile. When she stole a glance at his face she found him gazing at her steadily. She could not understand his silent adoration.

He eyed her lovely bare feet, her graceful arms and smooth neck and shining hair. Lovingly and wonderingly he regarded her sun-warmed cheeks and her chiseled

features. She could not utter a single word or move a muscle.

The cow returned alone to the barn that evening. Martha's master searched all through the valley but could not find her. His wife wept all that night. She said the next morning, "I saw Martha in my dream last night, and she was between the paws of a wild beast who lured her; the beast was about to kill Martha, but she smiled."

II

In the autumn of 1900, after a vacation in North Lebanon, I returned to Beyrouth. Before re-entering school I spent a week roaming the city with my classmates. We were like birds whose cage-door is unlocked, and who come and go as they please.

Youth is a beautiful dream, on whose brightness books shed a blinding dust. Will ever the day come when the wise link the joy of knowledge to youth's dream? Will ever the day come when Nature becomes the teacher of man, humanity his book and life his school? Youth's joyous purpose cannot be fulfilled until that day comes. Too slow is our march toward spiritual elevation, because we make so little use of youth's ardor.

One evening, as I was contemplating the jostling street crowds of Beyrouth, and feeling deafened by the shouts of the street vendors, I noticed a ragged boy of about five carrying some flowers on a tray. In a dispirited voice he asked me, "Will you buy some flowers, sir?" His mouth

was half-open, resembling and echoing a deep wound in the soul. His arms were thin and bare, and his frail body was bent over his flower tray like a branch of withering roses.

In my reply I tried to keep from my voice any intrusive edge of charity.

I bought some of his flowers but my chief purpose was to converse with him. I felt that his heart was a stage upon which a continuous drama of misery was being enacted.

At my careful, tactful words he began to feel secure and a smile brightened his face. He was surprised to hear words of kindness, for like all the poor he was accustomed to harshness. I asked his name, which was Fu'ad, and then, "Whose son are you?" He replied, "I am the son of Martha." "And who is your father?" I inquired. He shook his head, puzzled, as if unaware of the meaning of the word. I continued, "Where is your mother now, "Fu'ad?" He replied, weeping, "She is at home, sick."

Suddenly remembrance formed in my mind. Martha, whose unfinished story I had heard from an old villager, was ill nearby. That young woman who yesterday safely roamed the valley and enjoyed the beauty of nature was now suffering the anguish of destitution; that orphan who spent her early life in the haven of Nature was undergoing the tortures that city sophistication inflicts upon the innocent.

As the boy started to leave, I took hold of his hand saying, "Take me to your mother. I would like to see her."

He led the way silently, looking back now and then to see if I followed.

Through narrow, dirty streets with an odor of death in the air, and between houses of ill-fame, raucous with the sounds of sin, I walked behind Fu'ad, admiring the courage in his stride. It took courage to walk in these slums, where violence, crime and plague mocked the glory of this city, called "The Bride of Syria" and "The Pearl of the Sultan's Crown."

As we entered a particularly squalid quarter, the boy pointed to a hovel whose walls appeared to be collapsing. My heartbeats quickened and I followed Fu'ad into a sunless, airless room, unfurnished except for an oil lamp and a hard bed upon which Martha was lying, her face to the wall as if to hide from the oppression of the city. Fu'ad touched her shoulder and said, "Mama." As she turned painfully, he pointed at me. She moved her weak body under the ragged quilt, and with a despairing voice said, "What brings you here, stranger? What do you want? Did you come here to buy the last remnant of my soul and pollute it with your desire? Go away from here; the streets are full of women who sell themselves. What is left of my broken soul death shall soon buy. Go away from me and my boy."

Those few words completed her tragic story. I said, "Fear me not, Martha; I come here not as a devourer, but as a fellow sufferer. I am a Lebanese who lived near your valley by the cedars of Lebanon. Do not be frightened."

Realizing then that my words came from a feeling soul, she shook like a thin branch before a strong wind, and placed her hands upon her face, trying to hide away the terrible and beautiful memory whose sweetness was ravaged by bitterness.

Then in a strangely strong yet hopeless voice she said, "You have come here as a benefactor, and may God reward you; but I beg you to leave, for your presence here will bring disgrace upon you. Avoid being recognized. Your merciful heart does not restore my virtue; it neither effaces my shame nor protects me from the hands of death. My own sin brought this misery upon me; do not let your mercy bring you into shame. I am like a leper who must be avoided. Go, lest you be polluted! Do not mention my name in North Lebanon. The lamb with the mange is destroyed by the shepherd for fear he will infect the other lambs. If you speak of me, say I am dead."

Then she embraced her little boy and said: "People will taunt my son, saying he is the fruit of sin; the son of Martha the adulteress; Martha the prostitute. For they are blind and do not see that his mother gave him life through misery. I shall die and leave him as an orphan among other children, and his remembrance of me will bring him shame. But when he becomes a man, he will help heaven to end that which brought sin upon me; and when he dies in the trap of time, he will find me waiting for him in Eternity, where light and peace abide."

With a desolate heart I said, "Martha, you are not a

leper. You live in a grave yet you are clean. The filth of the body cannot reach a pure soul."

Hearing my heartfelt words, Martha's face brightened. But it was plain that her death was near. Yesterday she had roamed the valleys of Lebanon; today, weak and sorrowful, she awaited release from the shackles of life. Gathering her last fragments of strength she whispered, "I am everything you say, although my own weakness brought my agony . . . the horseman came . . . he spoke politely and cleverly . . . he kissed me . . . I knew nothing and relied on his words. He took me away and his fine words and smiles masked his ugly desires. After accomplishing my disgrace, he abandoned me. He split my life in two parts —my helpless self, and my baby. We were cold . . . we suffered. . . . For the sake of my child I took gold from men who bought my body. Many times I was close to taking my life. Now, at last, the hour has come and beloved death has arrived to enfold me under his sheltering wings."

Suddenly in a strong but calm voice she said, "Oh Justice, hidden behind those terrible images, hear the shrieking of my departing soul and the call of my broken heart! Have mercy on me by saving my child and taking me away!"

Her breathing became weak. She looked sorrowfully and sweetly at her son and then whispered, "Our Father which art in heaven, hallowed be Thy name. Thy kingdom come,

Thy will be done on earth as it is in heaven. . . . Forgive us our sins as we . . ."

Her voice gave out but her lips still moved. Then she breathed her last on earth. Her eyes remained open as if seeing the invisible.

As dawn came, the body of Martha was carried in a rough casket to a graveyard by two poor men. Far out from the City of Beyrouth they carried her. The priests refused to pray for her, and prohibited her interment in hallowed ground. And no one accompanied Martha to her resting place except her little son Fu'ad and a youth to whom life had taught mercy and kindness.

Vision

When Night came and Slumber spread its garment upon the face of the earth, I left my bed and walked toward the sea saying, "The sea never sleeps, and in its vigil there is consolation for a sleepless soul."

When I reached the shore, the mist from the mountains had engauzed the region as a veil adorns the face of a young woman. I gazed at the teeming waves and listened to their praise of God and meditated upon the eternal power hidden within them—that power which runs with the tempest and rises with the volcano and smiles through the lips of the roses and sings with the brooks.

Then I saw three phantoms sitting upon a rock. I stumbled toward them as if some power were pulling me against my will.

Within a few paces from the phantoms, I halted as though held still by a magic force. At that moment one of

the phantoms stood up and in a voice that seemed to rise from the depth of the sea said:

"Life without Love is like a tree without blossom and fruit. And love without Beauty is like flowers without scent and fruits without seeds. . . . Life, Love, and Beauty are three persons in one, who cannot be separated or changed."

A second phantom spoke with a voice that roared like cascading water and said:

"Life without Rebellion is like seasons without Spring. And Rebellion without Right is like Spring in an arid desert. . . . Life, Rebellion, and Right are three-in-one who cannot be changed or separated."

Then the third phantom in a voice like a clap of thunder spoke:

"Life without Freedom is like a body without a soul, and Freedom without Thought is like a confused spirit. . . . Life, Freedom, and Thought are three-in-one, and are everlasting and never pass away."

Then the three phantoms stood up together, and with one tremendous voice said:

> "That which Love begets,
> That which Rebellion creates,
> That which Freedom rears,
> Are three manifestations of God.
> And God is the expression
> Of the intelligent Universe."

At that moment Silence mingled with the rustling of

invisible wings and trembling of ethereal bodies; and it prevailed.

I closed my eyes and listened to the echoes of the sayings which I had just heard, and when I opened them I saw nothing but the sea wreathed in mist. I walked toward the rock where the three phantoms were sitting, but I saw naught save a column of incense spiralling toward heaven.

Communion of Spirits

Awake, my love, awake! For my spirit hails you from beyond the seas, and offers you her wings above the raging waves.

Awake, for silence has halted the clamor of the horses' hoofs and the tramp of the passers-by.

Slumber has embraced the spirits of men, while I alone remain awake; longing lifts me out of enveloping sleep.

Love brings me close to you but then, anxiety takes me far away.

I have left my bed, my love, for fear of the ghost of forgetfulness hiding in the quilts.

I have thrown my book aside, for my sighs silenced the words and left the pages blank before my eyes!

Awake, awake, my love, and hear me.

I hear you, my beloved! I heard your call from beyond the seas and felt the soft touch of your wings; I have left

my bed and walked upon the grass and the night dew has wet my feet and the hem of my garment. Here I stand under the blossoms of the almond tree, heeding the call of your spirit.

Speak to me, my love, and let your breath mount the breeze that comes towards me from the valleys of Lebanon. Speak. No one hears but me. Night has taken all others to their resting places.

Heaven has woven a veil of moonlight and drawn it over all Lebanon, my beloved.

Heaven has fashioned from the shadows of night a thick cloak lined with the fumes of workshops and the breath of Death, and laid it over the frame of the city, my love.

The villagers have surrendered to Slumber in their huts in the midst of the willow and walnut trees. Their spirits have sped towards the land of dreams, my beloved.

Men are bent under the burden of gold, and the steep road of green weakens their knees. Their eyes are heavy with trouble and weariness, and they drop on their beds as a haven, my love, from the Ghosts of Fear and Despair.

The ghosts of past ages walk in the valleys, and the spirits of the kings and prophets hover over the knolls and the hills. And my thoughts, fashioned by memory, show me the might of the Chaldeans, the splendor of the Assyrians, and the nobility of the Arabs.

In the sinister alleys walk the grim spirits of the thieves;

the heads of the vipers of lust appear from the crevices of the ramparts; and the ague of sickness, mingled with the agony of Death, shudders through the streets. Memory has removed the veil of forgetfulness from my eyes and shows me the loathsomeness of Sodom and the sins of Gomorrah.

The branches sway, my beloved, and their rustling joins the murmur of the rivulet in the valley, repeating to our ears the canticles of Solomon, the strains of David's harp, and the songs of Ishak al-Mausili.

The souls of the hungry children in the lodgings tremble; and the sighs of the mothers tossing upon the beds of misery and despair have reached the sky; and anxious dreams afflict the hearts of the infirm. I hear their bitter lamentations.

The fragrance of flowers has mingled with the pungent breath of the cedars. Brought by the frolicsome breeze over the hills, it fills the soul with affection and inspires longing for flight.

But the miasmas from the marshes also rise, steaming with disease. Like sharp secret arrows they have penetrated the senses and poisoned the air.

The morning has come, my beloved, and the soft fingers of wakefulness fondle the eyes of the dreamers. Rays of light force open the shutters and reveal Life's resolution and glory. The villages, reposing in peace and tranquility upon the shoulders of the valley, rise from their slumber; church bells fill the air with their pleasing summons to

morning prayer. And from the caves echo the chimes as if all Nature joins in reverent prayer. The calves have left their stalls, and the sheep and the goats their sheds, to graze upon the glittering, dewy grass. The shepherds walk before them, piping on their reeds; and behind them walk the damsels singing like the birds welcoming the morn.

And now the heavy hand of the Day lies upon the city. The curtains have been drawn from the windows and the doors are open. The fatigued eyes and drawn faces of toilers appear in the workshops. They feel death encroaching upon their lives, and on their shrivelled countenances appear Fear and Despair. The streets are congested with hurrying greedy souls; and everywhere are heard the clanking of iron, the rattling of wheels, and whistling of steam. The city has turned into a battlefield where the strong wrestle down the weak and the rich exploit and tyrannize over the poor.

How beautiful is life, my beloved; it is like the poet's heart, filled with light and tenderness.

And how cruel is life, my love, it is like a criminal's heart, throbbing with vice and fear.

Under the Sun

*I have seen all things that are done under the sun, and
behold all is vanity and vexation of spirit.*
ECCLESIASTES

O spirit of Solomon that hovers in the ethereal realm;
you, who cast aside the tattered garment of matter, have
left behind you these words, born of weakness and misery,
which deject those still imprisoned in bodies.

You know there is a meaning in this life which Death
does not conceal. But how could humanity attain a knowledge which comes only when the soul is freed from earthly
ties?

You realize now that life is not a vexation of spirit; that
things done under the sun are not all vanity; that somehow everything has ever marched and shall ever march
toward Truth. We miserable creatures have adhered to
your earthly sayings as words of great wisdom. But they
are shutters that darken the mind and obliterate hope.

582

You now understand that ignorance, evil, and despotism have their causes; and that Beauty is the revelation of wisdom, the product of virtue and the fruit of justice.

You now know that sorrow and poverty purify man's heart; though our weak minds see nothing worthy in the universe save ease and happiness.

You can see now that the spirit advances toward the light in spite of worldly hardships. Yet we repeat your words which teach that a man is but a toy in the hands of the unknown.

You have regretted your planting in our hearts a faintness toward life in the world and apprehension toward life in the hereafter. Yet we persist in heeding your earthly words.

O spirit of Solomon who now dwells in Eternity, reveal yourself to the lovers of wisdom and teach them not to walk the path of heresy and misery. Perchance this shall be an atonement for an unintended error.

A Glance at the Future

From behind the wall of the Present I heard the hymns of humanity. I heard the sounds of the bells announcing the beginning of the prayer in the temple of Beauty. Bells moulded in the metal of emotion and poised above the holy altar—the human heart.

From behind the Future I saw multitudes worshipping on the bosom of Nature, their faces turned toward the East and awaiting the inundation of the morning light—the morning of Truth.

I saw the city in ruins and nothing remaining to tell man of the defeat of Ignorance and the triumph of Light.

I saw the elders seated under the shade of cypress and willow trees, surrounded by youths listening to their tales of former times.

I saw the youths strumming their guitars and piping on their reeds and the loose-tressed damsels dancing under the jasmine trees.

I saw the husbandmen harvesting the wheat, and the wives gathering the sheaves and singing mirthful songs.

I saw woman adorning herself with a crown of lilies and a girdle of green leaves.

I saw Friendship strengthened between man and all creatures, and clans of birds and butterflies, confident and secure, winging toward the brooks.

I saw no poverty; neither did I encounter excess. I saw fraternity and equality prevailing among man.

I saw not one physician, for everyone had the means and knowledge to heal himself.

I found no priest, for conscience had become the High Priest. Neither did I see a lawyer, for Nature has taken the place of the courts, and treaties of amity and companionship were in force.

I saw that man knew that he is the cornerstone of creation, and that he has raised himself above littleness and baseness and cast off the veil of confusion from the eyes of the soul; this soul now reads what the clouds write on the face of heaven and what the breeze draws on the surface of the water; now understands the meaning of the flower's breath and the cadences of the nightingale.

From behind the wall of the Present, upon the stage of coming ages, I saw Beauty as a groom and Spirit as a bride, and Life as the ceremonial Night of the Kedre.*

* A night during the Moslem Lent when God is said to grant the wishes of the devout.

The Goddess of Fantasy

And after a wearying journey I reached the ruins of Palmyra. There I dropped, exhausted, upon the grass that grew among columns shattered and leveled by the ages. They looked like the debris left by invading armies.

At nightfall, as the black mantle of silence enfolded all creatures, I savored a strange scent in the air. It was as fragrant as incense and as inebriating as wine. My spirit opened her mouth to sip the ethereal nectar. Then a hidden hand seemed to press upon my senses and my eyelids grew heavy, while my spirit felt freed of its shackles.

Then the earth swayed under me and the sky trembled over me; whereupon I leaped up as though raised by a magic power. And I found myself in a meadow the like of which no human being has ever fancied. I found myself in the midst of a host of virgins who wore no other raiment than the beauty God gave them. They walked around me,

but their feet touched not the grass. They chanted hymns expressing dreams of love. Each maiden played on a lute framed with ivory and strung with gold.

I came upon a vast clearing in the center of which stood a throne inlaid with precious stones and illuminated with the rays of the rainbow. The virgins stood at both sides, raised their voices and faced the direction whence came the scent of myrrh and frankincense. The trees were in bloom and from between the branches, laden with blossoms, a queen walked majestically to the throne. As she seated herself, a flock of doves, white as snow, descended and settled around her feet and formed a crescent, while the maidens chanted hymns of glory. I stood there watching what no man's eyes had seen, and hearing what no man's ears had heard.

Then the Queen motioned, and silence fell. And in a voice that caused my spirit to quiver like the strings of the lute under a player's fingers, she said, "I have called you, man, for I am the Goddess of Fantasy. I have bestowed upon you the honor of standing before me, the Queen of the prairies of dreams. Listen to my commandments, for I appoint you to preach them to the whole human race: explain to man that the city of dreams is a wedding feast at whose door a mighty giant stands on guard. No one may enter unless he wears a wedding garment. Let it be known that this city is a paradise whose sentinel is the angel of Love, and no human may glance at it save he on whose forehead the sign of Love is inscribed.

Picture to them these beautiful fields whose streams flow with nectar and wine, whose birds sail in the skies and sing with the angels. Describe the aromatic scent of its flowers and let it be known that only the Son of Dream may tread its soft grass.

"Say that I gave man a cupful of joy; but he, in his ignorance, poured it out. Then the angels of Darkness filled the cup with the brew of Sorrow which he drank and became inebriated.

"Say that none can play the lyre of Life unless his fingers have been blessed by my touch and his eyes sanctified by the sight of my throne.

"Isaiah composed words of wisdom as a necklace of precious stones mounted on the golden chain of my love. Saint John recounted his vision in my behalf. And Dante could not explore the haven of souls save by my guidance. I am metaphor embracing reality, and reality revealing the singleness of the spirit; and a witness confirming the deeds of the gods.

"Truly I say to you that thoughts have a higher dwelling place than the visible world, and its skies are not clouded by sensuality. Imagination finds a road to the realm of the gods, and there man can glimpse that which is to be after the soul's liberation from the world of substance."

And the Goddess of Fantasy drew me toward her with her magic glance and imprinted a kiss upon my burning

lips and said, "Tell them that he who passes not his days in the realm of dreams is the slave of the days."

Thereupon the voices of the virgins rose again and the column of incense ascended. Then the earth began to sway again and the sky to tremble; and suddenly I found myself again among Palmyra's sorrowful ruins.

The smiling Dawn had already made its appearance, and between my tongue and my lips were these words: "He who passes not his days in the realm of dreams is the slave of the days."

History and the Nation

By the side of a rivulet that meandered among the rocks at the foot of Lebanon's Mountain sat a shepherdess surrounded by her flock of lean sheep grazing upon dry grass. She looked into the distant twilight as if the future were passing before her. Tears had jewelled her eyes like dew-drops adorning flowers. Sorrow had caused her lips to open that it might enter and occupy her sighing heart.

After sunset, as the knolls and hills wrapped themselves in shadow, History stood before the maiden. He was an old man whose white hair fell like snow over his breast and shoulders, and in his right hand he held a sharp sickle. In a voice like the roaring sea he said, "Peace unto you, Syria."*

The virgin rose, trembling with fear. "What do you wish of me, History?" she asked. Then she pointed to

* At the writing of this story Lebanon and Syria were one country known as Syria.

her sheep. "This is the remnant of a healthy flock that once filled this valley. This is all that your covetousness has left me. Have you come now to sate your greed on that?

"These plains that were once so fertile have been trodden to barren dust by your trampling feet. My cattle that once grazed upon flowers and produced rich milk, now gnaw thistles that leave them gaunt and dry.

"Fear God, oh History, and afflict me no more. The sight of you has made me detest life, and the cruelty of your sickle has caused me to love Death.

"Leave me in my solitude to drain the cup of sorrow— my best wine. Go, History, to the West where Life's wedding feast is being celebrated. Here let me lament the bereavement you have prepared for me."

Concealing his sickle under the folds of his garment, History looked upon her as a loving father looks upon his child, and said, "Oh Syria, what I have taken from you were my own gifts. Know that your sister nations are entitled to a part of the glory which was yours. I must give to them what I gave you. Your plight is like that of Egypt, Persia, and Greece, for each one of them also has a lean flock and dry pasture. Oh Syria, that which you call degradation is an indispensable sleep from which you will draw strength. The flower does not return to life save through death, and love does not grow except after separation."

The old man came close to the maiden, stretched forth

his hand and said, "Shake my hand, oh Daughter of the Prophets." And she shook his hand and looked at him from behind a screen of tears and said, "Farewell, History, farewell." And he responded, "Until we meet again, Syria, until we meet again."

And the old man disappeared like swift lightning, and the shepherdess called her sheep and started on her way, saying to herself, *"Shall there be another meeting?"*

The Speechless Animal

In the glance of the speechless animal there is a discourse that only the soul of the wise can really understand.

AN INDIAN POET

In the twilight of a beautiful day, when fancy seized upon my mind, I passed by the edge of the city and tarried before the wreck of an abandoned house of which only rubble was left.

In the rubble I saw a dog lying upon dirt and ashes. Sores covered his skin, and sickness racked his feeble body. Staring now and then at the setting sun, his sorrowful eyes expressed humiliation, despair, and misery.

I walked slowly toward him wishing that I knew animal speech so that I might console him with my sympathy. But my approach only terrified him, and he tried to rise on his palsied legs. Falling, he turned a look on me in which helpless wrath was mingled with supplication. In

593

that glance was speech more lucid than man's and more moving than a woman's tears. This is what I understood him to say:

"Man, I have suffered through illness caused by your brutality and persecution.

"I have run from your bruising foot and taken refuge here, for dust and ashes are gentler than man's heart, these ruins less melancholy than the soul of man. Begone, you intruder from the world of misrule and injustice.

"I am a miserable creature who served the son of Adam with faith and loyalty. I was man's faithful companion, I guarded him day and night. I grieved during his absence and welcomed him with joy upon his return. I was contented with the crumbs that fell from his board, and happy with the bones that his teeth had stripped. But when I grew old and ill, he drove me from his home and left me to merciless boys of the alleys.

"Oh son of Adam, I see the similarity between me and your fellow men when age disables them. There are soldiers who fought for their country when they were in the prime of life, and who later tilled its soil. But now that the winter of their life has come and they are useful no longer, they are cast aside.

"I also see a resemblance between my lot and that of a woman who, during the days of her lovely maidenhood enlivened the heart of a young man; and who then, as a mother, devoted her life to her children. But now, grown

594

old, she is ignored and avoided. How oppressive you are, son of Adam, and how cruel!"

Thus spoke the speechless animal whom my heart had understood.

Poets and Poems

If my fellow poets had imagined that the necklaces of verses they composed, and the stanzas whose meters they had strengthened and joined together, would some day become reins to hold back talent, they would have torn up their manuscripts.

If Al-Mutanabbi,* the prophet, had prophesied, and Al-Farid,** the seer, had foreseen that what they had written would become a source for the barren and a forced guide to our poets of today, they would have poured out their inks in the wells of Oblivion, and broken their quills with the hands of Negligence.

If the spirits of Homer, Virgil, Al-Maary,*** and

---

* The word Al-Mutanabbi means the one who divines or predicts. He was a famous Arabian poet whose poems were translated into several languages.

** An outstanding Arabian poet and philosopher.

*** A ninth century Arabian poet who became blind at the age of four and was looked upon as a genius.

Milton had known that poetry would become a lapdog of the rich, they would have foresaken a world in which this could occur.

I grieve to hear the language of the spirits prattled by the tongues of the ignorant. It slays my soul to see the wine of the muses flow over the pens of the pretenders.

Neither am I found alone in the vale of Resentment. Say that I am one of the many who see the frog puffed up to imitate the buffalo.

Poetry, my dear friends, is a sacred incarnation of a smile. Poetry is a sigh that dries the tears. Poetry is a spirit who dwells in the soul, whose nourishment is the heart, whose wine is affection. Poetry that comes not in this form is a false messiah.

Oh spirits of the poets, who watch over us from the heaven of Eternity, we go to the altars you have adorned with the pearls of your thoughts and the gems of your souls because we are oppressed by the clang of steel and the clamor of factories. Therefore our poems are as heavy as freight trains and as annoying as steam whistles.

And you, the real poets, forgive us. We belong in the New World where men run after worldly goods; and poetry, too, is a commodity today, and not a breath of immortality.

Among the Ruins

The moon dropped its gauzy veil over the gardens of the City of the Sun,* and silence swathed all beings. The fallen palaces looked menacing, like sneering monsters.

At that hour two phantoms, like vapor rising from the blue water of a lake, sat on a marble pillar pondering the scene which was like a realm of magic. One lifted his head, and with a voice that set echoes reverberating, said:

"These are the remnants of temples I built for you, my beloved, and this is the rubble of a palace I erected for your enjoyment. Nothing else remains to tell the nations of the glory to which I devoted my life, and of the pomp for which I exploited the weak.

"Think and ponder, my beloved, upon the elements that triumphed over my city, and upon Time that thus belittled my efforts.

"Oblivion has submerged the empire I established, and

* The ruined City of Baalbek.

naught is left save atoms of love which your beauty has created, and effects of beauty which your love has enlivened.

"I erected a temple in Jerusalem and the priests sanctified it, but time has destroyed it. But in my heart the altar I built for Love was consecrated by God and sustained against the powers of destruction.

"Men said of me, 'What a wise king he is!' The angels said, 'How trifling is his wisdom.' But the angels rejoiced when I found you, my beloved, and sang for you the song of Love and longing; though men heard no notes of my hymn. . . .

"The days of my reign were barriers to my understanding of Love and of the beauty of life, but when I saw you, Love awoke and demolished those barriers, and I lamented the life I spent considering everything under the sun as vanity.

"As Love enlightened me, I became humble both before the tribes who had feared my military might and before my own people.

"But when death came, it buried my deadly weapons in earth and carried my love to God."

And the other phantom said, "As the flower obtains life and aromatic scent from earth, so the soul extracts wisdom and strength from the weakness and errors of matter."

Then the two fused into one and walked away, saying:

> "Eternity keeps naught but Love,
> For Love is like Eternity."

At the Door of the Temple

I purified my lips with the sacred fire, to speak of Love, but could find no words.

When Love became known to me, the words lapsed into a faint gasping, and the song in my heart into deep silence.

Oh you who asked me about Love, whom I convinced of its mysteries and wonders, now since Love has wrapped me in its veil, I come to ask you about Love's course and merit.

Who can answer my questions? I ask about that which is in me; I seek to be informed about myself.

Who among you can reveal my inner self to myself and my soul to my soul?

Tell me, for Love's sake, what is that flame which burns in my heart and devours my strength and dissolves my will?

What are those hidden soft and rough hands that grasp my soul; what is that wine mixed of bitter joy and sweet pain that suffuses my heart?

What are those wings that hover over my pillow in the silence of Night, and keep me awake, watching no one knows what?

What is the invisible thing I stare at, the incomprehensible thing that I ponder, the feeling that cannot be sensed?

In my sighs is a grief more beautiful than the echo of laughter and more rapturous than joy.

Why do I surrender myself to an unknown power that slays me and revives me until Dawn rises and fills my chamber with its light?

Phantoms of wakefulness tremble between my seared eyelids, and shadows of dreams hover over my stony bed.

What is that which we call Love? Tell me, what is that secret hidden within the ages yet which permeates all consciousness?

What is this consciousness that is at once origin and result of everything?

What is this vigil that fashions from Life and Death a dream, stranger than Life and deeper than Death?

Tell me, friends, is there one among you who would not awake from the slumber of Life if Love touched his soul with its fingertip?

Which one of you would not leave his father and mother at the call of the virgin whom his heart loves?

Who among you would not sail the distant seas, cross

the deserts, and climb the topmost peak to meet the woman whom his soul has chosen?

What youth's heart would not follow to the ends of the world the maiden whose aromatic breath, sweet voice, and magic-soft hands have enraptured his soul?

What being would not burn his heart as incense before a god who listens to his supplications and grants his prayer?

Yesterday I stood at the temple door interrogating the passers-by about the mystery and merit of Love.

And before me passed an old man with an emaciated and melancholy face, who sighed and said:

"Love is a natural weakness bestowed upon us by the first man."

But a virile youth retorted:

"Love joins our present with the past and the future."

Then a woman with a tragic face sighed and said:

"Love is a deadly poison injected by black vipers, that crawl from the caves of hell. The poison seems fresh as dew and the thirsty soul eagerly drinks it; but after the first intoxication the drinker sickens and dies a slow death."

Then a beautiful, rosy-cheeked damsel smilingly said:

"Love is wine served by the brides of Dawn which strengthens strong souls and enables them to ascend to the stars."

After her a black-robed, bearded man, frowning, said:

"Love is the blind ignorance with which youth begins and ends."

Another, smiling, declared:

"Love is a divine knowledge that enables men to see as much as the gods."

Then said a blind man, feeling his way with a cane:

"Love is a blinding mist that keeps the soul from discerning the secret of existence, so that the heart sees only trembling phantoms of desire among the hills, and hears only echoes of cries from voiceless valleys."

A young man, playing on his viol, sang:

"Love is a magic ray emitted from the burning core of the soul and illuminating the surrounding earth. It enables us to perceive Life as a beautiful dream between one awakening and another."

And a feeble ancient, dragging his feet like two rags, said, in quavering tones:

"Love is the rest of the body in the quiet of the grave, the tranquility of the soul in the depth of Eternity."

And a five-year-old child, after him, said laughing:

"Love is my father and mother, and no one knows Love save my father and mother."

And so, all who passed spoke of Love as the image of their hopes and frustrations, leaving it a mystery as before.

Then I heard a voice within the temple:

"Life is divided into two halves, one frozen, the other aflame; the burning half is Love."

Thereupon I entered the temple, kneeling, rejoicing, and praying:

"Make me, O Lord, nourishment
for the blazing flame . . .
Make me, O God, food for the
sacred fire . . . Amen."

Narcotics and Dissecting Knives

"He is excessive and fanatic to the point of madness. Though he is an idealist, his literary aim is to poison the mind of the youths. . . . If men and women were to follow Gibran's counsels on marriage, family ties would break, society would perish, and the world would become an inferno peopled by demons and devils.

"His style is seductively beautiful, magnifying the danger of this inveterate enemy of mankind. Our counsel to the inhabitants of this blessed Mountain (Mount Lebanon) is to reject the insidious teachings of this anarchist and heretic and to burn his books, that his doctrines may not lead the innocent astray. We have read *The Broken Wings* and found it to be honeyed poison."

Such is what people say of me and they are right, for I am indeed a fanatic and I am inclined toward destruction as well as construction. There is hatred in my heart for

that which my detractors sanctify, and love for that which they reject. And if I could uproot certain customs, beliefs, and traditions of the people, I would do so without hesitation. When they said my books were poison, they were speaking truth about themselves, for what I say is poison to them. But they falsified when they said I mix honey into it, for I apply the poison full strength and pour it from transparent glass. Those who call me an idealist becalmed in clouds are the very ones who turn away from the transparent glass they call poison, knowing that their stomachs cannot digest it.

This may sound truculent, but is not truculence preferable to seductive pretense?

The people of the Orient demand that the writer be like a bee always making honey. They are gluttonous for honey and prefer it to all other food.

The people of the Orient want their poet to burn himself as incense before their sultans. The Eastern skies have become sickly with incense yet the people of the Orient have not had enough.

They ask the world to learn their history, to study their antiquities, customs and traditions, and acquire their languages. They also expect those who know them not to repeat the words of Baidaba the Philosopher, Ben Rished, Ephraim Al-Syriani, and John of Damascus.

In brief, the people of the Orient seek to make their past a justification and a bed of ease. They shun positive

thinking and positive teachings and any knowledge of reality that might sting them and awake them from their slumber.

The Orient is ill, but it has become so inured to its infirmities that it has come to see them as natural and even noble qualities that distinguish them above others. They consider one who lacks such qualities as incomplete and unfit for the divine gift of perfection.

Numerous are the social healers in the Orient, and many are their patients who remain uncured but appear eased of their ills because they are under the effects of social narcotics. But these tranquilizers merely mask the symptoms.

Such narcotics are distilled from many sources but the chief is the Oriental philosophy of submission to Destiny (the act of God). Another source is the cowardice of the social physicians who fear to aggravate pain by administration of drastic medicine.

Here are some samples of these social tranquilizers:

A husband and wife, for substantial reasons, find that hate has replaced love between them. After long mutual torment they separate. Immediately their parents meet and work out some agreement for the reconciliation of the estranged couple. First they ply the wife with falsehoods, then they work on the husband with similar deceits. Neither is convinced, but they are shamed into a pretense of peace. This cannot endure; soon the effects of the social

narcotics have worn off, and the miserable pair return for further doses.

Or a group or party revolts against a despotic government and advocates political reforms to free the oppressed from their shackles. They distribute manifestoes and deliver fiery speeches and publish stinging articles. But a month later, we hear that the government has either imprisoned the leader or silenced him by giving him an important position. And nothing more is heard.

Or a sect rebels against its religious leader, accusing him of misdeeds and threatening to adopt another religion, more humane and free of superstition. But shortly we hear that the wise men of the country have reconciled the shepherd and the flock, through the application of social narcotics.

When a weak man complains of oppression by a strong, his neighbor will quieten him, "Hush, the eye of the stubborn seer cannot withstand the blow of the spear."

When a villager doubts the holiness of the priest, he will be told, "Listen only to his teaching and disregard his shortcomings and misdeeds."

When a teacher rebukes a student, he will say, "The excuses that a lazy youth invents are often worse than the crime."

If a daughter refuses to adhere to her mother's customs, the mother will say, "The daughter is not better than the mother; she should follow in her mother's footsteps."

Should a young man ask a priest to enlighten him about

an ancient rite, the preacher will reprove him, "Son, he who does not look at religion with the eyes of Faith, will see nothing save mist and smoke."

Thus the Orient lies upon its soft bed. The sleeper wakes for an instant when stung by a flea, and then resumes his narcotic slumber.

Whoever tries to awaken him is berated as a rude person who neither sleeps himself nor lets others sleep. Shutting their eyes again, they whisper into the ears of their souls, "He is an infidel poisoning the mind of the youths and undermining the foundation of the ages."

Many times I have asked my soul, "Am I one of those awakened rebels who reject narcotics?" And my soul answered with cryptic words. But hearing my name and principles reviled, I was assured that I was awake and could count myself among those who do not surrender themselves to pipe dreams, that I belong with the strong-hearted who walk narrow and thorny paths where flowers are also to be found, amidst howling wolves—and singing nightingales.

If awakening were a virtue, modesty would prevent me from claiming it. But it is not a virtue, but a reality that appears suddenly to those who have the strength to rise. To be modest in speaking truth is hypocrisy. Alas that the people of the Orient call it education.

I will not be surprised if the "thinkers" say of me, "He is a man of excess who looks upon life's seamy side and reports nothing but gloom and lamentation."

To them I declare, "I deplore our Oriental urge to evade the reality of weakness and sorrow.

"I grieve that my beloved country sings, not in joy, but to still the quakings of fear.

"In battling evil, excess is good; for he who is moderate in announcing the truth is presenting half-truth. He conceals the other half out of fear of the people's wrath.

"I loathe the carrion mind; its stench upsets my stomach. I will not serve it with sweets and cordials.

"Yet I will gladly exchange my outcries for cheerful laughter, speak eulogies instead of indictments, replace excess with moderation, provided you show me a just governor, a lawyer of integrity, a religious hierarch who practices what he preaches, a husband who looks upon his wife with the same eyes as he looks upon himself.

"If you prefer me to dance, to blow the trumpet or beat the drum, invite me to a wedding feast and lead me out of the graveyard."

The Giants

We live in an era whose humblest men are becoming greater than the greatest men of preceding ages. What once preoccupied our minds is now of no consequence. The veil of indifference covers it. The beautiful dreams that once hovered in our consciousness have been dispersed like mist. In their place are giants moving like tempests, raging like seas, breathing like volcanoes.

What destiny will the giants bring the world at the end of their struggles?

Will the farmer return to his field to sow where Death has planted the bones of the dead?

Will the shepherd pasture his flock on fields mown by the sword?

Will the sheep drink from springs whose waters are stained with blood?

Will the worshipper kneel in a profaned temple at

611

whose altars Satanists have danced?

Will the poet compose his songs under stars veiled in gun smoke?

Will the musician strum his lute in a night whose silence was ravished by terror?

Will the mother at the cradle of her infant, brooding on the perils of tomorrow, be able to sing a lullaby?

Can lovers meet and exchange kisses on battlefields still acrid with bomb fumes?

Will Nisan* ever return to earth and dress the earth's wounds with its garment?

What will be the destiny of your country and mine? Which giant shall seize the mountains and valleys that produced us and reared us and made us men and women before the face of the sun?

Will Syria remain lying between the wolf lair and the pigsty? Or will it move with the tempest to the lion's den or soar to the eagle's eyrie?

Will the dawn of a new Time ever appear over Lebanon's peaks?

Every time I am alone I ask my soul these questions. But my soul is mute like Destiny.

Which one of you, people, does not ponder day and night on the fate of the world under the rule of the giants intoxicated with the tears of widows and orphans?

I am among those who believe in the Law of Evolution;

* The month of April.

I believe that ideal entities evolve, like brute beings, and that religions and governments are raised to higher planes.

The law of evolution has a severe and oppressive countenance and those of limited or fearful mind dread it; but its principles are just, and those who study them become enlightened. Through its Reason men are raised above themselves and can approach the sublime.

All around me are dwarves who see the giants emerging; and the dwarves croak like frogs:

"The world has returned to savagery. What science and education have created is being destroyed by the new primitives. We are now like the prehistoric cave dwellers. Nothing distinguishes us from them save our machines of destruction and our improved techniques of slaughter."

Thus speak those who measure the world's conscience by their own. They measure the range of all Existence by the tiny span of their individual being. As if the sun did not exist but for their warmth, as if the sea was created for them to wash their feet.

From the heart of life, from deep within the universe where the secrets of Creation are stored, the giants rise like winds and ascend like clouds, and convene like mountains. In their struggles age-old problems are being brought to solution.

But man, in spite of all his knowledge and skills, and notwithstanding the love and hatred in his heart, and the torments he endures, is but a tool in the hands of the

giants, to reach their goal and accomplish their inevitable high purpose.

The streams of blood shall some day become flowing rivers of wine; and the tears that bedewed the earth shall bring forth aromatic flowers; and the souls that left their abodes shall assemble and appear from behind the new horizon as a new Morn. Then man will realize that he had bought Justice and Reason in the slave market. He will understand that he who works and spends for the sake of Right will never lose.

Nisan shall come, but he who seeks Nisan without Winter's aid, will never find it.

Out of Earth

Wrathfully and violently earth comes out of earth;
and gracefully and majestically earth walks over
earth.
Earth from earth, builds palaces and erects towers
and temples,
And earth weaves on earth, legends, doctrines, and
laws.

Then earth becomes tired of the deeds of earth and
wreathes from its halo, dreams and fantasies.

And earth's eyes are then beguiled by earth's slumber
to enduring rest.
And earth calls unto earth:
"I am the womb and the sepulchre, and I shall
remain a womb and a sepulchre until the planets
exist no more and the sun turns into ashes.

O Night

O Night of lovers, inspirer of poets and singers,
O Night of phantoms, of spirits and fancies,
O Night of longing, of hopes and memories,
You are like a giant dwarfing the evening clouds
and towering over the dawn.
With the sword of fear you are armed, and with
the shining moon you are crowned, and with calm
and silence you are veiled.

With a thousand eyes you penetrate the depth
of life,
With a thousand ears you hear the moan
of death and non-existence.
The light of heaven shines through your darkness,
For Day is but light overwhelming us with the
obscurity of the earth.

Before the awe of eternity you open our eyes and
give us hope,
For Day is a deceiver that blinds us
with measures and quantities.
You are perfect silence revealing the secrets of
the awakened spirits in heaven,
But day is an uproar agitating the souls that
lie between the hooves of purpose and wonder.
You are Justice that brings unto the haven of
slumber the dreams of the weak, that they may be united
with the hopes of the strong.

You are a merciful monarch who closes with his
fingers of enchantment the eyes of the miserable,
and conveys their hearts into a gentler realm.

The lovers' spirits find refuge between the folds of
your blue garment,
And upon your feet, drenched with dew, the
forlorn shed their tears.

In the palms of your hands, where lies the fragrance
of the valleys, strangers find ease for their
yearnings.

You are the companion of lovers; you console the
desolate; you shelter the alien and the lonely.
In your shadow the poet's affections rest, and

the hearts of the prophets awaken,
And under your crown the
wisdom of the thinker takes form.
You inspire poets; you bring revelation to the
prophets; you instruct the philosophers

When my soul wearies of humanity, when my
eyes tire of staring into the face of the day,
I wander where the phantoms
of past ages sleep.

There I pause before a dim presence who strode
with a thousand feet over the earth, setting it
atremble.

There I look into the eyes of shadow, and
listen to the rustle of invisible wings, and feel
the soft touch of the unseen garment of silence,
and withstand the terrors of black darkness.

There I see you, Night, awful and beautiful,
poised between heaven and earth, veiled in
mist, cloaked in cloud, laughing at
the sun, ridiculing the day, taunting the slaves
who sleeplessly worship before the idols.

I see your wrath against kings sleeping upon beds of
velvet and silk;

I see thieves flinching before your vigilant gaze as
you guard the babes in slumber;
I see you weeping over the forced smiles of prostitutes
and smiling over tears of true lovers;
I see your right hand raising up the good and your
feet trampling the wicked.

There, I see you and you see me, Night. And though
terrible, you are like a father to me, and I,
dreaming, envision myself as your son.

The screen of distrust has been removed
from between us, and you reveal to me
your secrets and designs,
And I disclose to you my hopes and my desires.
Your terrors have turned into a melody sweeter and
more soothing to the heart than the whisper of the
flowers.

My fears are vanished and I am more tranquil
than birds.
You have lifted me unto you and held me between
your arms and taught my eyes to see, and my ears
to hear, and my lips to speak, and my heart to
love that which others hate, and to hate that
which others love.

You touch my thoughts with your
gentle fingers, and my contemplation flows like
a strong stream.

With your burning lips you print a kiss
upon the lips of my soul
and set it aflame like a torch.

I have accompanied you, O Night, and followed you
until we became akin.

I loved you until my being became a diminutive image
of your being.

In my dark self are glittering stars strewn
by my emotions.
And in my heart shines a moon lighting the processions
of my dreams.
In my sleepless soul a silence reveals
the lover's secrets and echoes the
worshipper's prayers,
And my face wears a magic mask. Torn by
the agony of death, it is mended by the songs of youth.
We are both alike in every way, Night.

Will man consider me boastful if I liken myself
unto you?
Does not man boast of his resemblance to the day?

I am like you, Night, and we are both accused of
being what we are not.
I am like you even though twilight does not crown me
with its golden clouds.
I am like you although morn does not adorn the
hem of my garment with its rosy rays.
I am like you though I am not encircled by the milky
way.
I am night boundless and calm; there is no beginning
to my obscurity and no end to my depth.

When the souls rise in the
light of their joy, my soul ascends glorified by the
dark of grief.
I am like you, Night! And when my morn comes, then
my time will end.

Earth

How beautiful you are, Earth, and how sublime!
How perfect is your obedience to the light, and
how noble is your submission to the sun!

How lovely you are, veiled in shadow, and how
charming your face, masked with obscurity!

How soothing is the song of your dawn, and how
harsh are the praises of your eventide!
How perfect you are, Earth, and how majestic!

I have walked over your plains, I have climbed your
stony mountains; I have descended into your valleys;
I have entered into your caves.
In the plains, I found your dream; upon the mountain
I found your pride; in the valley I witnessed your

622

tranquility; in the rocks your resolution; in the
cave your secrecy.

You are weak and powerful and humble and haughty.
You are pliant and rigid, and clear and secret.
I have ridden your seas and explored your rivers and
followed your brooks.
I heard Eternity speak through your ebb and flow,
and the ages echoing your songs among your hills.
I listened to life calling to life in your mountain
passes and along your slopes.
You are the mouth and lips of Eternity, the strings
and fingers of Time, the mystery and solution of
Life.
Your Spring has awakened me and led me to your fields
where your aromatic breath ascends like
incense.
I have seen the fruits of your Summer labor.
In Autumn, in your vineyards, I saw your
blood flow as wine.
Your Winter carried me into your bed, where the snow
attested your purity.
In your Spring you are an aromatic essence; in your
Summer you are generous; in your Autumn you are
a source of plenty.

One calm and clear night I opened the windows and
doors of my soul and went out to see you, my

heart tense with lust and greed.
And I saw you staring at the stars that smiled at
you. So I cast away my fetters, for I
found out that the dwelling place of the soul is in
your space.
Its desires grow in your desires; its peace rests in
your peace; and its happiness is in the golden
dust which the stars sprinkle upon your body.

One night, as the skies turned gray, and my soul was
wearied and anxious, I went out to you.
And you appeared to me like a giant, armed with
raging tempests, fighting the past with the present,
replacing the old with the new, and letting the
strong disperse the weak.

Whereupon I learned that the law of the people is
your law.
I learned that he who does not break his dry branches
with his tempest, will die wearily,
And he who does not use revolution, to strip
his dry leaves, will slowly perish.

How generous you are, Earth, and how strong is your
yearning for your children lost between that which
they have attained and that which they could not
obtain.
We clamor and you smile; we flit
but you stay!

We blaspheme and you consecrate.
We defile and you sanctify.
We sleep without dreams; but you
dream in your eternal wakefulness.

We pierce your bosom with swords and spears,
And you dress our wounds with oil and balsam.
We plant your fields with skulls and bones,
and from them you rear cypress
and willow trees.

We empty our wastes in your bosom, and you fill
our threshing-floors with wheat sheaves, and
our winepresses with grapes.

We extract your elements to make cannons and
bombs, but out of our elements you create
lilies and roses.

How patient you are, Earth, and how merciful!
Are you an atom of dust raised by
the feet of God when He journeyed from the east
to the west of the Universe?
Or a spark projected from the furnace
of Eternity?
Are you a seed dropped in the field of the
firmament to become God's tree reaching above
the heavens with its celestial branches?

Or are you a drop of blood in the veins of the
giant of giants, or a bead of sweat upon his
brow?

Are you a fruit ripened by the sun?
Do you grow from the tree of Absolute
Knowledge, whose roots extend through
Eternity, and whose branches soar through
the Infinite?

Are you a jewel placed by the God of Time in the
palm of the God of Space?

Who are you, Earth, and what are you?
You are "I," Earth!

You are my sight and my discernment.
You are my knowledge and my
dream.
You are my hunger and my thirst.
You are my sorrow and my joy.
You are my inadvertence and my wakefulness.
You are the beauty that lives in my eyes,
the longing in my heart, the everlasting life
in my soul.

You are "I," Earth.
Had it not been for my being,
You would not have been.

Perfection

You ask me, my brother, when will man reach
perfection. Hear my answer:
Man approaches perfection when he
feels that he is an infinite space and a sea
without a shore,
An everlasting fire, an unquenchable
light,
A calm wind or a raging tempest, a thundering sky or a rainy heaven,
A singing brook or a wailing rivulet, a tree abloom
in Spring, or a naked sapling
in Autumn,
A rising mountain or a descending valley,
A fertile plain or a desert.

When man feels all these, he has already
reached halfway to perfection. To attain his goal
he must then perceive

that he is a child dependent upon his mother,
a father responsible for his family,
A youth lost in love,
An ancient wrestling against his past,
A worshipper in his temple, a criminal in
his prison,
A scholar amidst his parchments,
An ignorant soul stumbling between the darkness of his
night and the obscurity of his day,
A nun suffering between the flowers of her faith and
the thistles of her loneliness,
A prostitute caught between the fangs of her
weakness and the claws of her needs,
A poor man trapped between his bitterness and his
submission,
A rich man between his greed and his conscience,
A poet between the mist of his twilight and the
rays of his dawn.

Who can experience, see, and understand
these things can reach perfection and
become a shadow of God's Shadow.

Yesterday, Today, and Tomorrow

I said to my friend,
       "See her leaning over his arm?
       Yesterday she leaned over my arm."
And he said:
       "Tomorrow she will lean over mine."
And I said,
       "See her sitting at his side;
       And yesterday she sat at my side."
And he said:
       "Tomorrow she will sit at mine."
And I said,
       "Don't you see her drinking from his
       Cup?
       And yesterday she sipped from mine."
And he said:
       "Tomorrow she will drink from mine."

629

And I said,

> "Look how she glances at him with eyes
> full of love!
> And with just such love, yesterday
> she glanced at me."

And he said:

> "Tomorrow she will glance at me
> likewise."

And I said,

> "Listen to her whispering songs of
> love in his ears.
> And yesterday she whispered the same songs
> in mine."

And he said:

> "Tomorrow she will whisper them
> in mine."

And I said,

> "Look at her embracing him; and yes-
> terday she embraced me."

And he said:

> "Tomorrow she will lie in my arms."

And I said,

> "What a strange woman she is!!"

And he said:

> "She is Life."

A Story of a Friend

I

I knew him as a youth lost on the paths of life, goaded by
wild impulse and following death in pursuit of his desires.
I knew him as a tender flower borne by the winds of rash-
ness into the sea of lust.

I knew him in that village as an ill-natured boy tearing with cruel hands at the birds' nests and slaying the
nestlings and trampling with his feet the beautiful crowns
of the sweet flowers.

I knew him at school as an adolescent averse to learning, arrogant, and an enemy of peace.

I knew him in the city as a young man trading his
father's honor in sinister markets, spending his father's
money in houses of ill-fame, and surrendering his mind to
the fruit of the vine.

However, I loved him. And my love for him was a

631

mingling of sorrow and sympathy. I loved him because his sins were not born of a small spirit, but rather the deeds of a lost and desperate soul.

The spirit, my dear people, strays from the path of wisdom unwillingly, but returns to it willingly. When the whirlwinds of youth blow dust and sand, the eyes are blind for a time.

I loved that youth because I saw the dove of his conscience struggling with the hawk of his evils. And I saw that the dove was subdued not by its own cowardice but by the strength of its enemy.

Conscience is a just but a weak judge. Weakness leaves it powerless to execute its judgment.

I said I loved him. And love comes in different shapes. Sometimes it comes in wisdom; at other times in justice; and oftentimes in hope. My love for him sustained my hope of seeing the light in him triumph over the darkness. But I knew not when and where would his defilement turn into purity, his brutality into meekness, his recklessness into wisdom. Man does not know in what manner the soul frees itself from the slavery of matter until after it is freed. Neither does man know how the flowers smile save after the coming of the morn.

2

The days passed, following the nights, and I remembered the youth with painful sighs; I repeated his name with

affection that made the heart bleed. Then yesterday a letter came from him saying:

"Come to me, my friend, for I wish to unite you with a young man whom your heart will rejoice to meet, and your soul will be refreshed to know."

I said, "Woe is me! Does he intend to mingle his sad friendship with another one similar to it? Is he not alone a sufficient example to the world of error and sin? Does he now wish to re-enforce his misdeeds with those of his companion so that I may see them in double darkness?"

Then I said to myself, "I must go; perhaps the wise soul shall reap figs from the brambles, and the loving heart shall extract light from the darkness."

When night came I found him alone in his room reading a book of verses. "Where is the new friend?" I said, and he answered, "I am he, my friend." And he displayed a calmness I had never seen in him before. In his eyes I could now see a strange light that penetrated the heart. Those eyes in which I had seen cruelty before, were radiant with the light of kindness. Then with a voice that I thought came from another, he said. "The youth whom you knew during childhood and with whom you walked to school, is dead. With his death I was born. I am your new friend; take my hand."

As I shook his hand I felt the existence of a gentle spirit circulating with the blood. His iron hand had become soft and kind. His fingers which yesterday tore like a tiger's claws, today caress the heart.

Then I spoke again. "Who are you, and what has happened? How have you become this kind of person? Has the Holy Spirit entered your heart and sanctified your soul? Or are you playing a part, the invention of a poet?"

And he said, "Ay, my friend, the spirit descended upon me and blessed me. A great love has made my heart a pure altar. It is woman, my friend—woman that I thought yesterday a toy in the hands of man—who has delivered me from the darkness of hell and opened before me the gates of Paradise where I have entered. A true woman has taken me into the Jordan River of her love and baptized me. The woman whose sister I disrespected through my ignorance has exalted me to the throne of glory. The woman whose companion I have defiled with my wickedness has purified my heart with her affections. The woman whose kind I have enslaved with my father's gold has freed me with her beauty. The woman who had Adam driven from Paradise by the strength of her will has restored me to Paradise by her tenderness and my obedience."

Ashes of the Ages and Eternal Fire

I

SPRING OF THE YEAR 116 B. C.

Night and silence had fallen over the slumbering City of
the Sun.* The lamps were extinguished in the dwellings
among the majestic temples standing amid olive and laurel
groves. The moon's silver light laved the marble columns
that stood like giant sentinels before the houses of the
gods.

At that hour, while souls succumbed to slumber,
Nathan, son of the High Priest, entered Ishtar's temple,
bearing a torch in quaking hands. He lit the lamps and
censors and soon the fragrance of myrrh and frankincense
rose to the uppermost corners. Then he knelt before the

---

* Baalbek, or the City of Baal, the sun god of ancient Syria; in
Graeco-Roman times its name was changed to Heliopolis, the Greek
term for City of the Sun. It was considered the most beautiful city in
the ancient Middle East. The ruins are mainly Roman.

altar, inlaid with ivory and gold, raised his hands toward Ishtar,* and with a choking voice cried out, "Have mercy upon me, O great Ishtar, goddess of Love and Beauty. Be merciful and hold back the hands of Death from my beloved, whom my soul has chosen by thy will. The potions of the physicians and spells of the wizards are of no avail. Naught is left save thy holy will. Thou art my guide and my aid. Gaze upon my crushed heart and aching soul with pity and grant my prayer. Spare my beloved's life so that together we may worship thee with the rites of love and devote to you our youth and beauty.

"Your servant Nathan, son of your High Priest Hiram, loves a maiden without peer and has made her his companion. But some female djin envied her loveliness and my passion for her and breathed into her a deadly plague, and now the messenger of Death stands at her bedside, spreading his black-ribbed wings over her, and unsheathing his sharp claws. Have mercy upon us, I beseech thee. Spare that flower which has not yet rejoiced in its summer.**

"Save her from the grasp of Death so that we may sing hymns of praise to thee and burn incense in thine honor and offer sacrifices at thine altar and fill thy vases with per-

---

* Ishtar, great goddess of the Phoenicians, was worshipped in the cities of Tyre, Sidon, Sur, Djabeil and Baalbek, and there called Burner of the Torch of Life, and Guardian of Youth. She was the counterpart of Aphrodite, the Greek goddess of Love and Beauty, and of the Roman goddess, Venus.

** During the "Era of Ignorance," (the period before the coming of Mohammed), the Arabs believed that if a female genie loved a human youth, she would prevent him from marrying, and if he did wed, she would bewitch the bride and cause her to die. This superstition persists today in isolated villages in Lebanon.

fumed oil and spread roses and violets upon the portico of thy temple. Let Love overcome Death in this struggle of Joy against Sorrow."

And Nathan, exhausted, could say no more.

At that moment his slave entered the temple, hastened to him, and whispered, "Master, she calls for you."

Nathan ran to his palace and entered the chamber of his beloved. He leaned over her bed, held her frail hand, and kissed her lips as if striving to breathe life into her body from his. Slowly she opened her eyes, and upon her lips appeared a faint smile, herald of a last heartbeat. With a feeble voice she said, "The goddess calls me, Oh Life of my Soul. Her servant, Death has come. The will of the goddess is sacred, and the errand of Death is just. I depart now, and I hear the rustle of the whiteness descending. But the cups of Love and Youth remain in our hands, and flowery paths of beautiful Life extend before us. I embark, my Beloved, upon an ark of the spirit, but I shall return to you; for great Ishtar will restore those souls of lovers who have not enjoyed their share of sweet Love and happy Youth."*

Weeping, Nathan bent down to kiss her and found her lips already cold. He cried out and began tearing his raiment, and his lamentations awoke the sleeping. At dawn

* This belief recurs in Asian thought. Mohammed said, "You were dead and He brought you back to life, and He will slay you again and revive you, whereupon you shall return to Him." Buddha said, "Yesterday we existed, and today, and we will return to this life, again and again, until we become perfect like God."

many came to Nathan's palace to offer their sympathy. But Nathan had disappeared. After a fortnight, the chief of a newly arrived caravan related that he had seen Nathan in the distant wilderness, wandering among a flock of gazelles.

The ages passed. In place of Ishtar, goddess of Love and Beauty, a destroying goddess reigned. She pulled down the magnificent temples of the City of the Sun; she demolished its beautiful palaces. She laid waste the orchards and fields. The land was scarred with ruins.

II

SPRING OF THE YEAR 1890 A. D.

The sun withdrew its golden rays from the plain of Baalbek. Ali El Hosseini* brought his sheep back to the sheds in the ruins of the temples. He sat among the ancient columns and piped to his flock.

Midnight came and heaven sowed the seeds of the following day in the deep furrows of the darkness. Ali's eyes became heavy and sleep captured his senses. He encountered his invisible self, who dwelt in a higher realm and the range of his vision broadened, bringing Life's hidden secrets to his view. His soul stood aside from Time rushing toward nothingness; it stood amid symmetrical thoughts and crystal ideas. For the first time in his life, Ali

* The Hosseinese are an Arabian tribe, living in tents pitched in the plains surrounding the ruins of Baalbek.

became aware of the causes of the spiritual hunger of his youth, the longing which neither the glory of the world nor passing time can still. Ali felt the ache of a centuries-old Memory, kindling like incense placed upon white-hot firebrands. A magic love touched his heart as a musician's delicate fingers touch quivering strings.

Ali looked at the ruins and then, like a blind man whose sight is suddenly restored, he recalled the lamps and the silver censers before the shrine of a goddess. . . . He recalled sacrifices at an altar of gold and ivory. . . . He saw again dancing maidens, tambourine players, singers who chanted hymns to the goddess of Love . . . and Beauty. . . . But how could such memories live in the heart of a simple shepherd youth born in a nomad's tent?

Suddenly the memories tore away the veil of oblivion and he rose and walked to the temple. At the cavernous entrance he halted as if a magnetic power had gripped his feet. Looking down, he saw a smashed statue on the ground, and the sight freed his soul's tears and they poured like blood from a deep wound. He also felt a stabbing loneliness and remoteness like an abyss between his heart and the heart from whom he had been torn before he entered upon this life.

"Who are you," Ali cried in anguish, "who stand close to my heart but unseen by my eyes? Are you a phantom from Eternity to show me the vanity of Life and the weakness of mankind? Or the spirit of a genie stolen out of earth's crevices to enslave me and render me an object of

mockery? What is your strange power which at one time prostrates and enlivens my heart? Who am I and what is this strange self whom I call "Myself"? Has the Water of Life which I have drunk made me an angel in communion with the universe and its mysteries? Or is it inebriating wine that blinds me to myself?

"Oh, what the soul reveals, and the night conceals. . . . Oh, beautiful spirit, hovering in the firmament of my dream, disclose yourself to me if you are human or command Slumber to shut my eyes so I can view your divine vastness. If you are human, let me touch you; let me hear your voice. Tear away this veil that conceals you from me. If I am worthy, place your hand upon my heart and possess me."

Thus an hour passed, with Ali shedding tears and voicing his yearnings.

Then Dawn appeared and the morning breeze stirred. The birds left their nests and sang their morning prayers.

Ali placed his cupped hand over his forehead. Like Adam, when God opened his eyes with his all-creating breath, Ali saw new objects, strange and fantastic. He called to his sheep and they followed him quietly toward the meadow. As he led them, he felt like a philosopher with the power to divine the secrets of the Universe. He reached a brook whose murmuring was soothing to his spirit, and sat under a willow tree whose branches dipped over the water as if drinking from the cool depths.

Here Ali felt the beating of his heart increase and through

his soul throbbed a strong and almost visible vibration. He sprang up like a mother suddenly awakened from her slumber by the scream of her child, and his eyes were magnetized by the sight of a beautiful maiden approaching from the opposite side, with a water jar on her shoulder. As she leaned over to fill the jar, her eyes and Ali's met. She cried out, distraught, dropped the jar, and ran off, but glanced back in agonizing disbelief.

Ali, compelled by the mysterious power, leaped across the brook, caught the maiden and embraced her. As if this caress had subdued her will she did not move, yielding to him as the fragrance of jasmine submits to the breeze. Both felt it to be the reunion of souls long separated by earth and now brought together by God.

The enamored pair walked amidst the willow trees, and the unity of the two selves was a speaking tongue for them; an eye to see the glory of Happiness; a silent auditor of the tremendous revelation of Love.

The sheep grazed; the birds of the sky hovered above their heads; the sun spread a golden garment upon the hills; and they sat by the side of a rock where the violets hid. The maiden looked into Ali's black eyes while the breeze caressed her hair, as though the shimmering wisps were fingertips craving kisses. Then she said: "Ishtar, oh my beloved, has restored both our spirits to this life from another, so that we shall not be denied the joy of Love and the glory of Youth."

Ali closed his eyes, as though her melodious voice had

brought to him images of a dream. Invisible wings bore him to a strange chamber where, upon her deathbed, lay the corpse of a maiden whose beauty had been claimed by Death. He uttered a fearful cry, then opened his eyes and found the maiden sitting by his side, a smile upon her lips and her eyes bright with the rays of Life. Then his heart was refreshed, and the phantom of his vision withdrew and the past and its cares vanished. The lovers embraced and drank the wine of sweet kisses. They slumbered, wrapped in each other's arms, until the last remnant of the shadow was dispersed by the Eternal Power which had awakened them.

A SELF-PORTRAIT

Gibran wrote this letter to his father in Bsharré to reassure him of the health of his two sisters, Miriana and Sultana. One of their relatives in the United States had written to Gibran's father and told him that both of his daughters were ill and the old man conveyed his worry to his son. Gibran's father had not noticed the date of the letter: April first, or April Fool's Day.

GIBRAN TO HIS FATHER

Beirut,
April, 1904

Dear Father:

I received your letter in which you express to me your anxiety over "sad and unexpected news." I would have felt the same way had I not known the intention of the writer and the purpose of the letter. They (may God forgive them) tell you in the letter that one of my sisters is critically ill, and again they say that the illness will involve a great deal of expense, which will make it difficult for my sisters to send you money. I have immediately found an explanation in noting that the letter was written on the first day of April. Our aunt has been accustomed to such funny and gentle jokes. Her saying that my sister has been ill for six months is as far from the truth as we are from her. During the last seven months I have received five letters from Mr. Ray who assures me that both of my sisters, Miriana and Sultana, are in excellent health. He extols their fine characters, marking Sultana's refined

manners; and speaks of the resemblance between her and me both in physique and in character.

These words came from the most honest man I have ever known; from a man who loathes April Fool jokes and dislikes any fabrication which saddens the heart of another. You may rest assured that all is well and let your mind be at ease.

I am still in Beirut, although I might be away from home for a whole month touring Syria and Palestine or Egypt and Sudan with an American family for whom I have great respect. For this reason I do not know how long my stay will last in Beirut. However, I am here for personal benefit which makes it necessary for me to remain in this country a while in order to please those who care for my future. Do not ever doubt my judgment regarding what is good for me and for the fortification and betterment of my future.

This is all I can tell you—with my affection to all my relatives and loving friends, and my respect to whoever inquires about me. May God prolong your life and protect you—

Your son,
GIBRAN

Jamil Malouf, a young Lebanese poet-writer, was a great admirer of Gibran. In this letter, Gibran reveals his concern and admiration for the young poet who had left Paris to live in São Paul, Brazil. Gibran pictures his friend Jamil as a torch from heaven illuminating the path of mankind, at the same time expressing his amazement at learning of his friend's move. He

presses him for a revelation of the motive that prompted him to go to São Paul and place himself among the "living dead."

TO JAMIL MALOUF

1908

Dear Brother Jamil:

When I read your letters I feel the existence of an enchanting spirit moving in this room—a beautiful and sorrowful spirit that attracts me by its undulation and makes me see you as two persons: one hovers over humanity with enormous wings similar to the wings of the seraphim whom Saint John saw standing before the Throne by the seven lamps; the other person is chained to a huge rock like Prometheus, who, in giving man the first torch of fire, brought on himself the wrath of the gods. The first person enlivens my heart and soothes my spirit because he sways with the sun rays and the frolicsome breeze of dawn; while the second person makes my heart suffer, for he is a prisoner of the vicissitudes of time. . . .

You have always been and still are capable of causing the torch of fire to come from heaven and light the path of mankind, but tell me what law or force has brought you to São Paul and fettered your body and placed you among those who died on the day of their birth and have not yet been buried? Do the Greek gods still practice their power in these days?

I have heard that you are going to return to Paris to live there. I, too, would like to go there. Is it possible that we both could meet in the City of Arts? Will we

meet in the Heart of the World and visit the Opera and the French theatre and talk about the plays of Racine, Corneille, Molière, Hugo, and Sardou? Will we meet there and walk together to where the Bastille was erected and then return to our quarters feeling the gentle spirit of Rousseau and Voltaire and write about Liberty and Tyranny and destroy every Bastille that stands in every city in the Orient? Will we go to the Louvre and stand before the paintings of Raphael, Da Vinci and Corot, and write about Beauty and Love and their influence on man's heart?

Oh, brother, I feel a gnawing hunger in my heart for the approach of the great works of art, and I have a profound longing for the eternal sayings; however, this hunger and longing come out of a great power that exists in the depth of my heart—a power that wishes to announce itself hurriedly but is unable to do so, for the time has not come, and the people who died on the day of their birth are still walking and standing as a barrier in the way of the living.

My health is, as you know, like a violin in the hands of one that does not know how to play it, for it makes him hear harsh melody. My sentiments are like an ocean with their ebb and flow; my soul is like a quail with broken wings. She suffers immensely when she sees the swarms of birds hovering in the sky, for she finds herself unable to do likewise. But like all other birds, she enjoys the silence of Night, the coming of Dawn, the rays of Sun, and the beauty of the valley. I paint and write now and then, and in the midst of my paintings and writings, I am like a small boat sailing between an ocean of an endless depth and a sky of limitless blue—strange dreams, sub-

lime desires, great hopes, broken and mended thoughts; and between all these there is something which the people call Despair, and which I call Inferno.

GIBRAN

In the month of May, 1903, Ameen Guraieb, editor and owner of *Almuhager,* daily Arabic newspaper published in New York, visited the city of Boston. Among the people who received Ameen was the young Kahlil Gibran who captured the journalist's regard with his kind manner and intelligence.

The following day Gibran invited Guraieb to his home. He showed him his paintings and presented him with an old notebook in which he had set down his thoughts and meditations. When Ameen saw the paintings and read the poems in the notebook he realized he had discovered a genius artist, poet, and philosopher. Thrilled by his discovery, the journalist offered to Gibran a position as columnist on his daily newspaper.

Thus Ameen Guraieb extracted Kahlil Gibran from his retreat in Boston and introduced him to his Arabic readers. "This newspaper is very fortunate," said Guraieb in one of his editorials, "to be able to present to the Arabic-speaking world the first literary fruit of a young artist whose drawings are admired by the American public. This young man is Kahlil Gibran of Bsharré, the famous city of the braves. We publish this essay without comments under the caption of *Tears and Laughter,* leaving it up to the readers to judge it according to their tastes." This was the first time that Gibran saw his name in print in a daily Arabic newspaper.

When Gibran wrote *Spirits Rebellious,* the book containing the story of Rose El Hanie which caused Gibran's expulsion from Lebanon and excommunica-

tion from the Church, it was his friend Ameen Guraieb who wrote the preface for the book.

As revealed in the following letter, Gibran's appreciation and love for Ameen went very deep. He wishes his friend *bon voyage*—Ameen was preparing for a trip to Lebanon—and confides in his friend traveling plans of his own.

TO AMEEN GURAIEB

Boston,
Feb. 12, 1908

Dear Ameen:

Only my sister Miriana knows something about this bit of news which I am going to tell you and which will make you and your neighbors rather happy: I am going to Paris, the capital of fine arts, in the late part of the coming spring, and I shall remain there one whole year. The twelve months which I am going to spend in Paris will play an important part in my every day life, for the time which I will spend in the City of Light will be, with the help of God, the beginning of a new chapter in the story of my life. I shall join a group of great artists in that great city and work under their supervision and gain a lot from their observation and benefit myself from their constructive criticism in the field of fine arts. It matters not whether they benefit me or not, because after my return from Paris to the United States, my drawings will gain more prestige, which makes the blind-rich buy more of them, not because of their artistic beauty, but because of their being painted by an artist who has spent a full year in Paris among the great European painters.

I never dreamed of this voyage before, and the thought of it never did enter into my mind, for the expense of the trip would make it impossible for a man like me to undertake such a venture. But heaven, my dear Ameen, has arranged for this trip, without my being aware of it, and opened before me the way to Paris. I shall spend one whole cycle of my life there at the expense of heaven, the source of plenty.

And now, since you have heard my story you will know that my stay in Boston is neither due to my love for this city, nor to my dislike for New York. My being here is due to the presence of a she-angel who is ushering me towards a splendid future and paving for me the path to intellectual and financial success. But it makes no difference whether I am in Boston or in Paris, *Almuhager* will remain the paradise in which my soul dwells and the stage upon which my heart dances. My trip to Paris will offer me an opportunity to write about things which I cannot find or imagine in this mechanical and commercial country whose skies are replete with clamor and noise. I shall be enlightened by the social studies which I will undertake in the capital of capitals of the world where Rousseau, Lamartine and Hugo lived; and where the people love art as much as the Americans adore the Almighty Dollar.

During your absence I shall continue to contribute to every issue of *Almuhager*. I shall pour upon its pages all the affections, hopes and ideas that my heart, soul and mind contain. I am not looking forward to receiving any compensation. All I want from you is your friendship. But if you feel like adding a material debt to the many moral debts which I owe you, you may tell your editorial staff to get behind my book *Tears and Laughter* and help me reap the harvest of the many nights I have spent on its writing. Tell them to assist me in selling the book to the Arabic readers and to the merchants in New York and other states. As you know, I cannot promote the book without the help of *Almuhager*.

Be at ease and do not occupy your mind with anything other than the joy of seeing your family and beholding the beautiful scenery of Lebanon. You have worked hard enough in the last five years and you deserve a little rest. Let not your worrying about the future interfere with your tranquility. No matter what happens, *Almuhager* will ever remain the pride of all Arabic papers. A message from you, a poem from Assad Rustum, and an article from Gibran every week will be sufficient to open the eyes of the Arab world and direct their attention to Twenty-one Washington Street.*

Your introduction to my book *Spirits Rebellious* made me happy because it was free from personal comment. Monday I sent you an article for *Almuhager*; has it arrived yet? Write me a few lines in answer to this letter. I shall write you more than one letter before you leave for Lebanon. Let nothing dampen your enthusiasm for your trip. We will be unable to meet and shake hands, but we will join each other in thoughts and spirits. Seven thousand miles are but one mile, and one thousand years are but one year in the eyes of the spirit.

Miriana sends you her regards and wishes you success. May God bless you and bring you back safe to me, and may heaven shower upon you blessings, the amount

* Address of the office and publishing house of *Almuhager*.

of which will equal the love and respect I have in my heart for you.

GIBRAN

It is a custom among the people of the Near East to call each other "brother" or "sister." Close friends and relatives other than those actually so related are often referred to in this manner.

This letter was written to Nakhli, Gibran's first cousin whom he addresses as brother. Gibran and Nakhli were inseparable companions in their early youth. They lived, slept, played, and ate together in their home town, Bsharré, close by the Holy Cedars of Lebanon.

Peter, Gibran's half-brother, a good singer and lute player, entertained Gibran and Nakhli and took good care of them. When Nakhli left Bsharré for Brazil in search of a livelihood, Gibran kept in close touch with him.

In the following letter, Gibran speaks to Nakhli of his struggles and complains of the Arabic-speaking conservative class which was accusing him of heresy because of their feeling that his writings were poisoning the mind of the youth. Gibran later published a story which he called "Kahlil the Heretic."

 TO NAKHLI GIBRAN

Boston,
March 15, 1908

Dear Brother Nakhli:

I have just received your letter which filled my soul with joy and sadness at the same time, for it brought

653

back to my memory pictures of those days that passed like dreams, leaving behind phantoms that come with the daylight and go with the darkness. How did those days undo themselves, and where did those nights, in which Peter lived, go? How did those hours, which Peter filled with his sweet songs and handsomeness pass away? Those days, nights and hours have disappeared like open flowers when dawn descends from the gray sky. I know that you remember those days with pain and I have noticed the phantoms of your affections between the lines of your missive, as if they came from Brazil to restore to my heart the echo of the valleys, the mountains and the rivulets surrounding Bsharré.

Life, my dear Nakhli, is like the seasons of the year. The sorrowful Autumn comes after the joyful Summer, and the raging Winter comes behind the sad Autumn, and the beautiful Spring appears after the passing of the awful Winter. Will the Spring of our life ever return so we may be happy again with the trees, smiling with the flowers, running with the brooks, and singing with the birds like we used to do in Bsharré when Peter was still alive? Will the tempest that dispersed us ever reunite us? Will we ever go back to Bsharré and meet by Saint George Church? I do not know, but I feel that life is a sort of debt and payment. It gives us today in order to take from us tomorrow. Then it gives us again and takes from us anew until we get tired of the giving and receiving and surrender to the final sleep.

You know that Gibran, who spends most of his life writing, finds enchanting pleasure in corresponding with the people he loves most. You also know that Gibran, who was very fond of Nakhli when he was a child, will

never forget the man that Nakhli has become. The things which the child loves remain in the domain of the heart until old age. The most beautiful thing in life is that our souls remain hovering over the places where we once enjoyed ourselves. I am one of those who remembers such places regardless of distance or time. I do not let one single phantom disappear with the cloud, and it is my everlasting remembrance of the past that causes my sorrow sometimes. But if I had to choose between joy and sorrow, I would not exchange the sorrows of my heart for the joys of the whole world.

And now let me drop the curtain upon the past and tell you something about my present and my future, for I know that you would like to hear something about the boy you have always loved. Listen to me, and I will read to you the first chapter of Gibran's story: I am a man of weak constitution, but my health is good because I neither think about it nor have time to worry about it. I love to smoke and drink coffee. If you were to come to see me now and enter my room, you would find me behind a screen of thick smoke mingled with the aromatic scent of Yamanite coffee.

I love to work and I do not let one moment pass without working. But the days in which I find myself dormant and my thought slothful are more bitter than quinine and more severe than the teeth of the wolf. I spend my life writing and painting, and my enjoyment in these two arts is above all other enjoyments. I feel that the fires that feed the affection within me would like to dress themselves with ink and paper, but I am not sure whether the Arabic-speaking world would remain as friendly to me as it has been in the past three years. I say this because the apparition of enmity has already appeared. The people in Syria are calling me heretic, and the intelligentsia in Egypt vilifies me, saying, "He is the enemy of just laws, of family ties, and of old traditions." Those writers are telling the truth, because I do not love man-made laws and I abhor the traditions that our ancestors left us. This hatred is the fruit of my love for the sacred and spiritual kindness which should be the source of every law upon the earth, for kindness is the shadow of God in man. I know that the principles upon which I base my writings are echoes of the spirit of the great majority of the people of the world, because the tendency toward a spiritual independence is to our life as the heart is to the body. . . . Will my teaching ever be received by the Arab world, or will it die away and disappear like a shadow?

Will Gibran ever be able to deflect the people's eyes from the skulls and thorns towards the light and the truth? Or will Gibran be like so many others who returned from this world to Eternity without leaving behind any reminders of their existence? I do not know, but I feel that there is a great power in the depth of my heart that wishes to come out, and it is going to come out some day with the help of God.

I have an important news for you. On the first day of the coming June I will be leaving for Paris to join a committee of artists, and I shall remain there a whole year after which I shall return to this country. My stay there will be filled with study and research and hard work; at the same time it will be the beginning of a new life.

Remember me when you and the family gather at the table to partake of your meals, and tell your wife

and the children that a certain relative, whose name is Gibran, has a loving place in his heart for every one of you.

My sister Miriana joins me in sending her regards. When I read your letter to her, it made her so happy that she was unable to hold back her tears when I ran across certain phrases. May God bless you and give you the best of health and keep you as a dear brother to

GIBRAN

TO AMEEN GURAIEB

Boston
March 28, 1908

Dear Ameen:

I have just locked myself up in my room behind a screen of cigarette smoke mingled with aromatic scent of Yamanite coffee to spend one hour talking to you. I am now enjoying my coffee and my smoke as well as our conversation.

You are now in the other part of the great, but small, globe, while I am still here. You are now in beautiful and peaceful Lebanon and I am in clamorous and noisy Boston. You are in the East and I am in the West, but no matter how far away you are from me, I feel that you are closer to me than ever. Man finds the expatriation of his beloved friends difficult to bear because his pleasure comes through the five senses. But Gibran's soul has already grown beyond that to a plane of higher enjoyment which does not require the mediation of the five senses. His soul

sees, hears, and feels, but not through the medium of eyes, ears, and fingers. His soul roams the whole world and returns without the use of feet, cars, and ships. I see Ameen far and near and I perceive everything around him as the soul regards many other invisible and voiceless objects. The subtlest beauties in our life are unseen and unheard.

How did you find Lebanon? Is it as beautiful as your yearnings promised? Or is it an arid spot where slothfulness dwells? Is Lebanon the same glorious Mountain whose beauty was sung and praised by poets like David, Isaiah, Farhat, Lamartine, and Haddad? Or is it a chain of mountains and valleys empty of geniality, aloof from beauty, and surrounded by loneliness?

Undoubtedly you shall answer all these questions in long articles to *Almuhager* and I shall read every word. But if there is something that you do not feel can be discussed publicly, tell it to me in a personal letter so that I may share your thoughts and see the reality of Lebanon through your eyes.

I am in these days like a man observing Lent and awaiting the coming of the dawn of the feast. My planned trip to Paris causes my dreams to hover around the great achievements I hope will be mine during my year in the City of Knowledge and Arts. I told you ere your departure to Lebanon that I would spend a whole year in Paris, and now I have also decided to visit Italy after the expiration of my time in Paris. I intend to spend another year visiting Italy's great museums and ruins and cities. I shall visit Venice, Florence, Rome, and Genoa; then I will return to Naples and board a boat to the United States. It will be a wonderful journey, for it will forge a

golden chain connecting Gibran's sorrowful past with his happy future.

I am sure that you will pass through Paris on your way back to the United States. In Paris we shall meet and be merry; in Paris we shall quench our soul's thirst for beautiful things created by famous artists. In Paris we shall visit the Panthéon and stop for a few minutes by the tombs of Victor Hugo, Rousseau, Chateaubriand, and Renan. In Paris we shall roam the Palace of the Louvre and look upon the paintings of Raphael, Michelangelo, and Da Vinci. In Paris we shall go to the Opera and hear songs and hymns revealed by the deity to Beethoven, Wagner, Mozart, and Rossini. . . . These names, whose pronunciation is rather difficult to an Arabic-speaking person, are names of great men who founded the civilization of Europe; these are the names of men whom the earth has swallowed, but whose deeds it could not fold or engulf. The tempest is capable of laying waste the flowers but unable to harm the seeds. This is the consolation that heaven delivers to the hearts of great men who love great deeds, and this is the light which causes us—the sons of knowledge—to walk proudly upon the path of life.

I was thrilled to receive your letter from Alexandria, Egypt, and I was proud to read in *Almuhager* about the reception you and our brother Assad Rustum met in Cairo. My heart and soul rejoice every time I hear a word from you or about you. But tell me, Ameen, did you mention my name when you met with the intelligentsia of Lebanon and Egypt? Did you speak of the third name in the Trinity who is still behind the ocean? I believe that my friend Saleem Sarkis had told you about the criticism I had received from Lutfi Al-Manfaluti concerning my

story about Madame Rose Hanie. It was published in *Al Muayad*. I was well pleased with the criticism because I feel that such persecution is a diet for new principles, especially when it comes from a learned man like Al-Manfaluti.

My work in these days is like a chain of many rings connected with one another. I have changed my way of living and I miss some of the joys of loneliness that embraced my soul before I dreamed about going to Paris. Yesterday I was contented with playing minor parts upon the limited stage of life, but today I have realized that such contentment is a sort of sluggishness. I used to look upon life through tears and laughter, but today I see life through golden and enchanting rays of light that impart strength to the soul and courage to the heart and motion to the body. I used to be like a bird imprisoned in a cage, contenting myself with seeds dropped down to me by the hands of Destiny. But today I feel like a free bird who sees the beauty of the fields and prairies and wishes to fly in the spacious sky, mingling its affections, its fancy and its hopes with the ether.

There is something in our life which is nobler and more supreme than fame; and this *something* is the great deed that invokes fame. I feel, within me, a hidden power that wishes to dress its nakedness with a beautiful garment of great deeds. This makes me feel that I came to this world to write my name upon the face of life with big letters. Such emotion accompanies me day and night. It is this sort of sentiment that causes me to see the future surrounded by light and encircled by rapture and triumph which I have been dreaming about since I was fifteen years of age. My dreams have just begun to be realized, and I

feel that my trip to Paris is going to be the first step on a ladder that reaches to heaven. I am intending to publish my book *The Broken Wings* next summer. This book is the best one I have ever written. But the one that is going to create a great movement in the Arabic-speaking world is a book of philosophy named *Religion and Religious-ness*,* which I started more than a year ago, and whose place to my heart is as the center to the circle. I shall finish this book in Paris, and probably will have it published at my own expense.

When you are in a beautiful spot or among learned people, or by the side of old ruins, or on the top of a high mountain, whisper my name so that my soul will go to Lebanon and hover around you and share with you the pleasure of life and all life's meanings and secrets. Remember me when you see the sun rising from behind Mount Sunnin or Fam El Mizab. Think of me when you see the sun coming down toward its setting, spreading its red garment upon the mountains and the valleys as if shedding blood instead of tears as it bids Lebanon farewell. Recall my name when you see the shepherds sitting in the shadow of the trees and blowing their reeds and filling the silent field with soothing music as did Apollo when he was exiled to this world. Think of me when you see the damsels carrying their earthenware jars filled with water upon their shoulders. Remember me when you see the Lebanese villager plowing the earth before the face of the sun, with beads of sweat adorning his forehead while his back is bent under the heavy duty of labor. Remember me when you hear the songs and hymns that Nature has woven from the sinews of moonlight, mingled with the aromatic scent

* This book was never finished or published.

of the valleys, mixed with the frolicsome breeze of the Holy Cedars, and poured into the hearts of the Lebanese. Remember me when the people invite you to their festivities, for your remembrance of me will bring to you pictures of my love and longing for your person and will add spiritual overtones and deeper meaning to your words and your speeches. Love and longing, my dear Ameen, are the beginning and the end of our deeds.

Now that I have written these lines to you, I feel like a child who wants to scoop the ocean water with a sea shell and place it in a small ditch he has dug in the sand of the shore. But do you not see between these lines other lines whose secrets you should inquire? They were written with the finger of the soul and the ink of the heart upon the face of love that hangs between the earth and the stars and hovers between the East and the West.

Remember me to your father, whom I admire and respect, and give my regards to your respected mother —that dear mother who gave the Arabic-speaking world a powerful figure, and bestowed upon Lebanon a brilliant torch, and enriched Gibran with a very dear and beloved brother. Kindly spread my salaam among your brothers, neighbors and admirers like the frolicsome breeze of Lebanon spreads its blossoms upon the apple trees in the month of Nisan.

Miriana greets you from behind the ocean and wishes you the best of health. My relative Melhem and his daughter Zahieh asked me to send you their regards. Everybody misses you and longs to see you, oh beloved brother of

GIBRAN

TO NAKHLI GIBRAN

Paris, France,
Sept. 27, 1910

My Beloved Brother Nakhli:

Do you recall those interesting tales we used to hear during the cold rainy days while sitting around the hearth with the snow falling outside and the wind blowing between the dwellings? Do you still remember the story about the gorgeous garden with beautiful trees bearing delicious fruits? Do you also remember the end of the story which tells how those bewitched trees turned into young men whom destiny had brought into the garden? I am sure you remember all these things even without knowing that Gibran is like those bewitched young men tied with unseen chains and ruled by invisible power.

I am, my dear, Nakhli, a bewitched tree, but Sid Aladin has not yet come from behind the Seven Seas to unshackle me and loosen the magic ties and make me free and independent.

On the 14th day of the coming month I shall leave Paris, but now I am busy arranging my work and planning for the future. I am like a spinning wheel turning day and night. God only knows how busy I am. Thus heaven directs my life, and thus destiny rotates me around a certain point from which I cannot get away.

Your letter just reached me this morning, and since then I have been thinking and thinking, but I do not know what to do. Do you believe that you can help me with your thoughts and affections? Can you look into the depth of my heart and understand the misery which God has placed in it? All I ask of you is to feel with me and

have faith and believe me when I tell you that I am a prisoner of time and circumstances. I am not lamenting my luck because I prefer to be like I am, and I refuse to exchange my plight for another one because I have chosen the literary life while being aware of all the obstacles and pains surrounding it.

Just think, my dear Nakhli, and ponder upon Gibran's life, for it reveals to you a sort of struggle and strife. It is a chain of connected links of misery and distress. I can say these things to you because I am very patient and glad of the existence of hardships in my life, for I hope to overcome all these difficulties. Had it not been for the presence of calamities, work and struggle would not have existed, and life would have been cold, barren and boresome.

GIBRAN

The ties of friendship were developed between Kahlil Gibran and the Lebanese artist, Yousif Howayek while they were studying art in Paris. Gibran was Howayek's inseparable friend who accompanied him to the opera, theatres, museums, galleries and other places of interest. Howayek was a great admirer of Gibran, and as a token of his admiration for the Prophet of Lebanon he worked several months on a beautiful oil portrait of Gibran and presented it to him.

TO YOUSIF HOWAYEK

Boston, 1911

Although this city is full of friends and acquaintances, I feel as if I had been exiled into a distant

land where life is as cold as ice and as gray as ashes and as silent as the Sphynx.

My sister is close by me, and the loving kin-folks are around me everywhere I go, and the people visit us every day and every night, but I am not happy. My work is progressing rapidly, my thoughts are calm, and I am enjoying perfect health, but I still lack happiness. My soul is hungry and thirsty for some sort of nourishment, but I don't know where to find it. The soul is a heavenly flower that cannot live in the shade, but the thorns can live everywhere.

This is the life of the oriental people who are afflicted with the disease of fine arts. This is the life of the children of Apolon who are exiled into this foreign land, whose work is strange, whose walk is slow, and whose laughter is cry.

How are you, Yousif? Are you happy among the human ghosts you witness every day on both sides of the road?

GIBRAN

In the preface of his Arabic book *May and Gibran,* Dr. Jamil Jabre wrote: "It is difficult to imagine a man and a woman falling in love without having known or met one another except by correspondence. But artists have their own unusual way of life which they themselves can only understand. This was the case of the great Lebanese woman writer, May Ziadeh and Kahlil Gibran.

"The literary and love relationship between Kahlil Gibran and May Ziadeh was not a myth or pre-

sumption, but a proven fact which was revealed to the public through some letters published by May Ziadeh after Gibran's death."

When *The Broken Wings* made its first appearance in Arabic, Gibran presented May Ziadeh with a copy of his novel and asked her to criticize it. Complying with his request, she wrote him the following letter:

FROM MAY ZIADEH

Cairo, Egypt,
May 12, 1912

. . . I do not agree with you on the subject of marriage, Gibran. I respect your thoughts, and I revere your ideas, for I know that you are honest and sincere in the defense of your principles that aim at a noble purpose. I am in full accord with you on the fundamental principle that advocates the freedom of woman. The woman should be free, like the man, to choose her own spouse guided not by the advice and aid of neighbors and acquaintances, but by her own personal inclinations. After choosing her life partner, a woman must bind herself completely to the duties of that partnership upon which she has embarked. You refer to these as heavy chains fabricated by the ages. Yes, I agree with you and I say that these *are* heavy chains; but remember that these chains were made by nature who made the woman what she is today. Though man's mind has reached the point of breaking the chains of customs and traditions, it has not yet reached the point of breaking the natural chains because the law of nature is above all laws. Why can't

a married woman meet secretly with the man she loves? Because by thus doing she will be betraying her husband and disgracing the name she has willingly accepted, and will be lowering herself in the eyes of the society of which she is a member.

At the time of marriage the woman promises to be faithful, and spiritual faithfulness is as important as physical faithfulness. At the time of matrimony she also declares and guarantees the happiness and well-being of her husband; and when she meets secretly with another man, she is already guilty of betraying society, family and duty. You may counter with, "Duty is a vague word that is hard to define in many circumstances." In a case like this we need to know "what is a family" in order to be able to ascertain the duties of its members. The roll which the woman plays in the family is the most difficult, the most humble, and the most bitter.

I myself feel the pangs of the strings that tie the woman down those fine silky strings are like those of a spider's web, but they are as strong as golden wires. Suppose we let Selma Karamy,* the heroine of your novel, and every woman that resembles her in affections and intelligence, meet secretly with an honest man of noble character; would not this condone any woman's selecting for herself a friend, other than her husband, to meet with secretly? This would not work, even if the purpose of their secret meeting was to pray together before the shrine of the Crucified.

MAY

* The beautiful girl of Beirut in Gibran's *The Broken Wings.*

Sarkis Effandi, one of Gibran's best friends, was considered a scholar among the intelligentsia of Lebanon. He owned a publishing house and a daily Arabic newspaper called *Lisan-Ul-Hal*. In the year 1912 the Arab League of Progress, an organization composed of many literary figures joined together for the purpose of promoting Arab unity and culture, decided to honor the great Lebanese poet Khalil Effandi Mutran, who a few years later became the poet laureate of Egypt and Syria.

Since Sarkis was the head of the committee honoring the poet, he extended an invitation to his friend Gibran in New York to join them on the honor day in Beirut. Gibran could not make the trip, but he sent to Sarkis a prose poem with instructions to read it in his behalf before the poet on the day of the event. The story, which is not published in this book, was entitled "The Poet from Baalbeck." It was a eulogy in which Gibran pictured the poet laureate of the two sister countries as a prince sitting on his golden throne and receiving wise men from the East. In the story, Gibran expressed his belief in the transmigration of souls and praises the great soul that was incarnated in the honored poet's body.

TO SALEEM SARKIS

New York,
Oct. 6, 1912

Dear Sarkis Effandi,

I am sending you a story that was revealed to me by the devilish muses to honor the poet Khalil Effandi Mutran. As you notice, the story is rather short compared with the dignity of the great prince and outstanding poet. But at the same time it is long in comparison to the ones written by other poets and writers who, of course, are

inclined to be brief and clever, especially when it comes to honoring poets. What shall I do when the muses inspire me to write on such a subject that needs a little expatiation?

Please accept my sincerest thanks for your invitation to join you in honoring a great poet who pours his soul as wine into the cups of the Arab League of Progress, and who burns his heart as incense before the two countries [Syria and Egypt] by strengthening the ties of friendship and love between them.

To you goes my salaam mingled with my sincerest respect and admiration.

GIBRAN

TO AMEEN GURAIEB

Boston,
Feb. 18, 1913

Brother Ameen:

This is the last word I say to you while you are in this country. It is a word emanating from the holy of holies of the heart, mingled with a sigh of longing and a smile of hope:

Be healthy every hour of the day, and every day of the month. Enjoy beautiful things wherever you see them, and let their memory and their echo remain in your heart until the day you return to your friends and well-wishers. Meet the admirers of *Almuhager* in Egypt, Syria, and Lebanon, and speak to them of the deeds of

their immigrant brethren; unfold before them that which the long distance has folded between our hearts and their hearts; and strengthen the ties that connect our souls with their souls.

Take a walk in the morning and stand on the top of one of the mountains in Lebanon and meditate upon the sun when it is rising and pouring its golden rays upon the villages and the valleys. Let these heavenly pictures remain inscribed upon your heart so that we can share them when you come back to us. Be kind enough to convey the longing of our souls and the wishes of our hearts to the youth of Lebanon. Tell the elderly men of Syria that our thoughts, affections, and dreams never leave our hearts and souls except when they fly towards them. When your boat reaches Beirut, stand on its prow and look towards Mount Sunnin and Fam El-Mizab and greet our forefathers who are sleeping under the layers of the earth, and salute the fathers and brothers who are living above the earth. Mention our works and endeavors in private and public meetings. Tell them that we are busy sowing seeds in America so that we may some day reap the harvest in Lebanon. Do and say whatever you wish provided you are happy, for your happiness is the wish and hope of every true Lebanese in the United States of America.

Miriana shakes your hand and wishes you happiness. Remember me to the well-wishers of *Almuhager* in Egypt, Syria, and Lebanon. Perchance when my name reaches their ears it will turn into a soothing tune. Goodbye, Ameen, goodbye, O dear brother of

GIBRAN

Every time Gibran published a book, he sent a copy to May for criticism. When *The Cortege* or *Procession,* and *The Madman* were published, May reviewed them in *Al-Hilal,* a magazine in Egypt, and wrote Gibran a special letter in which she discussed the above books. Gibran answered her and thanked her for the criticism, praising her cleverness, her vast knowledge, and her frankness. At the same time he tried to acquit himself of being in agreement with Nietzsche and to deny some ideas he wrote on passion in *The Madman.*

TO MAY ZIADEH

Dear May,

   ... All in all the madman is not I. The passion which I sought to bring out through the lips of a personage I had created does not represent my own feelings. The language that I found expressive of the desires of this madman is different from the language that I use when I sit down to converse with a friend whom I love and respect. If you really want to discover my reality through my writings, why don't you refer to the youth in the field and the soothing tune of his flute instead of the madman and his ugly cries? You will realize that the madman is no more than a link in a long chain made of metal. I do not deny that the madman was an unpolished link of rough iron, but this does not mean that the whole chain is rough. For every soul there is a season, May. The soul's winter is not like her spring, and her summer is not like her autumn. ...

> Then Gibran went on discussing his book *Tears and Laughter* whose dialogue May had criticized and enquired of its author what prompted him to write such a childish work, to which Gibran bravely answered:

. . . Now let us discuss *Tears And Laughter* for a moment. I am not afraid to tell you that this came out before the World War. At that time I sent you a copy and never heard from you whether you received it or not. The articles in *Tears And Laughter* were the first ones that I wrote in series and published them in *Almuhager* sixteen years ago. Nasseeb Arida (may Allah forgive him) was the one who collected these articles, to which he added two more which I wrote in Paris, and published them in one book. During my childhood and the days of my youth, before the writings of *Tears And Laughter*, I wrote enough prose and poetry to fill many volumes, but I did not, and shall not, commit the crime of having them published.

GIBRAN

As the name of Kahlil Gibran was, and still is, dear to every Lebanese heart or Arabic-speaking person, so the name of Mikhail Naimay today is dear to the hearts of the sons and daughters of Lebanon.

Naimy, who is a leading literary figure in Lebanon and the Middle East, lives in seclusion in his home town, Biskinta, near Mount Sunnin in Lebanon. While in New York, Naimy and Gibran were inseparable friends, and it was to Naimy that Gibran complained and entrusted his secrets. Even on his deathbed Gibran called for Naimy, who came to stay with him at the hospital until he breathed his last.

Born in Biskinta, Lebanon, Mikhail Naimy received his early education at a parochial school conducted by the Imperial Russian Palestine Society. In 1906 he was granted a scholarship to the Seminary of Poltava, in the Ukraine, where he made an extensive study of the Russian language in which he wrote poems and treatises that were widely admired. In 1916 Naimy

received two degress from the University of Washington. He wrote and published in Arabic many critical articles and stories while at the University. In 1916 he decided that the Arabic literary circle in New York, with the great Arabic writers, Ameen Rihani, Kahlil Gibran, Nassib Arida, and others, was to be his field.

In World War I, he served at the front with the AEF. After his honorable discharge in 1919 he returned to his literary career. In 1932 at the height of his fame he decided to return to Lebanon.

Among the works he published are *Two Generations*, a popular play; *The Cribble*, a series of critical essays; *Stages*, dealing with inner and outer life; *Once Upon a Time*, a collection of short stories; *Food for the Godward Journey*, his famous discourses; *Eyelid Whisperings*, philosophical poems; *Encounter*, a novel; *Threshing Floor* and *Light and Darkness*, philosophical contemplations; *The Memoirs of a Pitted Face*, a self-portrait of a bizarre personality; *Vineyard by the Road*, sayings and parables; *Present-Day Idols*, an analytical essay; *The World's Voice*, thoughts and meditations of life; *The Book of Mirdad*, a book for seekers after spiritual emancipation.

In his letters Kahlil Gibran addresses Mikhail Naimy sometimes as "Dear Meesha"—a diminutive for Mikhail. The long trip that Gibran refers to in the following letter was one of his usual trips to Boston where his sister Miriana lived. He also refers to *Al-Funoon*, an Arabic magazine which Gibran started, but which did not last long.

TO MIKHAIL NAIMY

New York,
Sept. 14, 1919

Dear Mikhail:

May God's peace be upon you. I have returned from my long trip and met with our brother Nasseeb

and had a long discussion with him about reviving *Al-Funoon*, and the ways and means of securing its future. I interviewed many educated and half-educated people in Boston and New York regarding this matter, but all of the talks stopped at a certain point. The point is this: Nasseeb Arida cannot take the responsibility alone. It is necessary that Mikhail Naimy return to New York and join Nasseeb in the project and put it on a working basis before the intelligentsia and the merchants of New York. By having these two men working together, the confidence of the Syrian people may be gained; for one alone cannot win. An entertainment should be given in New York, and the proceeds would go to the magazine. How can the entertainment be a success when the man who is capable of obtaining speakers and musicians is in Washington? A committee should be formed to start the work. The treasurer must be known to the Syrians in other states who will ask themselves a thousand and one questions before they answer the circular. But who else other than Mikhail Naimy is capable of forming this committee?

There are numerous things, Mikhail, that begin and end with you each time we discuss the subject of *Al-Funoon*. If you wish to revive the magazine, you should come to New York and be the trigger behind every move. Nasseeb is unable to do anything at present, and of all the admirers and well-wishers of *Al-Funoon* in New York, there is no one who is capable of taking the responsibility upon himself. It is my belief that five thousand dollars would be sufficient to guarantee the future of the magazine. However, I presume that a circular without the entertainment would not bring half of the proposed amount. In short, the success of the project depends upon your presence in New York. If your return to New York means a sacrifice on your part, that sacrifice must be considered as placing that which is dear, and offering the important upon the altar of that which is more important. To me the dearest thing in your life is the realization of your dreams, and the most important thing is the reaping of the fruit of your talents.

Write me if you will; and may God protect you for your brother

GIBRAN

Emil Zaidan was an outstanding scholar and well known throughout the Arabic-speaking world for his great works in the field of Arabic literature. Being a Lebanese and owner and editor of one of the best Arabic magazines in Egypt, he admired Gibran and looked upon him as a genius. He devoted many pages to him in his monthly magazine *Al-Hilal*, the Crescent. It was through this magazine and many others that Gibran won fame and became known as poet, artist, and philosopher.

In the following letter to his friend Zaidan, Gibran speaks of the circumstances that made it necessary for him to work ten hours a day despite his doctor's orders that he work no more than five. Gibran at that time was working on several projects that required many hours of daily work. He tells his friend that there is nothing more difficult than the existence of a strong spirit in a weak body.

 TO EMIL ZAIDAN

1919

My Brother Emil:

. . . My health is better now than it used to be. Yet it is still like a violin with broken strings. What is

bothering me most now is that circumstances have placed me in a position that require of me ten hours of daily work while I am forbidden to spend more than four or five hours writing or painting. There is nothing more difficult than the existence of a strong spirit in a weak body. I feel—I am not modest—that I am just at the beginning of a mountain road. The twenty years which I have spent as a writer and painter were but an era of preparation and desire. Up to the present time I have not yet done anything worthy of remaining before the face of the sun. My ideas have not ripened yet, and my net is still submerged in water.

GIBRAN

In this letter Gibran mentions his two friends, Abdul-Masseh and Nasseeb Arida. The former was the owner and editor of *As-Sayeh*, an Arabic newspaper published in New York, and the latter was a famous poet and owner and editor of *Al-Akhlak*, the Character, a monthly magazine published also in New York. Both Abdul-Masseh and Nasseeb were members of Arrabitah, a literary circle limited in membership to ten or thirteen, organized in New York with Gibran as president and Mikhail Naimy as secretary. Other members of Arrabitah were Catzeflis, an intimate of Gibran and an essayist of recognized accomplishments in the field of Arabian thought and literature, Ayoub, Hawie, Rihani, Abu-Mady, Nadra, Alkazin, Bahut, Atalla. Each one of these pioneers from Syria or Lebanon made a worthy contribution to poetry and literature. Gibran was the first of eight now dead. Arrabitah brought about a real renaissance in modern

Arabic literature. Many books in Arabic have already
been written about it, and many more will be written.

TO MIKHAIL NAIMY

Boston, 1920

My Brother Mikhail:

Peace be unto you and unto your big heart and
pure soul. I would like to know how you are and where you
are. Are you in the forest of your dreams or in the knolls
and hills of your thoughts? Or are you on the top of that
mountain where all dreams turn into one vision, and all
thoughts into a single ambition? Tell me where you are,
Mikhail.

As to myself, I am, between my confounded
health and the will of the people, like an out-of-tune musical instrument in the hands of a giant who plays on it
strange melodies devoid of harmony. God help me, Mikhail,
with those Americans! May God take both of us away
from them to the placid valleys of Lebanon.

I have just mailed to Abdul-Masseh a short
article for publication. Examine it, brother, and if it is
not fit for publishing, tell Abdul-Masseh to keep it for
me in an obscure corner until I return.

This article was written between midnight and
dawn, and I do not know whether it is good or not. But
the basic idea in it is not strange to the subject matter
we discuss during our evening gathering. Tell me, how is
Nasseeb and where is he? Each time I think of you and
him, I feel peaceful, calm and enchantingly tranquil, and
I say to myself, "Nothing is vanity under the sun."

A thousand greetings and salaams to our brethren in the spirit of truth. May God protect you and watch over you, and keep you a dear brother to your brother

GIBRAN

When Gibran published his Arabic book *The Tempest* in 1920, Naimy came out with an article praising the author and the outstanding works included in the volume.

TO MIKHAIL NAIMY

Boston, 1920

Brother Mikhail:

I have just read your article on *The Tempest*. What shall I say to you, Mikhail?

You have put between your eyes and the pages of my book a magnifying glass which made them appear greater than they really are. This made me feel ashamed of myself. You have placed, through your article, a great responsibility upon me. Will I ever be able to live up to it? Will I be able to vindicate the basic thought in the vision you have revealed of me? It seems to me that you wrote that wonderful article while looking upon my future, and not upon my past. For my past has consisted only of threads, not woven. It has also been stones of various sizes and shapes, but not a structure. I could see you looking upon me with the eye of hope, not of criticism, which

678

makes me regret much of my past and at the same time dream about my future with a new enthusiasm in my heart. If that was what you wanted to do for me, you have succeeded, Mikhail.

I liked the stationery for Arrabitah very much, but the motto "To God many a treasure beneath the throne, etc." should be more obvious. The printing of the names of the officers and members is necessary if we wish to create the desired result. Everyone looking at a missive from Arrabitah would wonder who the members of Arrabitah are. However, I prefer that the names be printed in the smallest Arabic type.

I am sorry, Mikhail, that I shall not return to New York before the middle of next week, for I am tied up with some important problems in this abominable city. What shall I do? You all go to Milford, and replenish your cups with the wine of the spirit and the wine of the grapes, but do not forget your loving brother who is longing to see you

GIBRAN

In the following letter Gibran speaks of the meeting he and other members of Arrabitah had at the home of Rasheed Ayoub. Plans had been made at the meeting for the publication of the *Anthology of Arrabitah*, an Arabic book containing a history of the literary organization as well as a collection of stories, articles, and poems written by its members.

Gibran refers to *Barren* and *Memoirs of a Pitted Face*. These were manuscripts of Mikhail Naimy, who

had asked Gibran to inquire of Nasseeb Aribda as to their whereabouts.

The word *inshallah* means "God willing."

TO MIKHAIL NAIMY

New York,
October 8, 1920

Dear Mikhail:

Each time I think of you traveling as a salesman in the interior for a business firm, I feel somehow hurt. Yet I know that this pain is the residue of an old philosophy. Today I believe in Life and in all that she brings upon us, and I confirm that all that the days and nights bring is good, and beautiful and useful.

We met last night at Rasheed's home, and we drank and ate and listened to songs and poetry. But our evening was not complete because you were not with us in person.

The materials for the *Anthology of Arrabitah* are all ready, if only in spirit! And they are all arranged, but only in words. When I ask for something from any of our brethren, he answers me saying, "In two days" or "At the end of this week," or "Next week." The philosophy of postponement, which is oriental, almost chokes me. And the strange thing about it, Meesha, is that some people consider coquettishness as a sign of intelligence!

I have asked Nasseeb through Abdul-Masseh to look for *Barren* and *Memoirs of a Pitted Face,* and he promised to do so, *inshallah.*

I was glad to hear that your absence will not be

prolonged. Perhaps I should not be glad. Come back to us, Meesha, when you want, and you shall find us as you want us to be.

May God watch over you and keep you for your brother

GIBRAN

◡◡ TO MIKHAIL NAIMY ◡◡

Boston,
May 24, 1920

Dear Mikhail:

May God shower your good soul and big heart with peace. Arrabitah shall hold its official meeting to-morrow (Wednesday) evening. Unfortunately I shall be far away from you. Had it not been for a lecture I am going to give Thursday night, I would return to New York for the sake of Arrabitah's love. If you consider the lecture a legal excuse, I will be grateful for your generosity and consideration; otherwise you will find me willing to pay the fine of five dollars with pleasure.

This city was called in the past the city of science and art, but today it is the city of traditions. The souls of its inhabitants are petrified; even their thoughts are old and worn-out. The strange thing about this city, Mikhail, is that the petrified is always proud and boastful, and the worn-out and old holds its chin high. Many a time I have sat and conversed with Harvard professors in

681

whose presence I felt as if I were talking to a sheik from Al-Azhar.*

On several occasions I have talked with Bostonian ladies and heard them say things which I used to hear from the ignorant and simple old ladies in Syria. Life is all the same, Mikhail; it declares itself in the villages of Lebanon as in Boston, New York, and San Francisco.

Remember me with best wishes to my brethren and fellow workers in Arrabitah. May God keep you as a dear brother to

GIBRAN

In many places throughout his writings Gibran refers to his studio in New York as "the hermitage." In this letter he speaks of his meeting there with Nasseeb Arida and Abdul-Masseh.

⤷ TO MIKHAIL NAIMY ⤶

New York, 1920

My Dear Meesha:

Good morning to you, oh wondering soul between the intent of the earth and the claim of heaven. I heard your voice calling the people's attention to "your goods" in the markets and squares. I heard you shouting softly, "We sell denims, we sell muslins," and I loved the soothing tone of your voice, Meesha, and I know that the angels hear you and record your calls in the Eternal Book.

---

* According to historians, Al-Azhar is the oldest university in the world whose sheiks (professors) stick to old traditions.

I was happy to hear about your great success. However, I fear this success! I am afraid it is going to lead you into the heart of the business world. He who reaches that heart will find it very difficult to return to our world!

I shall meet with Nasseeb and Abdul-Masseeh at the hermitage tonight and we shall discuss the *Anthology*. Wish you were with us.

I am in these days a man with a thousand and one things to do. I am like a sick bee in a garden of flowers. The nectar is ample and the sun is beautiful upon the flowers.

Pray for me and receive God's blessing, and remain a dear brother to

GIBRAN

TO MIKHAIL NAIMY

New York, 1920

Dear Meesha:

We have already missed you, though you have barely said goodby. What would happen to us if you stayed away three weeks?

The *Anthology*: What of it? It is a chain whose rings are made of postponement and hesitation. Every time I mention it to Nasseeb or Abdul-Masseeh, the first will say to me, "Tomorrow," and the second will respond "You are right." But in spite of all these delays, the *Anthology* will appear at the end of the year, *Inshallah*.

Write to me when you have nothing better to

683

do. If your new poem has already been completed, send me a copy of it. You have not given me a copy of your poem "Oh, Cup-Bearer." May God forgive you. Be as you wish and remain a dear brother to your brother

GIBRAN

TO MAY ZIADEH

Nov. 1, 1920

Dear May:

The soul, May, does not see anything in life save that which is in the soul itself. It does not believe except in its own private event, and when it experiences something, the outcome becomes a part of it. I experienced something last year that I intended to keep a secret, but I did not do so. In fact, I revealed it to a friend of mine to whom I was accustomed to reveal my secrets because I felt that I was in dire need of talking to someone. But do you know what she told me? She said to me without thinking, "This is a musical song." Suppose someone had told a mother holding her babe in her arms that she was carrying a wooden statue, what would be the answer, and how would that mother feel about it?

Many months had passed and the words ("a musical song") were still ringing in my ears, but my friend was not satisfied with what she had told me, but kept on watching me and reprimanding me for every word I uttered, hiding everything away from me and piercing my hand with a nail every time I attempted to touch her.

684

Consequently I became desperate, but despair, May, is an ebb for every flow in the heart; it's a mute affection. For this reason I have been sitting before you recently and gazing at your face without uttering a word or without having a chance to write you, for I said in my heart, "I have no chance."

Yet in every winter's heart there is a quivering spring, and behind the veil of each night there is a smiling dawn. Now my despair has turned into hope.

GIBRAN

May asked Gibran once how he wrote and how he ate and how he spent his everyday life, etc. She also inquired about his home and office and everything he did. Gibran answered some of her questions in the letter which follows.

TO MAY ZIADEH

1920

. . . How sweet are your questions, and how happy I am to answer them, May. Today is a day of smoking; since this morning I have already burned one million cigarettes. Smoking to me is a pleasure and not a habit. Sometimes I go for one week without smoking one single cigarette. I said that I burned one million cigarettes. It is all your fault and you are to blame. If I were by myself in this valley, I would never return . . .

As to the suit I am wearing today, it is cus-

tomary to wear two suits at the same time; one suit woven by the weaver and made by the tailor and another one made out of flesh, blood, and bones. But today I am wearing one long and wide garment spotted with ink of different colors. This garment does not differ much from the ones worn by the dervishes save that it is cleaner. When I go back to the Orient I shall not wear anything but old-fashioned Oriental clothes.

. . . As regards my office, it is still without ceiling and without walls, but the seas of sands and the seas of ether are still like they were yesterday, deep with many waves and no shores. But the boat in which I sail these seas has no masts. Do you think you can provide masts for my boat?

The book *Towards God* is still in the mist factory, and its best drawing is in *The Forerunner* of which I sent you a copy two weeks ago.

> After answering some of her questions he began to describe himself to her symbolically.

What shall I tell you about a man whom God has arrested between two women, one of whom turns his dream into awakeness, and the other his awakeness into dream? What shall I say of a man whom God has placed between two lamps? Is he melancholy or is he happy? Is he a stranger in this world? I do not know. But I would like to ask you if you wish for this man to remain a stranger whose language no one in the universe speaks. I do not know. But I ask you if you would like to talk to this man in the tongue he speaks, which you can understand better than anyone else. In this world there are

many who do not understand the language of my soul. And in this world there are also many who do not understand the language of your soul. I am, May, one of those upon whom life bestowed many friends and well-wishers. But tell me: is there any one among those sincere friends to whom we can say, "Please carry our cross for us only one day"? Is there any person who knows that there is one song behind our songs that cannot be sung by voices or uttered by quivering strings? Is there anyone who sees joy in our sorrow and sorrow in our joy?

... Do you recall, May, your telling me about a journalist in Buenos Aires who wrote and asked for what every newspaperman asks for—your picture? I have thought of this newspaperman's request many times, and each time I said to myself, "I am not a journalist; therefore I shall not ask for what the newspaperman asks for. No I am not a journalist. If I were the owner or editor of a magazine or newspaper, I would frankly and simply and without abashment ask her for her picture. No, I am not a journalist; what shall I do?"

GIBRAN

As-Sayeh was the name of an Arabic newspaper owned and edited by Abdul-Masseeh who was a member of Arrabitah, the literary circle. In that year Abdul-Masseeh was preparing a special issue of As-Sayeh and he called on Gibran and all the members of Arrabitah to contribute, which they did.

In that same year Gibran must have written an article under the caption of "The Lost One" and sent it to his friend Emil Zaidan to have it published in

his magazine, *Al-Hilal*, in Egypt. The translator of these letters has not yet succeeded in finding the article which Gibran speaks of in this letter. Gibran also refers to Salloum Mokarzel. He was at that time the owner of a publishing house in New York where he published his English magazine, *The Syrian World*.

TO MIKHAIL NAIMY

Boston,
Jan. 1, 1921

Dear Meesha:

Good morning, and a happy New Year. May the Lord burden your vines with bunches of grapes, and fill your bins with wheat, and replenish your jars with oil, honey, and wine; and may Providence place your hand upon the heart of Life in order to feel the pulse of Life's heart.

This is my first letter to you in the New Year. Were I in New York, I would ask you to spend the evening with me in the peaceful hermitage. But how far am I from New York, and how far is the hermitage from me!

How are you, and what are you writing or composing, and what are you thinking? Is the special issue of *As-Sayeh* about to come out, or is it still waiting for those machines which run fast when we wish them to slow down, and slow down when we wish them to run fast? The West is a machine and everything in it is at the mercy of the machine. Yes, Meesha, even your poem, "Do the Brambles Know," is at the mercy of Salloum Mokarzel's wheels. I was indisposed last week, and for this reason I

688

did not write anything new. But I have reviewed my article, "The Lost One," smoothed it out, and mailed it to *Al-Hilal.*

Remember me, Meesha, with love and affection to our comrades, and may God protect you as a dear brother to

GIBRAN

 TO MIKHAIL NAIMY

Boston, 1921

Brother Meesha:

After I read the last number of the Arrabitah's magazine and reviewed the previous issues, I was convinced that there is a deep abyss between us and them. We cannot go to them nor can they come to us. No matter what we endeavor to do, Mikhail, we cannot free them from the slavery of superficial literary words. Spiritual freedom comes from within and not from without. You know more about this truth than any man.

Do not endeavor to awaken those whose hearts God has put to sleep for some hidden wisdom. Do whatever you wish for them, and send them whatever you like, but do not forget that you shall place a veil of doubt and suspicion upon the face of our Arrabitah. If we have any power, this power exists in our unity and aloneness. If we must cooperate and work with other people, let our cooperation be with our equals who say what we say.

. . . So you are on the brink of madness. This is

a good bit of news, majestic in its fearfulness, fearful in its majesty and beauty. I say that madness is the first step towards unselfishness. Be mad, Meesha. Be mad and tell us what is behind the veil of "sanity." The purpose of life is to bring us closer to those secrets, and madness is the only means. Be mad, and remain a mad brother to your mad brother

GIBRAN

TO MIKHAIL NAIMY

Boston, 1921

Dear Meesha:

Here is a gentle missive from Emil Zaidan. Read it thoroughly and take care of it to the best of your knowledge as you have always done. The heat is killing in this city and its environs. How is it in New York, and what are you doing?

In my heart, Meesha, there are shadows and images that sway, walk, and expand like mist, but I am unable to give them the form of words. Peradventure it would be better for me to keep silent until this heart returns to what it used to be a year ago. Possibly silence is better for me, but, alas! How difficult and how bitter is silence in the heart of one who has become accustomed to talking and singing.

A thousand salaams to you and to our dear brothers. May you remain a dear brother to

GIBRAN

In this letter Gibran speaks of *Al-Barq* (The Lightning), which was one of the leading Arabic news-
papers in Beirut. Beshara El-Koury, the editor and
owner of *Al-Barq,* was a great admirer of Gibran,
and he devoted many columns in his paper to him.
Gibran also threatens his friend Naimy, saying that
if he (Naimy) did not mail him the snapshots which
they had taken at Cahoonzie he would file two suits
against him: one in the court of friendship and the
other in the court of El-Jazzar, a Turkish ruler
known for his despotism during his reign in Syria.

TO MIKHAIL NAIMY

Boston, 1921

Dear Mikhail:

Peace be unto you. Enclosing herewith a letter
addressed to the counsellor of Arrabitah from Beshara
El-Khoury editor of *Al-Barq.* As you notice, it is a brief
and gentle missive, and it demonstrates at the same time
a sort of pain in the soul of its author—and pain is a
good sign.

What happened to the snapshots we took at
Cahoonzie? You are hereby notified that I want a copy
of each. If I do not obtain my rights, I shall file two suits
against you—one with the court of friendship, the other
with the court of Ahmad Pasha El-Jazzar.

Remember me, Meesha, to our brethren and comrades, and may God keep you dear to your brother

GIBRAN

William Catzeflis has already been identified as one of Gibran's intimates and an essayist of recognized accomplishments in the field of Arabic thought and literature. He also was one of the members of Arrabitah.

The farewell party which Gibran refers to in this letter was given in Catzeflis' honor on the occasion of the latter's departure to Lebanon on a pleasure trip. He also refers to a special Arabic dish prepared by Nasseeb Arida consisting of meat, vegetables and spices.

TO MIKHAIL NAIMY

Boston, 1921

Dear Meesha:

A thousand salaams to your heart that neither beats, nor pities, nor palpitates, nor glitters. It seems that you are ridiculing me for that which has turned my hair white and my poetry black; and you blame me for my briefness in writing and my silence about myself; and you proceed gradually to scold me, entering through the door of blasphemy. Allah be my rescue!

As to myself, I do not see any fault in you. You are perfect with your black hair covering your temples and the top of your head, and with the abundance of your poetry and prose. It seems as if you were born just as you wished to be born when you were in the state of embryo, and that you attained your wish while in the cradle. From God we came and to God we return!

I regret to be absent while Nasseeb's *meddeh* (spread) is being prepared. But what can I do if the *meddeh* cannot be spread from one city to another? It is a shame that some people can be filled with delicious things

while others are hungry even for the grace of God, unable to obtain even a mouthful of it.

I am glad that Nasseeb insisted on your writing the preface to the *Anthology of Arrabitah.* Undoubtedly you have written or shall write that which shall be "a necklace about the neck of the *Anthology* and a bracelet about its wrist." May you remain, oh brother of the Arabs, a gem in the crown of literature, and a glittering star in its sky.

My health is better than it was last week. But I must keep away from working, from thinking, and even from feeling for a period of three months in order to regain my full health. As you know, Meesha, to quit working is harder than to work; and he who is accustomed to work finds rest the severest punishment.

I have done my duty towards William Catzeflis and those who wish to honor him by giving him a farewell party. I sent a telegram to William and another one to Anton Semman in response to their invitation to attend the reception in New York.

May God keep you and your brethren and mine, and may you remain a dear brother to

GIBRAN

TO MIKHAIL NAIMY

Boston, 1921

My Dear Meesha:

Good morning and good evening to you, and may God fill your days with songs and your nights with

dreams. I am enclosing herewith a good letter and a check, which is still better, from an adherent member of Arra-bitah. Will you answer the first in your good taste and perfect literary style, and accept the second as a burned incense and oil offering. Hoping that you do so, *inshallah*.

You say in your letter that you have told George* to send me the Spanish magazine and newspaper, but George has not sent them yet. May God forgive George, and may He mend George's memory with the threads of my patience and self-control. It seems to me, brother, that George has thrown the *Republic of Chile* [name of a magazine] into the waste-basket.

The cold in Boston is terrible. Everything is frozen, even the thoughts of the people are frozen. But in spite of the cold and the severe wind I am enjoying good health. My voice (or yell) is like the thunder of a volcano! And the tramping of my feet upon the ground is like a falling meteor that makes a big hollow in the ground. As to my stomach, it is like a mill whose lower stone is a file and whose upper one is a rattler! Hoping that your yell, your tramping, and your stomach are just as you like them to be whenever and wherever you want.

Give my regards to our brethren mingled with my love, my prayers, and longing. May God keep you dear to your brother

GIBRAN

When the doctors ordered Gibran in 1921 to leave New York for Boston to stay with his sister Miriana and
* A clerk in the office of *As-Sayeh*.

rest at home for a while, he carried with him on his way to Boston the English manuscript of *The Prophet* which he intended to publish that same year. When he arrived in Boston he was so sick that he had to postpone the publication of *The Prophet* until 1923. In the year 1918 he had published his first work in English, *The Madman,* and in 1920 *The Forerunner.* In this letter Gibran speaks of these two books and also of *Ad-Deewan,* which must have been an Arabic magazine or newspaper.

❧ TO MIKHAIL NAIMY ❧

Boston, 1921

Brother Meesha:

Ever since I arrived in this city I have been going from one specialist to another, and from one exhaustive examination to a more exhaustive one. It all happened because this heart of mine has lost its meter and its rhyme. And you know, Mikhail, the meter of this heart never did conform to the meters and rhymes of other hearts. But since the accidental must follow the constant as the shadow follows the substance, it was definitely decided that this lump within my chest should be in unison with that trembling mist in the firmament—that mist which is myself—called "I."

Never mind, Meesha, whatever is destined shall be. But I feel that I shall not leave the slope of this mountain before daybreak. And dawn shall throw a veil of light and gleam on everything.

When I left New York I put nothing in my valise except the manuscript of *The Prophet* and some raiments. But my old copy-books are still in the corners of

that silent room. What shall I do to please you and to please the Damascus Arrabitah? The doctors have ordered me to leave all mental work. Should I be inspired within the next two weeks, I shall take my pen and jot down the inspiration; otherwise my excuse should be accepted.

I do not know when I may return to New York. The doctors say I should not return until my health returns to me. They say I must go to the country and surrender myself to simple living free from every thought and purpose and dispute. In other words, they want me to be converted into a trifling plant. For that reason I see fit that you send the picture of Arrabitah to Damascus without me in it. Or you may send the old picture after you stain my face with ink. If it is necessary, however, that Arrabitah in New York should appear in full before the Damascus Arrabitah, how would you like for Nasseeb, or Abdul-Masseeh or you (if that were possible) to translate a piece from *The Madman* or *The Forerunner*? This may seem to be a silly suggestion. But what can I do, Mikhail, when I am in such a plight? He who is unable to sew for himself a new garment must go back and mend the old one. Do you know, brother, that this ailment has caused me to postpone indefinitely the publication of *The Prophet*? I shall read with interest your article in *Ad-Deewan*. I know it is going to be just and beautiful like everything else you have written.

Remember me to my brother workers of Arrabitah. Tell them that my love for them in the fog of night is not any less than in the plain light of the day. May God protect you and watch over you and keep you a dear brother to

GIBRAN

Gibran had always expressed his desire for and love of death. Although he wished at all times to attain such a goal, he was extremely affected when a dear friend of his or someone that he knew passed away. Saba, who was an intimate of Gibran and a dear friend of Naimy, was taken away by death while Gibran was in Boston suffering the pangs of a severe ailment. As soon as he heard of the death of his good friend Saba he wrote to Naimy expressing his sentiments toward his departed friend.

He also tells his friend Naimy of his dream of a hermitage, a small garden, and a spring of water on the edge of one of the Lebanese valleys. He loathed this false civilization and wished to be left alone in a solitary place like Yousif El-Fakhri, one of the characters of a story that he wrote under the name of "The Tempest." Yousif at thirty years of age withdrew himself from society and departed to live in an isolated hermitage in the vicinity of Kadeesha Valley in North Lebanon.

TO MIKHAIL NAIMY

Boston, 1922

Dear Meesha:

Saba's death affected me immensely. I know that he has reached his goal, and that he has now fortified himself against things we complain of. I also know that he has attained what I wish at all times to attain. I know all that, yet it is strange that this knowledge cannot lighten my burden of sorrow. What could be the meaning of this sorrow? Saba had hopes he wanted to fulfill. His lot of hopes and dreams was equal to the lot of each one of us. Is there something in his departure, before his hopes

697

blossomed and his dreams became fruitful, that creates this deep sorrow in our hearts? Is not my sorrow over him truly my grief over a dream I had in my youth when that youth passed away before my dream came true? Are not sorrow and regret at bereavement really forms of human selfishness?

I must not go back to New York, Meesha. The doctor has ordered me to stay away from cities. For this reason I rented a small cottage near the sea and I shall move to it with my sister in two days. I shall remain there until this heart returns to its order, or else becomes a part of the Higher Order. However, I hope to see you before summer is over. I know not how, where, or when, but things can be arranged somehow.

Your thoughts on "repudiating" the world are exactly like mine.* For a long time I have been dreaming of a hermitage, a small garden, and a spring of water. Do you recall Yousif El-Fakhri? Do you recall his obscure thoughts and his glowing awakening? Do you remember his opinion on civilization and the civilized? I say, Meesha, that the future shall place us in a hermitage on the edge of one of the Lebanese valleys. This false civilization has tightened the strings of our spirits to the breaking point. We must leave before they break. But we must remain patient until the day of departure. We must be tolerant, Meesha.

Remember me to our brethren and tell them that I love them and long to see them, and live in thought with them.

* Naimy was living at this time in a hermitage on the edge of one of the Lebanese valleys.

May God protect you, Meesha, and watch over you, and keep you a dear brother to your brother

GIBRAN

Nasseeb has already been identified as a member of Arrabitah—poet, editor and owner of *Al-Akhlak*, (the Character) which was a monthly Arabic magazine published in New York.

 TO MIKHAIL NAIMY

New York,
1922

Dear Meesha:

Good evening to you. I now bring you the glad tidings that our Nasseeb is remaining with us, in us, and of us indefinitely, and his voyage to Argentina has now become ancient history.

Arrabitah did not meet the last Wednesday of this month for two reasons: The first is that you are away, and second is the non-existence of anything that calls for a meeting. I believe that the first reason is sufficient, and is the creator of the second one.

I was glad to hear that you are coming back Thursday. You have stayed too long away from us, Meesha. In your absence our circle turns into something nebulous, misty, without form or shape.

I was not pleased with your saying, "May Izrael take Mikhail."* In my opinion Mikhail is stronger than

* May the angel of death take Mikhail.

Izrael. The first has authority over the second, but the second has no power over the first. There are secrets in names deeper than we imagine; and their symbols are more obvious and more important than that which we think of. Mikhail has been since the beginning more powerful and more exacting than Izrael.

Till we meet again, brother. May God keep you dear to

GIBRAN

A glimpse at the following letter will reveal that Gibran was to give two readings from his books: the first from *The Madman* and *The Forerunner,* and the second from *The Prophet.* Since this letter was written in 1922 and *The Prophet* was not published until 1923, it is obvious that the second reading was from the unpublished manuscript of *The Prophet.*

The reader will also realize that the money which the Syrians and the Lebanese in Brazil had spent on the gift (the translator does not know what kind) which they sent to the President of the United States was a waste of money. In Gibran's opinion, the money should have been sent to Arrabitah for the revival of *Al-Funoon,* the short-lived Arabic magazine which Gibran founded.

TO MIKHAIL NAIMY

Boston, 1922

Dear Meesha:

Do not say that the climate of Boston so agreed with me that I surrendered myself to relaxation and forgot New York and my comrades and my work and duties in

New York. God knows that never in my life did I spend a month more full of difficulties, disasters, problems, and sorrows than the last month. I have asked myself many times if my "djinnee" or my "follower" or my "double" has turned into a devil who opposes me and shuts doors in my face and places obstacles in my way. Since my arrival in this crooked city I have been living in a hell of worldly enigmas. Had it not been for my sister, I would have left everything and returned to my hermitage, dusting the dirt of the world off my feet.

When I received your telegram this morning I felt as if I were awakened from a terrible dream. I remembered the joyful hours we spent together talking about things spiritual and artistic. I forgot that I was in a battle and that my troops were in a critical situation. Then I remembered my past troubles and the coming ones and recalled that I was obliged to remain here to fulfill my promise and carry out my engagements. I am committed, Mikhail, to giving two readings from my books this coming week—the first from *The Madman* and *The Forerunner*, and the second one from *The Prophet*, before a "respectable" audience who likes this kind of thinking and this style of expression. But the things that have kept me in this city, and that will oblige me to remain here ten more days, have nothing to do with what I have written or read, or shall write or read. They have to do with dull and wearisome things, filling the heart with thorns and gall and grasping the soul with an iron hand as rough as a steel file.

I have not forgotten that next Wednesday is the date set for Arrabitah's meeting, but what shall I do when "the eye is far of view and the hand is short of reach?" I hope that you will meet and decide what is use-

ful, and that you will remember me with a kind word, for I am these days in dire need of good wishes from friends, and prayers from the devout. I am in need of a sweet glance from a sincere eye.

The gift from our brethren in Brazil will reach the White House, and the President of the United States will thank them for their generosity and kind intentions. All that shall be arranged in a beautiful manner. But a wave from the sea of oblivion shall submerge the matter from beginning to end. Meanwhile, *Al-Funoon* magazine is still asleep and Arrabitah is poor, and our brethren in Brazil and the United States neither remember the first, nor feel the presence of the second. How strange people are, Meesha, and what strangers we both are among them!

GIBRAN

Emil Zaidan was editor of *Al-Hilal,* an outstanding Arabic magazine published in Egypt, to which Gibran contributed many articles.

 TO EMIL ZAIDAN

In the late
part of 1922

My Brother Emil,

... I have intended to visit Egypt and Lebanon this year, but the indisposition which kept me away from work for twelve months has set me back two years and caused me to postpone those literary and technical treatises

which I once talked to you about. I must now remain in this country until my English book *The Prophet* comes out. At the same time I will be finishing some paintings that I promised to complete.

I am already longing for the Orient in spite of what some friends write to me, which sometimes makes me feel discouraged and causes me to prefer expatriation and living among strangers to the exile of living among relatives. Nevertheless, I shall return to my "old home" to see with my own eyes what has become of it.

Remain a dear brother to

GIBRAN

In introducing Mikhail Naimy, the translator referred to *The Cribble*, a series of critical essays, called *Algourbal* in Arabic.

Naimy and Nasseeb had written a poem together and promised to send it to Gibran. At the same time they must have asked Rasheed and Gibran to write something for publication. Rasheed, however, kept postponing, which made Gibran feel empty-handed also.

TO MIKHAIL NAIMY

Boston,
August 11, 1923

Dear Brother Meesha:

Good morning to you. I was glad to learn that your book *The Cribble* is out. But I do not mind telling you that I did not like for it to come at this time of the

year, although I know that the value of the book, which is unique of its kind, has nothing to do with the season or decade. Never mind, whatever is published is published.

I have spent many long hours with Archmandrite Beshir reviewing the translation of *The Madman* and *The Forerunner*. In spite of my rebellion, I was pleased with the man's enthusiasm and determination. When we finished reviewing and correcting he said to me, "I shall submit the translations of the two books to Mikhail Naimy and Nasseeb Arida and ask them to be unmerciful in their criticism." I liked his tact and I knew that he was truly seeking enlightenment.

I have not done anything worth mentioning since I left New York other than writing down some headings and renovating some old ideas. It seems to me, Meesha, that the orderly life in my sister's home pulls me away from creative writing. It is strange that chaotic living is the best sharpener for my imagination.

I shall be happy to receive your and Nasseeb's new poem, but I shall stand ashamed and empty-handed before both of you. I may not be the only one if Rasheed keeps on postponing. If he keeps this up, I do not know how he is going to have his book of poems published.

Give my salaam and love to our comrades and tell them that life without them is miserable. May God bless you, Meesha, and keep you a dear brother to your brother

GIBRAN

TO MIKHAIL NAIMY

Boston, 1923

Beloved Brother Meesha:

Forgive my long silence and help me obtain forgiveness from your brethren and mine. Early this summer the doctor told me to abstain from all kinds of writing, and I submitted to him after a great struggle between me and my will and the will of my sister and some friends. The result turned out to be good, for I am now closer to being in normal health than at any time during the last two years. My being away from the city, living a simple, quiet, and orderly life near the sea and the woods, has stilled the palpitations of my heart and altered my trembling hand to one that writes these lines.

I shall return to New York in two or three weeks and present myself to my brethren. If they take me into their midst, I shall know how affectionate they are. A beggar should not be demanding, and a criminal should make no conditions.

This is the first letter I have written to you for three months!

A thousand salaams to all, and may God protect you and keep you for your brother

GIBRAN

⟣ TO MIKHAIL NAIMY ⟢

Boston, 1923

I congratulate you and offer my felicitations upon *The Cribble*. Undoubtedly it is the first living breeze of that divine tempest which shall weed out all the dead wood in our literary forests. I have read the book thoroughly, from Aleph to Yey,* and I was reassured of a truth that I had long believed and which I once expressed to you. It is this: had you not been a poet and writer, you would not have reached your goal of critic, and you would not have succeeded in lifting the curtain to reveal the truth about poetry, poets, writing and writers. I say, Meesha, that had you not undertaken the task of poetry in your own heart, you could not have discovered the poetic experiences of others. And had you not taken a long walk in the garden of poetry, you would not have rebelled against those who walk only the dark and narrow paths of meters and rhymes. Sainte-Beuve, Ruskin and Walter Pater were artists before and after they criticised the artistic works of others and each one of them criticised through the help of the light of his own inner feelings, and not through the help of acquired taste. The spiritual light that comes from within is the source of everything beautiful and noble. This light turns criticism into a fine and magnificent art. Without this light, criticism is compulsive and boring and lacking the positive note of decisive persuasion.

Yes, Meesha, you are a poet and a thinker before everything else, and your unique power of criticism is the

* Aleph to Yey means A to Z.

outcome of your keen poetic thinking and feeling. Don't give the example of the "egg"*—I shall never accept it—for it smacks of empty controversy rather than demonstrable logic.

GIBRAN

In 1924, the Syrians apparently raised funds and built an orphanage, which Gibran calls "the noblest Syrian institution in the United States." He had planned to attend the dedication of the orphanage, but when the time came, he was ill in Boston with a stomach ailment.

TO MIKHAIL NAIMY

Boston,
Sept. 7, 1924

Dear Mikhail:

I have been locked in my room for several days and I have just left the bed to write you this letter. You know that I was indisposed when I left New York, and I have been fighting the poisoning in my stomach ever since. Had it not been for this, I would not have hesitated to go to the orphanage on the day of its dedication.

You realize, Meesha, that no matter how important and pressing my work is, it cannot keep me from absenting myself two or three days, especially when I am to take part in the dedication of the noblest Syrian insti-

* Gibran refers here to the old Arabic inquiry as to which came first—the egg or the hen.

tution in the United States. I beg you to offer my excuse to the Archbishop and to explain to him the real reason for my failure to come.

GIBRAN

Abdul-Masseh, owner and editor of *As-Sayeh,* had called on Gibran to make a special design for the annual special issue which came out in the form of a magazine rather than a paper and contained articles, poems, stories and pictures of the members of Arrabitah and other Arab writers.

☙ TO MIKHAIL NAIMY ❧

Boston, 1925

Dear Meesha:

Peace be unto your soul. As per your request, I have just mailed you the design for the cover of the special issue of *As-Sayeh.* The requests of princes are the princes of requests! I beg you to urge Abdul-Masseeh to keep the design for me after the engraver is finished with it.

I have been wondering if you have found solitude and peace in the hermitage! I was afraid that you might find it cold; and I should have told you of the electric apparatus which can warm one of its corners. Of course, warm hearts do not need outside heat.

I shall return to New York in a week, more or less, and we shall have long talks of things beneath the earth and above the clouds. May God keep you, Meesha, a beloved brother to

GIBRAN

P.S.   I shall return to New York in ten days, *inshal-lah*, and we shall have a long discussion and set the drawings for Rasheed's book and share many beautiful dreams.

Edmond Wehby translated "The Crucified" from the Arabic to French and published it in *La Syrie,* a daily French newspaper in Beirut. A copy of the translation was sent by the translator to the author accompanied by a nice letter to which Gibran wrote the following answer:

TO EDMOND WEHBY

New York,
March 12, 1925

Dear Brother:

Peace be unto you. I was very happy to receive your very kind letter. It revealed to me the abundance of your learning and the beauty of your spirit and your zeal for the arts and artists. I wish I were worthy of the praises and honor which you have accorded me in your missive, and I hope that I will be able to live up to the beautiful things you have said about me.

I have read with admiration your French translation of "The Crucified"—however, I was sorry to learn about the spiritual condition of Syrian and Lebanese youth today and their tendency towards learning foreign languages and neglecting their own tongue, which prompted your zeal to translate a piece especially written for that young generation in the language of their forefathers.

But your enthusiasm for Arrabitah and the deeds of its workers shows eagerness in your heart and willingness in your spirit for renovation, growth and enlightenment. Now in behalf of my brethren and fellow-workers of Arrabitah I offer to you thanks and gratitude.

Please accept my sincerest respect accompanied with my best wishes, and may Allah protect you and keep you.

GIBRAN

P.S. Please remember me to my great literary brother Felix Farris and give him my salaam.

TO MAY ZIADEH

1925

Dear May:

. . . What shall I say to you about my vicissitudes? A year ago I was living in peace and tranquility, but today my tranquility has turned into clamor, and my peace into strife. The people devour my days and my nights and submerge my life in their conflicts and desires. Many a time I have fled from this awful city* to a remote place to be away from the people and from the shadow of myself. The Americans are a mighty people who never give up or get tired or sleep or dream. If these people hate someone, they will kill him by negligence, and if they like or love a person, they will shower him with affection.

* New York.

He who wishes to live in New York must be a sharp sword in a sheath of honey. The sword is to repel those who are desirous of killing time, and the honey is to satisfy their hunger.

The day will come when I will be leaving for the Orient. My longing for my country almost melts my heart. Had it not been for this cage which I have woven with my own hands, I would have caught the first boat sailing towards the Orient. But what man is capable of leaving an edifice on whose construction he has spent all his life, even though that edifice is his own prison? It is difficult to get rid of it in one day . . .

. . . So you want me to smile and forgive. I have been smiling a lot since this morning, and I am now all smiles deep down in my heart. I smile as if I were born to smile. . . . But forgiveness is a horrible word which makes me stand in fear and shame. The noble soul that humbles herself to that extent is closer to the angels than to human beings. . . . I alone am to blame, and I have done wrong in my silence and despair. For this reason I ask you to forget what I have done and to forgive me.

GIBRAN

⌒ TO MAY ZIADEH ⌒

In the year 1926

Dear May:

. . . You say that I am an artist and a poet. I am neither an artist, May, nor a poet. I have spent my days

writing and painting, but I am not in accord with my days and my nights. I am a cloud, May—a cloud that mingles with objects, but never becomes united with them. I am a cloud, and in the cloud is my solitude, my loneliness, my hunger, and my thirst. But my calamity is that the cloud, which is my reality, longs to hear someone say, "You are not alone in this world but we are two together, and I know who you are."

. . . Tell me, May, is there any other person over there capable of and willing to say to me, "I am another cloud; O, cloud, let us spread ourselves over the mountains and in the valleys: let us walk between and above the trees, let us cover the high rocks, let us penetrate the heart of the human race, let us roam the unknown and the fortified distant places." Tell me, May, is there anyone who is capable of and willing to say at least one of these words?

GIBRAN

TO MAY ZIADEH

1928

Dear May:

I am indebted for all that I call "I" to women, ever since I was an infant. Women opened the windows of my eyes and the doors of my spirit. Had it not been for the woman-mother, the woman-sister, and the woman-friend, I would have been sleeping among those who seek the tranquility of the world with their snoring.

. . . I have found pleasure in being ill. This

pleasure differs with its effect from any other pleasure. I have found a sort of tranquility that makes me love illness. The sick man is safe from people's strife, demands, dates and appointments, excess of talking, and ringing of telephones . . . I have found another kind of enjoyment through illness which is more important and unmeasurable. I have found that I am closer to abstract things in my sickness than in health. When I lay my head upon the pillow and close my eyes and lose myself to the world, I find myself flying like a bird over serene valleys and forests, wrapped in a gentle veil. I see myself close to those whom my heart has loved, calling and talking to them, but without anger and with the same feelings they feel and the same thoughts they think. They lay their hands now and then upon my forehead to bless me.

. . . I wish I were sick in Egypt or in my country so I might be close to the ones I love.* Do you know, May, that every morning and every evening I find myself in a home in Cairo with you sitting before me reading the last article I wrote or the one you wrote which has not yet been published.

. . . Do you realize, May, that whenever I think of the Departure which the people call Death, I find pleasure in such thinking and great longing for such departure. But then I return to myself and remember that there is one word I must say before I depart. I become perplexed between my disability and my obligation and I give up hope. No, I have not said my word yet, and nothing but smoke has come out from this light. This is what makes me feel that cessation of work is more bitter than gall. I say this to you, May, and I don't say it to anyone else: If

* At the writing of this letter May was living in Cairo, Egypt.

I don't depart before I spell and pronounce my word, I will return to say the word which is now hanging like a cloud in the sky of my heart.

. . . Does this sound strange to you? The strangest things are the closest to the real truth. In the will of man there is a power of longing which turns the mist in ourselves into sun.

GIBRAN

This letter was written in the year 1928 when Gibran's book, *Jesus the Son of Man,* was published by Alfred A. Knopf. In this book Gibran speaks of Jesus in behalf of seventy-nine persons who saw him. The last man who speaks of Jesus in the book is a man from Lebanon who lives in the twentieth century.

As we notice in the following letter, Gibran wrote this book while he was ill.

TO MIKHAIL NAIMY

Boston, 1928

Dear Meesha:

Peace be unto your soul. How nice of you and typical of your big heart to inquire about my health. I was inflicted with a disease called summer rheumatism which departed from me with the departure of the summer and its heat.

I have learned that you returned to New Babylon* three weeks ago. Tell us, O Spring of Youth, what kind of treasures have you brought back with you as a

* New York.

result of your bodily and spiritual absence? I shall return to New York in a week, and I shall search your pockets to find out what you have brought with you.

The book of *Jesus* has taken all my summer, with me ill one day and well another. And I might as well tell you that my heart is still in it in spite of the fact that it has already been published and has flown away from this cage.

GIBRAN

The Garden of the Prophet, which Gibran speaks of in this letter, was published by Alfred A. Knopf in the year 1933, two years after Gibran's death. Gibran did not live to complete it. The book was later finished by Barbara Young, the author of *This Man from Lebanon,* a study of Kahlil Gibran.

TO MIKHAIL NAIMY

Boston,
March, 1929

Dear Meesha:

How sweet and how tender of you to ask about my health. I am at present in an "acceptable" state, Meesha. The pains of rheumatism are gone, and the swelling has turned to something opposite. But the ailment has settled in a place deeper than muscles and bones. I have always wondered if I was in a state of health or illness.

It is a plight, Meesha, to be always between health and illness. It is one of the seasons of my life; and

in your life and my life there are winter and spring, and you and I cannot know truly which one is preferable to the other. When we meet again I shall tell you what happened to me, and then you shall know why I once cried out to you, saying, "You have your Lebanon, and I have mine."

There is nothing like lemon among all the fruits, and I take lemon every day. . . . I leave the rest to God!

I have told you in a previous letter that the doctors warned me against working. Yet there is nothing I can do but work, at least with my mind, or at least for spite . . . What do you think of a book composed of four stories on the lives of Michelangelo, Shakespeare, Spinoza and Beethoven? What would you say if I showed their achievements to be the unavoidable outcome of pain, ambition, "expatriation" and hope moving in the human heart? What is your opinion of a book of this kind?

So much for that. But as to the writing of *The Garden of the Prophet*, it is definitely decided, but I find it wise to get away from the publishers at present.

My salaams to our beloved brethren. May God keep you a brother to

GIBRAN

TO MIKHAIL NAIMY

Telegram dated
March 26, 1929

Dear Meesha:

I was deeply touched by your telegram. I am better. The return of health will be slow. That is worse

than illness. All will be well with me gradually. My love to you and to all our comrades.

GIBRAN

TO MIKHAIL NAIMY

Boston,
May 22, 1929

Brother Meesha:

I feel better today than when I left New York. How great is my need for relaxation far away from the clamorous society and its problems. I shall rest and be away, but I would remain close to you and to my brethren in spirit and love. Do not forget me; keep in touch with me.

A thousand salaams to you, and Abdul-Masseeh, and to Rasheed and William and Nasseeb and to each one connected with us in Arrabitah.*

May heaven protect you and bless you, brother.

GIBRAN

TO MAY ZIADEH

1930

Dear May:

... I have many things to discuss with you concerning the transparent element and other elements. But

* Arrabitah means "bond" in Arabic, and since this is a literary society, the meaning here is "pen bond."

717

I must remain silent and say nothing about them until the cloud is dispersed and the doors of the ages are opened, whereupon the Angel of God will say to me: "Speak, for the days of silence are gone; walk, for you have tarried too long in the shadow of bewilderment." I wonder when will the doors open so that the cloud may be dispersed!

. . . We have already reached the summit, and the plains and the valleys and the forests have appeared before us. Let us rest, May, and talk a while. We cannot remain here long, for I see a higher peak from a distance, and we must reach it before sunset. We have already crossed the mountain road in confusion, and I confess to you that I was in a hurry and not always wise. But isn't there something in life which the hands of wisdom cannot reach? Isn't there something which petrifies wisdom? Waiting is the hoofs of time, May, and I am always awaiting that which is unknown to me. It seems sometimes that I am expecting something to happen which has not happened yet. I am like those infirms who used to sit by the lake waiting for the coming of the angel to stir the water for them. Now the angel has already stirred the water, but who is going to drop me in it? I shall walk in that awful and bewitched place with resolution in my eyes and my feet.

G<small>IBRAN</small>

∽ TO MAY ZIADEH ∼

1930

Dear May:

     . . . My health at present is worse than it was at
the beginning of the summer. The long months which I
spent between the sea and the country have prolonged the
distance between my body and my spirit. But this strange
heart that used to quiver more than one hundred times a
minute is now slowing down and is beginning to go back
to normal after having ruined my health and affected my
well-being. Rest will benefit me in a way, but the doctor's
medicines are to my ailment as the oil to the lamp. I am
in no need for the doctors and their remedies, nor for rest
and silence. I am in dire need f⸍ one who will relieve me
by lightening my burden. I am in need of a spiritual
remedy—for a helpful hand to alleviate my congested
spirit. I am in need of a strong wind that will fell my
fruits and my leaves.

     . . . I am, May, a small volcano whose opening
has been closed. If I were able today to write something
great and beautiful, I would be completely cured. If I
could cry out, I would gain back my health. You may say
to me, "Why don't you write in order to be cured; and
why don't you cry out in order to gain back your health?"
And my answer is: I don't know. I am unable to shout,
and this is my very ailment; it's a spiritual ailment whose
symptoms have appeared in the body . . . You may ask
again, "Then what are you doing for this ailment, and
what will be the outcome, and how long are you going to

remain in this plight?" And I say to you that I shall be cured, and I shall sing my song and rest later, and I shall cry out with a loud voice that will emanate from the depth of my silence. Please, for God's sake, don't tell me, "You have sung a lot, and what you have already sung was beautiful." Don't mention to me my past deeds, for the remembrance of them makes me suffer, and their triviality turns my blood into a burning fire, and their dryness generates thirst in my heart, and their weakness keeps me up and down one thousand and one times a day. Why did I write all those articles and stories? I was born to live and to write a book—only one small book—I was born to live and suffer and to say one living and winged word, and I cannot remain silent until Life utters that word through my lips. I was unable to do this because I was a prattler. It's a shame, and I am filled with regret because I remained a chatterbox until my jabbering weakened my strength. And when I became able to utter the first letter of my word, I found myself down on my back with a stone in my mouth . . . However, my word is still in my heart, and it is a living and a winged word which I must utter in order to remove with its harmony the sins which my jabbering has created.

The torch must come forth.

GIBRAN

When Felix Farris, a prominent Lebanese writer, heard about his beloved Gibran's illness, he felt so bad that he forgot about his own illness, and wrote to

Gibran the letter which follows. Gibran's answer is next included.

FROM FELIX FARRIS

1930

. . . Gibran, my seeing you ill was more painful to me than my own illness. Come let us go to the native land of the body and enliven it there. When the tempest of pain strikes a person, the body longs for its earth and the soul for its substance.

Come, my brother, let us discard what is broken, and fly away with the unbroken to the place where silence lives. There is a longing in my heart for you like the longing for the place in which I left my heart. There in Beirut, at the harbor, my eyes shall focus upon the heart of the Holy Cedars, the paradise of my country. With you by me, Gibran, my soul would look at its eternal Cedars as if it were on the shore of the true Universe. Let us triumph and remedy our ailments. This civilization which has tired you after many years, has exausted me many months ago. Come, let us withdraw and exploit our suffering under the shade of the Cedars and the pine trees, for there we shall be closer to the earth and nearer to heaven. . . . My eyes are anxious to see the dust of the earth and all that is within it of importance in the hidden world.

Believe me, Gibran, I have not seen a blooming flower, nor have I smelled an aromatic scent, nor heard the singing of a nightingale, nor felt the passing of a frolicsome breeze since the last time my eyes saw the Orient, your home and mine.

Come, let us awaken the dormant pains—come and let the pure skies of your country hear your beautiful songs, and let your brush and pen draw from the original what you are drawing now from the prints of memory.

FELIX FARRIS

⤳ TO FELIX FARRIS ⤳

1930

My dear Felix,

... It is not strange that we are both struck by the same arrow at the same time. Pain, my brother, is an unseen and powerful hand that breaks the skin of the stone in order to extract the pulp. I am still at the mercy of the doctors and I shall remain subject to their weights and measures until my body rebels against them or my soul revolts against my body. Mutiny shall come in the form of surrender and surrender in the form of mutiny; but whether I rebel or not, I must go back to Lebanon, and I must withdraw myself from this civilization that runs on wheels. However, I deem it wise not to leave this country before I break the strings and chains that tie me down; and numerous are those strings and those chains! I wish to go back to Lebanon and remain there forever.

GIBRAN

MIRRORS
OF THE SOUL

MIRRORS OF THE SOUL
IS IT ALL POSSIBLE?

KAHLIL GIBRAN was born in the shadow of the holy Cedars of Lebanon but spent the mature years of his life within the shadows of the sky-scrapers of New York. Gibran has been described as The Mystic, The Philosopher, The Religious, The Heretic, The Serene, The Rebellious and The Ageless. Is it possible to accumulate all these contradictory characteristics in one man?

Is it possible for some to burn his books because they are "dangerous, revolutionary and poisonous to youth," while others, at the same moment, are writing: "Gibran, at times, achieves Biblical majesty of phrase. There are echoes of Jesus and echoes of the Old Testament in his words."

One of Gibran's books, *The Prophet*, alone has been on the international best-seller lists for forty years; it has sold more than a million and a half copies and has been translated into more than twenty languages.

The Prophet is Gibran's best work in English, but *The Broken Wings*, his first novel, is considered his best in Arabic. It has been on the international best-seller list longer than *The Prophet*.

Biographers of Gibran, to date, have been his personal friends and acquaintances; they have thus been unable to separate his work from his personal life. They have written only of what they had seen of the Gibran with whom they lived; they were concerned only with the frailties of his life. Biographers, until now, have not tried to explain why the Gibran family migrated to America or

to explain the effect of such a migration upon Gibran's work, upon his revolutionary thought or upon his mysticism.

Gibran revolted against law, religion and custom. He advocated a society peaceful and mystical; but the world lacks the procedures and the formulae through which man can discard his present social orders to move into a Utopia full of love and eternal happiness.

Gibran wrote in two languages: Arabic for Lebanon, Syria and the Arabic world; English for the West. His admirers have translated his Arabic works into English, his English works into Arabic. Often, however, the translations have been like transporting an automobile to a country without roads or like training a horse to travel highways and expressways. To understand and justify some of Gibran's writing, a reader must study the unusual environment which influenced the dual Gibran. For example, his biographers have stated that he was exiled from Lebanon, but they have failed to explain that the Lebanese government did not expel Gibran. It was the Turkish Sultan who feared the rebellious Gibran and the introduction of modern Western ideas and Western methods of government into the Arab world which would accelerate the rebellion which was already fermenting agains Turkish rule in the Middle East.

THE ENVIRONMENT THAT
CREATED GIBRAN

EVEN BEFORE the birth of
Gibran, many men had fled from Syria and Lebanon,
some settling in Egypt, some in America, others in
Europe. Those who were not lucky enough to escape or
to be exiled were hanged in the public squares as examples to those who might have been tempted to revolt
against the Sultan.

Turkey had conquered Syria as early as the year 1517,
over 350 years before Gibran was born (1883). However,
the mountains of Lebanon were too treacherous to be
assaulted by the Turkish army; hence, Turkey occupied
the seashore and the plains and left the mountains and
their stubborn inhabitants in control of their own government under the supervision of an agent appointed by
Turkey, providing that they paid taxes to the treasury of
the Sultans.

The French Revolution

One of the ramifications of the French Revolution in
1789, nearly a century before the birth of Gibran, was the
expulsion of the Jesuits from France. Many of these religious were accepted, as refugees, in Lebanon.

The Christians of Lebanon are predominantly Maronites, who are Catholics with extraordinary privileges,
which are traditions preserved from the early practices of
the Church. The Patriarch, the head of the church in
Lebanon, is authorized to appoint bishops, an authority

which, of course, is not granted to even Cardinals in the Roman Rite. The Maronite Church uses Syriac, or Aramaic, in its liturgy, the same language spoken by Christ. A Maronite priest may marry. Gibran's mother was the daughter of a Maronite priest, educated in Arabic and French because the Jesuits who had settled permanently in Lebanon had opened schools and taught the French language and Western history, which had not been available in Arabic since the Turks took over three hundred years earlier.

The Sultans, Beautiful Women and Taxes

Turkey was once one of the mightiest nations on earth; it controlled all of the Arab World, North Africa and a great part of Europe. Proud of its military might, Turkey granted its army one-third of the spoils of war. The Sultan, according to law, owned the Empire. In return for good service or for a favor the Sultan was able to bestow an estate upon many of his subjects. This practice recreated and revitalized the feudal system in the Empire. All this favor and practice did not induce the Arab world to become a part of the Turkish Empire; local uprisings and small rebellions continued for many years. In 1860 Youssif Bey Karam, a member on the maternal side of this writer's family and from Gibran's district, led a great revolution for the independence of Lebanon. Although lacking manpower and ammunition, he out-maneuvered and defeated the Turkish Army in several engagements. In the end, however, the revolution failed.

The Sultans, generally speaking, did not help the economy of the Empire; their agents were busy selecting and transporting beautiful girls to the palace. If the girl

did not suit the Sultan, she pleased the Wazir or a secondary officer. If she happened to displease her benefactors, her hands were tied, she was placed in a sack and thrown in the sea to drown.

Tax collectors were not regular salaried employees of the government. They would submit bids to the Sultan for the privilege of collecting the tax in a certain country or countries. The tax rate was supposed to be 10 percent of the gross income. However, through intimidation and force those agents collected more than this percentage. If a farmer happened to harvest his wheat before the arrival of the tax collectors, he was accused of having disposed of some of the wheat. If the farmer waited for the tax collector, the wheat was estimated to have a higher yield and collection was made on the higher estimate. Tax collectors often walked into barns, seizing the livestock, and into houses, taking mattresses, cooking utensils and clothing, and selling them for payment of tax. This practice made the Turkish tax rate the highest in the world, without a single benefit accruing to the taxpayer.

The Sultan, as owner of the Empire, had full control of all mineral resources, which remained buried in the ground while the citizens remained in poverty.

The Suez Canal

A French engineer, Ferdinand de Lesseps, was in love with a beautiful girl who abandoned him to marry the Emperor Napoleon III. The Empress, to save her former lover from the Emperor's wrath, induced him to leave France.

The wandering lover, de Lesseps, went to Egypt, where he obtained from the Viceroy (who ruled in behalf of the Turkish Sultan) a charter to open a canal from the

Mediterranean to the Red Sea. This was not a new idea. Canals had been opened by the Pharaohs, the Arabs, and other rulers of Egypt, but in time they had become useless, being filled by sand drifts from the desert.

After many turbulent years, amid complications and financial difficulties which brought Egypt to the verge of bankruptcy, the Suez Canal was finally ready to be opened. The wandering lover, de Lesseps, anxious to impress his former sweetheart with his magnificent work, induced the Viceroy, Khedive Ismail, to invite the royalty and the dignitaries of Europe to attend the opening of the Canal.

The Khedive, not lacking in gaiety, pomp, or imagination, ordered the building of a new palace to house the guests, and since there was not time to grow trees around the building he ordered grown trees to be moved at a tremendous expense and replanted in the gardens of the new palace. As if this were not enough, he ordered the building of an opera house in which to entertain the guests; this building is the world's oldest opera house still in continuous use.

The Khedive commissioned Verdi, the Italian operatic composer, to set an Egyptian story to Western music. The opera was *Aida*.

What has all this to do with Gibran's life?

In 1869, just fourteen years before Gibran was born, the Empress Eugénie and her Emperor husband, Napoleon III, boarded the first ship at Port Said and the Canal was formally opened. While the emperors, kings and dignitaries of Europe sat in the opera house listening to the *Aida*, the bugle was sounding the death march for all caravan routes in India, Arabia, Syria, Lebanon, Turkey and even Egypt itself.

The hundreds of thousands of people who raised and sold horses and camels, managed inns and operated

caravans, and the merchants who carried on trade between the East and Europe (and all their attendant employees) were out of business. All these routes were within the domain of the Turkish Empire.

It was the straw that broke the camel's back. Until the present day, the Arab world has not recovered from this economically fatal blow. The Sultans of Turkey faced revolutions within their own palaces and brought about their own destruction. Egypt, in bankruptcy, surrendered to the English Army which came to protect English investments in the Canal, received no revenue from the Canal, and its economy never recovered. The Middle East became, theoretically, a sinking ship, its inhabitants abandoning their homes without life preservers.

It was not the poor but the majority of the intellectuals who migrated, the intellectuals who could understand that the economic upheaval was the disastrous result of the canal. Many of them were familiar with the idea of freedom and the Western world through their Jesuit education; many anticipated the permanency of the conditions created by the opening of the canal. Others rebelled against the tax collectors and the tyranny of the Turkish rulers.

Many Syrians and Lebanese migrated into Africa and opened the interior to white European settlers. Many simply boarded ships at Beirut and ended their migration wherever the ship left them, whether it was Australia, South America, New York or Boston.

The Gibran family was among them.

THE BIRTHPLACE OF GIBRAN

MAN is neither consulted about his birth nor about his death, and he will not be consulted about his eternal abode. Man registers his complaint about his arrival by crying at birth and registers his complaint about leaving this earth by his fear of death.

Gibran registered his birth complaint on the sixth day of December, 1883, at Bcherri in the Republic of Lebanon.

The city of Bcherri perches on a small plateau at the edge of one of the cliffs of Wadi Qadisha. Today there is a paved road to Bcherri, but in Gibran's day there was only a trail which led up the mountain, past the outskirts of the city, then, almost retracing itself, descended to the entrance of the city with its compact homes, built of ivory-hued stones and with rusty, red-tiled roofs.

Before the advent of the helicopter and modern transportation, no army or invader could have entered Bcherri; it was like an unwalled fortress.

Gibran's ancestors millennia ago must have angered the gods, particularly Baal, whose thunder, storm and roaring threw up the ocean bottom and created the chain of mountains from Europe to the Red Sea in Arabia. In the museum at Beirut, there is a rock imbedded with a fish eight or ten million years old. This fish was found in the mountains, not far from Bcherri. This work of the gods left deep canyons and cliffs, the deepest of which is Wadi Qadisha, meaning holy or sacred valley. It begins by the seashore and it ends near the summit, traveling along this great valley. Gibran as well as modern tourists

could not but ponder the force that raised the strata of rocks on its side thrusting toward the sky, and created out of the ocean floor a wave-like ribbon of mountains stretching out for miles.

Barbara Young, a friend and biographer of Gibran, wrote: "To visit the Wadi Qadisha is to leave the modern world and to be plunged body and spirit into an atmosphere both ancient and timeless.

"It is a beauty of a wild and unbridled quality, and it has a mighty force that compels the mind to dwell upon the words we have for eternity."

These mountains of Lebanon for centuries were covered with cedars, mentioned in the Bible more than 103 times. They are called the "cedars of God" and "the cedar in the paradise of God." Now the cedar forest near Gibran's home is called the holy cedar. If the guardianship of this forest were awarded to the nearest large city, Bcherri would be entitled to the honor. Gibran's grandfather being a priest, the family would have had the first claim to the keys of the "cedars of God." Gibran's ancestors, the Phoenicians, celebrated their religious rites among these cedars.

The oldest recorded stories, like those of Gelgamish, Eshtar and Tamuz, took place in the forest of the cedar.[1] Gibran walked, slept and meditated in the shadow of the cedars. He read about ancient gods and the history of the cedar and how it was used in the palaces of the ancient empires of Assyria, Babylonia and in the temples of Jerusalem and in the coffins of the Pharaohs. It was cedar wood that gave the Phoenician ships extra strength, resilience and resistance to the elements.

Gibran, living in the shadows of the skyscrapers of New York, never forgot the cedars in the paradise of

1. See the chapters on Gelgamish, Eshtar and Tamuz in the author's book *One White Race*.

God, and never forgot the gods who lived and played in that paradise. It was reflected in the mirror of his soul; it was reflected in his work. In a letter to his cousin Gibran wrote: "The things which the child loves remain in the domain of the heart until old age. The most beautiful thing in life is that our souls remain hovering over the places where we once enjoyed ourselves. I am one of those who remembers those places regardless of distance or time."

In his book *Jesus the Son of Man* in the chapter "The Woman from Byblos" Gibran wrote:

> Weep with me, ye daughters of Ashtarte, and all ye
>   lovers of Tamouz.
> Bid your heart melt and rise and run blood-tears,
> For He who was made of gold and ivory is no more.
> In the dark forest the boar overcame Him,
> And the tusks of the boar pierced His flesh.
> Now He lies stained with the leaves of yesteryear,
> And no longer shall His footsteps wake the seeds
>   that sleep in the bosom of Spring.
> His voice will not come with the dawn to my
>   window,
> And I shall be forever alone.
> Weep with me, ye daughters of Ashtarte, and all ye
>   lovers of Tamouz,
> For my Beloved has escaped me;
> He who spoke as the rivers speak;
> He whose voice and time were twins;
> He whose mouth was a red pain made sweet;
> He on whose lips gall would turn to honey.
>
> Weep with me, daughters of Ashtarte, and ye lovers
>   of Tamouz.
> Weep with me around His bier as the stars weep,

And as the moon-petals fall upon His wounded
    body.
Wet with your tears the silken covers of my bed,
Where my Beloved once lay in my dream,
And was gone away in my awakening.

I charge ye, daughters of Ashtarte, and all ye lovers
    of Tamouz,
Bare your breasts and weep and comfort me,
For Jesus of Nazareth is dead.

Byblos was not one of the mightiest Phoenician cities,
but it was the greatest religious center. The Old Testament was called the Book of Byblos. The head deity of
that city was El, the father of all gods. El is the name in
the Bible often called Elohim, and in Arabic is called Elah.
The earliest alphabetical writing was discovered in Byblos. Gibran, attending school in Beirut, must have
passed through Byblos and Tripoli each time he went
home on visits. Byblos is on the seashore, north of
Beirut, and a full day's journey on horseback from
Bcherri.
  Gibran's knowledge of geography and history was not
limited to his home town or the school route. His de-
scription of places, events, customs and history of the
Middle East prove that he had visited those places.
Gibran was twelve years of age when he came to the
United States. After two years of schooling in Boston he
was back in Lebanon finishing his education. During the
summer his father took him all over Lebanon, Syria and
Palestine. After four years of studying Arabic and
French, he left for Greece, Rome, Spain and then Paris to
do more studying. After two years of study in Paris,
Gibran returned to Boston.
  Among the places Gibran visited were Nazareth, Beth-

lehem, Jerusalem, Tyre (Sidon), Tripoli, Baalbek, Damascus, Aleppo and Palmyra. These names are but small dots on the map of the world, but they must have had profound effect on the thinking, the writings and philosophy of Gibran. They are reflected in the mirrors of his soul and in every word he wrote. It is reasonable to assume that while Gibran's feet were stumbling on the stones of Nazareth, he decided to write his book *Jesus the Son of Man*.

Baalbek is one of the wonders of the world; among its strewn stones and columns a man stands in humility, bowing his head to the skill, might and devotion of its builders to their gods. Baalbek was built east of one of the highest summits of the chain of mountains confining the Mediterranean; the cedar forest is on the west side of this summit, and Gibran's humble home was a short distance from both of them.

Baalbek was the oldest and the greatest religious center of the white man; the Egyptian Pharaohs placed boats of cedar wood near their tombs to transport them, on the day of resurrection, across the Mediterranean into Baalbek. The god Baal was found in all of the holy places of the white man, from Babylonia to the Baltic Sea.[2] The greatest competition to Jehovah came from Baal and his mother, Eshtar. Baal created the rain for everything living; but he was also temperamental and in his anger created storms, lightning and earthquakes. How could Gibran remove him from the mirrors of his soul when he gazed daily at Wadi Qadisha, created by the anger of this god? Who is to say that Gibran's book *The Earth's Gods* was not conceived on the cliffs of Bcherri, or amid the ruins of Baalbek? Within this book, Baalbek was the setting for many articles dealing with religion and mystic life.

2. See chapter on Baal in the book *One White Race*.

Damascus, the oldest continuously inhabited city in the world, was the capital of the golden period of Islam. While Europe was in its dark ages, its rulers unable to sign their own names, and while numbers and science were considered the work of the devil, the Ommiad dynasty at Damascus was gathering learned men from the four corners of the empire, which stretched from Spain to India, an area greater than any empire preceding it. These men translated the works of the Persians, the Greeks and the Romans and added their own. The outcome of this labor was preserved and translated into the modern languages after the Crusades. In other words, the works of the Greeks were translated into Arabic and from Arabic into English.

Wandering in the streets and mosques of Damascus, Gibran realized the absence of pictures of the great Arab leaders. This was due to the fact that Islam prohibits the use of images. Before he reached the age of sixteen, Gibran studied the works of the Arab philosophers and poets, and to match the written characters, he etched a set of pictures depicting those men and women.

Among the cities near the birthplace of Gibran were Tyre and Sidon. They were the main Phoenician cities which carried trade and civilization to the known world; they colonized and civilized Greece; they founded the city of Rome; they colonized North Africa and developed constitutional government in Carthage (this system originated in Tripoli, which is on the road between Bcherri and Beirut). It was carried thence into Carthage, and from that great Phoenician city was copied in America and became the great document known as the United States Constitution, under which Gibran lived to write in freedom for both Arabic and English readers. This small piece of land, the birthplace of Gibran, was the birthplace of Western Civilization and constitutional

government, and Gibran was one of its blessed sons and the latest contribution to this great United States of America.

WORDS OF CAUTION

Lebanon or Syria?

GIBRAN is known as the man from Lebanon, but he wrote *My Country Syria*. This discrepancy creates a most vexing problem for anyone writing about the Middle East.

As guideposts we offer the following:

As rivers bring sediment into the sea, new areas of land are created and new cities follow the land; in that case one city is older than another. In the Middle East the bottom of the ocean rose, carrying its petrified fish to the summit of a mountain. All the land east of the Mediterranean was created at the same time; no one section of it is older than another.

Man roamed the land as a hunter in the Middle East and North Africa for hundreds of thousands, if not millions of years. During this period of hunting there were no political subdivisions and man needed no passport to migrate.[1] Europe was covered with snow until twenty-five thousand years ago. Hence it was not conducive to human habitation; a few hardy savages lived in caves until the glacier receded. Then man changed his residence from a cave to a sur, or enclosure, and became a city dweller; this sur became the name of a city on the seashore known to the West as Tyre. This city, Sur (Tyre), and its goddess Suria, which is still worshiped in

1. See the book *One White Race*.

India, gave its name to the whole area east of the Mediterranean. As Sur was Latinized into Tyre, Suria was Latinized into Syria and included the mountains of Lebanon.

Those city dwellers developed a philosophy of the existence of the soul, its immortality and resurrection, along with the premise that the soul needed help or guidance in order that it might reach paradise (heaven). This idea was adopted by St. Augustine. Those city dwellers of Sur or Tyre traveled with their philosophy to Egypt, Babylonia, North Africa and Europe; they conquered the seas, colonized and founded the great cities of Europe, including London. They were nicknamed the Phoenicians or "the believers in immortality."

In the caves men developed the idea of fighting in groups to overcome the mighty animals; in the city they fought in groups to destroy each other.

The cave dwellers grouped together to protect a cave or a spring of water; the Suri or city dwellers built a sur to protect a city and an army to protect a country. Even now every country keeps an army.

What has all this to do with the nationality of Gibran?

It affects us in this respect: wars create new boundaries, new administrations and new philosophies of government. Hence the administrative divisions of Gibran's country during the Roman period varied greatly at different times. The Roman Emperor, Hadrian, divided it into three provinces: Syria, Syria-Phoenicia and Syria-Palestine. Gibran was born in Syria-Phoenicia; Christ was born in Syria-Palestine.

One historian writing about the birth of Christ has said: "It did not appear that one born in obscurity of a Syrian provincial village would be able to give a new date to history and change the religious belief of mankind."

After the Romans came the Arabs, after the Arabs

came the Turks, after the Turks came the French and the English. None of the armies of these invaders ever assaulted the mountains because they were treacherous, impregnable and not worth the cost. These mountains were like a besieged city; the armies would occupy the plains on the east and the cities along the seashore, and after a period of time the mountaineers would come down to join each new invader, bargaining but reserving for themselves certain rights and privileges.

When the Arabs conquered that part of the world from India to Spain and converted it to Islam, the mountaineers, Gibran's ancestors, were able to preserve their Christian religion, a tiny island of Christians in an ocean of Islam.

When Turkey overran the country, it divided Syria into districts (*Wilayah*), naming for each one a governor with the title of Pasha. The people, during the Turkish rule of four hundred years, refused to be assimilated by their conquerors. Hence the country of Gibran remained its Achilles' heel, and its numerous revolutions were supported by one European country or another until 1860, when a civil war broke out. England sent her fleet and France disembarked on Lebanese soil an army of six thousand men. After the landing of these armies, a special committee composed of diplomatic representatives of France, England, Russia and Austria convened in Beirut with the First Minister of Turkey. The outcome was the conferring upon Lebanon of an internal autonomy guaranteed by these European powers. The Sultan was to appoint a Christian governor for Lebanon and the European powers were to approve the appointment. This autonomous area included neither the plains of Bekka on the east nor the cities along the seashores, nor even Beirut, which is now the capital of Lebanon.

Therefore, the people who came to America from the

eastern shores of the Mediterranean were classified as Syrian nationals regardless of whether they came from Damascus or from the mountains by the cedars.

After the First World War Turkey was ousted and France received from the League of Nations a mandate over Syria and Lebanon, while England took over Palestine. Even then, people arriving in America were listed as Syrian nationals.

During the Second World War, Lebanon and Syria overthrew the French mandate and became separate, independent countries with full representation in the United Nations.

Therefore the words in Gibran's book *My Countrymen the Syrians* include both the Syrians and the Lebanese.

Youth

"During the days of my youth I wrote enough prose and poetry to fill many volumes, but I did not, and shall not, commit the crime of having them published."

Thus wrote Gibran to a friend. However, the admirers of Gibran are publishing anything and everything they can find. As a matter of fact, his best friend did the same thing while Gibran was still alive. Gibran protested, "Don't mention to me my past deeds, for the remembrance of them makes my blood into a burning fire."

This does not mean that all the early works of Gibran were trivial or unimportant, especially when we consider that Gibran died at the age of forty-seven (December 6, 1883–April 10, 1931).

A word of caution: Keep in mind that many items now in book form were originally written in a letter to a friend or in an article to a newspaper.

Reprints

Most, if not all, of Gibran's works have been through numerous reprints. Some of these reprints fail to carry the date of the original publication or the date and source of the material, particularly the Arabic editions, whose front page carries the year of reprint.

How can future biographers determine the time and circumstances under which a newspaper article was written?

For example, the Arabic edition reads: *"Spirits Rebellious* by Gibran, 1959." The English edition, published by Heinemann, reads: "The Spirits Rebellious by Gibran, translated from Arabic; first published 1949." But the introduction explains that the stories were completed in 1908.

Barbara Young wrote that the book was written and burned in the market place in Beirut between 1901 and 1903.

Quotation Marks

There are no quotation marks in Arabic writing. However, Arabic students of English or French do use quotation marks, often haphazardly.

One Lebanese biographer wrote some paragraphs in Arabic, using quotation marks, describing them as the work of Gibran. In reality, the quotation marks were meant to signify that they were figments of the biographer's own imagination. In translation these marks were not removed. A biographer writing in English, especially one who is not familiar with the Arabic

language, accepts the quotation marks as an indication that the statements are Gibran's own sayings and beliefs.

This confusion is unfair to Gibran, unfair to future writers and unfair to the reader. Therefore these words of caution become imperative.

GIBRAN'S DUAL PERSONALITY

MAN is the product of his environment. When Gibran was born, the economic conditions of the Middle East were bad and political conditions were even worse. For many years Turkey had been involved in wars, of which she was always the loser. Thus, the boundaries of the Empire were shrinking. Meanwhile, inside Turkey, the government grew more and more tyrannical. Minority groups in all parts of the Empire were abused and persecuted. It was true that the Lebanese were exempt from military service because of the local autonomy granted them in 1860 under pressure of the European nations, but it was also true that many families were moving from the cities into the mountains to avoid the dreaded military service. Many Moslem families changed to Christianity.

The whole Arab world became honeycombed with secret societies working to throw off the Turkish yoke. The Turkish government, trusting no one, systematically discharged non-Turks from government offices and replaced them with Turkish citizens; even judges were removed from their high offices. These secret societies even dared to send delegates to an Arab conference held in Paris. Many Syrian and Lebanese men from America attended the conference and made demands for reform. Many of the leaders paid with their lives. They were hanged in public squares for others to see and take heed.

Gibran, a young man in the United States and beyond the rope of the hangman, called his countrymen to revolt. He wrote articles for Arabic publication, using the

words, "my countrymen." These articles translated into English without benefit of explanations gave the impression that Gibran was calling the people of his adopted country of America to rebellion. Hence we find in Gibran a dual personality; he wrote in Arabic calling for arms, and in English calling for contentment and peace.

The following is an example of Gibran's writing to his countrymen, published in translation without explanation:

My Countrymen

by Kahlil Gibran

What do you seek of me my countrymen?
Do you wish that I falsely promise to build
For you great palaces out of words, and temples
    roofed with dreams?
Or would you rather I destroy the work of liars
    and cowards and demolish the work of
    hypocrites and tyrants?
What would you have me do, My Countrymen?

Shall I coo like a pigeon to please you,
Or shall I roar like a lion to please myself?
I sang for you but you did not dance;
I lamented but you did not cry.
Do you wish that I sing and lament at the same time?
Your souls are hungry and the bread of knowledge
    is more plentiful than the stones of the valleys,
    but you do not eat.
Your hearts thirst, yet the springs of life pour around
    your homes like rivers, and you do not drink.
The sea has its ebb and tide, the moon its crescent

and fullness, and the year has its seasons of
summer and winter, but Justice never changes,
never falters, never perishes.
Why, then, do you attempt to distort the truth?

I have called you in the quietness of the night
to point out to you the beauty of the moon and
the dignity of the stars. You arise, frightened,
and unsheathing your swords, cry, "Where is the
enemy—to be struck down?"
At dawn, when the horsemen of the enemy arrived,
I called again, but you refused to rise. You
remained asleep, at war with the enemy in your
dreams.

I told you, "Let us climb to the summit of the mountain
where I can show you the kingdoms of the world."
You answered saying, "In the bottom of the valley
of this mountain our fathers and forefathers lived;
and in its shadows they died; and in its caves
were they buried. How shall we leave and go to
places to which they did not go?" I told you,
"Let us go to the plains and I will show you
gold mines and treasures of the earth."
You refused, saying, "In the plains lurk thieves
and robbers."

I told you, "Let us go to the seashore where the sea gives
of its bounties." You refused, saying, "The tumult
of the abyss frightens us to death."

I loved you, My Countrymen, yet my love for you
distressed me and did not benefit you.

Today I hate you, and hate is a flood that carries away the
    dead branches and washes away crumbling
    buildings.
I pitied your weakness, but my pity encouraged your
    sloth. . . .

What are your demands from me, My Countrymen?
Rather what are your demands from Life,
Although no longer do I consider you children of Life.
Your souls cringe in the palms of soothsayers and
    sorcerers, while your bodies tremble in the paws of
    the bloody tyrants, and your country lies prostrate
    under the heels of the conquerors: what do you
    expect as you stand before the face of the sun? Your
    swords are rusty; the points of your spears are
    broken; your shields are covered with mud. Why,
    then, do you stand upon the battlefield?
Hypocrisy is your religion; Pretension, your life; dust,
    your end.
Why do you live? Death is the only rest for the wretched.

Life is determination in youth, strife during manhood,
    and wisdom in maturity. But you, My Countrymen,
    were born old and feeble, your heads shrunk,
Your skin withered, and you became as children, playing
    in the mire, and throwing stones at one
    another. . . .

Humanity is a crystalline river, singing, in a rippling
    rush, and carrying the secrets of the mountains to
    the depths of the sea. But you are as a swamp with
    worms in its dregs and snakes on its banks.

The soul is a sacred, blue-burning flame, illuminating the
    faces of the gods. But your souls, My Countrymen,
    are ashes for the wind to scatter over the snows, and
    for the tempest to dispel into the deep abysses.

I hate you, My Countrymen, because you despise glory
    and greatness.

I vilify you because you vilify yourselves.

I am your enemy because you are enemies of the gods
    and you do not know it.

The day of reckoning came during the First World
War. Turkey entered the war on the side of Germany and
the troops of both countries occupied the shores east of
the Mediterranean. This action was to prevent a landing
by the Allies and, more important, it was to protect the
railroad line that carried food to Turkey and Germany,
preventing a complete blockade of Germany.

Lebanon, demanding autonomy, had finally been
given that privilege. To start with, Lebanon was not
self-sufficient. Now that it was being blockaded, it was
deprived of the importation of food. Then the locusts
came, for two solid years, to eat everything from the
smallest blade of grass to the old oaks. The inhabitants
died of starvation on the roads and sidewalks and inside
their houses. The leaders were picked up and hanged in
the public squares; if the war had lasted longer the ex-
termination would have been complete and no one
would have been left to tell the story.

Gibran, reacting to this tragedy, wrote in Arabic the
article "My People Died," part of which follows:

My People Died

by Gibran

My people died of starvation and I came here alive,
lamenting them in my loneliness. . . .

749

I am told, "The tragedy of your country is only a part of the tragedy of the world; the tears and the blood shed in your country are only drops in the river of blood and tears pouring night and day in the valleys and the plains of the world."

This may be true, but the tragedy of my people is a silent one conceived in the heads of men, whom we should call snakes and serpents. The tragedy of my people is without music and without parades.

If my people had revolted against the tyrants and died in defiance, I would have said that death for liberty was more honorable than the life of servitude.

Whoever reaches eternity with sword in his hand lives as long as there is justice.

If my countrymen had entered the World War and were destroyed in battle to the last man, I would have said it was a wild hurricane destroying the green and the dead branches; I would have said death under the force of a hurricane is better than life in the arms of old age.

If an earthquake had swallowed my people and loved ones, I would have said it is the law of Nature directed by a power beyond the comprehension of man. It is foolish to attempt to solve its mysteries.

But my people did not die in rebellion, did not die in a battle and they were not buried by an earthquake.

My people died on the cross. My people died with their arms stretched toward both East and West and their eyes seeking in the darkness of the skies.

They died in silence because the ears of humanity had become deaf to their cry.

They died but they were not criminals.

They died because they were peaceful.

The died in the land that produced milk and honey.

They died because the hellish serpent seized all their flocks and all the harvest of their fields.

After the war France took over Syria and Lebanon, through a mandate from the League of Nations, to help them organize governments and become independent within three years.

The three years dragged into six, into twelve, and it appeared as though the French were to stay in Lebanon forever.

Gibran, in reaction to this situation, wrote his article, "You Have Your Lebanon and I Have My Lebanon."

"You Have Your Lebanon and I Have My Lebanon"

by Gibran

You have your Lebanon and its dilemma. I have my Lebanon and its beauty.

Your Lebanon is an arena for men from the West and men from the East.

My Lebanon is a flock of birds fluttering in the early morning as shepherds lead their sheep into the meadow and rising in the evening as farmers return from their fields and vineyards.

You have your Lebanon and its people. I have my Lebanon and its people.

Yours are those whose souls were born in the hospitals of the West; they are as a ship without rudder or sail upon a raging sea. . . . They are strong and eloquent among themselves but weak and dumb among Europeans.

They are brave, the liberators and the reformers, but only in their own area. But they cowards, always led backward by the Europeans. They are those who croak like frogs boasting that they have rid themselves of their ancient, tyrannical enemy, but the truth of the matter is

that this tyrannical enemy still hides within their own souls. They are the slaves for whom time had exchanged rusty chains for shiny ones so that they thought themselves free. These are the children of your Lebanon. Is there anyone among them who represents the strength of the towering rocks of Lebanon, the purity of its water or the fragrance of its air? Who among them vouchsafes to say, "When I die I leave my country little better than when I was born?"

Who among them dare to say, "My life was a drop of blood in the veins of Lebanon, a tear in her eyes or a smile upon her lips?"

Those are the children of your Lebanon. They are, in your estimation, great; but insignificant in my estimation.

Let me tell you who are the children of my Lebanon.

They are farmers who would turn fallow field into garden and grove.

They are the shepherds who lead their flocks through the valleys to be fattened for your table meat and your woolens.

They are the vine-pressers who press the grape to wine and boil it to syrup.

The are the parents who tend the nurseries, the mothers who spin silken yarn.

They are the husbands who harvest the wheat and the wives who gather the sheaves.

They are the builders, the potters, the weavers and the bell-casters.

They are the poets who pour their souls in new cups.

They are those who migrate with nothing but courage in their hearts and strength in their arms but who return with wealth in their hands and a wreath of glory upon their heads.

They are the victorious wherever they go and loved and respected wherever they settle.

They are the ones born in huts but who died in palaces of learning.

These are the children of Lebanon; they are the lamps that cannot be snuffed by the wind and the salt which remains unspoiled through the ages.

They are the ones who are steadily moving toward perfection, beauty and truth.

What will remain of your Lebanon after a century? Tell me! Except bragging, lying and stupidity? Do you expect the ages to keep in its memory the traces of deceit and cheating and hypocrisy? Do you think the atmosphere will preserve in its pockets the shadows of death and the stench of graves?

Do you believe life will accept a patched garment for a dress? Verily, I say to you that an olive plant in the hills of Lebanon will outlast all of your deeds and your works; that the wooden plow pulled by the oxen in the crannies of Lebanon is nobler than your dreams and aspirations.

I say to you, while the conscience of time listened to me, that the songs of a maiden collecting herbs in the valleys of Lebanon will outlast all the uttering of the most exalted prattler among you. I say to you that you are achieving nothing. If you knew that you are accomplishing nothing, I would feel sorry for you, but you know it not.

You have Your Lebanon and I have My Lebanon.

[As Gibran bitterly assailed the politicians in Lebanon he tenderly expressed his hopes and belief in the young people of Lebanese and Syrian origin in America. The following message is often found, framed and displayed on the walls in the homes of Gibran's countrymen:]*

*Sections in brackets are editor's interpolations within Gibran's text.

I Believe in You

by Gibran

I believe in you, and I believe in your destiny.

I believe that you are contributors to this new civilization.

I believe that you have inherited from your forefathers an ancient dream, a song, a prophecy, which you can proudly lay as a gift of gratitude upon the lap of America.

I believe that you can say to the founders of this great nation, "Here I am, a youth, a young tree whose roots were plucked from the hills of Lebanon, yet I am deeply rooted here, and I would be fruitful."

And I believe that you can say to Abraham Lincoln, the blessed, "Jesus of Nazareth touched your lips when you spoke, and guided your hand when you wrote; and I shall uphold all that you have said and all that you have written."

I believe that you can say to Emerson and Whitman and James, "In my veins runs the blood of the poets and wise men of old, and it is my desire to come to you and receive, but I shall not come with empty hands."

I believe that even as your fathers came to this land to produce riches, you were born here to produce riches by intelligence, by labor.

I believe that it is in you to be good citizens.

And what is it to be a good citizen?

It is to acknowledge the other person's rights before asserting your own, but always to be conscious of your own.

It is to be free in word and deed, but it is also to know that your freedom is subject to the other person's freedom.

It is to create the useful and the beautiful with your own hands, and to admire what others have created in love and with faith.

It is to produce by labor and only by labor, and to spend less than you have produced that your children may not be dependent upon the state for support when you are no more.

It is to stand before the towers of New York and Washington, Chicago and San Francisco saying in your heart, "I am the descendant of a people that builded Damascus and Byblos, and Tyre and Sidon and Antioch, and now I am here to build with you, and with a will."

You should be proud of being an American, but you should also be proud that your fathers and mothers came from a land upon which God laid His gracious hand and raised His messengers.

Young Americans of Syrian origin, I believe in you.

[Gibran did not live long enough to enjoy the realization of his hopes and dreams. The Lebanon of Gibran succeeded finally in becoming an independent nation.

In the summer of 1964, the Lebanese Government dedicated a four-lane boulevard stretching from Beirut to the gracious International Airport, the name of the avenue being Jadat Al Mogtaribeen (Lebanese Overseas). This boulevard is the path Gibran walked to meet his first love, and it encompasses the dreams toward which Gibran prodded his beloved homeland: the graceful resorts, modern skyscrapers and luxurious hotels of Beirut and the jet-age accommodations at the airfield. Each day, the emigrants born here in poverty travel Gibran's path. "The young trees, rooted in the hills of Lebanon, transplanted to various parts of the world, return, and they are fruitful."

In my mind's eye, I see Gibran watching this new passing parade. For did he not write:

"A little while, a moment to rest upon the wind, and another woman shall bear me."]

GIBRAN'S PAINTING AND POETRY

T HE RELIGION of Islam prohibited the use of images and idols, even the image of Mohammed. In the Christian countries it conquered, Islam converted many of the churches into mosques. Statues and paintings were easily removed; mosaic walls were covered with plaster. Hence the art of painting and carving vanished from the Islamic world. To enhance the appearance of new buildings, architects and decorators resorted to lines, geometrical designs and scenery.

As a young student in Lebanon, Gibran was not influenced by the art of one particular man or school of painters. Studying the work of the Arab philosophers, Gibran imagined their appearances and for the first time etched likenesses of these men appeared in books. Gibran created these at the age of seventeen. In the early days of his career as a painter, he exhibited his work in a studio in Boston. A fire destroyed the building and the entire collection of drawings and paintings. This was a great shock to a young man who needed to sell his work for a living. In later years he remarked that it was just as well that they were destroyed because he was not fully mature when he painted them. The paintings and drawings of Gibran are now scattered all over the Middle East, Europe and America.

Early in his career, Gibran wrote books, poetry and articles in Arabic. He created a new era in style, influenced by Western thought, and a revolution in the minds of the younger generation of his country. But all this did not give him a living income; therefore in his art he concentrated on portraits of famous or rich people. The

illustrations for his books consisted basically of naked bodies, shadows drawn in gray and black. Their movements and the settings were a clear attempt to relate the known to the unknown, to depict love, sorrow, and life in their relation to man and God. He used no clothes, no trees, no buildings, no churches, and nothing to identify the scene with any section of the earth or any religious denomination. What is revealed is Gibran and his own connection with the handiwork of God. Gibran's ancestors conceived of God as an ancient father with long beard and flowing clothes; this conception remained with the church which supported and financed the work of the great men of the Middle Ages. Gibran, not supported by the church, not affected by any specific style in his childhood, remained free to develop his own style.

Gibran left few poems because he learned how to write Arabic poetry before he knew how to write English. This has been the case of other Arabic writers in Gibran's circumstances. According to the rules of Arabic poetry, what we call a poem in English is considered only a rhymed phrase. In other words, if we accept the Arabic rules as standard, the English language has no poetry.

Gibran wrote most of his Arabic poetry in the early years of his life. Arab poets prided themselves in using words that could be understood only after consulting the dictionary. Gibran's Arabic poetry opened a new era and new horizons by using short and simple words.

In his later years, Gibran wrote for English readers. As we have said, according to Gibran's education, writing poetry in English would be like taking the work of Shakespeare and rewriting it in ordinary language. Hence, we find very little poetry among the voluminous work of Gibran.

In what poetry he wrote, the philosophy was the same as in his prose. The following translation gives an example of this philosophy:

During the ebb, I wrote a line upon the sand,
Committing to it all that is in my soul and mind;
I returned at the tide to read it and to ponder
   upon it,
I found naught upon the seashore but my
   ignorance.

One of Gibran's Arabic poems, "The Procession," has been translated into English by two different writers. Comparing the two works we find great variation and we feel that something is missing. If I were to attempt a translation, I could probably do no better. There remains something inherently untranslatable in the basic use of words and language. One of the translators wrote: "By reason of the nebulous, untranslatable character of the Arabic language . . . it required occasional departure from strict translation in order that Gibran's mighty message be captured intact."

A commentator who knew Arabic has said: "Arabic is a forceful language with a prolific vocabulary of pregnant words of fine shadings. Its delicate tones of warmth and color form with its melodies a symphony, the sound of which moves its listeners to tears or ecstasy."

Though we lose some of the forcefulness and melody, even a translation conveys the basic philosophy of Gibran, which reached its peak of expression in the later work, *The Prophet.*

The translator, G. Kheirallah, said of this work: "The poem represents the unconscious autobiography of Gibran: Gibran the sage, mellowed beyond his years, and Gibran the rebel, who had come to believe in the Unity and Universality of all existence and who longed for simple, impersonal freedom, merged in harmony with all things."

THE PHILOSOPHY OF GIBRAN

"**A** PHILOSOPHER is an ordinary person who thinks more deeply and obstinately than other people."

The American philosopher William James defines philosophy as "an unusually stubborn attempt to think clearly."

The word "philosophy" comes from Greek and means "love of wisdom." It is the process of observing the facts and events of life, in both the mental and the physical worlds, with intelligent analysis of their causes and effects, and especially laws that govern them, for the purpose of deducing sets of general principles and concepts, usually with some practical application of these as a final goal.

Because we live in a such a complex and distracting world, few of us see the effect of the principles of the great philosophers upon our lives, our relations with each other and indeed upon the very concepts we take for granted. For example, even hunger is a much more sophisticated process to man today than in the past: he measures his desire for food not merely by his appetite and the accessibility of foodstuffs, but also by his ability to pay for it and his peculiar tastes. This self-control is the result, of course, of thousands of years of legal, religious and political training.

Our world is so complex that we take for granted engineering processes that would dwarf any of the ancient Seven Wonders of the World; we ride railroad tracks that do not follow faithfully the curvature of the

earth, for the train would jump the tracks if they were level. We pass skyscrapers whose stress and strain are figured to the millionth of an inch, yet take for granted the fact that the Empire State Building actually sways constantly many feet. If we are religiously inclined, we take going to the church of our choice for granted; if we are non-believers, we give no second thought to the fact that we do not have to attend religious services if we do not choose. Yet the very privilege of non-belief represents the victory of philosophy; otherwise the non-churchgoer would still face the lions or the stake.

Gibran did not write treatises about philosophy, but as soon as he began his great book *The Prophet,* dealing with the question of birth and death, he placed himself within the Socratic maxim: "Know thyself."

A woman hailed him, asking, "Prophet of God . . . tell us all that has been shown you of that which is between birth and death."

As soon as Gibran wrote, "I did not love man-made laws and I abhor the traditions that our ancestors left us," he placed himself in the sphere of the theologians, illustrating particularly one of the principles of St. Augustine: "One could not doubt unless he were alive and thinking and aware that there is such a thing as truth."

Before man was able to read or write he pondered the meaning of his existence on earth. He came from where? He was going where? And why?

And as man learned to write, though in a simple and crude manner, he left for us his conception of life and death. Modern writers called this writing philosophy.

However, in these few pages, we cannot explore at length this great and vast subject, examples of which fill the shelves of libraries throughout the world. We will attempt to determine only the belief and reflections in the heart and soul of Gibran. Much of his writing reveals

that he asked himself the same perplexing questions as ancient man. He did accept the premise that there is a God, but was criticized for his definition of God.

Gibran's ancestors in Lebanon and the Middle East described God as a merciful Father and hewed His image from rock in the likeness of an old man with a long beard. This conception was expressed in the three great religions of the West: Judaism, Christianity and Islam.

Some philosophers, particularly the Arabic ones, searched for a more comprehensive definition of God.

Averröes (1126–1198), a great Arabic philosopher, wrote that a simple-minded believer would say, "God is in heaven." However, he said, "A man of trained mind, knowing that God must be represented as a physical entity in space, would say, 'God is everywhere, and not merely in Heaven.'

"But if the omnipresence of God be taken only in a physical and spatial sense, that formula, too, is likely in error.

"Accordingly, the philosopher more adequately expresses the purely spiritual nature of God when he asserts that God is nowhere but in Himself; in fact, rather than say that God is in space he might more justly say that space and matter are in God."

Gibran, educated in Lebanon, must have accepted the explanation of Averröes. In his *Garden of the Prophet*, he has one in a group of men ask, "Master, we hear much talk of God hereabout. What say you of God, and Who is He in very truth?" Gibran answered saying: "Think now, My Beloved, of a heart that contains all your hearts, a love that encompasses all your loves, a spirit that encompasses all your spirits, a voice enfolding all your voices, and a silence deeper than all your silences, and timeless.

"Seek now to perceive in your self-fullness a beauty

more enchanting than all things beautiful, a song more vast than the songs of the seas and the forest, a majesty. . . .

"It were wiser to speak less of God, Whom we cannot understand, and more of each other, whom we may understand. Yet I would have you know that we are the breath and the fragrance of God. We are God, in leaf, in flower, and oftentimes in fruit."

When it came to questions about the soul the biographers and critics of Gibran were at a loss. Some biographers said that Gibran believed in the transmigration of the soul, which is better known as the doctrine of Nirvana. Others, because Gibran assailed the activities of some religious men, accused him of being a heretic.

Therefore, to understand the philosophy of Gibran, we must discard part of what his biographers have written and consider objectively what Gibran himself wrote. He wrote many articles in Arabic about the great philosophers, among them Avicenna, Al Farid and Al Ghazali. Gibran regarded the belief of Avicenna nearest to his own. The following are Gibran's words translated from the Arabic:

"A Compendium on the Soul" by Avicenna

by Gibran

There is no poem written by the ancient poets nearer my own beliefs and my spiritual inclination than that poem of Avicenna, "A Compendium on the Soul."

In this sublime poem, the old sage embodies the greatest hopes engendered by man's aspiration and

knowledge, the deepest well of imagination created by man's thinking; and he raises those questions which are the first in man's quest and those theories which result from great thought and long meditation.

It is not strange for such a poem to come from the awareness of Avicenna, the genius of his age; but it is paradoxical for it to be the manifestation of the man who spent his life probing into the secrets of the body, into the peculiarities of physical matter. I believe he reached the mystery of the soul by studying physical matter, thus comprehending the unknown through the known. His poem, therefore, provides clear proof that knowledge is the life of the mind, and that practical experiments lead to intellectual conclusions, to spiritual feelings and to God.

The reader is bound to find, among the great writers of the West, passages which remind him of this sublime poem. For example, there are lines in Shakespeare's immortal plays similar to this one of Avicenna:

"I despised my arrival on this earth and I despise my departure; it is a tragedy."

There is a resemblance to the writing of Shelley in the following:

"I dozed, and in a revelation, I saw what it is not possible to see with open eyes."

There is in the writing of Browning this parallel thought: "It shone like lightning, but it vanished as if it had never shone."

Nonetheless, the sage preceded all these English writers by centuries, yet he embodied in a single poem ideas which have appeared in a variety of writers of many ages. This is what confirms Avicenna as the genius not only of his century but of the centuries following and makes his poem "A Compendium on the Soul" the most

sublime poem ever composed upon this most glorious subject.[1]

Al Farid

Al Farid was a devout poet. His unquenchable soul drank the divine wine of the spirit, wandering intoxicated through the exotic world where dwell the dreams of poets, lovers and mystics. Then, sobered, his soul returned to this earth to register what it saw and heard in words of beauty.

If we examine the merit of Farid's work, we find him a holy man in the temple of free thought, a prince in the great kingdom of the imagination and a general in the mighty army of mysticism. That mighty army inches steadily, nevertheless, toward the kingdom of God, conquering on its way the petty and mean things in life, ever seeking the magnificent and the majestic.

Al Farid lived in an era (1119–1220) void of creativity and original thinking. He lived among a people who parroted tradition, energetically commenting upon and explaining the great heritage of Islamic learning and philosophy.

He was a genius; a genius is a miracle. Al Farid deserted his times and shunned his milieu, seeking seclusion to write and to unite in his universal poetry the unknown with the known in life.

Al Farid did not choose his theme from daily events as

1. In the field of medicine, the books of Avicenna remained basic textbooks of the universities of Europe almost until the present day. About a hundred treatises are ascribed to him. He was great not only in his medical work, but in mathematics and astronomy, as well as philosophy. See *One White Race* by Joseph Sheban, page 241.

Al Mutanabbi[2] had done. He did not busy himself with the enigma of life as Maary[2] had done. Rather, he shut his eyes against the world in order to see beyond it, and he closed his ears against the tumult of the earth so that he could hear the eternal songs.

This, then, was Al Farid, a soul pure as the rays of the sun, a heart aflame, a mind as serene as a mountain lake, his poetry reaching beyond the dreams of those who came before and after him.

Al Ghazali

There exists between Al Ghazali and St. Augustine a spiritual unity. They represent two eras, but one idea despite the difference in the time, the religion and the society of their days. That idea is that there is a desire deep within the soul which drives man from the seen to the unseen, to philosophy and to the divine.

Al Ghazali gave up a life of ease and a high position to follow a life of asceticism and mysticism.[3] He searched for those thin lines which join the end of science to the beginning of religion. He searched for that hidden chalice in which the intelligence and experience of man is blended with his aspirations and his dreams.

St. Augustine had searched for the same chalice more than five centuries earlier. Whoever reads *The Confessions*

2. Both Matanabbi and Maary are great Arab poets.

3. Al Ghazali was a professor at the college in Bagdad. He gave up his chair suddenly, left his family and devoted himself to the ascetic life. He left 69 works, one of them in thirteen volumes. Al Ghazali wandered through Damascus, Jerusalem, Hebron, Mecca, Medina and Alexandria, but returned to Tas, Arabia, where he died.

of St. Augustine finds that he used the world and its fruit as a ladder to climb to consciousness of eternal truth.

However, I have found Al Ghazali nearer the secret and the heart of the matter than St. Augustine. This could be attributed to the difference in their eras; also to Al Ghazali's inheritance of the teaching and philosophies of the Arabs and Greeks who preceded him, as well as St. Augustine's bequest. By this I mean the matters that one mind hands down to another just as customs and dress represent certain eras.

I found in Ghazali a golden chain linking those mystics of India who preceded him with the deists who followed him. There is something of Al Ghazali in Buddhism and there is some of Ghazali's thinking in Spinoza and Blake.

Al Ghazali is highly respected among learned Orientalists of the West. The religious among them consider his the greatest and noblest concepts born of Islam. Strange as it seems, I saw on the wall of the fifteenth-century church in Venice a mural including Al Ghazali among the philosophers, saints and theologians whom, in the Middle Ages, the Church considered the cornerstones and pillars of its spiritual temple.

*   *

Gibran, in his articles about Avicenna, Al Farid and Al Ghazali, left no doubt about his admiration for these great Arabic philosophers and made clear his belief in the philosophy of Avicenna: "There is no poem . . . nearer my own beliefs and my spiritual inclination than that poem of Avicenna."

Gibran followed the definition of Averröes: "Space and matter are in God." Gibran said: "We are the breath and the fragrance of God." Gibran believed in the exis-

tence of God, in the existence of the soul and its rebirth, but not according to the doctrine of Nirvana.

Those who follow the doctrine of Nirvana believe that after death the soul enters the bodies of lower animals or the bodies of other human beings; and that it passes from one body to another until it is purified. It then returns to the dwelling place of its god.

Gibran did not accept the purification process. He believed that the soul comes back to finish what the man abandoned when he left the earth.

In an article about reincarnation and Nirvana, "The poet from Baalbek," written in Arabic, Gibran stated that the soul returns to an equal status. He wrote: "And the prince inquired, saying, 'Tell us, O sage, will the gods ever restore me to this world as a prince and bring back the deceased poet to life? Will my soul become incarnated in a body of a great king's son and the soul of the poet in the body of a great poet? Will the sacred laws permit him to face eternity composing poetry about life? Will I be able to shower him with gifts?' And the sage answered the prince saying: 'Whatever the soul longs for it will attain. The sacred laws which restore the spring after the passing of the winter will reinstate you a prince and will reinstate the poet as a poet.' "

Gibran wrote in *The Prophet*:

Fare you well, people of Orphalese
This day has ended.

Forget not that I shall come back to you.
A little while, and my longing shall
 gather dust and foam for another body.
A little while, a moment of rest upon
 the wind, and another woman shall
 bear me.

Gibran wrote in the last page of *The Garden of the Prophet*:

O, Mist, my sister, my sister, Mist,
I am one with you now.
No longer am I a selt.
The walls have fallen,
And the chains have broken;
I rise to you, a mist,
And together we shall float upon the sea until
    life's second day,
When dawn shall lay you, dewdrops in
    a garden,
And me a babe upon the breast of a woman.

In the late eighteenth century, materialism gained wide hold in Europe. The economic life of society became more important than religious ethics. The theory of natural selection was held to justify might against right, whether between individuals or nations.

Nietzsche and many other writers made the "self" the center of something approaching worship. Nietzsche even proclaimed that God was dead.

John A. T. Robinson maintained that Nietzsche was not an atheist, that he was trying to free man from the God who is a tyrant, who impoverishes, enslaves and annihilates man. He was trying to get rid of the kindly old man who could be pushed into one corner while men "got on with business."

One of Gibran's biographers has claimed that Gibran became acquainted with the work of Nietzsche and was even influence by it.

Gibran demanded that his people in the Middle East should revolt against Turkish rule. But at no time did he ever deny the existence of God.

We know that Gibran believed in God and in the immortality of the soul. But did he believe that man and his soul required guidance and, if so, what kind of guidance?

It is essential that we know the traditions and auspices of Gibran's background to answer the questions raised by his works. Gibran was born to the daughter of a Maronite priest, was baptized by his grandfather in rites employing Syriac, or Aramaic, the language Christ spoke. The Maronite Church is typical of Lebanon's tradition of being not only physically but philosophically and intellectually at the crossroads of the world. The Maronite rite came to Lebanon directly from the Church of Antioch, but it is Roman Catholic, preserving its ancient language and rituals through the Patriarch of Antioch and the Middle East, but preserving also its allegiance to Rome. Maronite priests are often married, for a married man may become a priest. A man may not, however, marry after he takes the Maronite vows of the priesthood.

At the age of five, Gibran was sent to a village school under the auspices of the Maronite Church. When he was eleven, he had memorized all the Psalms. At thirteen, he entered Al Hikmat, a church college, where he remained for five years. At Al Hikmat, he studied with Father Joseph Haddad, whom Gibran described as "the only man who ever taught me anything."

In his maturity, after he had written *The Prophet*, Gibran wrote *Jesus, the Son of Man*, a book which reflects Gibran's deep knowledge of the Bible and of both Western and Eastern thought; for Gibran wrote not only of Arab philosophers but also of such men as St. Augustine, whom the West considers the Father of Latin theology. Augustine, nevertheless, was of Lebanese origin (Punic or Phoenician); he had been educated in the

Phoenician schools of Carthage and was 33 before he accepted Christianity. Augustine accepted St. Paul's belief in man's original sin, but defined evil as that evil that man does voluntarily; St. Augustine wrote that only with help and through grace could man attain salvation, a premise which is now an orthodox doctrine of the Church.

Also, even a cursory review of Gibran's works reveals that he had familiarized himself with the works of the ancient Lebanese, the high priests of Eshtar, Baal and Tamuz; he knew, too, Moses, the Prophets, the Beatitudes, and had read deeply of both Christian and Islamic theology. Gibran's thirst had taken him to the fountains of Buddha, Zoroaster, Confucius, Voltaire, Rousseau, Nietzsche, Jefferson, Emerson and even to Lincoln. Gibran recognized that our religions advocate discipline and guidance, first through ceremonial practices, and secondly through prescribed ethical conduct.

Although religious rites vary greatly, Western ethics today are still those codified by Gibran's ancestors along the eastern shore of the Mediterranean, rules which advocate prudence, temperance, courage, justice, love, mercy and self-sacrifice.

Gibran was a rebel, but only against ceremonial practice, not against the ethos of his ancestors. Barbara Young, Gibran's secretary in the latter years of his life, has written, "Organized religion had no attraction for this man." But careful reading proves that Gibran was not agnostic; his anger was against religion as it was practiced, not against the religious man.

When Gibran was growing to manhood, the Turks ruled Lebanon, and the Maronite church accepted a feudal role in order to survive within an Islamic society. Buttressing the feudal position of the church, the Christian Lebanese, the Maronites, zealously donated more

lands to the church than it could cultivate; therefore, as the church turned more and more to the practice of sharecropping, it became increasingly a feudal master and employer of its own members. As the Church's secular power grew, some of its hierarchy, its bishops and priests, used their position and the Church's power to advance and enrich friends and relatives.

Gibran grew up too near the Church not to recognize its worldliness. He lost his first love to the nephew of a rapacious bishop. Then, leaving his own land, he saw the contrast provided by liberty, tolerance and freedom in America. His rebellion against the religious, then, was not only personal, but grew from the very ethos he had first learned from the religious.

Gibran later wrote a story in Arabic called "Kahlil the Heretic," in which a novice tries to convince the monks to distribute all their possessions and to go preach among the poor. "Let us restore to the needy the vast lands of the convent and let us give back the riches we have taken from them. Let us disperse and teach the people to smile because of the bounty of heaven and to rejoice in the glories of life and of freedom.

"The hardships we shall encounter among the people shall be more sanctifying and more exalting than the ease and serenity we accept in this place. The sympathy that touches a neighbor's heart is greater than virtue practiced unseen in this convent. A word of compassion for the weak, the criminal and the sinner is more magnificent than long, empty prayers droned in the temple."

The monks, of course, unable to make Kahlil obey their rules, throw him out of the monastery.

"The feudal lord proclaims from his castle that the Sultan has appointed him as overlord to the people and the priest proclaims from his altar that God has appointed him as guardian of their souls.

"The feudal lord binds the poor 'fellah's' arms while the priest filches from his pockets. Between the lord representing the law and the priest representing God, the bodies and the souls of the people of Lebanon wither and die."

In another story, also written in Arabic, "John the Madman," Gibran tells of John's reading the New Testament, which ordinary men were forbidden to read.

One day, reading and meditating, John neglected his herd, the heifers slowly wandering into the monastery's pasture. The monks kept the heifers and demanded payment for damages. Unable to pay, John's mother ransomed the herd by giving the monks her heirloom necklace in payment. Thus John became a crusader against the church, a preacher in the public square:

"Come again, O Jesus, to drive the vendors of thy faith from thy sacred temple. . . . They fill the skies with smoke from their candles and incense but leave the faithful hungry."

The monks had John arrested and refused to free him until his father testified that he was insane. Therefore no one listened to John because the public was led to believe he was a madman.

Gibran, writing a friend about "John the Madman," said, "I found that earlier writers, in attacking the tyranny of some of the clergy, attacked the practice of religion. They were wrong because religion is a belief natural to man. But using religion as an excuse for tyranny is wrong. That is why I made sure that John in my story was a powerful believer in Jesus, in his Gospel and in his teaching."

The ethics of the West are, of course, the products of religion. It is true that much of the Western world has separated the state from religion;[4] but our laws recognize

4. See *One White Race,* by Joseph Sheban.

Mosaic law in the prohibition against murder, theft and adultery and in recognition of each individual's property rights. Gibran, recognizing the traditions and ethos of religion, also urged prudence, temperance, courage, justice, love, mercy and self-negation. Nowhere, however, does he answer the question, "Is it possible to believe in God, to practice the ethics of religion and to admit salvation without the rites of religion?" He does, however, recognize the question in his short poem in Arabic, "O Soul":

O Soul

by Gibran

O Soul, if I did not covet immortality, I would never have learned the song which has been sung through all of time.

Rather, I would have been a suicide, nothing remaining of me except my ashes hidden within the tomb.

O soul! if I had not been baptized with tears and my eyes had not been mascaraed by ghosts of sickness, I would have seen life as through a veil, darkly.

O soul! life is a darkness which ends as in the sunburst of day.

The yearning of my heart tells me there is peace in the grave.

O soul! if some fool tell you the soul perishes like the body and that which dies never returns, tell him the flower perishes but the seed remains and lies before us as the secret of life everlasting.

"ASK NOT WHAT YOUR COUNTRY
CAN DO FOR YOU"

T HE FEUDAL system disappeared in both the political and religious life of Lebanon. It is now an independent state with its president and parliament elected by the people. Some of the stories and articles written by Gibran fifty years ago are a matter of history, but others are as modern as today's political situation, remaining timeless.

On the walls of many American homes hangs a plaque commemorating the statement of the late President John F. Kennedy:

Ask not what your country can do for you,
but ask what you can do for your country.

This statement appeared in an article written by Gibran in Arabic, over fifty years ago. The heading of that article can be translated either "The New Deal" or ' The New Frontier."

The article was directed to Gibran's people in the Middle East, but its philosophy and its lesson will continue as long as man lives in a free society. Hence we offer the translation of the whole article:

"The New Frontier"

by Gibran

There are in the Middle East today[1] two challenging ideas: old and new.

1. Fifty years before this translation.

The old ideas will vanish because they are weak and exhausted.

There is in the Middle East an awakening that defies slumber. This awakening will conquer because the sun is its leader and the dawn is its army.

In the fields of the Middle East, which have been a large burial ground, stand the youth of Spring calling the occupants of the sepulchers to rise and march toward the new frontiers.

When the Spring sings its hymn the dead of the winter rise, shed their shrouds and march forward.

There is on the horizon of the Middle East a new awakening; it is growing and expanding; it is reaching and engulfing all sensitive, intelligent souls; it is penetrating and gaining the sympathy of noble hearts.

The Middle East, today, has two masters. One is deciding, ordering, being obeyed; but he is at the point of death.

But the other one is silent in his conformity to law and order, calmly awaiting justice; he is a powerful giant who knows his own strength, confident in his existence and a believer in his destiny.

There are today, in the Middle East, two men: one of the past and one of the future. Which one are you? Come close; let me look at you and let me be assured by your appearance and conduct if you are one of those coming into the light or going into the darkness.

Come and tell me who and what are you.

Are you a politician asking *what your country can do for you* or a zealous one asking *what you can do for your country?*

If you are the first, then you are a parasite; if the second, then you are an oasis in a desert.

Are you a merchant utilizing the need of society for the necessities of life, for monopoly and exorbitant profit? Or a sincere, hard-working and diligent man facilitating the

exchange between the weaver and the farmer? Are you charging a reasonable profit as a middleman between supply and demand?

If you are the first, then you are a criminal whether you live in a palace or a prison. If you are the second, then you are a charitable man whether you are thanked or denounced by the people.

Are you a religious leader, weaving for your body a gown out of the ignorance of the people, fashioning a crown out of the simplicity of their hearts and pretending to hate the devil merely to live upon his income?

Or are you a devout and a pious man who sees in the piety of the individual the foundation for a progressive nation, and who can see through a profound search in the depth of his own soul a ladder to the eternal soul that directs the world?

If you are the first, then you are a heretic, a disbeliever in God even if you fast by day and pray by night.

If you are the second, then you are a violet in the garden of truth even though its fragrance is lost upon the nostrils of humanity or whether its aroma rises into that rare air where the fragrance of flowers is preserved.

Are you a newspaperman who sells his idea and his principle in the slave market, who lives on the misery of people like a buzzard which descends only upon a decaying carcass?

Or are you a teacher on the platform of the city gathering experience from life and presenting it to the people as sermons you have learned?

If you are the first, then you are a sore and an ulcer. If you are the second, then you are a balsam and a medicine.

Are you a governor who denigrates himself before those who appoint him and denigrates those whom he is to govern, who never raises a hand unless it is to reach

into pockets and who does not take a step unless it is for greed?

Or are you the faithful servant who serves only the welfare of the people?

If you are the first, then you are as a tare in the threshing floor of the nations; and if the second, then you are a blessing upon its granaries.

Are you a husband who allows for himself what he disallows for his wife, living in abandonment with the key of her prison in his boots, gorging himself with his favorite food while she sits, by herself, before an empty dish?

Or are you a companion, taking no action except hand in hand, nor doing anything unless she gives her thoughts and opinions, and sharing with her your happiness and success?

If you are the first, then you are a remnant of a tribe which, still dressing in the skins of animals, vanished long before leaving the caves; and if you are the second, then you are a leader in a nation moving in the dawn toward the light of justice and wisdom.

Are you a searching writer full of self-admiration, keeping his head in the valley of a dusty past, where the ages discarded the remnant of its clothes and useless ideas?

Or are you a clear thinker examining what is good and useful for society and spending your life in building what is useful and destroying what is harmful?

If you are the first, then you are feeble and stupid, and if you are the second, then you are bread for the hungry and water for the thirsty.

Are you a poet, who plays the tambourine at the doors of emirs, or the one who throws the flowers during weddings and who walks in processions with a sponge full of warm water in his mouth, a sponge to be pressed

by his tongue and lips as soon as he reaches the cemetery?

Or have you a gift which God has placed in your hands on which to play heavenly melodies which draw our hearts toward the beautiful in life?

If you are the first, then you are a juggler who evokes in our soul that which is contrary to what you intend.

If you are the second, then you are love in our hearts and a vision in our minds.

In the Middle East there are two processions: One procession is of old people walking with bent backs, supported with bent canes; they are out of breath though their path is downhill.

The other is a procession of young men, running as if on winged feet, and jubilant as with musical strings in their throats, surmounting obstacles as if there were magnets drawing them up the mountainside and magic enchanting their hearts.

Which are you and in which procession do you move?

Ask yourself and meditate in the still of the night; find if you are a slave of yesterday or free for the morrow.

I tell you that the children of yesteryears are walking in the funeral of the era that they created for themselves. They are pulling a rotted rope that might break soon and cause them to drop into a forgotten abyss. I say that they are living in homes with weak foundations; as the storm blows—and it is about to blow—their homes will fall upon their heads and thus become their tombs. I say that all their thoughts, their sayings, their quarrels, their compositions, their books and all their work are nothing but chains dragging them because they are too weak to pull the load.

But the children of tomorrow are the ones called by life, and they follow it with steady steps and heads high, they are the dawn of new frontiers, no smoke will veil

their eyes and no jingle of chains will drown out their voices. They are few in number, but the difference is as between a grain of wheat and a stack of hay. No one knows them but they know each other. They are like the summits, which can see and hear each other—not like caves, which cannot hear or see. They are the seed dropped by the hand of God in the field, breaking through its pod and waving its sapling leaves before the face of the sun. It shall grow into a mighty tree, its root in the heart of the earth and its branches high in the sky.

SOLITUDE AND SECLUSION

by Gibran

Life is an island in an ocean of solitude and seclusion.

Life is an island, rocks are its desires, trees its dreams, and flowers its loneliness, and it is in the middle of an ocean of solitude and seclusion.

Your life, my friend, is an island separted from all other islands and continents. Regardless of how many boats you send to other shores or how many ships arrive upon your shores, you yourself are an island separated by its own pains, secluded in its happiness and far away in its compassion and hidden in its secrets and mysteries.

I saw you, my friend, sitting upon a mound of gold, happy in your wealth and great in your riches and believing that a handful of gold is the secret chain that links the thoughts of the people with your own thoughts and links their feeling with your own.

I saw you as a great conqueror leading a conquering army toward the fortress, then destroying and capturing it.

On second glance I found beyond the wall of your treasures a heart trembling in its solitude and seclusion like the trembling of a thirsty man within a cage of gold and jewels, but without water.

I saw you, my friend, sitting on a throne of glory, surrounded by people extolling your charity, enumerating your gifts, gazing upon you as if they were in the presence of a prophet lifting their souls up into the planets and stars. I saw you looking at them, content-

ment and strength upon your face, as if you were to them as the soul is to the body.

On the second look I saw your secluded self standing beside your throne, suffering in its seclusion and quaking in its loneliness. I saw that self stretching its hands as if begging from unseen ghosts. I saw it looking above the shoulders of the people to a far horizon, empty of everything except its solitude and seclusion.

I saw you, my friend, passionately in love with a beautiful woman, filling her palms with your kisses as she looked at you with sympathy and affection in her eyes and the sweetness of motherhood on her lips; I said, secretly, that love has erased his solitude and removed his seclusion and he is now within the eternal soul which draws toward itself, with love, those who were separated by solitude and seclusion.

On the second look I saw behind your soul another lonely soul, like a fog, trying in vain to become a drop of tears in the palm of that woman.

Your life, my friend, is a residence far away from any other residence and neighbors.

Your inner soul is a home far away from other homes named after you. If this residence is dark, you cannot light it with your neighbor's lamp; if it is empty you cannot fill it with the riches of your neighbor; were it in the middle of a desert, you could not move it to a garden planted by someone else.

Your inner soul, my friend, is surrounded with solitude and seclusion. Were it not for this solitude and this seclusion you would not be you and I would not be I. If it were not for that solitude and seclusion, I would, if I heard your voice, think myself to be speaking; yet, if I saw your face, I would imagine that I were looking into a mirror.

THE SEA

by Gibran

In the still of the night
As man slumbers behind the folds,
the forest proclaims:
  "I am the power
  Brought by the sun from
  the heart of the earth."
The sea remains quiet, saying to itself,
  "I am the power."

The rock says,
  "The ages erected me as a monument
  Until the Judgment Day";
The sea remains silent saying to itself,
  "I am the monument."

The wind howls
  "I am strong,
  I separate the heavens from the earth."
The sea remains quiet, saying to itself,
  "The wind is mine."

The river says
  "I am the pure water
  That quenches the thirst of the earth";
The sea remains silent saying to itself,
  "The river is mine."

The summit says,
  "I stand high like a star

In the center of the sky."
The sea remains quiet saying to itself,
   "The summit is mine."

The brain says,
   "I am a ruler;
   The world is in those who rule";
The sea remains slumbering saying, in its sleep,
   "All is mine."

HANDFUL OF BEACH SAND

by Gibran

When you tell your trouble to your neighor you present him with a part of your heart. If he possesses a great soul, he thanks you; if he possesses a small one, he belittles you.

Progress is not merely improving the past; it is moving forward toward the future.

A hungry savage picks fruit from a tree and eats it; a hungry civilized man buys it from a man who, in turn, buys it from the man who picks it.

Art is one step from the visibly known toward the unknown.

The earth breathes, we live; it pauses in breath, we die.

Man's eye is a magnifier; it shows him the earth much larger than it is.

I abstain from the people who consider insolence, bravery and tenderness cowardice. And I abstain from those who consider chatter wisdom and silence ignorance.

They tell me: If you see a slave sleeping, do not wake him lest he be dreaming of freedom.

I tell them: If you see a slave sleeping, wake him and explain to him freedom.

Contradiction is a lower degree of intelligence.

Bravery is a volcano; the seed of wavering does not grow on its crater.

The river continues on its way to the sea, broken the wheel of the mill or not.

The greater your joy or your sorrow, the smaller the world in your eyes.

Learning nourishes the seed but it gives you no seed of its own.

I use hate as a weapon to defend myself; had I been strong, I would never have needed that kind of weapon.

There are among the people murderers who have never committed murder, thieves who have never stolen and liars who have spoken nothing but the truth.

Keep me away from the wisdom which does not cry, the philosophy which does not laugh and the greatness which does not bow before children.

O great intelligent Being! hidden and existing in and for the universe, You can hear me because You are within me and You can see me because You are all-seeing; please drop within my soul a seed of Your wisdom to grow a sapling in Your forest and to give of Your fruit. Amen!

THE SAYINGS OF THE BROOK

by Gibran

I walked in the valley as the rising dawn spoke the secret
    of eternity,
And there a brook, on its course, was singing, calling and
    saying:
Life is not only a merriment;
Life is desire and determination.
Wisdom is not in words;
Wisdom is meaning within words.
Greatness is not in exalted position;
Greatness is for he who refuses position.

A man is not noble through ancestry;
How many noblemen are descendants of murderers?

Not everyone in chains is subdued;
At times, a chain is greater than a necklace.

Paradise is not in repentance;
Paradise is in the pure heart.

Hell is not in torture;
Hell is in an empty heart.

Riches are not in money alone;
How many wanderers were the richest of all men?

Not all the poor are scorned;
The wealth of the world is in a loaf of bread and a cloak.

786

Beauty is not in the face;
Beauty is a light in the heart.

Perfection is not for the pure of soul;
There may be virtue in sin.

This is what the brook said to the tree upon its banks;
Perhaps what the brook sang was of some of the secrets
of the sea.

FOR HEAVEN'S SAKE, MY HEART!

by Gibran

For heaven's sake, my heart, keep secret your love,
   and hide the secret from those you see
   and you will have better fortune.
He who reveals secrets is considered a fool;
   silence and secrecy are much better for him
   who falls in love.
For heaven's sake, my heart, if someone asks,
"What has happened?" do not answer.
If you are asked, "Who is she?"
Say she is in love with another.
And pretend that it is of no consequence.
For heaven's sake, my love, conceal your passion;
   your sickness is also your medicine because love
   to the soul is as wine in a glass—what you
   see is liquid, what is hidden is its spirit.
For heaven's sake, my heart, conceal your troubles;
   then, should the seas roar and the skies fall,
   you will be safe.

THE ROBIN

by Gibran

O Robin, sing! for the secret of eternity
   is in song.

I wish I were as you, free from prisons and
   chains.

I wish I were as you; a soul flying over
   the valleys,
Sipping the light as wine is sipped from
   ethereal cups.

I wish I were as you, innocent, contented
   and happy,
Ignoring the future and forgetting the past.

I wish I were as you in beauty, grace and
   elegance
With the wind spreading my wings for
   adornment by the dew.

I wish I were as you, a thought floating
   above the land
Pouring out my songs between the forest
   and the sky.

O Robin, sing! and disperse my anxiety.
I listen to the voice within your voice
   that whispers in my inner ear.

THE GREAT SEA

by Gibran

Yesterday, the far and the near yesterday,
   my soul and I walked to the Great Sea to wash
   from ourselves, in its waters, the dust and dirt
   of the earth. Arriving at the shore, we searched
   for a secluded place far from the sight of others.

As we walked, we saw a man sitting upon a gray rock,
   in his hand a bag of salt from which he took one
   handful at a time and threw it into the sea.
     My soul said, "This man believes in bad omens;
     He sees nothing of life except its shadows.
     No beliver in bad omens should see our naked
       bodies.
     Let us leave; we can do no bathing here."

We left that spot and moved on to a bay.
There we saw a man standing on a white rock,
   and in his hand was a vase ornamented with precious
   stones.
From the vase he was taking cubes of sugar
   and throwing them into the sea.
     My soul said, "This man believes in good omens,
     and he expects to happen things which never
     happen.
     Beware, for neither should we let him
     see our naked selves.'

We walked on until we came to a man
   standing by the shore,

picking up dead fish and throwing them
back into the sea.
   My soul said, "This man is compassionate,
     trying to bring back life to those
     already dead. Let us keep away from him."

We continued on until we saw a man
  tracing his own shadow on the sand.
The waves rolled across his sketches and erased them,
  but he continued to retrace his work.
    My soul said, "He is a mystic, creating
      images to worship in his own imagination.
      Let us leave him alone also."

We walked on again until we saw a man
in a quiet bay skimming the foam off the waves
  and putting them into an agate jar.
    My soul said, "He is visionary like
      one who tries to weave a garment from
      spider threads. He is not worthy of
      seeing our naked bodies."

We moved ahead until suddenly we heard
  a voice calling, "This is the sea!
  This is the frightful sea!" We looked for
  the source of the voice, and we found a
  man with his back turned to the sea. In his
  hand he held a shell over his ear, listening
  to its murmur.
    My soul said, "He is a materialist,
      who closes his eyes to those things
      in the universe which he cannot understand
      and occupies himself with trifles."

My soul was saddened, and in a bitter voice said:
    "Let us leave these shores. There is no
      secluded place here for us to bathe.
      I will not comb my hair in this wind,
      nor will I open my bosom in this open space,
      nor will I undress and stand naked in this
      bright light."

My soul and I then left this great sea in search
  of a greater sea.

SEVEN REPRIMANDS

by Gibran

I reprimanded my soul seven times!

The first time: when I attempted to exalt
   myself by exploiting the weak.

The second time: when I feigned a limp
   before those who were crippled.

The third time: when, given a choice,
   I elected the easy rather than the difficult.

The fourth time: when I made a mistake
   I consoled myself with the mistakes of others.

The fifth time: when I was docile because of fear
   and then claimed to be strong in patience.

The sixth time: when I held my garments upraised
   to avoid the mud of Life.

The seventh time: when I stood in hymnal to God
   and considered the singing a virtue.

DURING A YEAR NOT REGISTERED IN HISTORY

by Gibran

. . . In that moment appeared from behind the willow trees a beautiful girl with hair that touched the ground. She stood beside the sleeping youth and touched his tender brow with her silken soft hand.

He looked at her through sleepy eyes as though awakened by the rays of the sun.

When he realized the Emir's daughter was standing beside him he fell upon his knees as Moses had done when he saw the burning bush.

He attempted to speak. Words failed him but his tearful eyes supplanted his tongue.

The young girl embraced him, kissed his lips; then she kissed his eyes, drying his copious tears and lips with her kisses.

In a voice softer than the tone of a reed, she said: "I saw you, sweetheart, in my dreams; I looked upon your face in my loneliness. You are the lost consort of my soul and the other better half from which I was separated when I was ordered to come into this world."

"I came here secretly to join you, sweetheart. Do not fear; you are now in my arms. I left the glory which surrounds my father and came to follow you to the end of the world, and to drink with you the cup of life and death."

"Come, sweetheart, let us go into the wilderness, away from civilization."

And the lovers walked into the forest, into the darkness of the night, fearing neither an Emir nor the phantoms of the darkness.

THE WOMEN IN THE LIFE OF GIBRAN

Gibran's Mother, Kamila

GIBRAN recognized the influence of women in his life. He once wrote: "I am indebted for all that I call 'I' to women ever since I was an infant. Women opened windows of my eyes and the doors of my spirit. Had it not been for the woman-mother, the woman-sister and the woman-friend, I would have been sleeping among those who disturb the serenity of the world with their snores."

There were many women in Gibran's life, his biographers agree.

Gibran's mother was especially important in his life because of circumstances which directed her own life. After she married, she and her husband migrated to Brazil, where he took sick and died, leaving her with her infant son, Peter. The mother returned with her son to the home of her father, Stephen Rahmy, a Maronite priest.

The man who was to become Gibran's father heard her singing one day in her father's garden, fell in love with her and soon they were married.

Kahlil Gibran was born December 6, 1883, followed by two sisters, Mariana and Sultana. Their mother taught them music, Arabic and French. As they grew older a tutor was brought into the home to teach them English.

Later they were sent to city schools. They were often taken to church, where their grandfather, a capable priest, served Mass and preached.

In the Maronite church, in certain ceremonies, the whole congregation participates, chanting in Syriac, the

language Christ spoke. The effect of the Maronite ceremonies remained with Gibran the rest of his life; a letter
he wrote in later years acknowledged his debt to the
church.

The religious bent of Gibran's mother, her beautiful
voice in church and the religious atmosphere of the family molded Gibran's character. This effect is apparent in
Gibran's book, *Jesus, the Son of Man.*

As Gibran reached the age of twelve, his half-brother,
Peter, reached the age of eighteen.

Peter was thus ready to go out on his own and, like all
the Lebanese (Phoenicians) who have used the seas as
their highways for thousands of years, set his heart on
America.

Gibran's mother, unwilling to have her children separate, brought Peter, Kahlil and the two girls to Boston.
Kahlil's father protested, for he owned large properties,
collected taxes for the government, and in season did
business as a cattle dealer. However, the fables from
America—that the streets were paved with gold and the
prospect of immediate riches—overwhelmed Peter,
and he decided to bring the family to America, Kahlil's
blond, blue-eyed father remaining in Lebanon.

Some of Gibran's biographers did not know that a
cattle dealer in the Middle East is actually a sheep dealer,
because sheep are imported to Lebanon, from Syria,
from Iraq and sometimes even from Turkey. Actually,
transporting sheep from Turkey without benefit of
trucks, with few rail facilities, with little feed and water,
is harder and more speculative than cattle droving in the
United States. Kahlil's biographers, in their confusion,
wrote that his father was a shepherd.

In Boston, Peter opened a grocery store, the other
children being sent to school. At the age of fourteen
Kahlil decided to go back to Lebanon to complete his

education in Arabic. His mother, realizing the talent and ambition of her son, consented to have him return to Beirut to enter the College of Al Kikmat.

Gibran remained in the college five years, spending the summers near the cedars and traveling with his father through the Middle East. After his five years were over, Gibran visited Greece, Italy and Spain on his way to Paris to study art (1901–1903).

Gibran was called back to the States because his younger sister, Sultana, had died and his mother was very sick. His mother remained bedridden nearly fifteen months before she died. During this time his half-brother Peter also died. It was the greatest shock in Gibran's life. The family was very close and its members had made great sacrifice to educate him. Mariana miraculously survived the tuberculosis which decimated Kahlil's family. Gibran's feelings toward his mother are more eloquently expressed by his own words from *The Broken Wings*:

"Mother is everything in this life; she is consolation in time of sorrowing and hope in time of grieving and power in moments of weakness. She is the fountainhead of compassion, forbearance and forgiveness. He who loses his mother loses a bosom upon which he can rest his head, the hand that blesses, and eyes which watch over him."

Micheline

One biographer has stated that Gibran met, in Boston, a beautiful and vivacious girl named Emilie Michel, nicknamed Micheline. He also stated that Micheline followed Gibran to Paris, that she asked him to marry her and when he refused she left Gibran's apartment and

vanished forever. Some biographers accepted this story; others did not mention the girl by name. Offered as proof by some who mentioned Micheline were two items: first, that Gibran had painted her before he left for Paris; second, the dedication of one of his books to Micheline.

I made a special effort to determine the existence of this beautiful girl. I visited the Museum of Gibran in Lebanon, where I asked the curator to direct me to the painting of Micheline. Pointing to one of the paintings on the wall he said, "This is what is considered to be the painting of Micheline."

This painting has no identifying marks whatsoever. It is not even signed by Gibran. But then only a few of his paintings are signed. I found no facts to show that this was the painting of Micheline; I found no correspondence between Gibran and Micheline.

The reprints of Gibran's Arabic books, as stated earlier, lack information as to the date of first publication. They also lack dedications. After a long search I obtained copies of the earlier editions which contain dedications; I found that Micheline was not mentioned.

The dedication I found read thus:

"To the soul that embraced my soul, to the heart that poured its secrets into my own heart, to the hand that kindled the flame of my emotions, I dedicate this book."

In Paris Gibran lived and worked with a close friend, Joseph Hoyek, who wrote a book about their two years together. The two young men did not live in the same apartment; however, they met daily and often shared the cost of a model for the sake of saving money. Hoyek wrote about the girls they met, the restaurants in which they ate. He named Olga, a Russian girl, another named Rosina, and an Italian girl who was the most beautiful model they hired, but Hoyek made no mention of Micheline.

Therefore, until further evidence is available, I withhold my decision that Micheline ever existed.

Mary Haskell or Mary Khoury?

In 1904 Gibran borrowed twenty dollars and arranged for an exhibition of his paintings. One of those who visited that exhibit was a Miss Mary E. Haskell, who became his friend. Later, she paid his way to Paris to further his art studies. One biographer said that Gibran thereafter asked her to check each of his manuscripts before he submitted it to his publisher.

Gibran's novel *The Broken Wings* was dedicated to M. E. H. However, the administrator of Gibran's estate insists that the woman who helped Gibran financially was a wealthy woman named Mary Khoury. The executor of the estate was the personal physician of Mary Khoury, and had seen in her apartment several of Gibran's paintings and statues on which Gibran had written in Arabic: "Do not blame a person for drinking lest he is trying to forget something more serious than drinking." The doctor further reports that she, Mary Khoury, agreed to have her letters from Gibran published. He also claims those letters were given to a friend for editing, and that both the friend and Mary Khoury have since died. Thus the letters and paintings fell into unknown hands.

According to Mary Khoury, Gibran spent many evenings, in the later days of his life, at her apartment.

The existence of letters from Gibran to Mary Khoury was verified independently by a reliable Lebanese reporter who explained that he had read some of them and that Mary Khoury had promised to have letters released after they were edited. When I asked the newsman if the letters were business or love letters, he emphasized that they were love letters.

Nevertheless, the mystery remains about the benefactress in Kahlil Gibran's life: Was she Mary Haskell or Mary Khoury—or both?

Barbara Young

Barbara Young knew Gibran the last seven years of his life, during which time she became the first of his disciples to shout his praise in a biography, *The Man From Lebanon*.

"If he, Gibran, had never written a poem or painted a picture, his signature upon the page of eternal record would still be inerasable. The power of his individual consciousness has penetrated the consciousness of the age, and the indwelling of his spirit is timeless and deathless. This is Gibran," wrote Barbara Young.

In 1923 Barbara heard a reading from *The Prophet*.

She wrote to Gibran expressing her admiration. She received "his gracious invitation to come to this studio 'to talk about poetry' and to see the pictures."

"So I went," she wrote, "to the old West Tenth Street building, climbed four flights of stairs and found him there, smiling, welcoming me as though we were old friends indeed."

Barbara was taller than Gibran, of light complexion, beautifully built. Her family came from Bideford, in Devon, England. By profession, she was an English teacher, she operated a book store, and she lectured about Gibran the rest of her life after that first climb of the four flights of stairs. After Gibran's death, she assembled and put together the chapters of his unfinished book, *Garden of the Prophet*, and arranged for its publication.

Barbara Young and other biographers have described Gibran as being slender, of medium height, five feet-four inches, as having large, sleepy, brown eyes fringed by

THE TREASURED WRITINGS OF KAHLIL GIBRAN

long lashes, chestnut hair, and a generous mustache framing full lips. His body was strong and he possessed a powerful grip. In some of his letters he mentioned that the beating of his heart was becoming normal again.

Barbara Young was with Gibran at the hospital when he passed away. Soon afterward she packed the precious paintings and effects left in the studio where Gibran had lived for eighteen years, and sent them to his home town of Bcherri in Lebanon.

During her speaking tours Barbara exhibited more than sixty paintings of Gibran's work. What became of this collection or any unfinished work, papers or letters she may have had depends on the generosity of those who bought, received or inherited these objects. Until they come forward, there will never be a complete biography of Gibran, particularly that part dealing with Barbara Young.

How close a relationship existed during these seven years can be answered, in part, by excerpts from Barbara's own writing.

Barbara never lived with Gibran. She kept her own apartment in the city of New York.

One Sunday, Barbara wrote, accepting an invitation from Gibran, she went to the studio. Gibran was writing a poem; he was at his desk when she arrived. While composing Gibran usually paced the floor and then he would sit down to write a line or two.

"I waited while he repeated his writing and his walking again and again. Then a thought came to me. The next time he walked I went and seated myself at his table and took up his pencil. When he turned he saw me sitting there.

" 'You make the poem and I'll write it,' I said."

After much protest Gibran consented to try it. He was pleased with the experiment.

" 'Well, you and I are two poets working together.' He paused. Then after a silence, 'We are friends,' he said. 'I want nothing from you, and you want nothing from me. We share life.' "

As they worked together and as she became more acquainted with his manner of thought and his work, she told him of her determination to write a book about him. Gibran was pleased and "it was from that time on that he talked often of his childhood, his mother and family, and some events in his life."

One day Gibran asked, "Suppose you were compelled to give up—to forget all the words you know except seven—what are the seven words that you would keep?"

"I named only five," Barbara wrote. "God, Life, Love, Beauty, Earth . . . and asked Gibran what other words would he select and he answered, 'The most important words to keep are: You and I . . . without these two there would need to be no others.' Then Gibran selected the seven words: You, I, Give, God, Love, Beauty, Earth."

"Gibran liked a frugal supper in the studio," Barbara wrote, "particularly during a period of his life when he was entertained and being feasted. This one evening Gibran said that 'in the East there is a custom of eating all from one huge vessel. Let us have our soup tonight in one bowl.' So we did and Gibran humorously drew an imaginary line through the soup and said, 'This is your half of the soup and this other is my half. See to it that we neither one trespass upon the soup of the other!' Then laughter and a thorough enjoyment, each of his own half of the soup."

In another chapter Barbara wrote: "One evening when we were doing the book 'Sea and Foam,' I piled cushions on the floor and sat upon them instead of occupying my usual chair. Then I had a strange feeling of a familiarity

about the gesture, and I said: 'I feel as if I've sat like this beside you many times—but I really haven't,' and Gibrar answered, 'We have done this a thousand years ago, and we shall do it a thousand years hence.'

"And during the writing of the book 'Jesus, the Son of Man' the drama of some incident, now and again, was so overwhelming that I felt, and said, 'It is so real. It seems as if I had been there.' And his answer came, almost like a cry, 'You were there! And so was I!' "

It is appropriate, here, to tell that two years after the death of Gibran, Barbara Young and this author met in the city of Cleveland. She asked: "How long would it take to learn the Arabic language?" I explained to her that for the purpose of translating any of Gibran's works it would take many years to learn the classical version of the language; just to speak Arabic would be a different matter. In any event Arabic is a difficult language.

At that time I was studying for my law degree. I was neither interested in teaching Arabic nor contemplating the writing of a book about Gibran. She also told me that whenever Gibran painted a hand it was hers.

The most famous hand Gibran painted is the one with an eye in its palm. This painting was meant to represent the Phoenician Goddess Tanit. In honor of this Goddess, there are two cities in Lebanon called Eyetanit meaning "Eye of Tanit."

This pose, the eye nestled in the palm of the hand, appeared in Carthage in North Africa, carried there by Gibran's ancestors (the Phoenicians). The Phoenicians left one of these carvings of the hand of Tanit in Alabama before the arrival of Columbus.

Did Gibran see one of these hands in Lebanon, was the similarity a coincidence, or were Gibran and Barbara there when the Temples of Tanit were being built in Lebanon and Carthage long before the birth of Christ?

Barbara Young wrote that once when some women came to visit Gibran, they asked why he did not get married. He replied: "Well . . . you see it is like this. If I had a wife, and if I were painting or making poems, I should simply forget her existence for days at a time. And you know well that no loving woman would put up with such a husband for very long."

One of the women, not satisfied with the smiling answer, prodded still deeper, "But have you never been in love?" Controlling himself with difficulty, he said, "I will tell you a thing you may not know. The most highly sexed beings upon the planet are the creators, the poets, sculptors, painters, musicians . . . and so it has been from the beginning. And among them sex is a beautiful and exalted gift. Sex is always beautiful, and it is always shy."

Barbara Young wrote the following paragraph, which we quote, without comment, leaving it to the reader to determine her place in the life of Gibran:

"It is always wise to be wary of the woman who appears out of nowhere and claims a great man for her own when he is dead. But if there be those who never say, 'Lord, Lord,' but who maintain a silence, doing his works, may it not be that these are the hands that have indeed ministered unto him, these the hearts that have perceived the intricacies of his myriad being? And for myself, I do not doubt that through the turbulent years of this man's life the ageless and universal cry for woman-comfort went out from his great loneliness, and that in the goodness of God, the cry was answered. To conclude otherwise would be the essence of stupidity."

Mariana

Mariana, being a younger sister of Gibran, was not consulted about her family's migration.

She was not asked whether her brother should be sent to Lebanon and Europe. However, when tragedy struck, and her mother, her sister and brother Peter, who was the breadwinner, died of tuberculosis within two years, Mariana found herself alone with her brother Kahlil, whose literary work was awakening the Arab world and upsetting the Ottoman Empire. Mariana realized that literary greatness and money do not often meet until, and if, late in life. Gibran's education was in Arabic; thus his articles and books were not bringing in sufficient cash to furnish the necessities of life.

Mariana refused to let her brother alter his plans or to take a job which would interfere with his literary and art career. She sewed and knit to keep a home for herself and for her brother. She encouraged him to paint until he had a collection ready for showing. Mariana did not have the money to pay for the display of his works, but Gibran managed to borrow twenty dollars from a Lebanese woman, who lived in Boston then, and is still living now, in Lebanon, and considers Gibran's note her greatest possession.

The investment in Gibran's education paid dividends, not only to the literary world but in money as well. The estimate of the royalties from Gibran's books is over a million and a half dollars. These royalties are sent to his home town, Bcherri. However, he left to his sister, Mariana (Mary), who still lives in Boston, sufficient money for her to retire with security for the rest of her life. She was on very good terms with Barbara Young, who dedicated the book *The Man From Lebanon* to her.

May Ziadeh

May Ziadeh was Gibran's love on paper only; he never saw her. May was a Lebanese girl, whose family had

moved to Egypt. An only child, she was educated in the Middle East and later went to Europe to study; later she wrote articles in her father's magazine and in other French and Arabic publications. Her parents' home was a meeting place for most of the prominent literary men in Egypt. Gibran's articles, appearing at this time, in many papers and magazines, were often a topic of discussion.

May, admiring Gibran's articles, decided to write to him. Fearing that he might disregard her letters as simply those from another admirer, she wrote, in the beginning, an introduction of herself. She explained that she wrote articles and books, and that much of her work appeared under the nom de plume, Isis Cubia. Then she proceeded to tell him the great effect his writing was having upon the Egyptian community.

Gibran was prompt in his answer. He wrote admiring her courage and thanking her for working toward the liberation of women in the Middle East. He told her that he was mailing her, in a separate package, a copy of his new book, *The Broken Wings*. And he tried to explain how he came to give it that title:

"I inherited from my mother ninety percent of my character and my disposition. This does not mean that I inherited her beauty and her humility, or her big heart. I recall that she told me once, when I was twenty years old, that it would have been much better for me and the people had I become a monk in one of the monasteries.

I said, 'It is true except that I took you as a mother before I came into this world.'

"She replied, 'If you had not come, you would have remained an angel.'

"I answered, 'I am still an angel.'

"She smiled and asked, 'But where are your wings?'

"I placed her arms on my shoulders and then said, 'These are my wings.'

"She responded, 'But they are broken.' "

Gibran added in his letter: "My mother, since passed beyond the blue horizon, but her words, 'the broken wings' remained with me and I used them for the title of the novel I am sending to you. I appreciate your personal opinion."

May sent her opinion, admiring the book, but sharply disagreeing with Gibran, because in the story he condoned a married woman meeting with her former lover.

"Regardless of how innocent it was," May wrote, "it is a betrayal of the husband, it is a betrayal of the name she carries and it is a betrayal of society."

In the meantime, the intelligentsia of Egypt were planning to honor a Lebanese poet and Gibran was to be one of the speakers. Unable to attend, mainly because he didn't have the money, Gibran sent an article "The Poet of Baalbek"[1] to be read at the affair. The toastmaster, knowing about the correspondence between Gibran and May, asked her to read the article.

Even though it was May's first attempt at public speaking, her reading earned an ovation. Thus, she had auctioned her heart to Gibran. They corresponded until his death. May's letters were not all of love, for she criticized his writing frequently and prodded him to write on certain subjects.

Once May wrote:

"The new Turkish governor arrived in Lebanon, and as usual, he began removing people from their jobs. He is following in the footsteps of his predecessors. The Lebanese people are prostrating themselves before his feet. When are we going to have among us men of courage? When are the Lebanese going to shake off the dust of insult? Why don't you write on this subject? The people respect your ideas, Gibran. Remind them they are men and men should not humble themselves."

1. Baalbek was the hometown of the poet being honored.

Writing on the subject Gibran said:

"Woe to the nation that receives her conquerors beating the drums. Woe to the nation that hates oppression in her sleep and accepts it in her awakening. Woe to the nation that raises her voice only behind a coffin and prides itself only in the cemetery. Woe to a nation that does not revolt until her neck is placed on the scaffold."

Gibran wrote and asked May to come to the United States. She refused because she was a woman and custom did not permit her; she asked him to come to Egypt. Part of Gibran's letter said: "What can I say about my economic condition?

"A year or two ago I had some peace and quiet. But now the quietness has turned into tumult and peace into struggle. The people are demanding my days and nights. I am overwhelmed by their demands. Every once in a while I leave this great city to elude the people and to escape from myself. The American public is mighty. It never wearies or gets tired, is never exhausted, never sleeps and never dreams. If it dislikes you it destroys you with neglect and if it likes you it destroys you with its affection and demand.

"The day may yet come when I can escape to the Middle East. If it were not for this cage, whose bars I have wrought with my own hands—I would have taken the first ship going East. What man would desert a building whose stones he had hewn and polished his entire life even though it had become a prison?"

In one of her letters May wrote:

"I do not know what I am doing but I know that I love you. I fear love. I expect too much of love, and I fear that I never will receive all my expectations. . . . How dare I write this to you . . . ? However, I thank God I am writing it and not saying it. If you were present I would have vanished after such a statement and disappeared until you had forgotten what I said.

THE TREASURED WRITINGS OF KAHLIL GIBRAN

"I blame myself for taking even this much liberty. Nevertheless, right or wrong, my heart is with you and the best thing it can do is to hover over you and guard you with compassion."

May's heart needed to hover only for a short time because Gibran's health was failing. He wrote:

"You know, May, every time I think of departing, that is, in death, I enjoy my thoughts and am contended to leave."

Gibran departed in 1931 at the age of forty-seven after nearly nineteen years of his love affair, on paper, with May Ziadeh.

Salma Karamy

Gibran was eighteen "when love opened his eyes by its magic rays and Salma was the first woman" to do it.

Gibran wrote a novel in Arabic about his first love. No other author could have narrated the events better than Gibran. However, biographers and Gibran's neighbors insist that Gibran's first girl was called Hala El-daher and that the events of the story took place in Bcherri instead of Beirut.

Gibran intended to buy the monastery of Mar Sarkis where Salma once met him. This monastery was actually carved in a cliff for a safe refuge. To enter it in the old days required either a rope or a ladder. Mariana, Gibran's sister, bought it. A footpath was built later for the convenience of visitors who now bow humbly before the resting place of Gibran, who had wished to retire there in life but reached his refuge only in death.

Among his last letters exists evidence of Gibran's desire to "to go to the Middle East, to Lebanon, to Bcherri, to Mar Sarkis, that hermitage carved in the rock and overlooking the most astonishing sight the eye could

ever see of the whole valley." Gibran was longing for the "new life in the heart of nature; among the golden fields of wheat, the green meadows, the flocks of sheep being led to pasture, the roaring falls and the rising mist reflecting in the rays of the sun."

Salma is presented to the reader in *The Broken Wings,* Gibran's own love story which has been on the best-seller list in Arabic for more than forty years.

THE WISDOM
OF KAHLIL GIBRAN

KEY

BW-ST: *Broken Wings* by Kahlil Gibran, in *A Second Treasury of Kahlil Gibran*, trans. by Anthony R. Ferris, Citadel Press, 1962.

KG-P: *Kahlil Gibran: A Biography* by Michael Naimy, in *The Parables of Gibran* by Annie Salem Otto, Citadel Press, 1963.

P: *The Procession* by Kahlil Gibran, trans. by George Kheirallah, Philosophical Library, 1958.

MS: *Mirrors of the Soul, Kahlil Gibran,* by Joseph Sheban, Philosophical Library, 1965.

S: In conversation and correspondence.

SH-P: *Secrets of the Heart* by Kahlil Gibran in *The Parables of Gibran.*

SH-T: *Secrets of the Heart* by Kahlil Gibran in *A Treasury of Kahlil Gibran*, trans. by Anthony Rizcallah Ferris, edited by Martin L. Wolf, Citadel Press, 1947.

SP-P: *Kahlil Gibran: A Self Portrait,* trans. by Anthony R. Ferris, in *The Parables of Gibran.*

SR-T: *Spirits Rebellious* by Kahlil Gibran in *A Treasury of Kahlil Gibran.*

T: *A Treasury of Kahlil Gibran.*

TL-T: *Tears and Laughter* by Kahlil Gibran in *A Treasury of Kahlil Gibran.*

VM-P: *The Voice of the Master* by Kahlil Gibran in *The Parables of Gibran.*

WM-ST: *The Words of the Master* by Kahlil Gibran in *A Second Treasury of Kahlil Gibran.*

A

ACTION

A little knowledge that *acts* is worth infinitely more than much knowledge that is idle.
WM-ST-63

Believing is a fine thing, but placing those beliefs into execution is a test of strength. Many are those who talk like the roar of the sea, but their lives are shallow and stagnant, like the rotting marshes. Many are those who lift their heads above the mountain tops, but their spirits remain dormant in the obscurity of the caverns.
SH-T-17

ADOLESCENCE

It is said that unsophistication makes a man empty and that emptiness makes him carefree. It may be true among those who were born dead and who exist like frozen corpses; but the sensitive boy who feels much and knows little is the most unfortunate creature under the sun, because he is torn by two forces. The first force elevates him and shows him the beauty of existence through a cloud of dreams; the second ties him down to the earth and fills his eyes with dust and overpowers him with fears and darkness.
BW-ST-18

ADVICE

He who does not seek advice is a fool. His folly blinds him to Truth and makes him evil, stubborn, and a danger to his fellow man.
WM-ST-67

AFFECTION

The heart's affections are divided like the branches of the cedar tree; if the tree loses one strong branch, it will suffer but it does not die. It will pour all its vitality into the next branch so that it will grow and fill the empty place.

BW-ST-93

AGE

Seek ye counsel of the aged, for their eyes have looked on the faces of the years and their ears have hearkened to the voices of Life. Even if their counsel is displeasing to you, pay heed to them.

WM-ST-68

AMBITION

> What good is there, pray thee tell me,
> In jostling through the crowd in life,
> 'Mid the argumental tumult,
> Protestation, and endless strife;

> Mole-like burrowing in darkness,
> Grasping for the spider's thread,
> Always thwarted in ambition,
> Until the living join the dead?

P-73

AMERICANS

The Americans are a mighty people who never give up or get tired or sleep or dream. If these people hate someone, they will kill him by negligence, and if they like or love a person, they will shower him with affection.

SP-ST-82

ANCESTRY

A man is not noble through ancestry;
How many noblemen are descendants of murderers?

MS-74

ANTHROPOMORPHISM

The mountains, trees, and rivers change their appearance with the vicissitudes of times and seasons, as a man changes with his experiences and emotions. The lofty poplar that resembles a bride in the daytime will look like a column of smoke in the evening; the huge rock that stands impregnable at noon will appear to be a miserable pauper at night, with earth for his bed and the sky for his cover; and the rivulet that we see glittering in the morning and hear singing the hymn of Eternity will, in the evening, turn to a stream of tears wailing like a mother bereft of her child.

BW-ST-78

APPEARANCE

The appearance of things changes according to the emotions, and thus we see magic and beauty in them, while the magic and beauty are really in ourselves.

BW-ST-51

> The purpose of the spirit in the
> Heart is concealed, and by outer
> Appearance cannot be judged.
> T-372

ART

Art must be a direct communication between the artist's imagination and that of the looker. For that reason, I avoid, so much as possible, busying the looker's eye with too many details in order that his imagination may roam wide and far. As to the physical molds, art is forced to create for expressing itself; they must be beautiful molds. Otherwise, art defeats its purpose.

KG-P-102

Is it really God that created Man, or is it the opposite? Imagination is the only creator, its nearest and clearest

manifestation is Art; yes, art is life, life is art; all else is trite and empty in comparison.
KG-P-97

Art is one step from the visibly known toward the unknown.
MS-71

ARTIST

I should be a traitor to my art if I were to borrow my sitter's eyes. The face is a marvelous mirror that reflects most faithfully the innermost of the soul; the artist's business is to see that and portray it; otherwise he is not fit to be called an artist.
KG-P-97

AUTHORITY

Selfishness, my brother, is the cause of blind superiority, and superiority creates clanship, and clanship creates authority which leads to discord and subjugation.

The soul believes in the power of knowledge and justice over dark ignorance; it denies the authority that supplies the swords to defend and strengthen ignorance and oppression — that authority which destroyed Babylon and shook the foundation of Jerusalem and left Rome in ruins. It is that which made people call criminals great men; made writers respect their names; made historians relate the stories of their inhumanity in manner of praise.
TL-T-8

B

BARRENNESS

How many flowers
Possess no fragrance from the day

Of their birth! How many clouds
Gather in the sky, barren of rain,
Dropping no pearls!
T-373

BEAUTY

Beauty is that which attracts your soul, and that which loves to give and not to receive. When you meet Beauty, you feel that the hands deep within your inner self are stretched forth to bring her into the domain of your heart. It is a magnificence combined of sorrow and joy; it is the Unseen which you see, and the Vague which you understand, and the Mute which you hear—it is the Holy of Holies that begins in yourself and ends vastly beyond your earthly imagination.
TL-T-407

Are you troubled by the many faiths that Mankind professes? Are you lost in the valley of conflicting beliefs? Do you think that the freedom of heresy is less burdensome than the yoke of submission, and the liberty of dissent safer than the stronghold of acquiescence?

If such be the case, then make Beauty your religion, and worship her as your godhead; for she is the visible, manifest and perfect handiwork of God. Cast off those who have toyed with godliness as if it were a sham, joining together greed and arrogance; but believe instead in the divinity of beauty that is at once the beginning of your worship of Life, and the source of your hunger for Happiness.

Do penance before Beauty, and atone for your sins, for Beauty brings your heart closer to the throne of woman, who is the mirror of your affections and the teacher of your heart in the ways of Nature, which is your life's home.
WM-ST-33

Only our spirits can understand beauty, or live and grow with it. It puzzles our minds; we are unable to describe it in words; it is a sensation that our eyes cannot see, derived from both the one who observes and the one who is looked upon. Real beauty is a ray which emanates from the holy of holies of the spirit, and illuminates the body, as life comes from the depths of the earth and gives color and scent to a flower.
BW-ST-34

Beauty is that harmony between joy and sorrow which begins in our holy of holies and ends beyond the scope of our imagination.
KG-P-93

> Beauty is not in the face;
> Beauty is a light in the heart.
> MS-75

BEING
It is impossible for the mirror of the soul to reflect in the imagination anything which does not stand before it. It is impossible for the calm lake to show in its depth the figure of any mountain or the picture of any tree or cloud that does not exist close by the lake. It is impossible for the light to throw upon the earth a shadow of an object that has no being. Nothing can be seen, heard, or otherwise sensed unless it has actual *being*.
SH-T-149

BELIEVER
When you *know* a thing, you *believe* it, and the true believer sees with his *spiritual discernment* that which the surface investigator cannot see with the eyes of his head, and he understands through his *inner* thought that which the outside examiner cannot understand with his demanding, acquired process of thought.

The believer acquaints himself with the sacred realities through deep senses different from those used by others. A believer looks upon his senses as a great wall surrounding him, and when he walks upon the path he says, "This city has no exit, but it is perfect within." The believer lives for all the days and the nights and the unfaithful live but a few hours.

SH-T-149

BODY

He who endeavours to cleave the body from the spirit, or the spirit from the body, is directing his heart away from truth. The flower and its fragrance are one, and the blind who deny the colour and the image of the flower, believing that it possesses only a fragrance vibrating the ether, are like those with pinched nostrils who believe that flowers are naught but pictures and colours, possessing no fragrance.

SH-T-139

Life is naked. A nude body is the truest and noblest symbol of life. If I draw a mountain as a heap of human forms and paint a waterfall in the shape of tumbling human bodies, it is because I see in the mountain a heap of living things, and in the waterfall a precipitate current of life.

KG-P-102

BOSTON

This city was called in the past the city of science and art, but today it is the city of traditions. The souls of its inhabitants are petrified; even their thoughts are old and worn-out. The strange thing about this city is that the petrified is always proud and boastful, and the worn-out and old holds its chin high.

SP-ST-53

BOUNTY

An eternal hunger for love and beauty is my desire; I know now that those who possess bounty alone are naught but miserable, but to my spirit the sighs of lovers are more soothing than music of the lyre.

T-413

BRAVERY

Bravery is a volcano; the seed of wavering does not grow on its crater.

MS-72

BROTHERHOOD

I love you because you are weak before the strong oppressor, and poor before the greedy rich. For these reasons I shed tears and comfort you; and from behind my tears I see you embraced in the arms of Justice, smiling and forgiving your persecutors. You are my brother and I love you.

TL-T-7

I love you, my brother, whoever you are — whether you worship in your church, kneel in your temple, or pray in your mosque. You and I are all children of one faith, for the divers paths of religion are fingers of the loving hand of one Supreme Being, a hand extended to all, offering completeness of spirit to all, eager to receive all.

WM-ST-69

C

CHAINS

Not everyone in chains is subdued;
At times, a chain is greater than a necklace.

MS-74

CHARITY

>The coin which you drop into
>The withered hand stretching toward
>You is the only golden chain that
>Binds your rich heart to the
>Loving heart of God. . . .
>   SH-T-345

CHATTER

I abstain from the people who consider insolence, bravery and tenderness cowardice. And I abstain from those who consider chatter wisdom and silence ignorance.
MS-71

CHILDHOOD

The things which the child loves remain in the domain of the heart until old age. The most beautiful thing in life is that our souls remain hovering over the places where we once enjoyed ourselves.
SP-ST-27

CHURCHES

Oh Jesus, they have built these churches for the sake of their own glory, and embellished them with silk and melted gold. . . . They left the bodies of Thy chosen poor wrapped in tattered raiment in the cold night. . . . They filled the sky with the smoke of burning candles and incense and left the bodies of Thy faithful worshippers empty of bread. . . . They raised their voices with hymns of praise, but deafened themselves to the cry and moan of the widows and orphans.

Come again, O Living Jesus, and drive the vendors of Thy faith from Thy sacred temple, for they have turned it into a dark cave where vipers of hypocrisy and falsehood crawl and abound.
SH-T-81

THE TREASURED WRITINGS OF KAHLIL GIBRAN

CITIZENSHIP

What is it to be a good citizen?

It is to acknowledge the other person's rights before asserting your own, but always to be conscious of your own.

It is to create the useful and the beautiful with your own hands, and to admire what others have created in love and with faith.

It is to create the useful and the beautiful with you own hands, and to admire what others have created in love and with faith.

It is to produce by labor and only by labor and to spend less than you have produced that your children may not be dependent upon the state for support when you are no more.
MS-35

CITY

Oh people of the noisome city, who are living in darkness, hastening toward misery, preaching falsehood, and speaking with stupidity . . . until when shall you remain ignorant? Until when shall you abide in the filth of life and continue to desert its gardens? Why wear your tattered robes of narrowness while the silk raiment of Nature's beauty is fashioned for you? The lamp of wisdom is dimming; it is time to furnish it with oil. The house of true fortune is being destroyed; it is time to rebuild it and guard it. The thieves of ignorance have stolen the treasure of your peace; it is time to retake it!
TL-T-403

CIVILIZATION

The misery of our Oriental nations is the misery of the world, and what you call *civilization* in the West is naught

but another spectre of the many phantoms of tragic deception.
SH-T-25

Inventions and discoveries are but amusement and comfort for the body when it is tired and weary. The conquest of distance and the victory over the seas are but false fruit which do not satisfy the soul, nor nourish the heart, neither lift the spirit, for they are afar from nature. And those structures and theories which man calls knowledge and art are naught except shackles and golden chains which man drags, and he rejoices with their glittering reflections and ringing sounds. They are strong cages whose bars man commenced fabricating ages ago, unaware that he was building from the inside, and that he would soon become his own prisoner to eternity.
SH-T-26

CLERGYMAN
The clergyman erects his temple upon the graves and bones of the devoted worshippers.
SR-T-269

CONCEALMENT
Conceal your passion; your sickness is also your medicine because love to the soul is as wine in a glass—what you see is liquid, what is hidden is its spirit. . . .

Conceal your troubles; then, should the seas roar and the skies fall, you will be safe.
MS-76

CONSCIENCE
Conscience is a just but weak judge. Weakness leaves it powerless to execute its judgment.
TM-ST-118

CONTENTMENT

Be not satisfied with partial contentment, for he who engulfs the spring of life with one empty jar will depart with two full jars.
SH-T-136

Fortune craves not Contentment, for it is an earthly hope, and its desires are embraced by union with objects, while Contentment is naught but heartfelt.
TL-T-92

CONTRADICTION

Contradiction is a lower degree of intelligence.
MS-72

COUNSEL

My brothers, seek counsel of one another, for therein lies the way out of error and futile repentance. The wisdom of the many is your shield against tyranny. For when we turn to one another for counsel we reduce the number of our enemies.
WM-ST-67

My soul is my counsel and has taught me to give ear to the voices which are neither created by tongues nor uttered by throats.

Before my soul became my counsel, I was dull, and weak of hearing, reflecting only upon the tumult and the cry. But, now, I can listen to silence with serenity and can hear in the silence the hymns of ages chanting exaltation to the sky and revealing the secrets of eternity.
MS-V

COUNTRY LIFE

We who live amid the excitements of the city know nothing of the life of the mountain villagers. We are swept into the current of urban existence, until we forget

the peaceful rhythms of simple country life, reap in au-
tumn, rest in winter, imitating nature in all her cycles.
We are wealthier than the villagers in silver or gold, but
they are richer in spirit. What we sow we reap not; they
reap what they sow. We are slaves of gain, and they the
children of contentment. Our draught from the cup of
life is mixed with bitterness and despair, fear and weariness; but they drink the pure nectar of life's fulfillment.
TM-ST-53

COURAGE
   The spirit who has seen the spectre of death cannot be
scared by the faces of thieves; the soldier who has seen
the swords glittering over his head and streams of blood
under his feet does not care about rocks thrown at him by
the children on the streets.
BW-ST-106

COURSER
   My soul, living is like a courser of the night; the swifter
its flight, the nearer the dawn.
WM-ST-69

CREEDS
                People's creeds come forth, then perish
                Like the shadows in the night.
                P-46

CRIMINAL
                For the Criminal who is weak and poor the
                Narrow cell of death awaits; but
                Honour and glory await the rich who
                Conceal their crimes behind their
                Gold and silver and inherited glory.
                T-364

D

DARKNESS

God has bestowed upon you intelligence and knowledge. Do not extinguish the lamp of Divine Grace and do not let the candle of wisdom die out in the darkness of lust and error. For a wise man approaches with his torch to light up the path of mankind.
WM-ST-62

DEATH

Man is like the foam of the sea, that floats upon the surface of the water. When the wind blows, it vanishes, as if it had never been. Thus are our lives blown away by Death.
WM-ST-31

The Reality of Life is Life itself, whose beginning is not in the womb, and whose ending is not in the grave. For the years that pass are naught but a moment in eternal life; and the world of matter and all in it is but a dream compared to the awakening which we call the terror of Death.
WM-ST-32

> The soul is an embryo in the body of
> Man, and the day of death is the
> Day of awakening, for it is the
> Great era of labour and the rich
> Hour of creation.
> T-373

> Death is an ending to the son of
> The earth, but to the soul it is
> The start, the triumph of life.
> T-374

> Death removes but the
> Touch, and not the awareness of

> All good. And he who has lived
> One spring or more possesses the
> Spiritual life of one who has
> Lived a score of springs.
> T-375

A child in the womb, no sooner born than returned to the earth—such is the fate of man, the fate of nations and of the sun, the moon, and the stars.
S

DESPAIR

Despair is an ebb for every flow in the heart; it's a mute affection.
SP-ST-57

Despair weakens our sight and closes our ears. We can see nothing but spectres of doom, and can hear only the beating of our agitated hearts.
BW-ST-98

DESPOT

The ignorant nations arrest their good men and turn them into their despots; and a country, ruled by a tyrant, persecutes those who try to free the people from the yoke of slavery.
SR-T-274

DESTINY

> Man possesses a destiny
> Which impels his thoughts and
> Actions and words, and that not
> Sufficing, directs his footsteps to
> A place of unwilling abode.
> T-376

DESTRUCTION

I am indeed a fanatic and I am inclined toward destruction as well as construction. There is hatred in my heart

for that which my detractors sanctify, and love for that which they reject. And if I could uproot certain customs, beliefs, and traditions of the people, I would do so without hesitation. When they said my books were poison, they were speaking truth about themselves, for what I say is poison to them. But they falsified when they said I mix honey into it, for I apply the poison full strength and pour it from transparent glass. Those who call me an idealist becalmed in clouds are the very ones who turn away from the transparent glass they call poison, knowing that their stomachs cannot digest it.

TM-ST-91

DEVIL

Remember, one just man causes the Devil greater affliction than a million blind believers.

WM-ST-62

DICHOTOMY

He who does not see the angels and devils in the beauty and malice of life will be far removed from knowledge, and his spirit will be empty of affection.

BW-ST-20

DIVINITY

Remember that Divinity is the true self of Man. It cannot be sold for gold; neither can it be heaped up as are the riches of the world today. The rich man has cast off his Divinity, and has clung to his gold. And the young today have forsaken their Divinity and pursue self-indulgence and pleasure.

WM-ST-65

DOCTORS

Since the beginning of the world, the doctors have been trying to save the people from their disorders; some

used knives, while others used potions, but pestilence spread hopelessly. It is my wish that the patient would content himself with remaining in his filthy bed, meditating his long-continued sores; but instead, he stretches his hands from under the robe and clutches at the neck of each who comes to visit him, choking him to death. What irony it is! The evil patient kills the doctor, and then closes his eyes and says within himself, "He was a great physician."
SH-T-23

E

EARTH
The earth that opens wide her mouth to swallow man and his works is the redeemer of our souls from bondage to our bodies.
WM-ST-79

EAST AND WEST
The West is not higher than the East, nor is the West lower than the East, and the difference that stands between the two is not greater than the difference between the tiger and the lion. There is a just and perfect law that I have found behind the exterior of society, which equalizes misery, prosperity, and ignorance; it does not prefer one nation to another, nor does it oppress one tribe in order to enrich another.
SH-T-25

EDIFICE
What man is capable of leaving an edifice on whose construction he has spent all his life, even though that edifice is his own prison? It is difficult to get rid of it in one day.
SP-ST-83

EQUALITY

One hour devoted to mourning and lamenting the
Stolen equality of the weak is nobler than a
Century filled with greed and usurpation.
TL-T-412

ETERNITY

Each thing that exists remains forever, and the very
existence of existence is proof of its eternity. But without
that realization, which is the knowledge of perfect being,
man would never know whether there was existence
or non-existence. If eternal existence is altered, then it
must become more beautiful; and if it disappears,
it must return with more sublime image; and if it sleeps,
it must dream of a better awakening, for it is ever greater
upon its rebirth.
SH-T-143

Only those return to Eternity
Who on earth seek out Eternity.
TL-T-410

EVOLUTION

The law of evolution has a severe and oppressive
countenance and those of limited or fearful mind dread
it; but its principles are just, and those who study them
become enlightened. Through its Reason men are raised
above themselves and can approach the sublime.
TM-ST-99

EXCESS

In battling evil, excess is good; for he who is moderate
in announcing the truth is presenting half-truth. He conceals the other half out of fear of the people's wrath.
TM-ST-96

I will not be surprised if the "thinkers" say of me, "He

is a man of excess who looks upon life's seamy side and reports nothing but gloom and lamentation."
TM-ST-95

EXILE

He who does not prefer exile to slavery is not free by any measure of freedom, truth and duty.
SR-T-224

EYE

I feel pity toward those who admit of the eternity of the elements of which the eye is made, but at the same time doubt the eternity of the various objects of sight which employ the eye as a medium.
SH-T-144

Man's eye is a magnifier; it shows him the earth much larger than it is.
MS-71

F

FACE

A look which reveals inward stress adds more beauty to the face, no matter how much tragedy and pain it bespeaks; but the face which, in silence, does not announce hidden mysteries is not beautiful, regardless of the symmetry of its features. The cup does not entice our lips unless the wine's color is seen through the transparent crystal.
BW-ST-67

FAITH

God has made many doors opening into truth which He opens to all who knock upon them with hands of faith.
SH-T-138

FAME

There is something in our life which is nobler and more supreme than fame; and this *something* is the great deed that invokes fame.

SP-ST-32

FATE

> Circumstances drive us on
>   In narrow paths by Kismet hewn.
>
> For Fate has ways we cannot change,
>   While weakness preys upon our Will;
> We bolster with excuse the self,
>   And help that Fate ourselves to kill.

P-74

Life takes us up and bears us from one place to another; Fate moves us from one point to another. And we, caught up between these twain, hear dreadful voices and see only that which stands as a hindrance and obstacle in our path.

WM-ST-46

FEAR OF DEATH

> Fear of death is a delusion
>   Harbored in the breast of sages;
> He who lives a single Springtime
>   Is like one who lives for ages.

P-71

FERTILITY

> The body is a womb to soul
>   In which it dwells until full term,
> When it ascends once more to soar,
>   While womb again recedes to germ.

P-67

FIRST LOVE

Every young man remembers his first love and tries to recapture that strange hour, the memory of which changes his deepest feeling and makes him so happy in spite of all the bitterness of its mystery.
BW-ST-12

FLOWERS

The flowers of the field are the children of sun's affection and nature's love; and the children of men are the flowers of love and compassion.
BW-ST-122

FOLLY

The fool sees naught but folly; and the madman only madness. Yesterday I asked a foolish man to count the fools among us. He laughed and said, "This is too hard a thing to do, and it will take too long. Were it not better to count only the wise?"
WM-ST-55

I once heard a learned man say, "Every evil has its remedy, except folly. To reprimand an obstinate fool or to preach to a dolt is like writing upon the water. Christ healed the blind, the halt, the palsied, and the leprous. But the fool He could not cure."
WM-ST-56

FORBIDDEN

When you behold a man turning aside from
Things forbidden that bring
Abysmal crime to self, look
Upon him with eyes of love, for
He is a preserver of God in him.
T-372

FREEDOM

> I love freedom, and my love for true
> Freedom grew with my growing knowledge
> Of the people's surrender to slavery
> And oppression and tyranny, and of
> Their submission to the horrible idols
> Erected by the past ages and polished
> By the parched lips of the slaves.
> But I love those slaves with my love
> For freedom, for they blindly kissed
> The jaws of ferocious beasts in calm
> And blissful unawareness, feeling not
> The venom of the smiling vipers, and
> Unknowingly digging their graves with
> Their own fingers.
> SH-T-100

> Dying for Freedom is nobler than living in
> The shadow of weak submission, for
> He who embraces death with the sword
> Of Truth in his hand will eternalize
> With the Eternity of Truth, for Life
> Is weaker than Death and Death is
> Weaker than Truth.
> SH-T-342

> The free on earth builds of his strife
>   A prison for his own duress,
> When he is freed from his own kin,
>   Is slave to thought and love's caress.
> P-55

Life without Freedom is like a body without a soul, and Freedom without Thought is like a confused spirit. . . . Life, Freedom, and Thought are three-in-one, and are everlasting and never pass away.
TM-ST-62

Freedom bids us to her table where we may partake of her savory food and rich wine; but when we sit down at her board, we eat ravenously and glut ourselves.
WM-ST-47

You may chain my hands and shackle my feet; you may even throw me into a dark prison, but you shall not enslave my thinking because it is free.
S

FRIENDSHIP
Friendship with the ignorant is as foolish as arguing with a drunkard.
WM-ST-62

G

GENTLENESS

      The gentleness of some is like
        A polished shell with silky feel,
  Lacking the precious pearl within
        Oblivious of the brother's weal.

      When you shall meet one who is strong
        And gentle too, pray feast your eyes;
      For he is glorious to behold,
        The blind can see his qualities.
P-59

GIANTS
We live in an era whose humblest men are becoming greater than the greatest men of preceding ages. What once preoccupied our minds is now of no consequence. The veil of indifference covers it. The beautiful dreams that once hovered in our consciousness have been dis-

persed like mist. In their place are giants moving like tempests, raging like seas, breathing like volcanoes.

What destiny will the giants bring the world at the end of their struggles? . . .

What will be the destiny of your country and mine? Which giant shall seize the mountains and valleys that produced us and reared us and made us men and women before the face of the sun? . . .

Which one of you people does not ponder day and night on the fate of the world under the rule of the giants intoxicated with the tears of widows and orphans?
TM-ST-97

GLORY

> One hour devoted to the pursuit of Beauty
> And Love is worth a full century of glory
> Given by the frightened weak to the strong.
> TL-T-411

I have seen you, my brother, sitting upon the throne of glory, and around you stood your people acclaiming your majesty, and singing praises of your great deeds, extolling your wisdom, and gazing upon you as though in the presence of a prophet, their spirits exulting even to the canopy of heaven.

And as you gazed upon your subjects, I saw in your face the marks of happiness and power and triumph, as if you were the soul of their body.

But when I looked again, behold I found you alone in your loneliness, standing by the side of your throne, an exile stretching his hand in every direction, as if pleading for mercy and kindness from invisible ghosts—begging for shelter, even such as has naught in it but warmth and friendliness.
WM-ST-42

GOD

Man has worshipped his own self since the beginning, calling that self by appropriate titles, until now, when he employs the word "God" to mean that same self.
SH-T-391

Most religions speak of God in the masculine gender. To me He is as much a mother as He is a Father. He is both the father and the mother in one; and Woman is the God-Mother. The God-Father may be reached through the mind or the imagination. But the God-Mother can be reached through the heart only—through love. And Love is that holy wine which the gods distill from their hearts and pour into the hearts of men. Those only taste it pure and divine whose hearts have been cleansed of all the animal lusts. For clean hearts to be drunk with love is to be drunk with God. Those, on the other hand, who drink it mixed with the wines of earthly passions taste but the orgies of devils in Hell.
KG-P-94

It were wiser to speak less of God, Whom we cannot understand, and more of each other, whom we may understand. Yet I would have you know that we are the breath and the fragrance of God. We are God, in leaf, in flower, and oftentimes in fruit.
MS-43

GOLD

Gold leads into gold, then into restlessness, and finally into crushing misery.
TL-T-403

The life that the rich man spends in heaping up gold is in truth like the life of the worms in the grave. It is a sign of fear.
WM-ST-65

GOOD

    The good in man should freely flow,
      As evil lives beyond the grave;
    While Time with fingers moves the pawns
      Awhile, then breaks the knight and knave.
    P-41

GOVERNOR

Are you a governor looking down on those you govern, never stirring abroad except to rifle their pockets or
to exploit them for your own profit? If so, you are like
tares upon the threshing floor of the nation.

Are you a devoted servant who loves the people and is
ever watchful over their welfare, and zealous for their
success? If so, you are a blessing in the granaries of the
land.
    WM-ST-35

H

HANDS

How small is the life of the person who places his
hands between his face and the world, seeing naught but
the narrow lines of his hands!
    SH-T-150

HAPPINESS

    I sought happiness in my solitude, and
    As I drew close to her I heard my soul
    Whisper into my heart, saying, "The
    Happiness you seek is a virgin, born
    And reared in the depths of each heart,
    And she emerges not from her birthplace."
    And when I opened my heart to find her,
    I discovered in its domain only her

Mirror and her cradle and her raiment,
And happiness was not there.
SH-T-101

Happiness is a myth we seek,
    If manifested surely irks;
Like river speeding to the plain,
    On its arrival slows and murks.

For man is happy only in
    His aspiration to the heights;
When he attains his goal, he cools
    And longs for other distant flights.
P-57

Happiness on earth is but a fleet,
Passing ghost, which man craves
At any cost in gold or time. And
When the phantom becomes the
Reality, man soon wearies of it.
T-371

HARDSHIP

Braving obstacles and hardships is nobler than retreat
to tranquillity. The butterfly that hovers around the lamp
until it dies is more admirable than the mole that lives in a
dark tunnel.
BW-ST-89

HATE

I use hate as a weapon to defend myself; had I been
strong, I would never have needed that kind of weapon.
MS-72

HEAVEN

The angels keep count of every tear shed by Sorrow;
and they bring to the ears of the spirits hovering in the
heavens of the Infinite each song of Joy wrought from
our affections.

There, in the world to come, we shall see and feel all the vibrations of our feelings and the motions of our hearts. We shall understand the meaning of the divinity within us, whom we contemn because we are prompted by Despair.
WM-ST-32

HELL

> Hell is not in torture;
> Hell is in an empty heart.
> MS-74

HERD

> Say not, "There goes a learned man"
>   Nor, "There a chieftain dignified."
> The best of men are in the herd,
>   And heed the shepherd as their guide.
> P-41

HONORS

> Honors are but false delusions
>   Like the froth upon the wave.
>
> Should the almond spray its blossoms
>   On the turf around its feet,
> Never will it claim a lordship,
>   Nor disdain the grass to greet.
> P-55

HOPE

> Hope is found not in the forest,
>   Nor the wild portray despair;
> Why should forest long for portions
>   When the ALL is centered there?
>
> Should one search the forest hopeful,
>   When *all nature* is the Aim?

For to hope is but an ailment,
So are station, wealth and fame.
P-58

HUMANITY

Humanity is the spirit of the Supreme Being on earth, and that humanity is standing amidst ruins, hiding its nakedness behind tattered rags, shedding tears upon hollow cheeks, and calling for its children with pitiful voice. But the children are busy singing their clan's anthem; they are busy sharpening the swords and cannot hear the cry of their mothers.

Humanity is the spirit of the Supreme Being on earth, and that Supreme Being preaches love and good-will. But the people ridicule such teachings. The Nazarene Jesus listened, and crucifixion was his lot; Socrates heard the voice and followed it, and he too fell victim in body. The followers of The Nazarene and Socrates are the followers of Deity, and since people will not kill them, they deride them, saying, "Ridicule is more bitter than killing."
TL-T-5

My soul preached to me and showed me that I am neither more than the pygmy, nor less than the giant.

Ere my soul preached to me, I looked upon humanity as two men: one weak, whom I pitied, and the other strong, whom I followed or resisted in defiance.

But now I have learned that I was as both are and made from the same elements. My origin is their origin, my conscience is their conscience, my contention is their contention, and my pilgrimage is their pilgrimage.

If they sin, I am also a sinner. If they do well, I take pride in their well-doing. If they rise, I rise with them. If they stay inert, I share their slothfulness.
TM-ST-31

HUNGER

A hungry man in a desert will not refuse to eat dry bread if Heaven does not shower him with manna and quails.
BW-ST-40

HUSBAND

Are you a husband who regards the wrongs he has committed as lawful, but those of his wife as unlawful? If so, you are like those extinct savages who lived in caves and covered their nakedness with hides.

Or are you a faithful companion, whose wife is ever at his side, sharing his every thought, rapture, and victory? If so, you are as one who at dawn walks at the head of a nation toward the high noon of justice, reason and wisdom.
WM-ST-35

I

IDEAS

How blind is the one who fancies and plans a matter in all true form and angles, and when he cannot prove it completely with superficial measurement and word proofs, believes that his idea and imagination were empty objects! But if he contemplates with sincerity and meditates upon these happenings, he will understand with conviction that his idea is as much a reality as is the bird of the sky, but that it is not yet crystallized, and that the idea is a segment of knowledge that cannot be proved with figures and words, for it is too high and too spacious to be imprisoned at that moment; too deeply imbedded in the spiritual to submit yet to the real.
SH-T-148

Every beauty and greatness in this world is created by a single thought or emotion inside a man. Every thing we see today, made by past generations, was, before its appearance, a thought in the mind of a man or an impulse in the heart of a woman. The revolutions that shed so much blood and turned men's minds toward liberty were the idea of one man who lived in the midst of thousands of men. The devastating wars which destroyed empires were a thought that existed in the mind of an individual. The supreme teachings that changed the course of humanity were the ideas of a man whose genius separated him from his environment. A single thought built the Pyramids, founded the glory of Islam, and caused the burning of the library at Alexandria.
BW-ST-49

IGNORANCE

In the house of Ignorance there is no mirror in which to view your soul.
SH-T-87

During the ebb, I wrote a line upon the sand,
Committing to it all that is in my soul and mind;
I returned at the tide to read it and to ponder upon it,
I found naught upon the seashore but my ignorance.
MS-39

ILLNESS

I have found pleasure in being ill. This pleasure differs with its effect from any other pleasure. I have found a sort of tranquility that makes me love illness. The sick man is safe from people's strife, demands, dates and appointments . . . I have found another kind of enjoyment through illness which is more important and unmeasurable. I have found that I am closer to abstract things in my sickness than in health.
SP-ST-84

I have pleasure in being ill. This pleasure differs with its effect from other pleasure. I have found a sort of tranquility that makes me love illness. The sick man is safe from people's strife, demands, dates and appointments, excess of talking and ringing of telephones. . . . I have found that I am closer to abstract things in my sickness than in health. When I lay my head and close my eyes and lose myself to the world, I find myself flying like a bird over serene valleys and forests, wrapped in a gentle veil. I see myself close to those whom my heart has loved, calling and talking to them, but without anger and with the same feelings they feel and the same thoughts they think. They lay their hands now and then upon my forehead to bless me.

SP-P-34

ILLUSION

> Man's will is a floating shadow
>   In the mind he conceives,
> And the rights of mankind pass and
>   Perish like the Autumn leaves.

P-51

IMAGINATION

Thoughts have a higher dwelling place than the visible world, and its skies are not clouded by sensuality. Imagination finds a road to the realm of the gods, and there man can glimpse that which is to be after the soul's liberation from the world of substance.

TM-ST-74

With one leap it [the imagination] would reach the core of life, divest it of all excrescences, then burn these excrescences and fling their ashes into the eyes of those who brought them into being. So must all imaginations be.

KG-P-24

IMITATION

> The people of the city feign great
> Wisdom and knowledge, but their
> Fancy remains false forever, for
> They are but experts of imitation.
> It gives them pride to calculate
> That a barter will bring no loss
> Or gain. The idiot imagines himself
> A king and no power can alter his
> Great thoughts and dreams. The
> Proud fool mistakes his mirror for
> The sky, and his shadow for a
> Moon that gleams high from the
> Heavens.
> T-368

IMMORTALITY

> Death on earth, to son of earth
>   Is final, but to him who is
> Ethereal, it is but the start
>   Of triumph certain to be his.
>
> If one embraces dawn in dreams,
>   He is immortal! Should he sleep
> His long night through, he surely fades
>   Into a sea of slumber deep.
>
> For he who closely hugs the ground
>   When wide awake will crawl 'til end.
> And death, like sea, who braves it light
>   Will cross it. Weighted will descend.
> P-70

If I did not covet immortality, I would never have learned the song which has been sung through all of time.

Rather, I would have been a suicide, nothing remaining of me except my ashes hidden within the tomb. . . .

Life is a darkness which ends as in the sunburst of the day.

The yearning of my heart tells me there is peace in the grave.

If some fool tells you the soul perishes like the body and that which dies never returns, tell him the flower perishes but the seed remains and lies before us as the secret of life everlasting.

MS-58

IMPERMANENCE

> Mankind is like verses written
> Upon the surface of the rills.

P-35

INDICTMENT

I will gladly exchange my outcries for cheerful laughter, speak eulogies instead of indictments, replace excess with moderation, provided you show me a just governor, a lawyer of integrity, a religious hierarch who practices what he preaches, a husband who looks upon his wife with the same eyes as he looks upon himself.

TM-ST-96

INFINITE

We are naught but frail atoms in the heavens of the infinite; and we cannot but obey and surrender to the will of Providence.

If we love, our love is neither from us, nor is it for us. If we rejoice, our joy is not in us, but in Life itself. If we suffer, our pain lies not in our wounds, but in the very heart of Nature.

WM-ST-23

INHERITANCE

The man who acquires his wealth by inheritance builds his mansion with the weak poor's money.

SR-T-269

INTOXICATION

> The human turns to drugging,
>   As to nursing from the breast;
> Coming to the age of weaning
>   Only when he's put to rest.
> P-39

ISLAND

Life is an island in an ocean of loneliness, an island whose rocks are hopes, whose trees are dreams, whose flowers are solitude, and whose brooks are thirst.

Your life, my fellow men, is an island separated from all other islands and regions. No matter how many are the ships that leave your shores for other climes, no matter how many are the fleets that touch your coast, you remain a solitary island, suffering the pangs of loneliness and yearning for happiness. You are unknown to your fellow men and far removed from their sympathy and understanding.
WM-ST-41

J

JESUS

Humanity looks upon Jesus the Nazarene as a poor-born Who suffered misery and humiliation with all of the weak. And He is pitied, for Humanity believes He was crucified painfully. . . . And all that Humanity offers to Him is crying and wailing and lamentation. For centuries Humanity has been worshipping weakness in the person of the Saviour.

The Nazarene was not weak! He was strong and is strong! But the people refuse to heed the true meaning of strength.
SH-T-154

Jesus came not from the heart of the circle of Light to destroy the homes and build upon their ruins the convents and monasteries. He did not persuade the strong man to become a monk or a priest, but He came to send forth upon this earth a new spirit, with power to crumble the foundation of any monarchy built upon human bones and skulls. . . . He came to demolish the majestic palaces, constructed upon the graves of the weak, and crush the idols, erected upon the bodies of the poor. Jesus was not sent here to teach the people to build magnificent churches and temples amidst the cold wretched huts and dismal hovels. . . . He came to make the human heart a temple, and the soul an altar, and the mind a priest.
SH-T-155

Surely you have prayed enough to last you to the end of your days, and hence forth you shall not enter a church as a worshipper; for the Jesus you love so dearly is not found in churches. Many are the places of worship, but few indeed are those who worship in Spirit and in truth.
KG-P-19

JOURNALIST
Are you a journalist who sells his principles in the markets of slaves and who fattens on gossip and misfortune and crime? If so, you are like a ravenous vulture preying upon rotting carrion.
WM-ST-35

JUDGMENT
The learned man who has not judgment is like an unarmed soldier proceeding into battle. His wrath will poison the pure spring of the life of his community and he will be like the grain of aloes in a pitcher of pure water.
WM-ST-54

JUSTICE

> Justice on earth would cause the Jinn
>   To cry at misuse of the word,
> And were the dead to witness it,
>   They'd mock at fairness in this world.
>
> Yea, death and prison we mete out
>   To small offenders of the laws,
> While honor, wealth, and full respect
>   On greater pirates we bestow.
>
> To steal a flower we call mean,
>   To rob a field is chivalry;
> Who kills the body he must die,
>   Who kills the spirit he goes free.
>   P-47

What justice does authority display when it kills the killer? When it imprisons the robber? When it descends on a neighbouring country and slays its people? What does justice think of the authority under which a killer punishes the one who kills, and a thief sentences the one who steals?
TL-T-9

When a man kills another man, the people say he is a murderer, but when the Emir kills him, the Emir is just. When a man robs a monastery, they say he is a thief, but when the Emir robs him of his life, the Emir is honourable. When a woman betrays her husband, they say she is an adulteress, but when the Emir makes her walk naked in the streets and stones her later, the Emir is noble. Shedding of blood is forbidden, but who made it lawful for the Emir? Stealing one's money is a crime, but taking away one's life is a noble act. Betrayal of a husband may be an ugly deed, but stoning of living souls is a beautiful sight. Shall we meet evil with evil and say this is the Law? Shall we fight corruption with greater corruption and say

this is the Rule? Shall we conquer crimes with more crimes and say this is Justice?
SR-T-315

The gifts which derive from justice are greater than those that spring from charity.
WM-ST-65

K

KIN

He who understands you is greater kin to you than your own brother. For even your own kindred may neither understand you nor know your true worth.
WM-ST-62

KINDNESS

From a sensitive woman's heart springs the happiness of mankind, and from the kindness of her noble spirit comes mankind's affection.
SR-T-262

> The kindness of the people is but an
> Empty shell containing no gem or
> Precious pearl. With two hearts do
> People live; a small one of deep
> Softness, the other of steel. And
> Kindness is too often a shield,
> And generosity too often a sword.
> T-367

KINGDOM OF HEAVEN

Vain are the beliefs and teachings that make man miserable, and false is the goodness that leads him into sorrow and despair, for it is man's purpose to be happy on this earth and lead the way to felicity and preach its gospel wherever he goes. He who does not see the king-

dom of heaven in this life will never see it in the coming life. We came not into this life by exile, but we came as innocent creatures of God, to learn how to worship the holy and eternal spirit and seek the hidden secrets within ourselves from the beauty of life.

SR-T-256

KINGDOMS

Humans are divided into different clans and tribes, and belong to countries and towns. But I find myself a stranger to all communities and belong to no settlement. The universe is my country and the human family is my tribe.

Men are weak, and it is sad that they divide among themselves. The world is narrow and it is unwise to cleave it into kingdoms, empires, and provinces.

TL-T-4

KNOWLEDGE

Learning follows various roads.
We note the start but not the end.
For Time and Fate must rule the course,
While we see not beyond the bend.

The best of knowledge is a dream
The gainer holds steadfast, uncowed
By ridicule, and moves serene,
Despised and lowly in the crowd.

P-52

L

LAW

What is Law? Who saw it coming with the sun from the depths of heaven? What human saw the heart of God and found its will or purpose? In what century did the

angels walk among the people and preach to them, saying, "Forbid the weak from enjoying life, and kill the outlaws with the sharp edge of the sword, and step upon the sinners with iron feet"?
SR-T-316

Are you a soldier compelled by the harsh law of man to forsake wife and children, and go forth into the field of battle for the sake of *Greed*, which your leaders mis-call *Duty*?

Are you a prisoner, pent up in a dark dungeon for some petty offense and condemned by those who seek to reform man by corrupting him?

Are you a young woman on whom God has bestowed beauty, but who has fallen prey to the base lust of the rich, who deceived you and bought your body but not your heart, and abandoned you to misery and distress?

If you are one of these, you are a martyr to man's law. You are wretched, and your wretchedness is the fruit of the iniquity of the strong and the injustice of the tyrant, the brutality of the rich, and the selfishness of the lewd and the covetous.
WM-ST-44

> Man is weak by his own hand, for he
> Has refashioned God's law into his own
> Confining manner of life, chaining
> Himself with the coarse irons of the
> Rules of society which he desired; and
> He is steadfast in refusing to be aware
> Of the great tragedy he has cast upon
> Himself and his children and their sons.
> Man has erected on this earth a prison
> Of quarrels from which he cannot now
> Escape, and misery is his voluntary lot.
> T-366

LAWS

People are saying that I am the enemy of just laws, of family ties and old tradition. Those people are telling the truth. I do not love man-made laws . . . I love the sacred and spiritual kindness which should be the source of every law upon the earth, for kindness is the shadow of God in man.
MS-V

Human society has yielded for seventy centuries to corrupted laws until it cannot understand the meaning of superior and eternal laws. . . . Spiritual disease is inherited from one generation to another until it becomes a part of the people, who look upon it, not as a disease, but as a natural gift, showered by God on Adam. If these people found someone free from the germs of this disease, they would think of him with shame and disgrace.
SP-P-31

LEARNING

Learning nourishes the seed but it gives you no seed of its own.
MS-72

Reason and learning are like body and soul. Without the body, the soul is nothing but empty wind. Without the soul, the body is but a senseless frame.

Reason without learning is like the untilled soil, or like the human body that lacks nourishment.
WM-ST-55

Learning is the only wealth tyrants cannot despoil. Only death can dim the lamp of knowledge that is within you. The true wealth of a nation lies not in its gold or silver but in its learning, wisdom, and in the uprightness of its sons.
WM-ST-61

LIARS

There are among the people murderers who have never committed murder, thieves who have never stolen and liars who have spoken nothing but the truth.
MS-72

LIBERTY

I walked lonely in the Valley of the Shadow of Life, where the past attempts to conceal itself in guilt, and the soul of the future folds and rests itself too long. There, at the edge of Blood and Tears River, which crawled like a poisonous viper and twisted like a criminal's dreams, I listened to the frightened whisper of the ghosts of slaves, and gazed at nothingness.

When midnight came and the spirits emerged from hidden places, I saw a cadaverous, dying spectre fall to her knees, gazing at the moon. I approached her, asking, "What is your name?"

"My name is Liberty," replied this ghastly shadow of a corpse.

And I inquired, "Where are your children?"

And Liberty, tearful and weak, gasped, "One died crucified, another died mad, and the third one is not yet born."

She limped away and spoke further, but the mist in my eyes and cries of my heart prevented sight or hearing.
SH-T-66

Everything on earth lives according to the law of nature, and from that law emerges the glory and joy of liberty; but man is denied this fortune, because he set for the God-given soul a limited and earthly law of his own. He made for himself strict rules. Man built a narrow and painful prison in which he secluded his affections and desires. He dug out a deep grave in which he buried his heart and its purpose. If an individual, through the dic-

tates of his soul, declares his withdrawal from society and violates the law, his fellowmen will say he is a rebel worthy of exile, or an infamous creature worthy only of execution. Will man remain a slave of self-confinement until the end of the world? Or will he be freed by the passing of time and live in the Spirit for the Spirit? Will man insist upon staring downward and backward at the earth? Or will he turn his eyes toward the sun so he will not see the shadow of his body amongst the skulls and thorns?

SR-T-228

LIFE

Man struggles to find life outside himself, unaware that the life he is seeking is within him.

SH-T-144

Life is a woman bathing in the tears of her lovers and anointing herself with the blood of her victims. Her raiments are white days, lined with the darkness of night. She takes the human heart to lover, but denies herself in marriage.

> *Life is an enchantress*
> *Who seduces us with her beauty—*
> *But he who knows her wiles*
> *Will flee her enchantments.*
> WM-ST-85

How often I talked with Harvard professors, yet felt as if I were talking to a professor from Al-Azhar! How often I have conversed with some Bostonian ladies and heard them say things I used to hear from simple and ignorant old women in Syria! Life is one, Mikhail; it manifests itself in the villages of Lebanon as in Boston, New York, and San Francisco.

KG-P-37

LIGHT

The true light is that which emanates from within man, and reveals the secrets of the heart to the soul, making it happy and contented with life.
SR-T-255

LIMITATION

The person who is limited in heart and thought is inclined to love that which is limited in life, and the weak-sighted cannot see more than one cubit ahead upon the path he treads, nor more than one cubit of the wall upon which he rests his shoulder.
SH-T-129

LONGING

In the will of man there is a power of longing which turns the mist in ourselves into sun.
SP-ST-86

LOVE

The power to
Love is God's greatest gift to man,
For it never will be taken from the
Blessed one who loves.
SH-T-99

Love lies in the soul alone,
Not in the body, and like wine
Should stimulate our better self
To welcome gifts of Love Divine.
P-61

Man cannot reap love until after sad and revealing separation, and bitter patience, and desperate hardship.
TL-T-115

Yesterday I stood at the temple door interrogating the passersby about the mystery and merit of Love.

And before me passed an old man with an emaciated and melancholy face, who sighed and said:

"Love is a natural weakness bestowed upon us by the first man."

But a virile youth retorted:

"Love joins our present with the past and the future."

Then a woman with a tragic face sighed and said:

"Love is a deadly poison injected by black vipers, that crawl from the caves of hell. The poison seems fresh as dew and the thirsty soul eagerly drinks it; but after the first intoxication the drinker sickens and dies a slow death."

Then a beautiful, rosy-cheeked damsel smilingly said:

"Love is a wine served by the brides of Dawn which strengthens strong souls and enables them to ascend to the stars."

After her a black-robed, bearded man, frowning, said:

"Love is the blind ignorance with which youth begins and ends."

Another, smiling, declared:

"Love is a divine knowledge that enables men to see as much as the gods."

Then said a blind man, feeling his way with a cane:

"Love is a blinding mist that keeps the soul from discerning the secret of existence, so that the heart sees only trembling phantoms of desire among the hills, and hears only echoes of cries from voiceless valleys."

And a feeble ancient, dragging his feet like two rags, said, in quavering tones:

"Love is the rest of the body in the quiet of the grave, the tranquility of the soul in the depth of Eternity."

And a five-year-old child, after him, said laughing:

"Love is my father and mother, and no one knows Love save my father and mother."

And so, all who passed spoke of Love as the image of

their hopes and frustrations, leaving it a mystery as
before.
TM-ST-88

Those whom Love has not chosen as followers do not
hear when Love calls.
BW-ST-75

Love is the only flower that grows and blossoms without the aid of seasons.
BW-ST-54

Love is the only freedom in the world because it so
elevates the spirit that the laws of humanity and the
phenomena of nature do not alter its course.
BW-ST-35

Love passes by us, robed in meekness; but we flee
from her in fear, or hide in the darkness; or else pursue
her, to do evil in her name.
WM-ST-46

Love that comes between the naivete and awakening
of youth satisfies itself with possessing, and grows with
embraces. But Love which is born in the firmament's lap
and has descended with the night's secrets is not contented with anything but Eternity and immortality; it
does not stand reverently before anything except deity.
BW-ST-114

> If humanity were to
> Lead love's cavalcade to a bed of
> Faithless motive, then love there
> Would decline to abide. Love is a
> Beautiful bird, begging capture,
> But refusing injury.
> T-369

> Love,
> When sought out, is an ailment
> Between the flesh and the bone,

And only when youth has passed
Does the pain bring rich and
Sorrowful knowledge.
T-369

Darkness may hide the trees and the flowers from the eyes but it cannot hide love from the soul.
S

LUST
Beauty reveals itself to us as she sits on the throne of glory; but we approach her in the name of Lust, snatch off her crown of purity, and pollute her garment with our evil-doing.
WM-ST-46

M

MADNESS
Madness is the first step towards unselfishness. Be mad and tell us what is behind the veil of "sanity." The purpose of life is to bring us closer to those secrets, and madness is the only means.
SP-ST-62

MAIDEN
There is no affection purer and more soothing to the spirit than the one hidden in the heart of a maiden who awakens suddenly and fills her own spirit with heavenly music that makes her days like poets' dreams and her nights prophetic.
SR-T-264

MANKIND
I love mankind and I love equally all
Three human kinds . . . the one who

Blasphemes life, the one who blesses
It, and the one who meditates upon it.
I love the first for his misery and
The second for his generosity and the
Third for his perception and peace.
    SH-T-101

MARRIAGE

Marriage is the union of two divinities that a third might be born on earth. It is the union of two souls in a strong love for the abolishment of separateness. It is that higher unity which fuses the separate unities within the two spirits. It is the golden ring in a chain whose beginning is a glance, and whose ending is Eternity. It is the pure rain that falls from an unblemished sky to fructify and bless the fields of divine Nature.
    WM-ST-50

MERCHANT

Are you a merchant, drawing advantage from the needs of the people, engrossing goods so as to resell them at an exorbitant price? If so, you are a reprobate; and it matters naught whether your home is a palace or a prison.

Or are you an honest man, who enables farmer and weaver to exchange their products, who mediates between buyer and seller, and through his just ways profits both himself and others?

If so, you are a righteous man; and it matters not whether you are praised or blamed.
    WM-ST-34

MERCY

Do not be merciful, but be just, for mercy is bestowed upon the guilty criminal, while justice is all that an innocent man requires.
    SR-T-276

860

MERRIMENT
> Life is not only a merriment;
> Life is desire and determination.
>
> MS-74

MIDDLE EAST

There are in the Middle East today two challenging ideas: old and new.

The old ideas will vanish because they are weak and exhausted.

There is in the Middle East an awakening that defies slumber. This awakening will conquer because the sun is its leader and the dawn is its army. . . .

There is on the horizon of the Middle East a new awakening; it is growing and expanding; it is reaching and engulfing all sensitive, intelligent souls; it is penetrating and gaining the sympathy of noble hearts.

The Middle East, today, has two masters. One is deciding, ordering, being obeyed; but he is at the point of death.

But the other one is silent in his conformity to law and order, calmly awaiting justice; he is a powerful giant who knows his own strength, confident in his existence and a believer in his destiny.

MS-60

MIMIC

He who repeats what he does not understand is no better than an ass that is loaded with books.

WM-ST-63

MODERN GENERATION

This strange generation exists between sleeping and waking. It holds in its hands the soil of the past and the seeds of the future.

BW-ST-84

MODERN POETRY

Oh spirits of the poets, who watch over us from the heaven of Eternity, we go to the altars you have adorned with the pearls of your thoughts and the gems of your souls because we are oppressed by the clang of steel and the clamor of factories. Therefore our poems are as heavy as freight trains and as annoying as steam whistles.

And you, the real poets, forgive us. We belong in the New World where men run after worldly goods; and poetry, too, is a commodity today, and not a breath of immortality.

TM-ST-83

MODERN WOMAN

Modern civilization has made woman a little wiser, but it has increased her suffering because of man's covetousness. The woman of yesterday was a happy wife, but the woman of today is a miserable mistress. In the past she walked blindly in the light, but now she walks open-eyed in the dark. She was beautiful in her ignorance, virtuous in her simplicity, and strong in her weakness. Today she has become ugly in her ingenuity, superficial and heartless in her knowledge. Will the day come when beauty and knowledge, ingenuity and virtue, and weakness of body and strength of spirit will be united in a woman?

BW-ST-83

MODESTY

To be modest in speaking truth is hypocrisy.

TM-ST-95

MONEY

Money! The source of insincere love; the spring of false light and fortune; the well of poisoned water; the desperation of old age!

TL-T-175

Money is like a stringed instrument; he who does not know how to use it properly will hear only discordant music. Money is like love; it kills slowly and painfully the one who withholds it, and it enlivens the other who turns it upon his fellow men.

TL-T-404

MOTHER

The mother is every thing—she is our consolation in sorrow, our hope in misery, and our strength in weakness. She is the source of love, mercy, sympathy, and forgiveness. He who loses his mother loses a pure soul who blesses and guards him constantly.

Every thing in nature bespeaks the mother. The sun is the mother of the earth and gives it its nourishment of heat; it never leaves the universe at night until it has put the earth to sleep to the song of the sea and the hymn of the birds and brooks. And this earth is the mother of trees and flowers. It produces them, nurses them, and weans them. The trees and flowers become kind mothers of their great fruits and seeds. And the mother, the prototype of all existence, is the eternal spirit, full of beauty and love.

BW-ST-92

MUSIC

When God created Man, he gave him Music as a language different from all other languages. And early man sang her glory in the wilderness; and she drew the hearts of kings and moved them from their thrones.

WM-ST-58

> The moaning flute is more divine
> Than the golden cup of deep, red wine.
> T-368

God created music as a common language for all men. It inspires the poets, the composers and the architects. It

lures us to search our souls for the meaning of the mysteries described in ancient books.

    S

N

NATURE

> In the wild there is no Credo
>   Nor a hideous disbelief;
> Song-birds never are assertive
>   Of the Truth, the Bliss, or Grief.
> P-46

When I began to draw and paint, I did not say to myself, "Behold Kahlil Gibran. There are ahead of you so many ways to art: The classic, the modern, the symbolistic, the impressionistic, and others. Choose for yourself one of them." I did nothing of the sort. I simply found my pen and brush, quite of themselves, recording symbols of my thoughts, emotions, and fancies. Some think the business of art to be a mere imitation of nature. But Nature is far too great and too subtle to be successfully imitated. No artist can ever reproduce even the least of Nature's surpassing creations and miracles. Besides, what profit is there in imitating Nature when she is so open and so accessible to all who see and hear? The business of art is rather to understand Nature and to reveal her meanings to those unable to understand. It is to convey the soul of a tree rather than to produce a fruitful likeness of the tree. It is to reveal the conscience of the sea, not to portray so many foaming waves or so much blue water. The mission of art is to bring out the unfamiliar from the most familiar.

Pity the eye that sees no more in the sun than a stove to keep it warm and a torch to light its way between the

home and the business office. That is a blind eye, even if capable of seeing a fly a mile away. Pity the ear that hears no more than so many notes in the song of the nightingale. It is a deaf ear, even if capable of hearing the crawling of ants in their subterranean labyrinths.
KG-P-100

Nature reaches out to us with welcoming arms, and bids us enjoy her beauty; but we dread her silence and rush into the crowded cities, there to huddle like sheep fleeing from a ferocious wolf.
WM-ST-47

> To Nature all are alive and all are
> Free. The earthly glory of man is an
> Empty dream, vanishing with the bubbles
> In the rocky stream.
> T-367

NATURE AND MAN

I heard the brook lamenting like a widow mourning her dead child and I asked, "Why do you weep, my pure brook?"

And the brook replied, "Because I am compelled to go to the city where Man contemns me and spurns me for stronger drinks and makes of me a scavenger for his offal, pollutes my purity, and turns my goodness to filth."

And I heard the birds grieving, and I asked, "Why do you cry, my beautiful birds?" And one of them flew near, and perched at the tip of a branch and said, "The sons of Adam will soon come into this field with their deadly weapons and make war upon us as if we were their mortal enemies. We are now taking leave of one another, for we know not which of us will escape the wrath of Man. Death follows us wherever we go."

Now the sun rose from behind the mountain peaks, and gilded the treetops with coronals. I looked upon this beauty and asked myself, "Why must Man destroy what Nature has built?"
WM-ST-83

NEIGHBOR

When you tell your trouble to your neighbor you present him with a part of your heart. If he possesses a great soul, he thanks you; if he possesses a small one, he belittles you.
MS-71

NEW YORK

He who wishes to live in New York must be a sharp sword in a sheath of honey. The sword is to repel those who are desirous of killing time, and the honey is to satisfy their hunger.
SP-ST-83

NIGHTINGALE

The nightingale does not make his nest in a cage lest slavery be the lot of its chicks.
BW-ST-122

O

OLD AGE

An old man likes to return in memory to the days of his youth like a stranger who longs to go back to his own country. He delights to tell stories of the past like a poet who takes pleasure in reciting his best poem. He lives spiritually in the past because the present passes swiftly, and the future seems to him an approach to the oblivion of the grave.
BW-ST-24

Many are the men who curse with venom the dead days of their youth; many are the women who execrate their wasted years with the fury of the lioness who has lost her cubs; and many are the youths and maidens who are using their hearts only to sheath the daggers of the bitter memories of the future, wounding themselves through ignorance with the sharp and poisoned arrows of seclusion from happiness.

Old age is the snow of the earth; it must, through light and truth, give warmth to the seeds of youth below, protecting them and fulfilling their purpose.

T-302

ONENESS

All things in this creation exist within you, and all things in you exist in creation; there is no border between you and the closest things, and there is no distance between you and the farthest things, and all things, from the lowest to the loftiest, from the smallest to the greatest, are within you as equal things. In one atom are found all the elements of the earth; in one motion of the mind are found the motions of all the laws of existence; in one drop of water are found the secrets of all the endless oceans; in one aspect of *you* are found all the aspects of *existence*.

SH-T-140

OPPORTUNITY

He who tries to seize an opportunity after it has passed him by is like one who sees it approach but will not go to meet it.

WM-ST-56

OPPRESSION

Woe to the nation that receives her conquerors beating the drums. Woe to the nation that hates oppression in

her sleep and accepts it in her awakening. Woe to the nation that raises her voice only behind a coffin and prides itself only in the cemetery. Woe to a nation that does not revolt until her neck is placed on the scaffold.
MS-99

ORIENT

The people of the Orient demand that the writer be like a bee always making honey. They are gluttonous for honey and prefer it to all other food.

The people of the Orient want their poet to burn himself as incense before their sultans. The Eastern skies have become sickly with incense yet the people of the Orient have had not enough. . . .

Numerous are the social healers in the Orient, and many are their patients who remain uncured but appear eased of their ills because they are under the effects of social narcotics. But these tranquilizers merely mask the symptoms.

Such narcotics are distilled from many sources but the chief is the Oriental philosophy of submission to Destiny (the act of God).
TM-ST-92

P

PACIFISM

Beware of the leader who says, "Love of existence obliges us to deprive the people of their rights!" I say unto you but this: protecting others' rights is the noblest and most beautiful human act; if my existence requires that I kill others, then death is more honourable to me, and if I cannot find someone to kill me for the protection of my honour, I will not hesitate to take my life by my

own hands for the sake of Eternity before Eternity comes.
TL-T-8

PAIN

Pain is an unseen and powerful hand that breaks the skin of the stone in order to extract the pulp.
SP-ST-94

PAST AND FUTURE

I tell you that the children of yesteryears are walking in the funeral of the era that they created for themselves. They are pulling a rotted rope that might break soon and cause them to drop into a forgotten abyss. I say that they are living in homes with weak foundations; as the storm blows — and it is about to blow — their homes will fall upon their heads and thus become their tombs. I say that all their thoughts, their sayings, their quarrels, their compositions, their books and all their work are nothing but chains dragging them because they are too weak to pull the load.

But the children of tomorrow are the ones called by life, and they follow it with steady steps and heads high, they are the dawn of new frontiers, no smoke will veil their eyes and no jingle of chains will drown out their voices. They are few in number, but the difference is as between a grain of wheat and a stack of hay. No one knows them but they know each other. They are like the summits, which can see and hear each other — not like caves, which cannot hear or see. They are the seed dropped by the hand of God in the field, breaking through its pod and waving its sapling leaves before the face of the sun. It shall grow into a mighty tree, its root in the heart of the earth and its branches high in the sky.
MS-64-65

PATRIOT

Are you a politician who says to himself: "I will use my country for my own benefit"? If so, you are naught but a parasite living on the flesh of others. Or are you a devoted patriot, who whispers into the ear of his inner self: "I love to serve my country as a faithful servant." If so, you are an oasis in the desert, ready to quench the thirst of the wayfarer.

WM-ST-34

PATRIOTISM

What is this duty that separates the lovers, and causes the women to become widows, and the children to become orphans? What is this patriotism which provokes wars and destroys kingdoms through trifles? And what cause can be more than trifling when compared to but one life? What is this duty which invites poor villagers, who are looked upon as nothing by the strong and by the sons of the inherited nobility, to die for the glory of their oppressors? If duty destroys peace among nations, and patriotism disturbs the tranquility of man's life, then let us say, "Peace be with duty and patriotism."

SH-T-379

I have a yearning for my beautiful country, and I love its people because of their misery. But if my people rose, stimulated by plunder and motivated by what they call "patriotic spirit" to murder, and invaded my neighbour's country, then upon the committing of any human atrocity I would hate my people and my country.

TL-T-4

PEACE

Will peace be on earth while the sons of misery are slaving in the fields to feed the strong and fill the

stomachs of the tyrants? Will ever peace come and save them from the clutches of destitution?

What is peace? Is it in the eyes of those infants, nursing upon the dry breasts of their hungry mothers in cold huts? Or is it in the wretched hovels of the hungry who sleep upon hard beds and crave for one bite of the food which the priests and monks feed to their fat pigs?

SH-T-82

PERPETUITY

I am saddened by the one who gazes upon the mountains and plains upon which the sun throws its rays, and who listens to the breeze singing the song of the thin branches, and who inhales the fragrance of the flowers and the jasmine, and then says within himself, "No . . . what I see and hear will pass away, and what I know and feel will vanish." This humble soul who sees and contemplates reverently the joys and sorrows about him, and then denies the perpetuity of their existence, must himself vanish like vapour in the air and disappear, for he is seeking darkness and placing his back to truth. Verily, he is a living soul denying *his* very existence, for he denies *other* of God's existing things.

SH-T-144

PERPLEXITY

Perplexity is the beginning of knowledge.

WM-ST-87

PERSECUTION

Persecution cannot harm him who stands by Truth. Did not Socrates fall proudly a victim in body? Was not Paul stoned for the sake of the Truth? It is our inner self that hurts us when we disobey and kills us when we betray.

SH-T-77

PHILOSOPHY

There is a desire deep within the soul which drives man from the seen to the unseen, to philosophy and to the divine.
MS-49

PILGRIMAGE

For every seed that autumn drops into the heart of the earth, there exists a different manner of splitting the shell from the pulp; then are created the leaves and then the flowers, and then the fruit. But regardless of the fashion in which this takes place, those plants must undertake one sole pilgrimage, and their great mission is to stand before the face of the sun.
SH-T-141

POET

Poet, you are the life of this life, and you have
Triumphed over the ages despite their severity.

Poet, you will one day rule the hearts, and
Therefore, your kingdom has no ending.

Poet, examine your crown of thorns; you will
Find concealed in it a budding wreath of laurel.
TL-T-301

Are you a poet full of noise and empty sounds? If so, you are like one of those mountebanks that make us laugh when they are weeping, and make us weep, when they laugh.

Or are you one of those gifted souls in whose hands God has placed a viola to soothe the spirit with heavenly music, and bring his fellow men close to Life and the Beauty of Life? If so, you are a torch to light us on our way, a sweet longing in our hearts, and a revelation of the divine in our dreams.
WM-ST-36

Poets are unhappy people, for, no matter how high their spirits reach, they will still be enclosed in an envelope of tears.
BW-ST-41

POETRY

Poetry, my dear friends, is a sacred incarnation of a smile. Poetry is a sigh that dries the tears. Poetry is a spirit who dwells in the soul, whose nourishment is the heart, whose wine is affection. Poetry that comes not in this form is a false messiah.
TM-ST-83

If the spirits of Homer, Virgil, Al-Maary, and Milton had known that poetry would become a lapdog of the rich, they would have forsaken a world in which this could occur.
TM-ST-82

POOR

Not all the poor are scorned;
The wealth of the world is in a loaf of bread and a cloak.
MS-75

POPULAR KNOWLEDGE

Present knowledge of the people
Is a fog above the field;
When the sun mounts the horizon
To its rays the mist will yield.
P-54

POSITION

Greatness is not in exalted position;
Greatness is for he who refuses position.
MS-74

POSSESSIVENESS

Limited love asks for possession of the beloved, but the unlimited asks only for itself.
BW-ST-114

POVERTY

My fellow poor, Poverty sets off the nobility of the spirit, while wealth discloses its evil. Sorrow softens the feelings, and Joy heals the wounded heart. Were Sorrow and Poverty abolished, the spirit of man would be like an empty tablet, with naught inscribed save the signs of selfishness and greed.
WM-ST-65

My poor friend, if you only knew that the Poverty which causes you so much wretchedness is the very thing that reveals the knowledge of Justice and the understanding of Life, you would be contented with your lot.

I say knowledge of Justice: for the rich man is too busy amassing wealth to seek this knowledge.

And I say understanding of Life: for the strong man is too eager in his pursuit of power and glory to keep to the straight path of truth.

Rejoice then, my poor friend, for you are the mouth of Justice and the book of Life. Be content, for you are the source of virtue in those who rule over you and the pillar of integrity of those who guide you.
WM-ST-64

PRAISE

My soul preached to me and said, "Do not be delighted because of praise, and do not be distressed because of blame."

Ere my soul counseled me, I doubted the worth of my work.

Now I realize that the trees blossom in Spring and bear fruit in Summer without seeking praise; and they drop their leaves in Autumn and become naked in Winter without fearing blame.
TM-ST-31

PRAYER

Prayer is the song of the heart. It reaches the ear of God even if it is mingled with the cry and the tumult of a thousand men.
S

PREACHING

How painful is the preaching of the fortunate to the heart of the miserable! And how severe is the strong when he stands as advisor among the weak!
SH-T-381

PRIEST

The priest is a traitor who uses the Gospel as a threat to ransom your money . . . a hypocrite wearing a cross and using it as a sword to cut your veins . . . a wolf disguised in lambskin . . . a glutton who respects the tables more than the altars . . . a gold hungry creature who follows the Dinar to the farthest land . . . a cheat pilfering from widows and orphans. He is a queer being, with an eagle's beak, a tiger's clutches, a hyena's teeth and a viper's clothes. Take the Book away from him and tear his raiment off and pluck his beard and do whatever you wish unto him; then place in his hand one Dinar, and he will forgive you smilingly.
SR-T-281

When a villager doubts the holiness of the priest, he will be told, "Listen only to his teaching and disregard his shortcomings and misdeeds."
TM-ST-94

PROGRESS

Progress is not merely improving the past; it is moving forward toward the future.
MS-71

PROPHET

>The Prophet arrives
>   Veiled in the cloak of future thought,
>'Mid people hid in ancient garb,
>   Who could not see the gift he brought.

>He is a stranger to this life,
>   Stranger to those who praise or blame,
>For he upholds the Torch of Truth,
>   Although devoured by the flame.
P-52

R

REASON

When Reason speaks to you, hearken to what she says, and you shall be saved. Make good use of her utterances, and you shall be as one armed. For the Lord has given you no better guide than Reason, no stronger arm than Reason. When Reason speaks to your inmost self, you are proof against Desire. For Reason is a prudent minister, a loyal guide, and a wise counsellor. Reason is light in darkness, as anger is darkness amidst light. Be wise—let Reason, not Impulse, be your guide.
WM-ST-54

REBELLION

Life without Rebellion is like seasons without Spring. And Rebellion without Right is like Spring in an arid

THE TREASURED WRITINGS OF KAHLIL GIBRAN

desert. . . . Life, Rebellion, and Right are three-in-one who cannot be changed or separated.
TM-ST-62

Did God give us the breath of life to place it under death's feet? Did He give us liberty to make it a shadow for slavery? He who extinguishes his spirit's fire with his own hands is an infidel in the eyes of Heaven, for Heaven set the fire that burns in our spirits. He who does not rebel against oppression is doing himself injustice.
BW-ST-112

REGRET

Be not like him who sits by his fireside and watches the fire go out, then blows vainly upon the dead ashes. Do not give up hope or yield to despair because of that which is past, for to bewail the irretrievable is the worst of human frailties.
WM-ST-68

RELIGION

If we were to do away with the various religions, we would find ourselves united and enjoying one great faith and religion, abounding in brotherhood.
SH-T-135

Religion is a well-tilled field,
　　Planted and watered by desire
Of one who longed for Paradise,
　　Or one who dreaded Hell and Fire.

Aye, were it but for reckoning
　　At Resurrection, they had not
Worshipped God, nor did repent,
　　Except to gain a better lot—

As though religion were a phase
　　Of commerce in their daily trade;

Should they neglect it they would lose—
Or persevering would be paid.
P-44

Religion to man is like a field,
For it is planted with hope and
Tended by the shivering ignorant,
Fearing the fire of hell; or it is
Sowed by the strong in wealth of
Empty gold who look upon religion
As a kind of barter, ever seeking
Profit in earthly reward. But
Their hearts are lost despite
Their throbbing, and the product
Of their spiritual farming is but
The unwanted weed of the valley.
T-364

RELIGIOUS LEADER

Are you a leader of religion, who weaves out of the simplicity of the faithful a scarlet robe for his body; and of their kindness a golden crown for his head; and while living on Satan's plenty, spews forth his hatred of Satan? If so, you are a heretic; and it matters not that you fast all day and pray all night.

Or are you the faithful one who finds in the goodness of people a groundwork for the betterment of the whole nation; and in whose soul is the ladder of perfection leading to the Holy Spirit? If you are such, you are like a lily in the garden of Truth; and it matters not if your fragrance is lost upon men, or dispersed into the air, where it will be eternally preserved.
WM-ST-34

REPENTANCE

Paradise is not in repentance;
Paradise is in the pure heart.
MS-74

RICHES

Riches are not in money alone;
How many wanderers were the richest of all men?
MS-75

RULER

Between the frown of the tiger and the smile of the wolf the flock is perished; the ruler claims himself as king of the law, and the priest as the representative of God, and between these two, the bodies are destroyed and the souls wither into nothing.
SR-T-269

S

SANITY

Eagles never display wonder,
Or say, " 'Tis marvel of the age."
For in nature we the children
Only hold the sane as strange.
P-64

SCIENCE

All around me are dwarves who see giants emerging; and the dwarves croak like frogs:

"The world has returned to savagery. What science and education have created is being destroyed by the new primitives. We are now like the prehistoric cave dwellers. Nothing distinguishes us from them save our machines of destruction and our improved techniques of slaughter."

Thus speak those who measure the world's conscience by their own. They measure the range of all Existence by the tiny span of their individual being. As if the sun did not exist but for their warmth, as if the sea was created for them to wash their feet.
TM-ST-99

THE TREASURED WRITINGS OF KAHLIL GIBRAN

SECRETS

>My heart, keep secret your love,
>　and hide the secret from those you see
>　and you will have better fortune.
>He who reveals secrets is considered a fool;
>　silence and secrecy are much better for him
>　who falls in love.
>　MS-76

SEED

>The seed which
>The ripe date contains in its.
>Heart is the secret of the palm
>Tree from the beginning of all
>Creation.
>　T-374

SEGREGATION

A God Who is good knows of no segregation amongst words or names, and were a God to deny His blessing to those who pursue a different path to eternity, then there is no human who should offer worship.
　SH-T-142

SELF

Man is empowered by God to hope and hope fervently, until that for which he is hoping takes the cloak of oblivion from his eyes, whereupon he will at last view his real self. And he who sees his real self sees the truth of real life for himself, for all humanity, and for all things.
　SH-T-140

It is vain for the wayfarer to knock upon the door of the empty house. Man is standing mutely between the non-existence within him and the reality of his surroundings. If we did not possess what we have within ourselves we could not have the things we call our environs.
　SH-T-145

THE TREASURED WRITINGS OF KAHLIL GIBRAN

SELF-EXPRESSION

Is it not true, that every time we draw Beauty we approach a step nearer to Beauty? And every time we write the Truth we become one with it? Or do you propose to muzzle poets and artists? Is not self-expression a deeply seated need in the human soul?

KG-P-95

SELF-KNOWLEDGE

Know your own true worth, and you shall not perish. Reason is your light and your beacon of Truth. Reason is the source of Life. God has given you Knowledge, so that by its light you may not only worship him, but also see yourself in your weakness and strength.

WM-ST-55

SENSES

How ignorant are those who see, without question, the abstract existence with *some* of their senses, but insist upon doubting until that existence reveals itself to *all* their senses. Is not faith the sense of the heart as truly as sight is the sense of the eye? And how narrow is the one who hears the song of the blackbird and sees it hovering above the branches, but doubts that which he has seen and heard until he seizes the bird with his hands. Were not a *portion* of his senses sufficient? How strange is the one who dreams in truth of a beautiful reality, and then, when he endeavours to fashion it into form but cannot succeed, doubts the dream and blasphemes the reality and distrusts the beauty!

SH-T-148

SEX

The most highly sexed beings upon the planet are the creators, the poets, sculptors, painters, musicians . . . and so it has been from the beginning. And among them

sex is a beautiful and exalted gift. Sex is always beautiful, and is always shy.
MS-94-95

SHADOWS

How unjust to themselves are those who turn their backs to the sun, and see naught except the shadows of their physical selves upon the earth!
SH-T-150

SHEPHERD

In the city the best of
Man is but one of a flock, led by
The shepherd in strong voice. And he
Who follows not the command must soon
Stand before his killers.
T-361

SIGHT

Not all of us are enabled to see with our inner eyes the great depths of life, and it is cruel to demand that the weak-sighted see the dim and the far.
SH-T-129

SILENCE

Great truth that transcends Nature does not pass from one being to another by way of human speech. Truth chooses Silence to convey her meaning to loving souls.
WM-ST-75

There is something greater and purer than what the mouth utters. Silence illuminates our souls, whispers to our hearts, and brings them together. Silence separates us from ourselves, makes us sail the firmament of spirit, and brings us closer to Heaven; it makes us feel that

bodies are no more than prisons and that this world is only a place of exile.
BW-ST-48

SIN

Perfection is not for the pure of soul;
There may be virtue in sin.
MS-75

SINCERITY

Many a time I have made a comparison between nobility of sacrifice and happiness of rebellion to find out which one is nobler and more beautiful; but until now I have distilled only one truth out of the whole matter, and this truth is sincerity, which makes all our deeds beautiful and honorable.
BW-ST-117

SLAVERY

I accompanied the ages from the banks of the Kange to the shores of Euphrates; from the mouth of the Nile to the plains of Assyria; from the arenas of Athens to the churches of Rome; from the slums of Constantinople to the palaces of Alexandria. . . . Yet I saw slavery moving over all, in a glorious and majestic procession of ignorance. I saw the people sacrificing the youths and maidens at the feet of the idol, calling her the God; pouring wine and perfume upon her feet, and calling her the Queen; burning incense before her image, and calling her the Prophet; kneeling and worshipping before her, and calling her the Law; fighting and dying for her, and calling her Patriotism; submitting to her will, and calling her the Shadow of God on earth; destroying and demolishing homes and institutions for her sake, and

calling her Fraternity; struggling and stealing and work-
ing for her, and calling her Fortune and Happiness;
killing for her, and calling her Equality.

She possesses various names, but one reality. She has
many appearances, but is made of one element. In truth,
she is an everlasting ailment bequeathed by each generation unto its successor.

SH-T-64

> They tell me: If you see a slave sleeping, do not wake
> him lest he be dreaming of freedom.
> I tell them: If you see a slave sleeping, wake him and
> explain to him freedom.
> MS-72

SLEEP

> Life is but a sleep disturbed
> By dreaming, prompted by the will;
> The saddened soul with sadness hides
> Its secrets, and the gay, with thrill.
> P-42

SOBRIETY

> Few on this earth who savor life,
> And are not bored by its free gifts;
> Or divert not its streams to cups
> In which their fancy floats and drifts.
>
> Should you then find a sober soul
> Amidst this state of revelry,
> Marvel how a moon did find
> In this rain cloud a canopy.
> P-37

SOCIETY

> Society
> Is of naught but clamour and woe

THE TREASURED WRITINGS OF KAHLIL GIBRAN

And strife. She is but the web of
The spider, the tunnel of the mole.
T-376

SOLITUDE

The sorrowful spirit finds relaxation in solitude. It
abhors people, as a wounded deer deserts the herd and
lives in a cave until it is healed or dead.
BW-ST-87

Solitude has soft, silky hands, but with strong fingers
it grasps the heart and makes it ache with sorrow. Solitude is the ally of sorrow as well as a companion of
spiritual exaltation.
BW-ST-19

Your life, my brother, is a solitary habitation separated
from other men's dwellings. It is a house into whose
interior no neighbor's gaze can penetrate. If it were emptied of provisions, the stores of your neighbors could not
fill it. If it stood in a desert, you could not move it into
other men's gardens, tilled and planted by other hands.
If it stood on a mountaintop, you could not bring it down
into the valley trod by other men's feet.

Your spirit's life, my brother, is encompassed by loneliness, and were it not for that loneliness and solitude,
you would not be *you*, nor would I be *I*. Were it not for
this loneliness and solitude, I would come to believe on
hearing your voice that it was my voice speaking; or
seeing your face, that it was myself looking into a mirror.
WM-ST-43

SONG

Give to me the reed and sing thou!
For the song is gracious shade,
And the plaint of reed remaineth
When illusions dim and fade.
P-39

THE TREASURED WRITINGS OF KAHLIL GIBRAN

SORROW

> Sorrow is the shadow of a God who
> Lives not in the domain of evil hearts.
> SH-T-86

> Sorrow, if able to speak, would
> Prove sweeter than the joy of song.
> SH-T-99

He who has not looked on Sorrow will never see Joy.
WM-ST-88

The sorrowful spirit finds rest when united with a similar one. They join affectionately, as a stranger is cheered when he sees another stranger in a strange land. Hearts that are united through the medium of sorrow will not be separated by the glory of happiness.
BW-ST-42

> The secret of the heart is encased
> In sorrow, and only in sorrow is
> Found our joy, while happiness serves
> But to conceal the deep mystery of life.
> T-362

SOUL

> The reason why the soul exists
> Is folded in the soul itself;
> No painting could its essence show,
> Nor manifest its real self.
> P-65

The soul does not see anything in life save that which is in the soul itself. It does not believe except in its own private event, and when it experiences something, the outcome becomes a part of it.
SP-ST-56

SOUNDS OF NATURE

When the birds sing, do they call to the flowers in the fields, or are they speaking to the trees, or are they echoing the murmur of the brooks? For Man with his understanding cannot know what the bird is saying, nor what the brook is murmuring, nor what the waves whisper when they touch the beaches slowly and gently.

Man with his understanding cannot know what the rain is saying when it falls upon the leaves of the trees or when it taps at the window panes. He cannot know what the breeze is saying to the flowers in the fields.

But the Heart of Man can feel and grasp the meaning of these sounds that play upon his feelings. Eternal Wisdom often speaks to him in a mysterious language; Soul and Nature converse together, while Man stands speechless and bewildered.

Yet has not Man wept at the sounds? And are not his tears eloquent understanding?

WM-ST-58

SPIRIT

The spirit in every being is made manifest in the eyes, the countenance, and in all bodily movements and gestures. Our appearance, our words, our actions are never greater than ourselves. For the soul is our house; our eyes its windows; and our words its messengers.

WM-ST-62

> The strength of the spirit alone is
> The power of powers, and must in time
> Crumble to powder all things opposing
> It. Do not condemn, but pity the
> Faithless and their weakness and their
> Ignorance and their nothingness.
>
> T-365

Through the spirit,
Not the body, love must be shown,
As it is to enliven, not to deaden,
That the wine is pressed.
T-371

You may deprive me of my possessions; you may shed my blood and burn my body, but you cannot hurt my spirit or touch my truth.
S

SPIRITS

Between the people of eternity and people of the earth there is a constant communication, and all comply with the will of that unseen power. Oftentimes an individual will perform an act, believing that it is born of his own free will, accord, and command, but in fact he is being guided and impelled with precision to do it. Many great men attained their glory by surrendering themselves in complete submission to the will of the spirit, employing no reluctance or resistance to its demands, as a violin surrenders itself to the complete will of a fine musician.

Between the spiritual world and the world of substance there is a path upon which we walk in a swoon of slumber. It reaches us and we are unaware of its strength, and when we return to ourselves we find that we are carrying with our real hands the seeds to be planted carefully in the good earth of our daily lives, bringing forth good deeds and words of beauty. Were it not for that path between our lives and the departed lives, no prophet or poet or learned man would have appeared among the people.
SH-T-146

SPIRITUAL AFFINITY

It is wrong to think that love comes from long companionship and persevering courtship. Love is the offspring

THE TREASURED WRITINGS OF KAHLIL GIBRAN

of spiritual affinity and unless that affinity is created in a moment, it will not be created in years or even generations.
BW-ST-52

SPIRITUAL AWAKENING

Spiritual awakening is the most essential thing in man's life, and it is the sole purpose of being. Is not civilization, in all its tragic forms, a supreme motive for spiritual awakening? Then how can we deny existing matter, while its very existence is unwavering proof of its conformability into the intended fitness? The present civilization may possess a vanishing purpose, but the eternal law has offered to that purpose a ladder whose steps can lead to a free substance.
SH-T-29

SPIRITUALITY

Time and place are spiritual states, and all that is seen and heard is spiritual. If you close your eyes you will perceive all things through the depths of your inner self, and you will see the world physical and ethereal, in its intended entirety, and you will acquaint yourself with its necessary laws and precautions, and you will understand the greatness that it possesses beyond its closeness.
SH-T-139

SPRING

In every winter's heart there is a quivering spring, and behind the veil of each night there is a smiling dawn.
SP-ST-57

STRENGTH

The very strength that protects the heart from injury is the strength that prevents the heart from enlarging to its

intended greatness within. The song of the voice is sweet, but the song of the heart is the pure voice of heaven.

SH-T-121

SUBMISSION

Men, even if they are born free, will remain slaves of strict laws enacted by their forefathers; and the firmament, which we imagine as unchanging, is the yielding of today to the will of tomorrow and submission of yesterday to the will of today.

BW-ST-118

SWORD

Whoever reaches eternity with sword in his hand lives as long as there is justice.

MS-29

SYMPATHY

The sympathy that touches the neighbour's heart is more supreme than the hidden virtue in the unseen corners of the convent. A word of compassion to the weak criminal or prostitute is nobler than the long prayer which we repeat emptily every day in the temple.

SR-T-257

T

TALK

I am bored with gabbers and their gab; my soul abhors them. . . .

Is there in this universe a nook where I can go and live happily by myself?

Is there any place where there is no traffic in empty talk?

Is there on this earth one who does not worship himself talking?

Is there any person among all persons whose mouth is not a hiding place for the knavish Mister Gabber?
TM-ST-40-42

TEACHER

Whoever would be a teacher of men let him begin by teaching himself before teaching others; and let him teach by example before teaching by word. For he who teaches himself and rectifies his own ways is more deserving of respect and reverence than he who would teach others and rectify their ways.
KG-P-27

TEARS

He who is seared and cleansed once with his
Own tears will remain pure forevermore.
SH-T-86

The tears you shed are purer than the laughter of him that seeks to forget and sweeter than the mockery of the scoffer. These tears cleanse the heart of the blight of hatred, and teach man to share the pain of the brokenhearted. They are the tears of the Nazarene.
WM-ST-65

Love that is cleansed by tears will remain eternally pure and beautiful.
BW-ST-42

The tears of young men are the overflow of full hearts. But the tears of old men are the residue of age dropping upon their cheeks, the remains of life in weakened bodies. Tears in the eyes of young men resemble drops of dew upon a rose, but the tears of old men resemble yellow autumn leaves, blown and scattered by the wind as the winter of life approaches.
S

TEARS AND LAUGHTER

I would not exchange the laughter of my heart for the fortunes of the multitudes; nor would I be content with converting my tears, invited by my agonized self, into calm. It is my fervent hope that my whole life on this earth will ever be tears and laughter.

T-413

TEETH

In the mouth of Society are many diseased teeth, decayed to the bones of the jaws. But Society makes no efforts to have them extracted and be rid of the affliction. It contents itself with gold fillings. Many are the dentists who treat the decayed teeth of Society with glittering gold.

Numerous are those who yield to the enticements of such reformers, and pain, sickness, and death are their lot. . . .

Visit the courts and witness the acts of the crooked and corrupted purveyors of justice. *See* how they play with the thoughts and minds of the simple people as a cat plays with a mouse.

Visit the homes of the rich where conceit, falsehood, and hypocrisy reign.

But don't neglect to go through the huts of the poor as well, where dwell fear, ignorance, and cowardice.

Then visit the nimble-fingered dentists, possessors of delicate instruments, dental plasters and tranquilizers, who spend their days filling the cavities in the rotten teeth of the nation to mask the decay.

TM-ST-38

THINGS

Substantial things deaden a man without suffering; love awakens him with enlivening pains.

TL-T-3

If your knowledge teaches you not the value of things, and frees you not from the bondage to matter, you shall never come near the throne of Truth.
WM-ST-63

THIRST
The thirst of soul is sweeter than the wine of material things, and the fear of spirit is dearer than the security of the body.
BW-ST-69

THRONG
Life amid the throngs is but brief
And drug-laden slumber, mixed with
Mad dreams and spectres and fears.
T-362

TIME
This world is but a winery,
Its host and master Father Time,
Who caters only to those steep'd
In dreams discordant, without rhyme.

For people drink and race as though
They were the steeds of mad desire;
Thus some are blatant when they pray,
And others frenzied to acquire.
P-39

The people
Of the city abuse the wine of Time,
For they think upon it as a temple,
And they drink of it with ease and
With unthinking, and they flee,
Scurrying into old age with deep
But unknowing sorrow.
T-363

How strange Time is, and how queer we are! Time has really changed, and lo, it has changed us too, It walked one step forward, unveiled its face, alarmed us and then elated us.

Yesterday we complained about Time and trembled at its terrors. But today we have learned to love it and revere it, for we now understand its intents, its natural disposition, its secrets, and its mysteries.

Yesterday we crawled in fright like shuddering ghosts between the fears of the night and the menaces of the day. But today we walk joyously towards the mountain peak, the dwelling place of the raging tempest and the birthplace of thunder. . . .

Yesterday we honored false prophets and sorcerers. But today Time has changed, and lo, it has changed us too. We can now stare at the face of the sun and listen to the songs of the sea, and nothing can shake us except a cyclone.

Yesterday we tore down the temples of our souls and from their debris we built tombs for our forefathers. But today our souls have turned into sacred altars that the ghosts of the past cannot approach, that the fleshless fingers of the dead cannot touch.

We were a silent thought hidden in the corners of Oblivion. Today we are a strong voice that can make the firmament reverberate.

TM-ST-33

TORCH

The human soul is but a part of a burning torch which God separated from Himself at Creation.

WM-ST-67

TREASURE

Knowledge and understanding are life's faithful companions who will never prove untrue to you. For knowl-

edge is your crown, and understanding your staff; and when they are with you, you can possess no greater treasures.
WM-ST-62

TRUTH
Truth is like the stars; it does not appear except from behind obscurity of the night. Truth is like all beautiful things in the world; it does not disclose its desirability except to those who first feel the influence of falsehood. Truth is a deep kindness that teaches us to be content with our everyday life and share with the people the same happiness.
SR-T-255

He who would seek truth and proclaim it to mankind is bound to suffer. My sorrows have taught me to understand the sorrows of my fellow men . . . persecution . . . [has not] dimmed the vision within me.
VM-P-86

Truth calls to us, drawn by the innocent laughter of a child, or the kiss of a loved one; but we close the doors of affection in her face and deal with her as with an enemy.
WM-ST-47

U

UNAWARENESS
The human heart cries out for help; the human soul implores us for deliverance; but we do not heed their cries, for we neither hear nor understand. But the man who hears and understands we call mad, and flee from him.
Thus the nights pass, and we live in unawareness; and

the days greet us and embrace us. But we live in constant dread of day and night.

WM-ST-47

UNSEEN

The subtlest beauties in our life are unseen and unheard.

SP-ST-30

The Jews, my beloved, awaited the coming of a Messiah, who had been promised them, and who was to deliver them from bondage.

And the Great Soul of the World sensed that the worship of Jupiter and Minerva no longer availed, for the thirsty hearts of men could not be quenched with that wine.

In Rome men pondered the divinity of Apollo, a god without pity, and the beauty of Venus already fallen into decay.

For deep in their hearts, though they did not understand it, these nations hungered and thirsted for the supreme teaching that would transcend any to be found on the earth. They yearned for the spirit's freedom that would teach man to rejoice with his neighbor at the light of the sun and the wonder of living. For it is this cherished freedom that brings man close to the Unseen, which he can approach without fear or shame.

WM-ST-92

V

VIRGIN

There is no secret in the mystery of life stronger and more beautiful than that attachment which converts the silence of a virgin's spirit into a perpetual awareness that

makes a person forget the past, for it kindles fiercely in the heart the sweet and overwhelming hope of the coming future.
SR-T-264

W

WAR

You are my brother, but why are you quarreling with me? Why do you invade my country and try to subjugate me for the sake of pleasing those who are seeking glory and authority?

Why do you leave your wife and children and follow Death to the distant land for the sake of those who buy glory with your blood, and high honour with your mother's tears?

Is it an honour for a man to kill his brother man? If you deem it an honour, let it be an act of worship, and erect a temple to Cain who slew his brother Abel.
TL-T-7

Can lovers meet and exchange kisses on battlefields still acrid with bomb fumes?

Will the poet compose his songs under stars veiled in gun smoke?

Will the musician strum his lute in a night whose silence was ravished by terror?
TM-ST-98

WAY TO GOD

Perhaps we are nearer to Him each time we try to divide Him and find Him indivisible. Yet do I say that art, through drawing a line between the beautiful and the ugly, is the nearest way to God. Pure meditation is another way. But it leads to silence and to self-

confinement. Silence is truer and more expressive than speech; and the hour shall come when we shall be silent. But why muzzle our tongues before that hour has struck? There is your friend Lao Tze; he became silent, but when? After he gave to the world the gist of his faith in words.

KG-P-96

WEAKNESS

That deed which in our guilt we today call weakness, will appear tomorrow as an essential link in the complete chain of Man.

WM-ST-32

WEALTH

In some countries, the parent's wealth is a source of misery for the children. The wide strong box which the father and mother together have used for the safety of their wealth becomes a narrow, dark prison for the souls of their heirs. The Almighty Dinar which the people worship becomes a demon which punishes the spirit and deadens the heart.

BW-ST-64

WILL

To Will belongs the Right. For Souls
　　When strong prevail, when weak become
Subject to changes, good and bad,
　　And with the wind may go and come.

Then, deny not that Will in Soul
　　Is greater than the Might of Arm,
And weakling only mounts the throne
　　Of those beyond the good and harm.

P-50

WINGS

God has given you a spirit with wings on which to soar into the spacious firmament of Love and Freedom. Is it not pitiful then that you cut your wings with your own hands and suffer your soul to crawl like an insect upon the earth?
WM-ST-67

WISDOM

The wise man is he who loves and reveres God. A man's merit lies in his knowledge and in his deeds, not in his color, faith, race, or descent. For remember, my friend, the son of a shepherd who possesses knowledge is of greater worth to a nation than the heir to the throne, if he be ignorant. Knowledge is your true patent of nobility, no matter who your father or what your race may be.
WM-ST-61

Keep me away from the wisdom which does not cry, the philosophy which does not laugh and the greatness which does not bow before children.
MS-72

WOMAN

A woman whom Providence has provided with beauty of spirit and body is a truth, at the same time both open and secret, which we can understand only by love, and touch only by virtue; and when we attempt to describe such a woman she disappears like a vapor.
BW-ST-39

Women opened the windows of my eyes and the doors of my spirit. Had it not been for the woman-mother, the woman-sister, and the woman-friend, I would have been sleeping among those who seek the tranquility of the world with their snoring.
SP-P-31

Writers and poets try to understand the truth about woman. But until this day they have never understood her heart because, looking upon her through the veil of desire, they see nothing except the shape of her body. Or they look upon her through a magnifying glass of spite and find nothing in her but weakness and submission.
S

WOMAN'S HEART

A woman's heart will not change with time or season; even if it dies eternally, it will never perish. A woman's heart is like a field turned into a battleground; after the trees are uprooted and the grass is burned and the rocks are reddened with blood and the earth is planted with bones and skulls, it is calm and silent as if nothing has happened; for the spring and autumn come at their intervals and resume their work.
BW-ST-71

WORDS

Wisdom is not in words;
Wisdom is meaning within words.
MS-74

WORSHIP

God does not like to be worshipped by an ignorant man who imitates someone else.
SR-T-267

WORTH

If your knowledge teaches you not to rise above human weakness and misery and lead your fellow man on the right path, you are indeed a man of little worth and will remain such till Judgment Day.
WM-ST-63

WRITER

Are you a writer who holds his head high above the crowd, while his brain is deep in the abyss of the past, that is filled with the tatters and useless cast-offs of the ages? If so, you are like a stagnant pool of water.

Or are you the keen thinker, who scrutinizes his inner self, discarding that which is useless, outworn and evil, but preserving that which is useful and good? If so, you are as manna to the hungry, and as cool, clear water to the thirsty.
WM-ST-36

Y

YOUTH

Youth is a beautiful dream, on whose brightness books shed a blinding dust. Will ever the day come when the wise link the joy of knowledge to youth's dream? Will ever the day come when Nature becomes the teacher of man, humanity his book and life his school? Youth's joyous purpose cannot be fulfilled until that day comes. Too slow is our march toward spiritual elevation, because we make so little use of youth's ardor.
TM-ST-55

Beauty belongs to youth, but the youth for whom this earth was made is naught but a dream whose sweetness is enslaved to a blindness that renders its awareness too late. Will ever the day come when the wise will band together the sweet dreams of youth and the joy of knowledge? Each is but naught when in solitary existence.
T-302

YOUTH AND AGE

Mankind divided into two long columns, one composed of the aged and bent, who support themselves on

crooked staves, and as they walk on the path of Life, they pant as if they were climbing toward a mountaintop, while they are actually descending into the abyss.

And the second column is composed of youth, running as with winged feet, singing as if their throats were strung with silver strings, and climbing toward the mountaintop as though drawn by some irresistible, magic power.

WM-ST-36

Until when shall the people remain asleep?
Until when shall they continue to glorify those
Who attained greatness by moments of advantage?
How long shall they ignore those who enable
Them to see the beauty of their spirit,
Symbol of peace and love?
Until when shall human beings honor the dead
And forget the living, who spend their lives
Encircled in misery, and who consume themselves
Like burning candles to illuminate the way
For the ignorant and lead them into the path of light?

TL-T-300